QUEERING THE RENAISSANCE

Edited by

Michèle Aina Barale,

Jonathan Goldberg,

Michael Moon,

and Eve Kosofsky

Sedgwick

QUEERING THE
RENAISSANCE

EDITED BY JONATHAN GOLDBERG

Duke University Press   Durham and London 1994

© 1994 Duke University Press
All rights reserved
Printed in the United States of America
on acid-free paper ∞
Typeset in Centaur by Keystone Typesetting Inc.
Library of Congress Cataloging-in-Publication Data
appear on the last printed page of this book.

Contents

QUEERING THE RENAISSANCE

Introduction

JONATHAN GOLDBERG

I N the more ordinary understanding of the title of this collection of essays, the process of queering the Renaissance has been under way for some time. Perhaps since Joan Kelly resolutely answered the question "Did Women Have a Renaissance?" in the negative, the period has been under scrutiny in ways that have called into question the accomplishments of the Renaissance as foundational for modernity, or, at any rate, that have revealed aspects of that foundation that need to be scrutinized.[1] Thus, to take one example, it is now often observed that the humanism of the Renaissance—an accomplishment so often celebrated in the past—was available to only a limited segment of the population (not to all of "humanity"), for the most part males within fairly limited socioeconomic strata and a small number of women, almost all from the highest social stratum.[2] Hence, in the past decade and more, various antihumanist agendas have been brought to bear upon the period, and the collective work of feminists, materialists, new historicists, and theorists of a variety of kinds has made it difficult to turn to the Renaissance as a site for the creation of an "individual" (to recall Burckhardt's thesis) whose nature is a site for celebration; rather, for contestation. Indeed, as Margaret Hunt suggests in her afterword in this volume, it is precisely when anyone other than a privileged white heterosexual male makes claims to a supposed "universal" individuality and humanity that the contestatory nature of the claim is most clear. It is, in part, for that very reason, as Hunt urges, that more work is needed to investigate the relations between questions of race, gender, and sexuality as they intersect with the projects of nation-building, colonialism, and imperial expansion that mark the Renaissance. The recent deluge of important work on the New World, it has to be remarked, while attentive to some aspects of these questions, has remained all but silent on the questions of sexuality that this volume raises.

It is nonetheless the case that the essays gathered here draw some of their energies from the pressure that has been put on Renaissance studies in the last decade or so. Allegiances to feminism shape many of them, and their commitment to historicization couldn't be clearer. Antifoundational work of the kind I have invoked is also continued in this volume, in Jeff Masten's essay, for example, when it calls into question the very notion of the availability of the concept of the individual for the Renaissance texts he considers; in Carla Freccero's essay, whose inquiry into the conditions of national subject-formation and textual formations is informed by a historicizing gesture that seeks to mark a crucial and potentially disruptive moment in the foundations of a modern sociosexual order guaranteed by the Phallus; in the essays by Valerie Traub and Graham Hammill, where the non-self-identity of the subject, familiar enough from psychoanalytic or Derridean theory, requires a rereading in a historic period that does not operate under the aegis of the homo/hetero divide, where the divisions, as Freccero suggests, cross boundaries of gender and class.

Hence, the kinds of questions these essays seek to raise, and the ways in which they would queer the Renaissance, go well beyond the ordinary protocols of a great deal of the criticism in the field. Valerie Traub, in "Desire and the Difference It Makes," an essay related to the one that appears here, has shown, for instance, how heterosexist the assumptions of much feminist criticism have been, and therefore how kinds of lesbian possibilities in Renaissance texts have gone unread or, at times when recognized, have been demeaned.[3] This is a critique that I follow in my contribution to this volume, showing how straitening such views can be when considering ways of organizing desire, even in a text as fundamental for the heterosexual imaginary as *Romeo and Juliet* is taken to be. Richard Rambuss makes a parallel point in his essay on devotional poetry, noting how the policing of sexuality in earlier periods (when "they couldn't have meant *that*") is often most stringent when the sexuality in question is not straight. Thus, while considering how enabling Caroline Walker Bynum's work has been in proposing cross-gender transformations in medieval piety, he takes her to task for drawing back from countenancing considerations of sexuality, for instance in the spectacle of a female worshiper contemplating a feminized Christ, and above all, it would appear, from granting the lesbian possibilities at play in such devotion. Of course, one would not want to give the impression that feminists err most in this area (indeed, criticism of such work proceeds from the opposite assumption, that feminist critics working in the Renaissance should have no investment in the reinforcement of compulsory heterosexuality), and in her essay in this volume, Traub pauses to note how Stephen Greenblatt's efforts in the field of gender and sexuality have operated within the syntax of a normative heterosexuality; Rambuss similarly treats a range of critics of seventeenth-century devotional poetry (including Stanley Fish) who seek to efface the homoerotics that he powerfully suggests surrounds images of the penetrated male body in the texts of Crashaw, Herbert, and Donne, while I look at ways in which a supposedly neutral formalist criticism carries heterosexist assumptions. These are lapses that can be performed in the name of being true to the texts at hand, but it is more often the case that they arise from a failure to scrutinize presumptions that we carry all too unthinkingly. Thus, I am happy to stand corrected, as I am in Dorothy Stephens's essay, for my own blindness in *Endlesse Worke* to female-female sexual possibilities in *The Faerie Queene.*

What I would therefore suggest is that however much we have learned to queer the Renaissance in the past couple of decades, we are still on the verge of a major reassessment of the field to which these essays seek to contribute. As Alan K. Smith points out in his essay on Burchiello, sodomy in fifteenth-century Italy was associated with modernity; Alan Bray suggests in his essay that the disruption of the traditional parameters of friendship by the emergence, however limited, of the so-called new men in the course of the sixteenth century in England brought sodomy into visibility as the emblem of social disruption; Graham Hammill argues that the new model of scientific knowledge that Bacon offers is intimately bound up with sodomitical sex; Carla Freccero glimpses a utopian possibility for lesbian separatism even as a compulsory heterosexuality seems to be legislated as a condition of the modern state; Michael Warner contends that there is a warrant for sodomy in the founding of the new nation on this side of the Atlantic. All of these might be seized as our license here for yet another rewriting of the Renaissance—one that, I believe, answers the caution voiced in Margaret Hunt's afterword, that such a rewriting must not be a reinscription of the Renaissance or a discovery there of some realm of freedom lost with the advent of modernity and its carceral regimes.

It would be a falsification to claim that questions about sexuality in the Renaissance have been raised only quite recently. However, it is true that the engagement with such subjects by academics is new, and it would be uncontentious to state that the impetus behind this work lies with the introductory volume to Foucault's *History of Sexuality*. Its conceptualization of the field announced in its title opened a domain for study and provided tools for analysis. In Foucault's work, as in this volume, the aim is not to "find" gays and lesbians hidden from history, which is to say that the assumption of a transhistorical homosexual identity is not the motivation behind this work. Jeff Masten's programmatic statement at the end of his essay, avowing that the task of criticism in queering the Renaissance is not that of "outing" authors (not even Beaumont and Fletcher, who wrote together, kept house together, and, as Aubrey reported, "lay together"), is a position to which most of the contributors to this volume would subscribe. It explains why Valerie Traub's essay, which delivers possibilities for a number of kinds of lesbianism across a range of sites—differentiated by nationality, literary genres, disciplinary domains—nonetheless puts the word *lesbian* in scare quotes (Carla Freccero ventures a question mark after she invokes the word to describe the Virgilian warrior Camilla that lurks on the edge of the tale from Marguerite de Navarre's *Heptameron* upon which she focuses). So too it motivates the call for tact and caution in Forrest Tyler Stevens's essay when facing the question of Erasmus's alleged homosexuality; Stevens argues that by vacating that term and its definitional relation to heterosexuality a route to an answer about Erasmus's sexuality can be found. It is with similar concerns and with an equal display of tact that Dorothy Stephens observes of the highly charged night that Amoret and Britomart spend together at the opening of Book Four of *The Faerie Queene* that "it is wonderfully puzzling that the one happy bed scene in the whole poem appears here," the puzzle—and the delight—lying precisely in how far one can impute sexual activity to this moment and how one is to read it.

As these examples might suggest, the work of Alan Bray has been indispensable for most of the contributors to this volume; his *Homosexuality in Renaissance England*[4] remains the groundbreaking and unsurpassed historical investigation for the period; its signal contribution was to find ways of talking about homosexuality before the advent of *the homosexual*. Bray charts a path to the unacknowledged availability of homosexuality that is coextensive with social organization itself. Thus, in his essay, recast for inclusion in this volume, it is the unspeakable proximity of the most exalted bonds between men—friendship—and the most excoriated terms for male-male relations—sodomy—that concerns him, and the task of his essay is to articulate and make visible relations which the period sought to occlude and yet could not help seeing. As my framing of Bray's work might suggest, his investigations, keenly attuned to historic differences as they are, also formidably engage and provoke theoretical and epistemological questions. It is thus not all that surprising to find that many of the contributors to this volume move between his work and that of Eve Kosofsky Sedgwick, whose paradigm of homosocial relations complements Bray's sense of the ways in which male-male intimacies were furthered by the power structures that organized households, schools, and patronage networks. These are a few examples of the social domains that come under consideration in his work as well as in the volume at hand—sites enlarged in Carla Freccero's consideration of a text authored by a woman in which a group of women serve as narrator and audience, and register thereby an alternative social scene. Moreover, Sedgwick's elaboration of an epistemology of the closet provides a supple analytic tool for investigating the regimes of unknowing and unacknowledgeability that structure the place of homosexuality in Renaissance culture.[5] Her work is valuably skeptical about any form of historical knowledge that makes the past unusable for the present; it also highlights, thanks to its rich engagement with the texts it treats, the coordinates of modes of social organization and ways of knowing that are anything but transhistorical.

If *Epistemology of the Closet* problematizes even as it details the installment of the modern regimes of homo/hetero difference, the essays in this volume work within and through the complex terrain of a period that does not know those organizing terms. Indeed, to follow Foucault à la lettre, the Renaissance comes before the regimes of sexuality, and to speak of sexuality in the period is a misnomer. This is indeed the case if sexuality is taken as a marker of identity, definitional of a core of the person, and these essays, as I have already suggested, take great care not to suggest that gay or lesbian identity can be found in the texts at hand. Yet this does not mean that the anachronism of speaking of sexuality in the Renaissance is not to be risked, especially if the failure to invoke sexuality means acting as if texts of the period can always be explained in other terms, and in ways in which anything like sex disappears—into the "convention" of friendship, for instance, to take up a point in Forrest Tyler Stevens's essay, or into a *lapsus calami*, to take the extreme instance Elizabeth Pittenger notes, involving an editor's decision that where the record of the Privy Council on the case of Nicholas Udall reads *buggery*, it should have *burglary* instead. These essays do not know in advance where sexuality is or how it will manifest itself (indeed, there is pressure in several of these essays on the very crucial question of whether there is any such thing as sexuality in itself beyond its variegated historical manifestations), but they know that the failure to raise questions of sexuality in these texts has often meant nothing less than the tacit assumption that the only sexuality that ever obtains is a transhistorical heterosexuality. Moreover, to return to the examples just cited, these essays recognize that because something is a convention is no reason to assume that it bears no relation to experience (Bray's essay demonstrates how the idealized literary image of the friend, for instance, served real social—and, I would add, ideological—purposes), while, as Pittenger argues, the point is not to decide between *buggery* and *burglary* but to recognize the complicities between the supposed separate domains those words suggest, differentiated by scarcely more than a letter.

The point is that sexuality is only phantasmatically cordoned off to some private sphere; in truth, sexuality structures and destructures the social. In the Renaissance, as Bray points out, bedfellows were publicly known; if it is not always clear what shared beds meant—whether the "right" or the "wrong" persons were in bed together—it is always the case that exchanges of power are anything but disembodied acts. Although Bray's work looks only at men, as has been suggested already, a number of essays in this volume are alert to possibilities between women hitherto overlooked. It is in Spenser's book of friendship that Amoret and Britomart share a bed, and everyone knows it, for the phenomenon was not uncommon: ladies and their servants slept together, and so too did women friends, as the impassioned speech that Hermia delivers in *A Midsummer Night's Dream* (considered by Valerie Traub) certainly makes clear.

The language of that speech approaches the language of marriage. This is indicative of another sort of phenomenon noted by many of the essays here. For in addition to extending queer territory beyond the all-male limits that mark much of the work in the field, the way in which these essays engage the sociohistorical imbrication of sexuality necessitates readings that are not confined to "discovering" homosexuality or to the supposition that such unearthings would take place within some confined, marginalized position or locus.[6] These essays focus on homosexual relations in the full recognition that they cannot be studied outside questions of gender or aside from the understanding of the powerful interests that are served by the social organizations that shape sexual difference: reproduction, familial structures, and the like. That these are not structures that ought simply to be equated with each other or treated as if their definitional and institutional energies answered fully to their desire to map the social is suggested, for instance, by Jeff Masten when he details the ways in which male-male engendering (the phenomenon of joint, collaborative authorship that was a regular feature of writing for the English Renaissance theater) conflict with patriarchal and absolutist paradigms of authorship and textual ownership that emerge in the seventeenth century; his argument gains further resonance and complexity through its consideration of how male-male relations are related to the emergence of an ideal of companionate heterosexual relations, but also how the Beaumont and Fletcher folio may be compared to the limits and enablements that shaped Margaret Cavendish's literary production and her folio publications.

A broadly related point emerges from an examination of the divided terrain that puritan America bequeaths to the liberal social imagination, as Michael Warner argues, contemplating the conflicts between principles of hierarchy and a potential egalitarianism. Likewise, the complexities in Marguerite de Navarre's texts, as Carla Freccero shows, are instances of a series of crossings: between a bourgeois character celebrated for her resistance to the attentions of a prince, and a prince thereby celebrated for his restraint—characters, however, who meet in a name, François/Françoise, that is not only the name of Marguerite's brother and the future François I, but the name of the nation. Implicated in the celebration of separate spheres are crossings that suggest incestuous desires, a displacement of the paternal Phallus, and the impossibilities of compulsory heterosexuality. The place of the sexual—or of multiplying sexualities—within such social terrains suggests something about the kinds of crossings these essays broach, syntaxes that are not confined within the oppositional and hierarchical understanding of gender difference that is the legacy of heterosexual organization. Thus, to take one further instance, Marcie Frank looks at how Dryden deploys differentially same-sex male and female scenes in *All for Love* as a way of expressing his relation to Shakespeare, deflecting the animus against his predecessor in a scene in which two rival queens fight it out; yet they fight for the position of wife, and as Frank argues, Dryden also (thanks to his belatedness vis-à-vis Shakespeare, and to his lower class status in comparison to that of various court wits, for instance, not to mention the king) casts himself in this feminine position. These identifications across gender are thus also repudiations and deflections meant to shore up or to contribute to an emerging heterosexual and bourgeois sphere in which Dryden nonetheless remains something of a queer interloper, though not quite the site of queerbashing, which Frank also sees as emergent in this period.

Elsewhere in this volume, the lines of identification across gender which disrupt the plotting of desire as heterosexual seem more closely allied to a paradigm of substitution in which male sexual desire can take both boys and women as its object (this is a paradigm at work to a certain extent in my discussion of anal erotics in *Romeo and Juliet*, and it also operates in Forrest Tyler Stevens's consideration of the relation between the letters Erasmus wrote to a young acolyte and his formulas for "proper" love letters). That such replacements can also function to efface women is a point that is not ignored in these readings across gender; it is broached in my own essay and in Jeff Masten's, for instance, and engaged most forthrightly in Elizabeth Pittenger's analysis of complicities between male homosocial arrangements and misogyny. Yet, to recur to an earlier point, there are moments in these essays—for example those by Richard Rambuss and Graham Hammill—when such arguments, when they have been made in the effort to delegitimate male-male sexual relations, and when the defense of women turns out to be a defense of heterosexuality, are faced. It is, in short, only by thinking beyond the claims of heterosexual organization (recognizing that it too is a historic phenomenon and not to be assumed to be at work in Renaissance texts) that same-sex and cross-sex relations can be thought of in less deforming ways. Indeed, this is part of the point of the essays by Valerie Traub, Carla Freccero, and Dorothy Stephens. While all three are acutely aware of the limits upon female sexuality in the period, they seek the sites of evasion and enablement that open spaces for female-female erotics—sites, for instance, in friendship before marriage, or even within it, always in peril, but nonetheless possible. Not surprisingly, as Traub suggests, it is the woman with a strap-on—the woman who can, from a hetero perspective, be understood as attempting to usurp male prerogatives—who can most easily call up the frightening image of the sodomite. Or, rather, as Traub argues, on the Continent she can be so imagined and named; no woman in Renaissance England ever was charged with sodomy (though as Stephens details, male writers were hardly reticent about supposing the rampancy of female desire whenever women were left untended, and Marcie Frank's essay brings such Renaissance misogyny into early modern perspective, suggesting, as does Jeff Masten's essay, some of the complex routes from Renaissance organizations of desire to ones that seem closer to the modern regimes of hetero and homosexuality).

These essays, as I have been suggesting, productively engage the complex questions involving male domination, misogyny, and the possibilities for male-male and female-female erotics from a number of vantage points that open areas of further debate and discussion. What the essays share is an acute awareness of the multiplicities of acts that can be sexualized, the ever-shifting terrains between texts, across national and generic borders (to mix some more categories) that make available and opaque the sites upon which sexual possibilities fasten. As Janet E. Halley argues, in an essay that comes first in this volume because of the forcefulness with which it locates the political pressures upon work queering the Renaissance, it is precisely through such multiplications that it would be possible to halt the presumptions of knowingness that led to the 1986 U.S. Supreme Court decision in *Bowers v. Hardwick* that denied the right to private consensual acts of what the court termed "homosexual sodomy." As Halley argues, that decision was rooted in English law that goes back to the time of Henry VIII and in presumptions about the univocal and transhistorical nature of sodomy. These essays do not make that presumption, and while it may be wishful to suppose that a Supreme Court Justice (or clerk) ever might find her or his way to this book, it is nonetheless through the production of such knowledge as this volume aims at that the lethal energies of the law can at least be shown to be motivated by ignorance and prejudice.

Most instructive in this regard is Donald N. Mager's essay here, which looks at John Bale's *Comedy Concernynge thre lawes, of Nature, Moses, & Christ* to discover in this unpromisingly titled venture the only English Renaissance play to my knowledge to feature a character called Sodomy. As Mager shows, this figure catches up much of the incoherence of the concept in the period (though Mager also usefully suggests that the meaning of sodomy in an early-sixteenth-century text is not quite that to be found a century later, much as Valerie Traub suggests, looking from England to the Continent, that there are at the same historical period multiple sodomies at work, a point extended in Jeff Masten's essay, which ventures a multiplicity of homoeroticisms in the period). But beyond this—since simply to reveal the powerful inconsistencies of the term is not enough—Mager shows how sodomy is marshaled precisely through its multiplicities to serve to do more than regulate male-male sexual behavior. As he argues, Bale's play is part of a propaganda effort that has everything to do with the reorganization of state / church relations under Henry VIII and therefore also has to do with possibilities for marriage and divorce, with extensions of the royal prerogative and thus with ways conceiving of heterosexual and reproductive rights (the terrain that Foucault calls alliance). Mager thus looks at a literary text fully embedded within the historic period that produced the first secular sodomy statute in England and shows that that statute is not legible simply as a pronouncement about a form of sexuality and that Bale's play is more than a reflection of a historic situation.

To revert to the argument of Alan K. Smith: what Mager's essay and many of the others reveal thereby is an intractability, the impossibility of delivering arguments about sexuality in the period without recognizing how fully embedded they are in the political. Smith coins the term *fraudomy* to suggest that the texts he considers are equally and endlessly decipherable in a double register that is at once sexual and social. There is no surprise here, for as both Smith and Alan Bray argue, sodomy in the period is seen as an assault on the sovereign, instances of *laesae majestatis*, a wounding that is most assaultive because it is so constitutive of the very structures of power. Hence, equally unsurprisingly, sodomy can be found lurking everywhere and nowhere in these texts. This is a point that Elizabeth Pittenger argues in an exacting discussion of methodological questions about evidence in which she takes exception to ways in which the terms that Bray uses can seem to suggest that homosexuality in the Renaissance is a separate and self-defining domain to be discovered (or uncloseted); so, too, Pittenger calls into question the availability of a notion of secrecy that might presume that there is something to hide. It is precisely the point that the terrains explored in these essays are elusive because they could be anywhere. Thus Smith records his initial skepticism that the poems his essay considers were written in a code that could be deciphered to make legible sexual acts, and while his essay makes use of this deciphering technique to decode sodomy in the work of Burchiello, sodomy is as it were recoded as the nonce word *fraudomy* to register that sexuality in the period does not stand apart as a separate domain. Such complex hermeneutic motions of revealing and reveiling are performed many times in this volume (Smith's essay ends, for instance, by beginning to open paths from psychoanalytic theory to the particularities of the historic and social features of fifteenth-century Florence, a trajectory that might bear comparison with those explored in Graham Hammill's and Carla Freccero's essays, the latter engaging the social anthropology of Jean-Joseph Goux to deliver a complex revaluation of the historicity of phallocracy). It leads one to remark how insistently textual many of the essays are, how, to borrow Freccero's title, they engage in practices of queer philology, contesting the work of, as she terms them, *phallologists*.

Here are some further instances: Richard Rambuss's essay on the erotic possibilities offered by the spectacle of penetrable (penetrating and penetrated) male bodies in religious poetry finds that one of the ways in which such actions are imagined is as scenes of inscription, the pen penetrating the flesh. So too Graham Hammill's consideration of the erotics of a new pedagogy involves a scene of writing, not one of making the slate clean, but rather a palimpsest effect which also doubles a scene of purgation that Bacon performed on his own body. Which is to say that for Hammill as for Rambuss the connections between bodies are anal. This is a point I come to as well and also through a textual crux in *Romeo and Juliet* where a blank or a mistranscription in one of the authoritative texts for the play, or an "etc." in the other, marks a spot which, however unnameable it may be, nonetheless is reported to circulate among young women when they speak to each other. What they whisper is a secret that everyone knows: that men and women both have anuses, and that they are for both sexes sites of sexual pleasure. If this secret is literal, it is literally literal: conveyed by letters. Thus it is through the traces of letters that duplicate each other and yet can be differentiated from each other that Elizabeth Pittenger considers scenes of letter writing and reading in *Ralph Roister Doister* and the rhetorical performances of Nicholas Udall as he deflects and makes explicit his mode of (not) being a sodomite. It is also through the exchange of letters and the theory of letter writing that Forrest Tyler Stevens gauges questions of sexuality in Erasmus, making a point that these essays often share, that the materiality of the letter is not to be discounted as a site for sexuality. This is a supposition that joins many of the essays although it is reached from a number of different trajectories: psychoanalytic theory in the case of Hammill, for instance; bibliographical concerns for Pittenger or for Jeff Masten in his consideration of the textual apparatus of the Beaumont and Fletcher folio; both of these in Carla Freccero's discussion of textual variants among three manuscripts of Marguerite de Navarre's *Heptameron* and the ways in which they continually reconfigure questions of gender and open possibilities of proscribed sexualities as the phallic law is located on a maternal and sororal site. As Freccero further argues, these textual/sexual questions challenge both male humanist traditions and feminist critiques of them. The transfer of letters is another name for literary history too, and these essays look at that domain as well, Alan Smith charting paths from Dante to Burchiello, for instance, Marcie Frank from Shakespeare to Dryden. Indeed, Frank's essay ends with a call to extend the terrains of queer inquiry back to an understanding of literary and critical formations, and it is clear that such questions motivate Masten's essay as well, or Smith's, which raises explicitly also questions of canons and classrooms.

If the domain in which these essays can best hope to make a difference is the classroom and the university, Janet E. Halley's initial essay and Michael Warner's closing piece (framed as it is by the decision in *Bowers v. Hardwick*) suggest that the spheres in which we operate are not to be regarded as thereby limited. These essays share Halley's agenda, which seeks to problematize the ways in which much gay historiography has been shaped as if the sole question were when a recognizable homosexual minority first emerged. This is a subject treated at length and with acuity in Margaret Hunt's afterword; if the answer to the question of origins is not singular, as these essays and much other historical work suggest, and if something like a recognizable identity formation was available much earlier on the Continent than it was in England, part of the point would be, to follow Hunt's argument, that what has been misguided in the privileging of the question of identity among historians has been the regulatory function that sexual identity tends to have in such accounts. One must not discount the inestimable value of histories of *communities* as part of the work of resisting homogenizing definitions of identity. As Halley argues here and in earlier essays on *Bowers v. Hardwick*, it was the court's presumption to know what a homosexual is, and to assume that identity as a transhistorical category transhistorically excoriated, that can be read in the majority decision written by Byron White (or in the equally nasty concurring opinion issued by Warren Burger, which quotes Blackstone with relish as he pronounces sodomy a crime worse than rape or murder).[7] These suggest that to shape gay historiography only in terms of the emergence of a minority can feed into horribly lethal energies. While Halley's work by no means advocates a return to the closet, it seeks, as these essays also do, to problematize questions of identity.

If a "universalizing" definition is at work here (to recall Sedgwick's terms in *Epistemology of the Closet*), it has its warrant in Renaissance notions of sodomy as a range of desires and acts that the period thought anyone could have or do, sodomy in its most capacious definition including just about anything but unprotected vaginal intercourse between a married couple. If this is the historical warrant for the nonidentitarian tack of this volume, there are other more contemporary reasons for it. As Halley suggests, one answer to the U.S. Supreme Court would lie in the recognition that the sexual acts it wishes to condemn and to cordon off as done only by homosexuals are undertaken in the face of quite other facts: that everyone does them (or could do them) and that sexual identity is far more mutable than the Court recognizes. The Court declares that nothing in the founding documents of this nation finds a place for sodomy, but as Warner argues, looking at some of those texts, they are riddled with the proximity of the city on the hill (to recall Winthrop's phrase for the puritan endeavor) and the city on the plain (to recall the biblical locus for Sodom and Gomorrah); indeed, as he argues, these protonational texts resonate with the fearful and thrilling recognition of the virtual identity of those supposedly opposite sites. The colonial imaginary, as I have argued elsewhere, is particularly prone to a desire to other its own desires.[8] This is one legacy of the national imaginary, but not its only one. For, as Warner argues too, the spheres the founding fathers would keep separate in fact interpenetrate. The desire of this volume to queer the Renaissance is undertaken in the recognition that queer identity is far less easily regulated or defined in advance than legislatures and courts imagine, and that literary texts are far more available to queer readings than most critics would allow or acknowledge. If there is a path from the Renaissance to modernity, or, within the U.S. national imaginary, from the founding fathers to the present, it leads to a queer nationhood whose borders we have yet to determine, and which may in fact not be determinable. Or, to pick up a figure of speech deployed by Alan Bray, this volume is not a glimpse at activities on the margins or in the shadows, but works to redefine the center. Or, better, to locate a center without a center: these essays really queer the Renaissance.

Notes

1. Kelly's essay first appeared in *Becoming Visible: Women in European History*, ed. Renate Bridenthal and Claudia Koonz (New York: Houghton Mifflin, 1977), and is reprinted in Joan Kelly, *Women, History, and Theory* (Chicago: University of Chicago Press, 1984).

2. For one version of the argument, see Anthony Grafton and Lisa Jardine, *From Humanism to the Humanities* (Cambridge: Harvard University Press, 1986).

3. See Valerie Traub, "Desire and the Difference It Makes," in *The Matter of Difference*, ed. Valerie Wayne (Ithaca: Cornell University Press, 1991), 81–114, and the fuller discussion of erotic possibility in her *Desire and Anxiety: Circulations of Sexuality in Shakespearean Drama* (London: Routledge, 1992), 91–144.

4. London: Gay Men's Press, 1982.

5. See Eve Kosofsky Sedgwick, *Between Men: English Literature and Male Homosocial Desire* (New York: Columbia University Press, 1985), which includes a powerful chapter on Shakespeare's sonnets; and *Epistemology of the Closet* (Berkeley: University of California Press, 1990), which considers questions of historicity among its initial axioms.

6. Such minoritizing views (to borrow Sedgwick's term) can be found in Joseph Pequigney's *Such Is My Love* (Chicago: University of Chicago Press, 1985), as well as in two more recent books in the field: Gregory Bredbeck's *Sodomy and Interpretation* (Ithaca: Cornell University Press, 1991), and Bruce R. Smith's *Homosexual Desire in Shakespeare's England* (Chicago: University of Chicago Press, 1991), both of which, however, are more attentive than is Pequigney to historical and discursive formations of (homo)sexuality in the Renaissance.

7. See Janet E. Halley, "The Politics of the Closet: Towards Equal Protection for Gay, Lesbian, and Bisexual Identity," *UCLA Law Review* 36 (1989): 915–76, and her "Misreading Sodomy: A Critique of the Classification of 'Homosexuality' in Federal Equal Protection Law," in *Body Guards*, ed. Julia Epstein and Kristina Straub (New York: Routledge, 1991), 351–77.

8. See "Sodomy in the New World: Anthropologies Old and New," *Social Text* 29 (1991): 45–56, and "Bradford's 'Ancient Members' and 'A Case of Buggery . . . Amongst Them,' " in *Nationalisms and Sexualities*, ed. Andrew Parker et al. (New York: Routledge, 1991). Both essays form the basis for a discussion of the New World in my *Sodometries: Renaissance Texts, Modern Sexualities* (Stanford: Stanford University Press, 1992).

BOWERS V. HARDWICK

in the Renaissance

JANET E. HALLEY

ISTORIANS queering the Renaissance occupy a particularly auspicious vantage point for probing the social fictions spun by the United States Supreme Court's notorious decision in *Bowers v. Hardwick*. After all, both Justice White writing for the majority and Justice Burger concurring in his own opinion trace Georgia's statute to the state's reception of English law, positing an unmediated codification of Henry VIII's statute prohibiting buggery and Elizabeth I's reinstatement of it[1] in the criminal law of the United States. The historiography of sodomy proposed by the Supreme Court in *Hardwick*—one in which sodomy is always and everywhere the same, always and everywhere opprobriated, always and everywhere joined in a purportedly stable equation with homosexual identity—provides an important contemporary context for the essays collected here. It is the purpose of this essay to examine that historiography, and to make some suggestions about how cultural history can contribute to the dis-authorization of the *Hardwick* opinion and its cultural meanings.

In *Bowers v. Hardwick* the United States Supreme Court held that constitutional privacy and substantive due process rights are not violated when a state criminalizes what the Court was pleased to call "homosexual sodomy."[2] Courts, legislators, and executive officials have repeatedly cited this baneful decision to justify the official denomination of a class of homosexuals and its equation with criminalizable sodomy. Several federal courts have held that *Hardwick* forecloses meaningful equal protection for gay men, lesbians, and bisexuals because sodomy is the "behavior that defines the class" of homosexuals.[3] Others have refused to acknowledge that a gay public employee who comes out of the closet has engaged in First Amendment protected speech, or indeed any speech at all, because to acknowledge gay identity is to admit membership in a criminal class.[4] The Alabama legislature has banned public funding of any student group "that fosters or promotes a lifestyle or actions prohibited by the [state's] sodomy and sexual misconduct laws,"[5] relying on the state attorney general's opinion that, under *Hardwick*, Alabama's sodomy statute—a prohibition of oral/genital and genital/anal contacts between *any* unmarried persons[6]—constitutionally prohibits "homosexuality."[7]

In the face of these category implosions equating sodomy with the personhood of individuals identified as gay or lesbian, it is well to recall Jonathan Goldberg's conclusion that "sodomy, 'that utterly confused category,' as Foucault memorably put it, identifies neither persons nor acts with any coherence or specificity. This is one reason why the term can be mobilized—precisely because it is incapable of exact definition; but this is also how the bankruptcy of the term, and what has been done in its name, can be uncovered."[8] Presiding over this regime of incoherence, the *Hardwick* decision exploits confusion about what sodomy is in ways that create opportunities for the Court's exercise of homophobic power. And yet *Hardwick* represents sodomy as a self-evident unit of thought, *an* act rather than many. Indeed, the very logic of the decision depends on a representation of sodomy as immutable, as a historical monolith, the unitary object of an uninterrupted continuity of historical condemnation running forward, according to Justice White's majority opinion, from the date of the Bill of Rights to the date of Hardwick's arrest,[9] running back, according to Justice Burger's concurring opinion, through the "millennia" to the very origins of "Western civilization."[10]

Two questions, both important for the shared project of the essays collected here, arise from this conjuncture of history making with definitional politics: how did the *Hardwick* majority manage the definitional relationship between sodomy and gay identity, and how did it deploy history in doing so? The *Hardwick* Court's historical/definitional practices suggest that the most useful questions for cultural historians to explore may not be precisely the same as the ones that have energized historical examinations of gay, lesbian, and bisexual practices and identities in recent years. I would argue that *Hardwick's* invocation of legal and cultural tradition can best be critiqued by queer historiography that asks not whether and when gay and lesbian identities and subjectivities became historically available to people who did (or did not) engage in same-sex erotic contacts, but how contests to control the meaning of sodomy have involved shifting, opportunistic, sometimes ontologically coherent and sometimes inchoate deployments of the relationship between act and identity.

As courts of limited jurisdiction, federal courts are constitutionally empowered (they themselves have held) to answer only the specific legal questions that litigants present to them. But what are those questions? The process of framing the question is a second-order constitutive activity, in which the court defines its own power and the context in which (the court hopes) that power will operate. By the time the *Hardwick* majority framed the question it then proceeded to answer, most of its work of deciding, and much of its work of situating itself in relation to the question it would answer, was done. It's important, then, to describe quite carefully the definitional implications of the question the Supreme Court purported to answer:

> The issue presented is whether the Federal Constitution confers a fundamental right *upon homosexuals* to engage in sodomy and hence invalidates the laws of the many States that still make *such conduct* illegal and have done so for a very long time.[11]

This question has struck many readers as odd, because the Georgia sodomy statute provides that "a person commits the offense of sodomy when he performs or submits to any sexual act involving the sex organs of one person and the mouth or anus of the other"[12]—that is, it is a facially neutral prohibition of the specified bodily contacts notwithstanding the gender of the actors. Not only is it not limited to "homosexuals": it does not even mention them. To be sure, Michael Hardwick was charged with sodomy after a Georgia police officer entered his bedroom and beheld him engaged in fellatio with another man.[13] But Hardwick raised a facial challenge to the Georgia sodomy statute, alleging that the statute violated rights he held not as a gay man but as a person.[14] The Court attempted to contain that objection by asserting that the record before it was devoid of any actual issue of heterosexual sodomy, and that it would therefore treat Hardwick's claim not as a facial challenge to the statute but as a challenge to the statute "as applied" to Hardwick alone.[15] But as Kendall Thomas deftly observes, the core of Hardwick's claim to standing was his fear that the state of Georgia would develop further facts incriminating him under the sodomy statute, and in raising this claim he nowhere clarified whether those facts would emerge from acts of homosexual or heterosexual sodomy.[16]

By refusing to review the full question before them, the majority justices occluded from the case every trace of felonious heterosexual fellatio, cunnilingus, and anal intercourse. As a result "the homosexual"—"a personage, a past, a case history, a childhood, in addition to being a type of life, a life form, . . . a morphology . . . [and, in sum,] a species"[17]—looms forward as the subject of judicial knowledge and power. And yet the Court never abandons its simultaneous focus on sodomy—that not-yet-superseded "category of forbidden acts"[18]—and indeed finally defines the crux of the issue at stake as "such conduct."

Definitional instability attends the notion of "such conduct" throughout the majority opinions. Are "homosexuals" definitive of "such conduct" or not? The Court remains ready to answer yes *or* no. Sodomy can receive its definitive characteristic from the "homosexuals" who do it, or can stand free of persons and be merely a "bad act." As a result the majority justices have enabled themselves to treat sodomy as a metonym for homosexual personhood—or not, as they wish. The question Justice White sets out to answer is thus apparently single but actually multiple: "such conduct" represents not a purely act-based categorical system but an unstable hybrid one, in which identity and conduct simultaneously appear as logical alternates and implicate one another.

When Justice White asks whether the Constitution "confers a fundamental right upon homosexuals to engage in sodomy" and then situates his question in a historical tradition of criminalizing "such conduct," then, he not only doubles his analytic focus but represents the resulting duplicity as a historical given. For this reason I would argue that *Hardwick* cannot be explained by invoking the periodization proposed by Foucault, in his story of how a taxonomy of acts before the nineteenth century was transformed into one of persons thereafter.[19] Rather, the Court in *Hardwick* conducts its analysis as though this transformation were somehow not yet complete. It poses a double problem: historically volatile definitions of sodomy operate in a context of two simultaneously available but substantially incommensurable articulations of their significance, sodomitical act and personal identity.[20]

To be sure, the Court's overarching strategy is to represent these complex matters as simple. It represents "such conduct" as a stable, univocal signifier for act(s) that have a monolithic history: the states "still make such conduct illegal and have done so for a very long time."[21] This representation of sodomy as univocal and continuous over time becomes the prerequisite for one of the three crucial holdings in this case, the one rejecting Hardwick's "fundamental rights" claim.[22] Hardwick argued that Georgia had violated a right so fundamental to the relationship between the state and its residents that a federal court must intervene to protect him even though the U.S. Constitution nowhere verbally specifies this obligation.[23] Setting forth the doctrinal analysis under which he would adjudicate this claim, Justice White wrote for the Court that Hardwick could assert no "fundamental right to engage in homosexual sodomy" unless he could show that the liberty he aspired to is *"deeply rooted in this Nation's history and tradition."*[24] The doctrinal prerequisite for denying Hardwick's claim is the attribution of an unadulterated historical pedigree to Georgia's sodomy statute.

Here are the lines in which the majority justices make that attribution and defeat Hardwick's fundamental rights claim:

> It is obvious to us that [this formulation] would [not] extend a fundamental right to homosexuals to engage in acts of consensual sodomy. Proscriptions against that conduct have ancient roots. See generally, Survey on the Constitutional Right to Privacy in the Context of Homosexual Activity, 40 U. Miami L. Rev. 521, 525 (1986). Sodomy was a criminal offense at common law and was forbidden by the laws of the original thirteen States when they ratified the Bill of Rights. In 1868, when the Fourteenth Amendment was ratified, all but 5 of the 37 States in the Union had criminal sodomy laws. In fact, until 1961, all 50 States outlawed sodomy, and today, 24 States and the District of Columbia continue to provide criminal penalties for sodomy performed in private and between consenting adults. See Survey, U. Miami L. Rev., *supra*, at 524, n.9. Against this background, to claim that a right to engage in such conduct is 'deeply rooted in this Nation's history and tradition' . . . is, at best, facetious.[25]

In the interpretive apparatus Justice White implicitly invokes here, the basic moving parts are two simplifying and unifying claims. Bits of constitutional text can have only the meanings attributed to them at the time of their ratification; and those attributed meanings can be recovered on the premise that no bit of constitutional text would have been ratified if it were in any way inconsistent with the then-existing positive law of the states taken as a whole. The first of these interpretive devices will work only if the Court can represent the right asserted as identical with the right denied by early statutes. And the second will work only if the Court can represent the ratifying intentionality as an agent of authoritarian deference, not only in the sense that it operated as a monolithic social entity, but also in the sense that it necessarily assented in all its acts to the entire corpus of then-existing positive law.[26]

As will shortly become apparent, the broader problems of interpreting criminal sodomy statutes raised by Justice White's authoritarianism are everywhere implicit in the more specifically historical problem raised by his decision to equate past with present definitions of sodomy. Defects in this purportedly act-based history of sodomy appear immediately. Let's assume that the right Hardwick asserted is indeed the right of "homosexuals to engage in acts of consensual sodomy."[27] One would suppose that, in order to determine whether a right to commit sodomy was denied at constitutionally significant moments in the past, one would have to know what an act of sodomy is. But no. Throughout Justice White's footnote history of sodomy, and even more sweepingly in Justice Burger's concurring opinion, sodomy is always and only "sodomy"; "homosexual sodomy" is treated as its equivalent, and no specification of bodily contacts is offered.

The most acute instance of this pattern emerges in the Court's statement of the facts of Hardwick's case. There the Court informs us that "Hardwick . . . was charged with violating the Georgia statute criminalizing *sodomy* by committing *that act* with another adult male."[28] As the Court proposes to use it, the term *sodomy* is not a general analytic category that includes more specific bodily acts; it is not a legal fiction devised to describe a set of physical practices; rather, it *is* the act: "sodomy" is what Michael Hardwick *did.* But Hardwick was arrested for and charged with engaging in *fellatio*—and, at the time the relevant constitutional amendments were ratified, sodomy statutes then in effect had not yet been interpreted to prohibit that specific bodily contact.

It would be convenient to argue here that fellatio was not sodomy at the time the Bill of Rights and the Fourteenth Amendment were adopted— 1791 and 1868, respectively. This is the argument advanced by Anne B.

Goldstein, who infers from certain late-nineteenth- and early-twentieth-century cases holding that oral-genital conduct was not sodomy then, that it had not been sodomy before either.[29] Such an argument, if it could be proven, would break the continuity of sodomy upon which the Supreme Court's reasoning depends for its constitutional justification of the Georgia statute "as applied" to Hardwick's act of fellatio.

The legal historical record is too equivocal to support that claim—and yet the ways in which it is equivocal constitute an even stronger refutation of the Court's historiography. Fellatio emblematizes the way in which the volatility of sodomy makes it impossible to make provable assertions of its transhistorical continuity even as it creates the possibility of cobbling together simulacra of such proof.

Courts have diverged sharply in their willingness to define fellatio as sodomy. In some states, late-nineteenth- and early-twentieth-century judicial decisions refused to interpret sodomy statutes to include oral-genital conduct. In many other states, courts were willing to take this step—even though their statutes were not discernibly different in scope.[30] Georgia courts, oddly enough, did both.

Georgia's sodomy prohibition makes its first unequivocal appearance as a criminal statute in 1817, though that early statute did not define the crime. The first legislative definition, offered in 1833, limited the prohibition to "the carnal knowledge and connection against the order of nature by man with man, or in the same unnatural manner with woman."[31] In its 1904 decision *Herring v. State* the Georgia supreme court held that that statute prohibited fellatio, coyly described as an "infamous act . . . committed . . . not per anum, but in even a more disgusting way."[32] A worried court noted that various authorities on the English common law excluded fellatio from the definition of sodomy, but proceeded to hold that the lack of a positive historical basis for its holding was of no importance because present views could be imputed to past courts:

> After much reflection, we are satisfied that, if the baser form of the abominable and disgusting crime against nature—i.e., by the mouth—had prevailed in the days of the early common law, the courts of England *could well have held* that that form of the offense *was* included in the *current definition* of the crime of sodomy. . . . We therefore think that it made no difference in this case whether Herring . . . had in mind one or the other form of the crime [when he

made the false accusation of sodomy upon which his perjury conviction was based].[33]

This is almost a prediction of the past on the basis of the present—a strategy familiar to the close reader of the strange time-reversals attempted by Justice White in *Hardwick*.[34] The present construction of a figure of the past is treated *as* the past, and emboldens a traditionalist court to commit what it clearly worries is an act of innovation.

No claim about the noncriminalization of fellatio before 1904 should be made on the basis of a case this equivocal as to its basis in precedent. As the subsequent history of sodomy in Georgia unfolds, moreover, it becomes clear that this equivocation is endemic to the statutory history of sodomy in Georgia. The first lesson is that even a positive judicial holding defining sodomy to include (or exclude) a certain act is subject to re-negotiation if the legal landscape changes. What happened after *Herring* was this: Georgia courts went on to hold in *Comer v. State* that the 1833 statute also prohibited cunnilingus performed by a man on a woman ("carnal knowledge and connection . . . by man . . . in the same unnatural manner with woman"),[35] *and*, in *Thompson v. Aldredge*, that the statute did not encompass cunnilingus committed by two women.[36] This created the intolerable anomaly that a man and a woman were subject to life imprisonment for doing together what two women could do together with impunity. Decades later this anomaly was removed, when the state supreme court in *Riley v. Garrett* reversed *Comer* and held that heterosexual cunnilingus was not sodomy in Georgia.[37] The judicial decisions re-enact rather than resolve the problem of whether Georgian sodomy included oral-genital contacts in 1868, when the Fourteenth Amendment was adopted.

What happened next points even more sharply to the duplicity of sodomy's historiography. Within five years after *Riley* the Georgia legislature amended the 1833 statute, issuing the present prohibition on all oral-genital and genital-anal contacts notwithstanding the gender of the participants.[38] This statute clearly has the effect of reversing *Riley* and *Aldredge*. But what does this change tell us about the meaning of the 1833 act? Does it tend to prove that fellatio and cunnilingus were always already sodomy in Georgia, or that the legislature has just now added them to the roster of sodomitical acts?

If we take this question as a problem in legislative intent, it cannot be resolved. The legislature itself wrote a rationale for the 1968 amendment that squints, looking to both continuity and innovation for justifications:

> Although appearing widely dissimilar to present Georgia provisions, the proposal on sodomy *substantially restates, in modern language, the prevailing law* with respect to sodomy.
>
> *Added* to the coverage of the proposal are Lesbian acts of sexual gratification. *The omission of these situations* has been commented on adversely by past judicial decisions where the court has felt itself obligated to follow the reading of [the 1833 statute].[39]

The most relevant canons of statutory interpretation cut both ways too.[40] On one hand, the canonists tell us, "any material change in the language of the original act is presumed to indicate a change in legal rights," so that "it is presumed that the provisions added by the amendment were not included in the original act."[41] We are also told, however, that no purpose to change the law "is indicated by the mere fact of an amendment of an ambiguous provision,"[42] a principle of interpretation that might apply if the explicit naming of body parts is seen as an effort to disambiguate the 1833 terms "carnal knowledge and connection against the order of nature." Moreover, the canons of statutory interpretation continue, "the time and circumstances surrounding the enactment of the amendment may indicate that the change wrought by the amendment was formal only—that the legislature intended merely to interpret the original act."[43] Such "time and circumstances" may be supplied by the Georgia legislature's relatively swift action after the *Riley* decision came down: "If the amendment was enacted soon after controversies arose as to the interpretation of the original act, it is logical to regard the amendment as a legislative interpretation of the original act—a formal change—rebutting the presumption of substantial change."[44]

The *Herring* decision, the subsequent shifting judicial interpretations of the 1833 statute, and the contradictory inferences created by the 1968 amendment all undermine any assumption that the 1833 statute had a single determinate meaning when it was adopted, at any one time thereafter, or over the entire fool's progress of its (non)reformulation. That is, these moments in the history of sodomy in Georgia threaten the idea that sodomy has *a* history. The volatility of sodomy is a problem: Anne Goldstein tames it by giving sodomy a clearer historical transformation than the record will support. And the Supreme Court goes to the other ex-

treme: it ignores the volatility altogether, attempting to forget that sodomy changes by eliding the acts into which it dis- and re-aggregates.

Important elements of the Court's decision—its focus on acts, its
promise to decide the constitutionality of the Georgia statute "as applied"
to Michael Hardwick, and its historical claim that Hardwick sought constitutional protection for an act which had been subject to criminal punishment at the time the Bill of Rights and Fourteenth Amendment were
adopted—all depend on this elision of the historically difficult relationship between sodomy and oral sex. Each of these legally crucial steps in
the decision is plausible only to the extent that *sodomy* functions not as a
legal term of art open to a range of concrete applications, not as a signifier
with construable signifieds, but as a signifier that is identical and coter-
minous with, that is undifferentiatable from, its signified. Only in this way
is the Court able to represent sodomy as identical to its meanings contem-
poraneously and across time.

There is more at work here than a naive nominalism that deems any
conduct called sodomy to be sodomy. For example, imagine citing to the
Court a sodomy case, tried in colonial Massachusetts, in which judicial
officers appear to have been quite willing to interpret the biblical prohibition of sodomy to include vaginal intercourse of an adult man with a
young girl.[45] What made such conduct *not* sodomy in that case, it appears,
was lack of proof of penetration. The records as we have them provide a
fairly sound basis on which to claim that, in circumstances which we
would categorize either as child sexual abuse or statutory rape, colonial
courts were willing to attach the name "sodomy" to vaginal heterosexual
intercourse. But we can be almost certain that the *Hardwick* majority would
have rejected this case as a meaningful precedent, refusing to be bound by
the "mere" terminology of sodomy. That is, they would not agree that
such a contact is sodomy merely because settled and antique authority was
willing to give it that name.

Nor does the majority's word-magic make the referential complexity of
sodomy go away. The centrifugal forces of sodomy's internal differences
are there, within the field of the Court's decision: the distinctive move the
Court makes to contain these forces is not to eliminate but to sidestep the
discourse of acts that engenders them. What gives definitional coherence
to the *Hardwick* Court's sodomy, and makes possible its legally crucial
equation of past with present prohibitions, is not conduct (for the classes
of conduct defined as sodomy are demonstrably mutable) but the *person of*

the homosexual. The Court's apparent focus on acts, that is, depends on a less obvious focus on persons. Its strict act-based traditionalism covertly implies a transhistorical homosexual person who has always been the real target of legal condemnation and who alone can unite within the tentative grasp of logical coherence the vast array of different sodomy statutes and of different sorts of conduct which the Court treats as the same.

The fundamental-rights holding quoted above begins with the same gesture Justice White made in framing the question he now answers: he sets up his binocular vision of the case—"a fundamental right [of] *homosexuals* to engage in *acts of consensual sodomy*"—and then refers to this un-settled agglomeration of identity with conduct as *"that conduct."* The bi-vocality of "that conduct" is key to the historical claim that "[p]roscrip-tions against *that conduct* have ancient roots." Antihomophobic critique of this decision should not now take up the questions of whether the Court's analysis is more fundamentally act based or identity based, and whether it can be better refuted from an act- or identity based position. Instead we should examine how the Court's *simultaneous* deployment of act- and identity-based theories creates opportunities for doctrinal and represen-tational legerdemain.

The advantages to the Court of an act-based theory are manifold. First, by insisting on sodomy as an act—indeed, by using it not as a term referring to act(s) but as the act itself—the Court manages to inaugurate a kind of infinite expansion of the present into the past, in which historical condemnations of "sodomy" can be represented as identical to Georgia's and in which any holding invalidating the statute would take on the char-acter of raw judicial innovation. As we have seen, this act-based approach makes it possible for the Court not only to defeat Hardwick's funda-mental-rights claim but to do so in the name of Western moral authority in general. The jurisprudential payoff is a posture of judicial restraint. Framed as a case about mere bodily acts and not messy, contested, re-lentlessly political identities, *Hardwick* purports to take the justices out of politics. Inasmuch as it is about acts and not identity, their ruling is a gesture of deference to majority sentiment: they carry their posture of neutrality so far that they even claim to refrain from deciding whether criminal prohibitions of "sodomy . . . between homosexuals in particu-lar . . . are wise or desirable."[46] By purporting to focus on specific, morally bad acts the majority justices attempt to deflect attention from their own involvement in the dynamics of homo/heterosexual definition and to shake off Justice Blackmun's accusation that their ruling reveals an "almost obsessive focus on homosexual activity."[47]

And yet, as we have seen, the Court's act-based approach not only distinguishes itself from but is dependent upon an identity-based approach. The historical argument itself can be made to appear coherent only if "that conduct" refers not to acts but to persons. If "sodomy" means "homosexuals," then the Court need not worry about the complex series of historical mutations by which Georgia came to include within its sodomy statute the conduct for which Hardwick was arrested. Indeed, by its focus on persons the Court manages to occlude the historical volatility of Georgian sodomy, and thus the provisional status of its own historical fiction. This volatility threatens to interrupt the monolithic history of sodomy upon which the Court's fundamental-rights holding rests only if sodomy is a species of acts; if sodomy is instead a metonym for homosexual persons the problem goes away.

As an example of queer history, *Hardwick* is most usefully studied as an example of what *not* to do. I have suggested in the last section that one cautionary lesson of *Hardwick* is that sodomy is not identical to itself; that the relationships between sodomy and homosexual identities need to be specified with great care and precision, and without the assumption that discourses of act and of identity cannot operate together in the same temporal frame. In closing, I'd like to describe a corollary warning sounded by *Hardwick*: that sodomy statutes may not univocally bespeak a social consensus that the thing they prohibit (assuming it can be coherently ascertained) is bad. That is, they may not have the same social target; and they may not transparently express majority disapprobation of whatever it is they do target.

It is now commonplace to disparage the *Hardwick* justices' performance as historians, though it is less common to specify what was wrong with it.[48] At first blush the problem is simply that the Court makes a sweeping historical claim on the basis of a single, unexamined secondary source: "Proscriptions against that conduct have ancient roots. See generally, Survey on the Constitutional Right to Privacy in the Context of Homosexual Activity, 40 U. Miami L. Rev. 521, 525 (1986)."[49]

Justice White (or his law clerk) has given only the lightest copyediting to the University of Miami survey's conclusion that "[c]urrent state laws prohibiting homosexual intercourse are ancient in origin."[50] The Court adopts this posture of slavish dependency unwisely, as even a cursory examination of the University of Miami article (which I will call, for shorthand, the Survey) indicates.

The Survey authors claimed that we may find what Plato "believed" about "homosexuality" in his *Laws*—and failed to mention the *Symposium*.[51] They asserted that "[t]hroughout the middle ages" sodomy was a capital crime equivalent to heresy—even though John Boswell's *Christianity, Social Tolerance, and Homosexuality*, published six years earlier, had made a strong argument that capital punishment of sodomy and its assimilation to heresy were legal innovations of the twelfth and thirteenth centuries.[52] They reported that "homosexuals" were burned at the stake by medieval ecclesiastical courts—ignoring the well-documented institutional relationships of church and state, in which secular officials administered punishments even when ecclesiastical officials convicted.[53] And they stated that this most severe sanction was consistently applied—it wasn't; less severe sanctions were more common.[54]

Every single historical claim about the ancient and medieval periods can be impeached, and each impeachment points to a single underlying fallacy: the assumption that the history of sodomy is one thing. I suggested above that this assumption takes the interpretive turn when Justice White assumes that the historical meaning of the U.S. Constitution is always the meaning-of-the-ratifiers, and that the ratifiers can be thought to have formed no intention inconsistent with the entire panoply of majoritarian sentiments expressed in then-existing positive law taken as a whole. Justice White's method treats majoritarian decisionmaking as the expression of a single, nondiverse intentionality: whether it operates to ratify a constitutional amendment or to ban an erotic practice, it is unitary, and it consistently embraces the similarly unitary intention of past authoritative decisionmakers.

When the Survey turns from the Middle Ages to the Renaissance, and to the beginning of a more fully secular and statutory tradition, it indicates that this assumption is particularly decisive for the interpretation of statutes.[55] At this juncture, the Survey—and the Court—fail to notice the manifold inferential gaps that open up between a criminal statute and popular (or, for states lacking effective universal franchise, authoritative) will. The enactment of a criminal statute need not suggest pervasive social disapproval; it may indicate a temporary and local triumph of one social or institutional constituency in its contest with another. And we should try to remember that the *Hardwick* Court's own effort to voice a transhistorical moral commitment apparently provoked a noticeable up-tick in public acceptance of gay men, lesbians, and bisexuals in the United States.[56] Authoritative expressions of moral condemnation can backfire, and engender rather than stifle resistance.[57]

Moreover, continued criminalization does not prove the existence of settled and immovable social attitudes: statutes are notoriously more diffi-cult to repeal than to enact, and may long outlive any will that may be said to have promulgated them.[58] It is almost impossible to repeal a criminal statute in the present political climate, in which even a gesture in that direction may be seized upon by political opponents as a demonstration of "softness on crime." The resulting lack of political will erodes rather than confirms one's confidence that the criminal code reflects the will of a contemporary majority.

If they stay on the books, what do old criminal statutes do? Martha Fineman's careful empirical study of the enforcement of Wisconsin's co-habitation statute suggests that they may be assigned "purposes" quite different from those imagined for them when they were adopted. Fineman discovered that, though a statute banning unmarried partners from co-habiting was widely thought to be desuetudinous (the doctrinal equiva-lent of "blue"), and thus "merely symbolic," some local district attorneys relied on it quite heavily—to regulate welfare fraud, to preempt the need for paternity proceedings by forcing admissions of paternity, to regulate domestic violence and neglect, and in some cases to enforce private con-tracts to pay overdue rent.[59] Such newly acquired purposes are familiar to those living under the sodomy statutes, and are pandemic in the historical record of sodomy enforcement. And it may be especially true for sodomy statutes, for two reasons. The criminalization and prosecution of sod-omitical conduct have often appeared to target something ever so slightly distinguishable from the acts or identities that supposedly give meaning to the law in this area: they may be about political personality,[60] about religious identity,[61] or about the effort to reinforce conventions about privacy.[62] And the unnameability trope, according to which sodomy is (as Justice Burger reminds us in celebratory cadences) "a heinous act 'the very mention' of which is a disgrace to human nature' and 'a crime not fit to be named,'"[63] directly erodes the correspondence between a sodomy pro-hibition and any culturally pervasive condemnation, by providing that many otherwise well-informed people will have no idea what sodomy is.

As Samuel Pepys, a busy-bodied know-it-all well ensconced in the governing elite of seventeenth-century London, wrote to his diary, "blessed be God, I do not to this day know what is the meaning of this sin, nor which is the agent nor which the patient."[64]

Even if we could assume that a historical sodomy statute expressed a substantial, abiding condemnation of something, the evidence of the statute alone wouldn't enable us to say for sure what that was. The evolving scope of sodomy in Georgia exemplifies this problem. Shifting the historiographical focus to this problem is not without its costs, and it is only prudent to acknowledge that it calls into question a critical practice widespread in antihomophobic analysis. This is the practice of reading sodomy statutes to confirm the Foucaultian hypothesis that, during the late nineteenth century, a discourse of homosexual persons displaced a discourse of bad acts. For those seeking to establish a terminus *a quo* for homosexual personhood, a time-honored litmus test has been to seek evidence that homosexual *and not* heterosexual sodomy is the object of legal control: where heterosexual sodomy is targeted as well, the logic goes, one has evidence that an identity-based discourse had yet to make its debut. Anne Goldstein thus argues that, because the colonial and state sodomy statutes cited by the Court are gender neutral, they tend to prove the claim that "[b]efore the late 1800s, sexuality—whether tolerated or condemned—was something a person did, not what he or she was."[65] To support the claim of actual, pervasive, social-historical gender neutrality, Goldstein argues that English buggery statutes incorporated into American colonial law applied indifferently to anal intercourse between two men and between a man and a woman on the grounds of the facially neutral scope of some early statutes, like that adopted by Georgia in 1833, and on the strength of an early-eighteenth-century English case, *R. v. Wiseman*, holding that buggery with a woman "is a crime exactly of the same nature, as well as it is the same action, as if committed upon a male[.]"[66]

But a close reading of *Hardwick* indicates that an explicitly act-based, gender-neutral sodomy statute can be deployed, even in the same text, to target bad acts *and/or* bad persons. The cultural effect of such a sodomy statute over the range of its non/enforcement is exceedingly complex and difficult to measure. Published cases are likely to reveal novel legal circumstances and to misrepresent the full range of police and prosecutorial practices,[67] while it may very often happen that a virtually unenforced positive law mediates, facilitates, and authorizes, even though it does not explicitly administer, a more finely dispersed but potentially even more sharply violent cultural exercise of power.[68] In the contemporary United States, the relationship between personhood and felony sodomy is likely to remain inchoate, volatile, subject to moments of terrible fixity and others of disorienting rearrangement. The instability of act and identity detected within the *Hardwick* Court's reasoning should be hypothesized to infect the historical record as well.

For these reasons, a certain skepticism should attend any project of reading the history of sodomy to decide when and where a homosexual, gay, lesbian, or queer subjectivity came into existence. To deny that homosexual subjectivity existed in sixteenth-, seventeenth-, or eighteenth-century England on the ground of a judicial decision approving a conviction for heterosexual sodomy merely inverts the claim (which it is hard to imagine anyone making) that homosexual subjectivity exists today because the Supreme Court is pleased to excoriate it. The history of sexual subjectivity may be unrecoverable from legal records: better, I would argue, to focus on the legal deployment of the *idea* that sexual subjectivities exist. What's wrong with the historiography of *Hardwick*, finally, is not that it mistakenly imagines a modern personhood as the object of past sodomy prohibitions, but that it attempts to hide even while it exploits the ways in which act and identity, past and present, bear diacritical relations to one another in the categorical practices of sodomy.[69]

Notes

I want to thank colleagues Robert W. Gordon, Thomas C. Grey, Deborah L. Rhode, William H. Simon, and Robert Weisberg for their comments on this essay. In addition, I am pleased to thank Laura Dickinson for her relentlessly rigorous contributions at the inception of this project; and Kathleen Ansari, Andy Eisenberg, Lisa Hayden, Martha Kegel, Nicolai Ramsey, and Iris Wildman for bibliographical assistance. Research was funded by a bequest from the Dorothy Redwine Estate.

Legal citations in this essay are current to May 18, 1993, and conform to *A Uniform System of Citation* (15th ed.)—the "Bluebook"—modified somewhat to include information of interest to scholars in the humanities and to eliminate some of the more ornate features of Bluebook citation. That means that volume numbers precede and page numbers follow titles. In citations to articles and cases, where more than one page number follows a title, the first number is the item's initial page and all others are the page numbers of quoted passages. Dates refer to dates of publication: for judicial decisions this will be the year the court rendered the opinion under discussion, but for statutes it indicates the year the statute reporter was published, and not necessarily the year the statute was adopted or last amended.

1. 25 Hen. VIII ch. 6 (1533); 5 Eliz. ch. 17 (1562).

2. *Bowers v. Hardwick*, 478 U.S. 186, 106 S. Ct. 2841 (1986).

3. *Padula v. Webster*, 822 F.2d 97, 103 (D.C. Cir. 1987); see also *High Tech Gays v. Defense Indus. Security Clearance Office*, 895 F.2d 563, 571 (9th Cir. 1990); *BenShalom v. Marsh*, 881 F.2d 454, 464–65 (7th Cir. 1989), *cert. denied*, 110 S. Ct. 1296 (1990); *Woodward v. United States*, 871 F.2d 1068, 1076 (Fed. Cir. 1989), *cert. denied*, 110 S. Ct. 1295 (1990).

4. Cf. the First Amendment analysis in *BenShalom v. Marsh*, 881 F.2d 454, 458–62; *Pruitt v. Cheney*, 963 F.2d 1160, 1163–64 (9th Cir. 1991), *cert. denied*, 113 S. Ct. 655 (1992). Michael J. Bowers, the attorney general of Georgia and, not coincidentally, the triumphant defendant in *Bowers v. Hardwick*, goes further, construing a spoken acknowledgment of lesbian identity not just as an admission of past or future sodomitical conduct, but as sodomy itself. Bowers fired Robin J. Shahar from her position as staff attorney in his office when she announced that she intended to marry another woman. Discussing his motion to dismiss her constitutional challenge, Bowers argued that "by admitting her marriage to another woman and making it public knowledge, Shahar had violated the state's anti-sodomy law." "Court Allows Lesbian Lawyer to Proceed with Suit over Withdrawal of Job Offer," 49 BNA *Daily Labor Report* A-7 (March 12, 1992).

5. Ala. Laws Act 92-439 (H.B. 454) (1992).

6. Ala. Code § 13A-6-65(a)(3), 13A-6-60(2) (1982).

7. Alabama Attorney General Opinion, "Colleges and Universities—State Funds—Sexual Misconduct," March 19, 1992.

8. Jonathan Goldberg, "Sodomy in the New World: Anthropologies Old and New," 29 *Social Text* 46, 46 (1991), quoting Michel Foucault, I *The History of Sexuality* 101 (Robert Hurley, trans.) (New York: Vintage Books, 1980).

9. *Hardwick*, 478 U.S. at 191–94, 106 S. Ct. 2844–46.

10. *Hardwick*, 478 U.S. at 196–97, 106 S. Ct. at 2847.

11. *Hardwick*, 478 U.S. at 190, 106 S. Ct. at 2843 (emphasis added).

12. Georgia Code Ann. § 16-6-2 (1984).

13. For a discussion of the facts leading to Hardwick's arrest, see Kendall Thomas, "Beyond the Privacy Principle," 92 *Columbia Law Review* 1431, 1437–39 (1992); see also Note, "Constitutional Law—An Imposition of the Justices' Own Moral Choices," 9 *Whittier L. Rev.* 115, 130–32 n.101 (1987); Art Harris, "The Unintended Battle of Michael Hardwick," *Washington Post*, August 21, 1986, at C1.

14. See especially "Brief for Respondent in *Bowers v. Hardwick*," in *Landmark Briefs and Arguments of the Supreme Court of the United States: Constitutional Law: 1985 Term Supplement* 404, 411, and passim (Philip B. Kurland and Gerhard Casper, eds.) (Frederick, Md.: University Publications of America, 1987).

15. *Hardwick*, 478 U.S. at 187 n.2, 106 S. Ct. at 2842 n.2.

16. Kendall Thomas, "Beyond the Privacy Principle," 92 *Columbia Law Review* at 1431–32 n.3.

17. Foucault, 1 *The History of Sexuality*, at 43.

18.   Ibid.

19.   Ibid.

20.   As Eve Kosofsky Sedgwick has argued, the application of gender-neutral sodomy statutes in a culture that simultaneously punishes disfavored identities creates a "threat of . . . juxtaposition [that] . . . can only be exacerbated by the insistence of gay theory that the discourse of acts can represent nothing but an anachronistic vestige." Sedgwick, *Epistemology of the Closet* 47 (Berkeley: Univ. of California Press, 1990).

21.   *Hardwick*, 478 U.S. at 190, 106 S. Ct. at 2843.

22.   The other two are rulings that prior privacy cases protecting marriage and procreative decisionmaking don't apply to Hardwick's claim; and that the Georgia statute survives any claim that it violates due process because it is irrational.

23.   Hardwick relied on privacy rights "emanating from" rather than "enumerated in" the various provisions of the Bill of Rights that protect the privacy of the home (especially the Third Amendment, which limits the power of government to quarter soldiers in people's homes, and the Fourth Amendment, which limits governmental power to make "unreasonable searches and seizures" of the "persons, houses, papers and effects" of the people), and the guarantee made in Section 1 of the Fourteenth Amendment, that no state may deprive any person of liberty without due process of law.

24.   *Hardwick*, 478 U.S. at 192, 106 S. Ct. at 2844 (quoting *Moore v. City of East Cleveland*, 431 U.S. 494, 503, 97 S. Ct. 1932, 1937 [1977]; emphasis added). Formally, White also asked whether the liberties asserted were " 'implicit in the concept of ordered liberty,' such that 'neither liberty nor justice would exist if [they] were sacrificed.' " *Hardwick*, 478 U.S. at 191–92, 106 S. Ct. at 2844, quoting *Palko v. Connecticut*, 302 U.S. 319, 325–26, 58 S. Ct. 149, 151 (1937). But Justice White devoted no separate analysis to this test, and relied for his conclusion as to Hardwick's entire fundamental-rights claim only on the history of sodomy analyzed below.

25.   *Hardwick*, 478 U.S. at 192–194, 106 S. Ct. at 2844–46. I have deleted footnotes in which the Court painfully lists every state sodomy statute in effect in 1791 (when the Bill of Rights was ratified) and in 1868 (when the Fourteenth Amendment was ratified). I also delete a sloppy and misleading footnote on the modern repeal of sodomy statutes: though twenty-six states had repealed their sodomy statutes by 1986, the Court cites only one.

26.   Frank Michelman provides not only the terminology I adopt here, but a scorching analysis of the jurisprudence that emerges when the *Hardwick* Court becomes the agent of the authoritarianism it attributes to the ratifiers: "The devastating effect in *Bowers* of a judicial posture of deference to external authority appears in the majority's assumption, plain if not quite explicit in its opinion, that public values meriting enforcement as law are to be uncritically equated with either the formally enacted preferences of a recent legislative or past constitutional majority, or with the received teachings of an historically dominant, supposedly civic, orthodoxy. I will call such a looking backward jurisprudence *authoritarian* because it regards adjudicative actions as legitimate only insofar as dictated by the prior normative

utterance, express or implied, of extra-judicial authority." Michelman, "Law's Republic," 97 *Yale Law Journal* 1493, 1496 (1988).

27. *Hardwick*, 478 U.S. at 192, 106 S. Ct. 2844. In vigorous dissent, Justice Blackmun denied that the majority had accurately described the right at stake. Hardwick's challenge, Justice Blackmun would have ruled, called for protection of "the right to be let alone," the right to "control[] the nature of [one's] intimate associations with others," and "the right . . . to conduct intimate relationships in the intimacy of [one's] own home[.]" *Hardwick*, 478 U.S. at 199, 206, 208; 106 S. Ct. at 2848, 2852, 2853 (Blackmun, J., dissenting).

28. *Hardwick*, 478 U.S. at 188, 106 S. Ct. at 2842; emphasis added.

29. See her important article "History, Homosexuality, and Political Values Searching for the Hidden Determinants of *Bowers v. Hardwick*," 97 *Yale Law Journal* 1073, 1084–85, and 1085 n.71 (1988).

30. For attempts to taxonomize these developments, see Note, "The Crimes against Nature," 16 *Journal of Public Law* 159 (1967), and James R. Spence, "The Law of Crime against Nature," 32 *North Carolina Law Review* 312 (1954). An analysis that differentiates among states with different statutory language and among states with different presumptions about how narrowly criminal statutes should be construed is offered by *State v. Morrison*, 25 N.J. Super. 534, 96 A.2d 723 (1953). I am engaged in state-by-state research intended to test these and other attempted explanations for the wide variety of state approaches to the interpretation of sodomy statutes. In the interim, I offer the following close look at Georgia as a case study, one that is of particular importance because the *Hardwick* Court so signally missed its nuances.

31. When Georgia first prohibited sodomy is as unclear as what Georgian sodomy has been. Justice White in his opinion for the majority in *Hardwick* blithely concluded that sodomy was a crime at common law when, in 1784, Georgia adopted the common law of England. *Hardwick*, 478 U.S. at 192 n.5, 106 S. Ct. at 2844 n.5. But as Goldstein points out, all Georgia did in 1784 was to adopt "the common laws of England and such of the statute laws as were usually in force," An Act for Reviving and Enforcing Certain Laws Therein Mentioned, 1784, reprinted in R. Watkins, *Digest of the Laws of Georgia* 289 (Phil. 1800), and it cannot be conclusively shown either that sodomy was a common law crime in England (all the sources in favor of this position are hornbooks summarizing English common law, while the presence of a sodomy *statute* from the time of Henry VIII would seem to argue that the crime was entirely statutory in nature), or that the English sodomy statute was "usually in force" in Georgia in 1784. See Goldstein, 97 *Yale Law Journal* at 1084 n.65. Jonathan Ned Katz does report a sodomy conviction in Georgia in 1734, but it is not clear how that bears on whether a sodomy proscription was "usually in force" fifty years later, in 1784. Katz, *Gay / Lesbian Almanac* 133, 680 n.67 (New York: Harper and Row, 1983). Goldstein concludes that Georgia's first explicit prohibition of sodomy was enacted in 1817. Goldstein, 97 *Yale Law Journal* at 1084, n.65. She appears to be right. 1817 Session Laws of Georgia, 101 § 35, 36, rpt. in Prince, *A Digest of the Laws of the State of Georgia* 350 (Milledgeville, 1822). An almost identical statute was apparently adopted in 1816, 1816 Session Laws of Georgia, 151 § 35, 36, but according to the

Georgia Court of Appeals in a 1949 decision, that statute never went into effect. *Barton v. State*, 53 S.E.2d 707, 709 (Ga. Ct. App. 1949). A final wrinkle: when in 1826 William Schley compiled the English statutes then in force in Georgia pursuant to the 1784 Act, he made no mention of sodomy. Schley, *A Digest of the English Statutes in Force in the State of Georgia* vii (Philadelphia, 1826). Goldstein cites this as further evidence that sodomy was not implicitly included in the 1784 Act, 97 *Yale Law Journal* at 1084 n.65, but it is conceivable that Schley omitted sodomy because he thought the 1816/17 legislation preempted the earlier, more general legislation on this point.

   With Justice White on one side, so confident that Georgia did prohibit sodomy in 1784, and Professor Goldstein on the other, equally sure that it did not, I must admit to uncertainty. As I argue above, it is an uncertainty that I think is endemic to the problem of interpreting sodomy. As I attempt to demonstrate in the text, uncertainty pervades even Georgia's first amended sodomy statute, adopted in 1833 and providing Georgia's first statutory definition of sodomy: "the carnal knowledge and connection against the order of nature by man with man, or in the same unnatural manner with woman." Ga. Laws 1833, Penal Code, 4th Div. § 36. The focus of uncertainty now shifts: what one cannot determine with certainty is no longer *whether* "sodomy" is banned, but *what* sodomy will be deemed to encompass.

32. *Herring v. State* 119 Ga. 709, 46 S.E. 876, 881 (1904).

33. Ibid. at 881–82 (emphasis added).

34. The following, for instance: "the laws of the many states that *still* make such conduct illegal and [then? therefore?] *have done so for a very long time.*" *Hardwick*, 478 U.S. at 190, 106 S. Ct. at 2843; emphasis added.

35. *Comer v. State* 21 Ga. App. 306, 94 S.E. 314 (1917).

36. *Thompson v. Aldredge*, 187 Ga. 467, 200 S.E. 799 (1939).

37. *Riley v. Garrett*, 219 Ga. 345, 133 S.E.2d 367 (1963).

38. 1968 Ga. Laws § 26-2002, Ga. Code Ann. § 16-6-2(a) (1988) ("A person commits the offense of sodomy when he performs or submits to any sexual act involving the sex organs of one person and the mouth or anus of another.").

39. Ga. Code Ann. Ch. 26-2002 (1968) (Committee Notes).

40. Reciprocal cancellation is a feature of statutory interpretation under the recognized interpretive canons; see Karl Llewellyn's celebrated send-up of the canons, "Remarks on the Theory of Appellate Decisions & the Rules of Canons about How Statutes Are to Be Construed," 3 *Vanderbilt Law Review* 395 (1950). My argument here concerns the particular effect of this indeterminacy in the context of sodomy statutes and their historiography.

41. Norman J. Singer, 1A *Sutherland's Statutes and Statutory Construction* § 22-30 (4th ed.) (Wilmette, Ill.: Callaghan & Co., 1985).

42. Ibid.

43. Ibid.

44. *Sutherland* § 22.31.

45. Robert Oaks has gathered materials on a revealing sodomy case tried in Massachusetts in 1641. Oaks, "Defining Sodomy in Seventeenth-Century Massachu-

setts," 6:1 / 2 *J. of Homosexuality* 79 (1980 / 81) (special edition entitled *Historical Perspectives on Homosexuality*, ed. Salvatore J. Licata and Robert P. Petersen); see also Nan D. Hunter, "Life after Hardwick," 27 *Harvard Civil Rights—Civil Liberties Law Review* 531, 533—34 (1992), for an analysis of this case similar to that advanced here. The defendants were adult men, charged with repeatedly engaging in vaginal intercourse with two young sisters, one of them only seven years old. Because the defendants refused to admit penetration, however, they could be tried only on an accusation of having engaged in masturbatory contacts with the girls ("contactus et fricatio usque ad seminis effusionem sine penetratione corporis"—"contact and friction producing the emission of semen without penetration of the body"). Massachusetts then had a capital prohibition of sodomy that tracked, word for word, the definition given in Leviticus: "If a man lyeth with mankinde, as he lyeth with a woman, both of them have committed abomination" (Leviticus 20:13). The legal question was whether the defendants could be capitally punished under this provision.

The defendants were severely punished but not put to death, as they would have been if the judges had been confident that the sodomy ban applied. Oaks, at 81; II *Records of the Governor and Company of the Massachusetts Bay in New England* 12—13 (Nathaniel B. Shurtleff, ed.) (Boston: Commonwealth of Massachusetts, 1853—54). The problem that vexed the judges, and the ministers from other states whom they consulted, seems to have been the lack of penetration. See John Winthrop, *The History of New England from 1630 to 1649* 56 (James Savage, ed.) (Boston: Little, Brown, 1853) (reporting that most of the ministers consulted advised that the sodomy ban did not apply, apparently because "there must be such an act as must make the parties one flesh"); William Bradford, *Of Plymouth Plantation, 1620—1647*, Appendix X (Samuel Eliot Morison, ed.) (New York: Modern Library, 1967) (printing letters from three ministers concluding that the sodomy statute did apply because penetration was not crucial). Oaks somehow concludes from these records that "many of the responding ministers clearly and understandably equated 'sodomy' with male-male sexual activity and found it difficult to apply the term to [this] case" because it involved heterosexual contacts. Oaks, at 80—81; see also Jonathan Goldberg, *Sodometries: Renaissance Texts, Modern Sexualities* 240—41 (Stanford: Stanford Univ. Press) (chapter entitled "Bradford's 'Ancient Members' and 'A Case of Buggery . . . Amongst Them,' " also available in *Nationalisms and Sexualities*, ed. Andrew Parker, Mary Russo, Doris Sommer, and Patricia Yeager [New York: Routledge, 1991], p. 60) for a similar reading. But Oaks and Goldberg seem to be mistaken. The more probable inference from the records, and the one reached by Hunter, is that sodomy would have been interpreted to include what we would now call heterosexual child molestation and/or statutory rape if legally sufficient proof of vaginal penetration had been available.

46. *Hardwick*, 478 U.S. at 190, 106 S. Ct. at 2843.

47. *Hardwick*, 478 U.S. at 200, 106 S. Ct. at 2849.

48. As Judge Posner correctly notes, the avalanche of law review commentary on *Hardwick* provides vastly more doctrinal than historical analysis. Richard A. Posner, *Sex and Reason* 347 (Cambridge: Harvard Univ. Press, 1992). Anne B. Goldstein's article,

with which I differ at some points in this essay, is a remarkable, pathbreaking exception—as Judge Posner has noted.

49. *Hardwick*, 478 U.S. at 192, 106 S. Ct. at 2844.

50. "Survey on the Constitutional Right to Privacy in the Context of Homosexual Activity," 40 *University of Miami Law Review* 521, 525 (1986).

51. For considerations of the importance of the *Symposium* in the history of erotic relations between men, see K. J. Dover, *Greek Homosexuality*, 11–13, 162–170 (Cambridge: Harvard Univ. Press, 1978), and David M. Halperin, "Was Diotima a Woman?," in Halperin, *One Hundred Years of Homosexuality and Other Essays on Greek Love* 113 (New York: Routledge, 1990). Though the latter was published after 1986, the former was readily available to the Survey authors and to the Court. Of course, they could have read the *Symposium* anytime.

52. John Boswell, *Christianity, Social Tolerance, and Homosexuality: Gay People in Western Europe from the Beginning of the Christian Era to the Fourteenth Century* (Chicago: Univ. of Chicago Press, 1980). Boswell's book was widely reviewed, even in the popular press. See *Newsweek*, "Homosexuality Since Rome," Sept. 29, 1980, at 79. It received a well-publicized American Book Award from the Association of American Publishers, and was named a "best book" of 1980 by the *New York Times Book Review*. *N.Y. Times Book Rev.*, "Paperbacks: New and Noteworthy," July 19, 1981, Section 7, p. 23; *N.Y. Times Book Rev.*, "Editors' Choice 1980," Nov. 30, 1980, Section 7, p. 3. Even if the Survey authors or the Justices agreed with those reviewers of Boswell's study who challenged his claim on this point (e.g., J. Robert Wright, "Boswell on Homosexuality: A Case Undemonstrated," 66 *Anglican Theological Review* 79 [1989]), they should have understood themselves to be under some duty of scholarly care requiring an explanation of why they took a contested position.

53. Pollock and Maitland derive this tradition from the First Lateran Councils of 1179 and 1215, which concluded that "[t]he impenitent heretic when convicted by the ecclesiastical court is to be handed over to the lay power for due punishment." Sir Frederick Pollock and Frederic William Maitland, 2 *The History of English Law Before the Time of Edward I* 545 (2d ed.) (Cambridge: Cambridge Univ. Press, 1968). The punishment of sodomy, understood as a species of heresy, "was a subject for ecclesiastical cognizance, and apparently there was a prevailing opinion that, if the church relinquished the offenders to the secular arm, they ought to be burnt." Ibid. at 556. Whether in fact such a punishment was assigned, as Pollock and Maitland note, is another question: "As a matter of fact we do not believe that in England they were thus relinquished." Ibid.; see note 54 below.

54. The Survey depends for this point on Derrick Sherwin Baily, *Homosexuality and the Western Christian Tradition* 146–47 (London: Archon Books, 1955). But at this very point Baily asserts the opposite: he relies on the passage from Pollock and Maitland quoted in note 53 above, and concludes that "as a matter of fact persons in England who were guilty of homosexual acts were not . . . relinquished" by the church to secular officials for capital punishment by burning. Ibid., at 147, citing F. Pollock and F. W. Maitland, 2 *The History of the English Law before the Time of Edward I* 556–57 (Cambridge: Cambridge Univ. Press, 1898). Brundage reports that the sever-

ity of punishment increased during the thirteenth century, but that even then the sanctions varied widely. Ecclesiastical sanctions included fasting and other ascetic disciplines, expulsion from religious orders, and the requirement that penance be made not before an ordinary confessor but before a bishop. To be sure, the municipalities provided for terrible punishments—some alternatives were castration and hanging or hanging by "the virile members"—but there was more to it than death at the stake. Brundage, *Law, Sex, and Christian Society* at 472–73. And Brundage concludes that, during the late medieval period when these severe sanctions became available, they were rarely invoked: young offenders had to pay fines, and "[c]ase records show that the most horrendous statutory punishments were reserved for particularly vicious cases, such as homosexual rape[,] and that ordinary offenders were more likely to be whipped, fined and exiled." Ibid., at 534–35.

55. Survey, 40 *University of Miami Law Review* at 525 ("The first secular legislation forbidding sodomy was not passed until the English Reformation when Henry VII removed jurisdiction from the ecclesiastical courts and granted it to the king's courts"—a historical turning point which the authors interpret in light of their claim that "[t]raditionally, . . . sodomy statutes have been aimed primarily at homosexuals.").

56. "The Gallup Poll reported that in 1985, 47 percent of those polled thought homosexual relations between consenting adults should not be legal, up from 39 percent in 1982—the difference presumably reflecting awareness of the AIDS epidemic. The percentage who thought that homosexual relations should be legal fell in the same period from 45 to 44 percent. Gallup Report nos. 244–245, January–February 1986, 3. The Supreme Court's decision in *Bowers v. Hardwick* was approved by 51 percent of the respondents, while 41 percent disapproved. Gallup Report no. 254, November 19[8]6, 26. Yet between 1986 and 1989, the percentage of Gallup Poll respondents who believed that homosexual relations between consenting adults should be illegal fell from 54 to 36 percent, and the percentage thinking they should be legal rose from 33 to 47 percent. Gallup Report no. 289, October 1989, 13." Posner, *Sex and Reason* 347 n.56.

57. See Thomas B. Stoddard, "Lesbian and Gay Rights before a Hostile Federal Judiciary," 27 *Harvard Civil Rights–Civil Liberties Law Review* 555, 568–73 (1992), for a discussion of this effect of "losing" gay-rights litigation.

58. Guido Calabresi, *A Common Law for the Age of Statutes* 6 (Cambridge: Harvard Univ. Press, 1982). For a useful survey of the problem of statutes that have survived the legislative will that purportedly adopted them, see William Eskridge, Jr., and Philip P. Frickey, *Cases and Materials on Legislation: Statutes and the Creation of Public Policy* 844–91 (St. Paul: West Publishing Co., 1988).

59. Martha L. Fineman, "Law and Changing Patterns of Behavior: Sanctions on Non-Marital Cohabitation," 1981 *Wisconsin Law Review* 275, 287–93. This study also documents the impediments to repeal set up by a "tough on crime" political rhetoric. Ibid., 299, 299 n.98.

60. Brundage, "The Politics of Sodomy: Rex v. Pons Hugh de Ampurias (1311)," in Joyce E. Salisbury, ed., *Sex in the Middle Ages* (Garland, 1991) (concluding that the

prosecution of Count Pons Hugh by James II of Aragon offers "another episode . . . in the political use of sodomy as an instrument of royal as well as ecclesiastical power"); Brundage, *Law, Sex and Christian Society* at 473; Alan Bray, *Homosexuality in Renaissance England* 37 (London: Gay Men's Press, 1982) (arguing that early Stuart accusations of homosexual conduct actually targeted "the Court—the extravagant, overblown, parasitic Renaissance court"); B. R. Burg, "Ho Hum, Another Work of the Devil: Buggery and Sodomy in Early Stuart England" 6:1/2 *J. of Homosexuality* 69, 77 (1980/81) (special edition entitled *Historical Perspectives on Homosexuality*, ed. Salvatore J. Licata and Robert P. Petersen) (concluding from a survey of seventeenth-century sodomy prosecutions in England that the decisions to prosecute same-sex conduct and to impose severe penalties for it were usually taken only "when public figures were involved and political motives were present").

61.   Consider an argument to the lords assembled to try Mervyn Touchet, Earl of Castlehaven for (*inter alia*) sodomy. Anticipating Castlehaven's defense that the essential element of penetration was unproven against him, the Lord Steward asserted that: "As to [the charge of sodomy] there is no other Question, but whether it be *Crimen Sodomiticum penetratione*, whether he penetrated the Body, or not; to which I answer, the Fifth of *Elizabeth*, sets it down in general Terms, and *ubi Lex non distinguit, ibi non distinguendum* [where the law does not distinguish, let there be no distinction made]; and I know you will be cautious how you give the least Mittigation to such abominable Sins; for when once a Man indulges his Lust, and Prevaricates with his Religion, as my Lord *Audley* has done, by being a Protestant in the Morning and a Papist in the Afternoon, no wonder he commits the most abominable Impieties; for when Men forsake their God, 'tis no wonder he leaves them to themselves." *The Tryal and Condemnation of Mervin Lord Audley, Earl of Castle-Haven, at Westminster, April the 5th 1631. For abetting a rape upon his Countess, committing sodomy with his servants, and commanding and countenancing the Debauching of His Daughter*, rpt. in *Sodomy Trials* (ed. Randolph Trumbach) (New York: Garland, 1986), at 12. Sir Edward Coke, in a roughly contemporaneous synthesis of British law, states that penetration (though not emission) was then an essential element of felony sodomy. Coke, *The Third Part of the Institutes of the Laws of England* (London, 1644), 59 ("there must be *penetratio*, that is, *res in re*"). Personhood thus functioned to redefine sodomy in Castlehaven's case—but it is religious, not sexual, personhood that was decisive.

62.   As Judge Posner observes, recent nonmilitary prosecutions for sodomy reflected in reported judicial opinions tend to involve elements of "public indecency." Posner, *Sex and Reason*, at 344 n.52.

63.   *Hardwick*, 478 U.S. at 197, 106 S. Ct. 2847 (Burger, J., concurring) (quoting 4 William Blackstone, *Commentaries on the Laws of England* 215 (1769; facsimile edition, Chicago: Univ. of Chicago Press, 1979).

64.   4 *The Diary of Samuel Pepys* 209–10 (ed. Robert Latham and William Matthews) (London, 1971), quoted in Randolph Trumbach, "The Birth of the Queen: Sodomy and the Emergence of Gender Equality in Modern Culture, 1660–1750," in *Hidden from History: Reclaiming the Gay and Lesbian Past* 129, 131 (ed. Martin Duberman, Martha Vicinus, and George Chauncey, Jr.) (New York: Meridian, 1990). Brundage

reports on twelfth-century penitential manuals which advise confessors "to be exceptionally careful in questioning penitents about these matters. Robert of Flamborough noted that his own practice in confession was to allude to unnatural sex only in the most vague and general terms, in order to avoid giving penitents ideas that had not already occurred to them." Brundage, *Law, Sex, and Christian Society* at 399.

65. Goldstein, "History, Homosexuality, and Political Values," at 97 *Yale Law Journal* at 1087.

66. Ibid., 1082–83 n.62, discussing *R. v. Wiseman*, 91 *Fortes* 92–93, 92 Eng. Rep. 774, 774 (1716).

67. See Posner, *Sex and Reason* at 345 n.52 ("it is for the most part only cases that are appealed that get reported. Not all convicted persons appeal. Defendants who plead guilty have in general no right to appeal," creating the possibility that sodomy convictions obtained on pleas go unreported). Scholars working with historical records will encounter different contextual limits to the social referentiality of printed reports of sodomy prosecutions—but it seems wise to assume that limits of this kind are ubiquitous.

   A converse problem in the relation between statutory prohibition and enforcement practices arises when state officials seek to disavow a desuetudinous statute on the ground that it is not enforced, and to prove that it is not enforced by the absence of appellate litigation under the statute. The Georgia attorney general, responding to questions about discriminatory enforcement of the Georgia statute at oral argument in *Hardwick*, asserted that it had not been enforced against heterosexual sodomy for about fifty years, but then was forced to concede that he had relied for this claim on research among reported appellate decisions. "Oral Argument in *Bowers v. Hardwick*," in *Landmark Briefs* at 643. Such a claim should not have reassured the justices that heterosexual privacy was safe in Georgia.

   For an unusually exacting social study of how sodomy laws have been enforced, see "Project: The Consenting Adult Homosexual and the Law: An Empirical Study of Enforcement and Administration in Los Angeles County," 13 *UCLA Law Review* 643 (1966).

68. Kendall Thomas, for instance, draws on Foucault's theory of power to argue that sodomy statutes constitute cruel and unusual punishment in violation of the Eighth Amendment because they encourage and legitimate homophobic attacks in the private sector. Thomas, "Beyond the Privacy Principle."

69. For a more detailed description of the diacritical relations between the discourse of acts and the discourse of identity in the *Hardwick* opinion and its legal surround, see my article "Reasoning about Sodomy," forthcoming in the *Virginia Law Review*.

Homosexuality and the Signs of Male
Friendship in Elizabethan England

ALAN BRAY

Dreams, Fantasies, and Fears

THIS essay is a commentary on two images that exercised a compelling grip on the imagination of sixteenth-century England, if the many references to them are a reliable guide to its dreams and fears. One is the image of the masculine friend. The other is the figure called the sodomite. The reaction these two images prompted was wildly different; the one was universally admired, the other execrated and feared: and yet in their uncompromising symmetry they paralleled each other in an uncanny way. Why this was and what it tells us of early modern England is what I have set out to explore here.

This symmetry appears among the shadows, on the edge of social life, in the fears and fantasies of Elizabethan England. But I shall argue that if we press it we will quickly emerge into the daylight, in the very center of early modern England. But we will go by a road, which I hope to lay open in this essay, which the Elizabethans themselves were unwilling to acknowledge was there.

The Sodomite

Elizabethan society was one of those which lacked the idea of a distinct homosexual minority, although homosexuality was nonetheless regarded with a readily expressed horror. In principle it was a crime which anyone was capable of, like murder or blasphemy. This is the New England minister Thomas Shepard in his *The Sincere Convert* of 1641:

Thy heart is a foul sink of all atheism, sodomy, blasphemy, murder, whoredom, adultery, witchcraft, buggery; so that, if thou hast any good thing in thee, it is but as a drop of rosewater in a bowl of poison; where fallen it is all corrupted.

It is true thou feelest not all these things stirring in thee at one time . . . but they are in thee like a nest of snakes in an old hedge. Although they break not out into thy life, they lie lurking in thy heart.

It was, according to John Rainolds, not only a "monstrous sin against nature" but also one to which "men's natural corruption and viciousness is prone." It is why it was sometimes attributed to drunkenness and why a sixteenth-century minister accused of sodomy said when first confronted that what he had done he had done in his sleep. The logic is the same as that of Thomas Shepard. It was not part of the individual's nature: it was part of all human nature and could surface when the mind was dulled or sleeping, much as someone might commit murder in a drunken fit or in a dream.[1]

But the Elizabethan "sodomy" differed from our contemporary idea of "homosexuality" in a number of other ways also. It covered more hazily a whole range of sexual acts, of which sexual acts between people of the same sex were only a part. It was closer, rather, to an idea like debauchery. But it differed more fundamentally also in that it was not only a sexual crime. It was also a political and a religious crime and it was this that explains most clearly why it was regarded with such dread, and it is this point that I propose to investigate.

One can see this sharply outlined in the accusations made in Elizabeth's reign against the rebellious nobleman Edward de Vere by his erstwhile fellow conspirators. The picture they draw is of a man who was not only a sodomite but also an enemy of society: a traitor and a man given to lawless violence against his enemies. He was also, they tell us, a habitual liar, an atheist, and a blasphemer. The charge of sodomy was not merely added to the list. It symbolized it. If this man was a rebel against nature, was it surprising that he was also a rebel against society and the truth (or the Truth) that supported it? Sodomy, the jurist Edward Coke wrote, was "crimen laesae majestatis, a sin horrible committed against the king: and this is either against the king celestial or terrestrial." It was one of those horrible crimes according to James I that a king was bound in conscience

never to forgive. It was in this way that the ubiquitous association of
sodomy with treason and heresy was put together and why one encounters
it so commonly in the polemics of Reformation Europe.[2]

The Masculine Friend

The image of the masculine friend was an image of intimacy between men
in stark contrast to the forbidden intimacy of homosexuality. It is an
image which will be very familiar to students of Elizabethan poetry and
drama, where it frequently appears; but the image there is misleading, for
when we see how it was used in the tumble of daily life we see something
more immediately practical than the literary images at first glance reveal.
The "voices of yourselves, your tenants and such other friends as you can
procure" was how a northern landowner was asked for his support in an
election early in the seventeenth century. "It were pity to lose him" wrote
an Elizabethan commander in the Low Countries about the possible loss
of an influential supporter "for he is indeed marvelously friended."[3]

It is in this way we see the word *friend* being used in such mundane
documents, and behind it is a web of social relations which will be recognized readily by students of Elizabethan society. What it points to is
that network of subtle bonds amongst influential patrons and their clients, suitors, and friends at court.

A concept so necessary to social life was far removed from the "uncivil"
image of the sodomite, yet there was still between them a surprising
affinity, as in some respects they occupied a similar terrain. An illustration
of this is the way each required a physical closeness, although after four
centuries have passed it is perhaps not immediately obvious how crucial
this was to the way friendship worked. One striking expression of this is
what it meant in early modern England to be someone's "bedfellow." This
was a society where most people slept with someone else and where the
rooms of a house led casually one into the other and servants mingled
with their masters. Such a lack of privacy usually made who shared a bed
with whom into a public fact. It was also a potentially meaningful one, for
beds are not only places where people sleep: they are also places where
people talk. To be someone's "bedfellow" suggested that one had influence and could be the making of a fortune.

It is in that sense that the Countess of Oxford used the word when she complained about the influence a certain John Hunt was exercizing over her son: "Hunt hath impudently presumed to be his bedfellow and otherwise used him most unrespectively." Anne Bacon uses "bed-companion" in the same sense in a letter to Anthony Bacon in 1594: "Your brother . . . keepeth that bloody Pérez, as I told him then, yea as a coach-companion and bed-companion." But the most striking illustration I know of is an entry Archbishop Laud made in his diary in August 1625: "That night in a dream the Duke of Buckingham seemed to me to ascend into my bed, where he carried himself with much love towards me, after such rest wherein wearied men are wont exceedingly to rejoice; and likewise many seemed to me to enter the chamber who did see this." Archbishop Laud's dream is of his patron the great Duke of Buckingham but the point of the dream is in its conclusion, that the powerful mark of favor he was dreaming of was public. It is in this sense also that we should read the now famous remark of George Villiers when he looked back with gratitude in a letter to James I, to that night when first "the bed's head could not be found between the master and his dog."[4]

The common bed shared in the public eye was only one expression of this. When two men kissed or embraced, the gesture had the same meaning. "But I doubt not so soon as his name shall come into the knowledge of men and his worthiness be sounded in the trump of fame, but that he shall be not only kissed but also beloved of all, embraced of the most, and wondered at of the best." That is the editor of the *Shepheardes Calender* in 1579 introducing its hopeful author, and such a public kiss carried the same meaning as the equally public fact of being a powerful man's bedfellow. At the beginning of Davenant's play *The Cruel Brother* of 1627, one of the characters points to just such public embraces as evidence of a certain Lucio's influence with the duke; and it is in such terms that Thomas Howard recorded Robert Carr's rise to power at the court of James I: "The Prince leaneth on his arm, pinches his cheek, smooths his ruffled garment . . . We are almost worn out in our endeavours to keep pace with this fellow in his duty and labour to gain favour, but all in vain; where it endeth I cannot guess, but honours are talked of speedily for him." This publicly displayed intimacy is part of what Francis Bacon in his essay *Of Followers and Friends* called "countenance," the appearance of a patron's evident favor; and its withdrawal could mean ruin. This is what Henry Howard later advised the now greatly powerful Robert Carr: "There is no better way to pare their nails . . . than by some withdrawing of your favourable countenance, which I do assure you is a groundyard to their boldness and a discharge of many watchful ears and eyes."[5]

Such kisses and embraces were for such "watchful ears and eyes" as these, as was the common bed Archbishop Laud dreamed of; but the physical intimacy they expressed was not the only sign of a friendship between two men that was recognized by the Elizabethans. It was expected to be matched by an equivalent emotional bond, and this had a part in the conventions of friendship as deep as the physical intimacy I have been describing. One can see this at length in the letters written by Antonio Pérez, the renegade secretary of Philip II, while he was part of the circle around the Earl of Essex during his visit to England in the 1590s. Love between men is the theme of these letters, which are suffused by an understood emotional attachment both between Essex and his servants and among them. Typical of many more is the letter in which a mere note arranging a meeting in the morning becomes an elaborate reflection, as moving now as it was then, on the nature of one man's desire for another. We should not be misled, though, by Pérez's neoplatonic decorations: this is in essence the same language that a great earl uses when he signs a stern note to one of his clients "Your loving master" or a great lord when he closes a message with the injunction to love this messenger, adding significantly that the recipient of the letter should also receive its bearer into his protection. In these letters Pérez was merely using the ubiquitous convention.[6]

One might well wonder, of course, how genuine were such expressions of affection. Antonio Pérez was a man on the make, and those he scattered about rarely convince. But one can see alongside his friendships others which had all the utilitarian functions the Elizabethans expected of friendship and yet did contain within them obviously genuine emotion. The correspondence of Michael Hickes, the patronage secretary of Lord Burghley, and his friend John Stubbe in the Lansdowne Manuscripts is one of these. We see Michael Hickes putting out money on John Stubbe's behalf. We see him trying to obtain payment of a debt due to him. We also see Stubbe asking Hickes to use his influence on behalf of a friend. But these letters document also an intense personal friendship which began when they were students together in Cambridge and in its time included both passion and jealousy. In 1570 we see Hickes writing Stubbe an emotional and jealous letter complaining of his friendship with a friend of their Lincoln's Inn days. Which of the two, he asks angrily, do you love the best? And one can see from a teasing letter Stubbe sent him in 1575 that he was still prickly about the friendship several years later. There are also in these letters evident expressions of affection in quieter times and a glimpse in a late letter of Stubbe of that youth, as he put it, that they spent together.[7]

One can see the same combination of usefulness and affection in the letters of Tobie Matthew and Francis Bacon, but there is a striking isolated illustration of the same thing in the emotion evident in a letter written to Casiodoro de Reina, the minister for several years of the Spanish Protestant congregation in London, by his friend and collaborator Antonio del Corro after a long and anxious separation. If it had not been for his wife, he writes, he would have hastened to him long ago, the very day "I saw and realised how impossible it was for me to live without you." He then goes on to explain that in desperation he had set off impetuously to find Reina, without even knowing where to set out for, when "almost miraculously" he received Reina's letter. He then turns from this emotional introduction to the business in hand: the arrangements he is making for the printing of Reina's translation of the Bible into Spanish.[8]

Emotional bonds such as these had their place alongside the physical links of friendship, but in contrast these were directed inward to the participants themselves, not outward to the world at large. They were an assurance that their friendship would remain, in good fortune or bad: a sign and a telling guarantee that they could indeed rely on each other.

Such comments give us a vantage point from which to judge the elegant garments in which friendship was often dressed in Elizabethan England, as much in its daily use as in a poem or a play or a piece of imaginative literature. Typical of the carefully beautiful manner in which it was usually presented is the picture of Euphues's friendship with his friend Philautus in John Lyly's Elizabethan novel *Euphues*:

> But after many embracings and protestations one to another they walked to dinner, where they wanted neither meat, neither music, neither any other pastime; and having banqueted, to digest their sweet confections they danced all that afternoon. They used not only one board but one bed, one book (if so be it they thought not one too many). Their friendship augmented every day, insomuch that the one could not refrain the company of the other one minute.

> All things went in common between them, which all men accounted
> commendable.

This is idealized, of course; and there are literary echoes here, especially of
Cicero's essay on friendship, *De Amicitia*, and of the numerous ornate
treatises on love which popularized Ciceronian and neoplatonic ideas
on friendship. Indeed, the same could be said of all the letters between
friends I have referred to. But when one looks at the details of this account
one sees something surprisingly more mundane. Its material is made up
virtually entirely of the conventions I have been writing of: the embraces
and the protestations of love, the common bed and the physical closeness,
the physical and emotional intimacy. All had their ready parallels in the
accustomed conventions of Elizabethan friendship. Its idealization consisted rather in what it left out: its tactful omission of those bonds of
mutual interest of which the everyday signs were such conventions. The
engaging artifice is part of a tough reality, and the realistic comment to set
by it is that of Francis Bacon at the end of his essay on followers and
friends when he says that such friendship as there is in this world is in
truth between those who have the same material interests, those "whose
fortunes" as he puts it "may comprehend the one the other."[9]

But John Lyly was fully right to declare such intimacy to be accepted by
all. There was no suggestion at all about it of the possible signs of a sodomitical relationship. When William Prynne edited Archbishop Laud's
diary he tried to read into it the sodomitical sin one would expect of the
papist in heart that Prynne presented him as being, but when he came to
his dream of sleeping with the Duke of Buckingham he merely transcribed
it. Its meaning was too obvious to do otherwise. And one would be greatly
mistaken to assume a softness toward sodomy on the part of these writers.
Sodomy for Tobie Matthew was one of "those crimes which are against
nature . . . ever to be detested and punished," and the sodomite for John
Lyly was "a most dangerous and infectious beast." So also when Antonio
del Corro preached in London on the sin of the sodomites in Paul's letter
to the Romans he elaborated the horror of the sin with all the exuberance
of a popular preacher.[10]

The great distance between sodomy and friendship and the nature of
that distance is well illustrated by a sodomitical joke Antonio Pérez includes in one of his letters to the Earl of Essex, in which he likens himself
to the girlfriend of his newly arrived assistant. One can see that this is a

joke but it seems rather a dangerous one, for the Inquisition charged Pérez with being a sodomite as well as a heretic and a traitor; and yet it was quite out of character for him to have added fuel to the charge by a rash remark. But how rash was this remark? The joke rested securely on a real distinction between the joke itself and the actuality. It turned the world upside down. In it, it is the patron who becomes the conventionally weaker part and the servant the powerful: it is Pérez and not the servant who becomes the girl. That was why the joke was only a joke and not to be taken seriously.[11]

In the same way, how seriously could one then take the apparent similarity between the sodomite and the masculine friend? The signs of the one were indeed sometimes also the signs of the other, but the conventions of friendship were set a world away from the wild sin of Sodom by the placid orderliness of the relationships they expressed. The anarchic crime of which Edward Coke wrote was a clearly different thing.

An Unnatural Intimacy

The distinction between the two kinds of intimacy was then apparently sharp and clearly marked: the one was expressed in orderly "civil" relations, the other in subversive; and this simple distinction explains a good deal of what we see. But it does not explain quite all. On occasion one can also come across a document that appears—against all our expectations—to be putting the two together and reading a sodomitical meaning by such a monstrous image into just those conventions of friendship which elsewhere seemed protected from that interpretation.

Rare though they are, these documents are not to be dismissed as mere curiosities, and I propose to look at two such documents closely, for they suggest that this distinction was neither as sharp nor as clearly marked as the Elizabethans would have us believe. They cast by this an unexpectedly bright light on that hidden road I mentioned: the unacknowledged connection between the unmentionable vice of Sodom and the friendship which all accounted commendable.

One of these two documents is a denunciation made in 1601 by a paid informer by the name of William Reynolds, whose subject was a certain Piers Edmonds, a soldier who had been in Ireland with the Earl of Southampton before Southampton joined Essex's ill-fated rebellion of that year. Piers Edmonds, he implies, was likely to have been a rebel as his master had been; and into this implication William Reynolds weaves a story of an unnatural intimacy between the two men that told its own tale.

> I do marvel also what became of Piers Edmonds, called Captain Piers or Captain Edmonds, the Earl of Essex man, born in Strand near me, one which has had many rewards and preferments by the Earl Essex. His villainy I have often complained of.
>
> He dwells in London. He was corporal general of the horse in Ireland under the Earl of Southampton. He ate and drank at his table and lay in his tent. The Earl of Southampton gave him a horse which Edmonds refused a hundred marks for him. The Earl Southampton would coll [embrace] and hug him in his arms and play wantonly with him.
>
> This Piers began to fawn and flatter me in Ireland, offering me great courtesy, telling me what pay, graces and gifts the earls bestowed upon him, thereby seeming to move and animate me to desire and look for the like favour. But I could never love and affect them to make them my friends, especially Essex, whose mind I ever mistrusted.

Behind this account is the familiar Elizabethan stereotype that the man guilty of "unnatural filthiness" would be also very likely a traitor. But the evidence William Reynolds points to so menacingly—the common tent in which they slept, the embraces William Reynolds saw—were all the conventional signs of friendship; and that the characters in this drama understood them in this way is strongly suggested by the openness of Piers Edmonds's boasting and the public nature of these embraces, for they must indeed have been public if someone like William Reynolds could have been a witness of them.[12]

A document such as this poses an interesting question about what its author is doing, but first the other such document I mentioned. This works in a similar way but is far more famous. The relationship of Edward and Gaveston in Marlowe's play *Edward II* is of a piece with all that I have said of friendship and is the spectacular center of the play, in that it is Edward's love for Gaveston and Gaveston's rise to power which prompt the rebellion of Edward's resentful nobles and his ensuing tragedy and death. Modern critics of the play have recognized that its conventions are those of sixteenth-century, not fourteenth-century, England. But the many who have written of the apparently openly "homosexual" nature of the play have not grasped its irony or that the intense emotion, the passionate language, and the embraces we see between these two men have ready parallels in Elizabethan England in the daily conventions of friendship without being signs of a sodomitical relationship.[13]

When we look for signs of overt sexuality, what we see are rather Edward as a father and his determination to marry Gaveston to his niece. The latter is no incidental detail, nor is it an accident that she is referred to quite simply as the king's niece, as her role is to unite Gaveston and Edward as well as to give Gaveston a wife. In the same way Henry Howard in the daylight world of Jacobean England sought to bind himself to the powerful Robert Carr by Carr's marriage to his grandniece Frances Howard. An expression in one of Howard's letters puts the point neatly. If he has any pain, he writes, in reading Carr's last letter it is but "like the pain which my Lady Frances shall feel when the sweet stream follows." The image extends the erotic relationship to include Howard and it is entirely appropriate that it should, for though this was a heterosexual relationship it united also two men.[14]

Yet there are in the relationship of Edward and Gaveston dark suggestions of sodomy. It is there in the sexual ambiguity of the opening. When the naked and lovely boy in Gaveston's entertainment for Edward holds a bush "to hide those parts which men delight to see" is it the body of the boy which is being hidden or of the goddess he is playing? It is there in the later comparison of Gaveston to the classical Ganymede, the beautiful youth caught up by Zeus to be his cupbearer. Giles Fletcher could compare Christ's ascension without embarrassment to the fate of Ganymede, but a "ganymede" was also used more crudely as a synonym for a catamite. It is there also in Gaveston's foreign birth and Italianate ways, both of which were associated in Elizabethan England with sodomy. It is there most clearly but most disturbingly in the hideous sodomitical murder of Edward at the end of the play. Yet this one clear statement of Edward's sodomitical sin is put in the hands of a man called Lightborne, whose name is but an Anglicized echo of Lucifer, the father of all lies.[15]

Marlowe describes in this play what could be a sodomitical relationship, but he places it wholly within the incompatible conventions of Elizabethan friendship, in a tension which he never allows to be resolved. The image we see is simultaneously that of both friendship and its caricature.

A Changing Context

Such unlikely texts as these of William Reynolds's denunciation and Christopher Marlowe's play prompt the same question. These texts appear to be bringing together images which were usually kept quite detached from each other. Why, we might well then ask, did their authors think they would be believed? The answer casts a light on the society in which these documents were put together quite as much as it does on the documents themselves. The answer in short is this. As a contemporary would have seen far more readily than we do, some of the conventions of friendship are missing in these accounts and the missing ones are precisely those that ensured that the intimacy of these conventions was read in an acceptable frame of reference; but they were not only missing in these accounts: by the end of the sixteenth century they were also often missing in society at large. It is this that these documents point up.

One of these conventions was the assumption that both masters and their close servingmen would be "gentle," men (as a work published in 1598 entitled *A Health to the Gentlemanly Profession of Seruingmen* puts it) "made of their own metal, even a loaf of their own dough, which being done . . . the gentleman received even a gentleman into his service." It is this missing propriety that William Reynolds indirectly alludes to when he describes Piers Edmonds as a man born in the Strand "near me"; another description of Piers Edmonds puts it more bluntly as, "a man of base birth," and the nobles' frequently repeated complaints of Gaveston's "base" birth in *Edward II* make the same point.[16]

A second assumption which is missing is that the bond between a master and such an intimate servingman was personal, not mercenary. Such a servant did not seek a reward, although both master and servant would rightly care for the interests of the other. Rather the relationship was like that of father and son, to which it was habitually compared. The convention is well expressed in a letter home in 1595 of the secretary of Antonio Pérez, in a description he gives of a conversation he had one day with his master.

> My master called me unto him the other day and amongst many promises he willed me to tell him what thing I would most desire he should do for me. I answered for him that I only desired him to love me. He again asked me (as not being satisfied with that answer) and

I answered him again the same. He then assured me that he loved me as his own son and would do as much for me as for his own son.

It is this missing assumption which William Reynolds alludes to in the damning commentary he quietly adds to Piers Edmonds's boasting, beginning with that simple but all important participle "seeming to move and animate me to desire and look for the like favour." His motives were as base as his origins; that is what William Reynolds indirectly is telling his reader.[17]

Gaveston's motives are as suspect as William Reynolds would have us believe Piers Edmonds's were. The opening scene in the play makes that all too clear, as does the image Marlow later has him unconsciously lapse into. It begins with the same—eminently proper—sentiment which Antonio Pérez's servant professed. Its end is brutally different:

> It shall suffice me to enjoy your love,
> Which whiles I have I think myself as great
> As Caesar riding in the Roman streets
> With captive kings at his triumphant car.[18]

The absence of these two reassuring conventions left what remained open to a darker interpretation. What then was it that one was seeing? If someone had acquired a place in society to which he was not entitled by nature and could then perhaps even lord it over those who were naturally his betters, the specter likely to be conjured up in the mind of an Elizabethan was not the orderly relationship of friendship between men but rather the profoundly disturbing image of the sodomite, that enemy not only of nature but of the order of society and the proper kinds and divisions within it. Perhaps, it darkly suggested, it was the signs of *this* that one was seeing? It is this fear that William Reynolds and Christopher Marlowe played on with such skill.

Such documents warn one against making a mistake one might otherwise easily fall into; they clarify that what one is seeing in such a structure of ideas as I have described is not a collective and automatic mentality, of any kind. It is rather a kind of code: the difference between the two lay in that a code was something individuals were still free to manipulate. They may not have done it very often, but the possibility of consciously manipulating the signs of this code, for their own benefit, was always there; and it is not an accident that the two clearest examples I have seen were created by authors whose task was to shape and manipulate meaning: to tell tales.

But this was not merely sleight of hand, and it is this that makes these documents so revealing. These two authors were able to present such credible pictures precisely because the conventions which were so crucially absent in these accounts were also in practice often absent in daily life. It was because contemporaries were often *not* following the ideals of service that Elizabethans wrote their tracts expounding them, as the tracts themselves make clear. A master looking for a useful servant might well prefer the industrious servant who was poor but able and anxious to better himself to the better born one, and the protestations of disinterested service one reads so frequently were often hollow. After the pious protestations of the secretary of Antonio Pérez I quoted earlier, he then coldly sets about adding up how much he is likely to make through his master's influence. Hardly more convincing are the protestations of affection for his dearest friends with which his master himself recommends various rich merchants to the Earl of Essex.[19]

These proprieties are the conventional niceties that all too often were no more than pretense. "You may boldly write for his favour in this matter," a lawyer in Elizabethan London was well able to write. "You paid well for it."[20]

Such cynicism was probably always likely to have been justified, but there is something wider at work here also. A broad hint of this is given in the *Health to the Gentlemanly Profession of Seruingman*, which I quoted from earlier. The decay in the conventions of service, its author tells us, was something that he could still describe. The Lisle letters support that judgment; in them we see the conventions of personal service still very much alive in the 1530s. Why then the change? According to the anonymous author of this work, the change was brought about by the decline in the open-handed "housekeeping" of the great house. It was also due, he tells us, to the replacement of gentlemen retainers by servants drawn from outside the gentry, a change which was referred to by Walter Darell in his conduct book for servingmen published in 1572. The gentleman servingman was being replaced by the gentry with "the rich farmer's son," as Darell puts it, a man who will "drudge in their business."[21]

Behind these complaints lies the sixteenth-century decline in the hordes of retainers in the great houses of an earlier and different England

and the conventions of personal service associated with them, a change these tracts closely document. Such great households were by no means extinct in Elizabeth's reign. Lord Burghley was still able to say that it was his disease to have too many servants although there was little he could do about it, and early in the following century we still see the Earl of North-ampton taking into his household the sons of his gentry supporters. But servingmen like these were increasingly an anachronism. The able and hard-working secretaries of the Earl of Essex or Lord Burghley, men such as Michael Hickes (who was the son of a mercer), were altogether more suited to their times.[22]

As a social form the personal service of early Tudor England was in decay by the end of the sixteenth century, but as a cultural form it was not; here the language of "friendship," as a set of assumptions and expecta-tions, was still very much alive. There was, though, now a disparity be-tween the two in precisely those elements that protected the intimacy it involved from a charge of sodomy, and it was this that provided a conve-nient inlet to charges of the kind that were laid at the prison door of the Earl of Southampton and the hapless Piers Edmonds. William Rey-nolds's account and the picture Christopher Marlowe gives in *Edward II* are in fact more accurate pictures of the ties of friendship in the late sixteenth century than the conventional ideal the Elizabethans were still apt to present, and it was this fact that made these descriptions so fright-eningly effective.

The Weapon

To take William Reynolds's allegations as evidence of a covert sexual relationship is to follow a phantom, cunningly made. But they do put in a different light many of the charges of homosexuality we see in early mod-ern England. We cannot say whether there was a sexual relationship be-tween Piers Edmonds and the Earl of Southampton, and the malice of their accuser should make us cautious; but to leave the matter there is to miss the nature of such accusations. They did not need such a sexual relationship. They turned rather on a sharp-eyed recognition that the public signs of a male friendship—open to all the world to see—could be read in a different and sodomitical light to the one intended. But although we cannot say whether there was a sexual relationship between the Earl of Southampton and the man who served under him in Ireland as corporal general of the horse, we can see within the accusation a familiar social outline. This relationship is not alone in that. It is true also of a good many others: of Charles I's bishop John Atherton and Atherton's proctor, who were accused of sodomy in 1640 at the onset of the ruin of the Caroline church; of the Casiodoro de Reina mentioned earlier and the servant who shared his bed, with whom he was accused of sodomy in a tale spread by his enemies in the émigré community; of the popish Earl of Castlehaven, who in 1631, in a prosecution full of anti-Catholic prejudice, was accused of sodomy with his servants; and, indeed, of James I in the famous accusations made against him and companions such as Robert Carr or the Duke of Buckingham. We will misunderstand these accusations if, beguiled by them, we uncritically assume the existence of the sexual relationship which they appear to point to, for the material from which they could be constructed was rather open and public to all. What such accusations have in common is rather the outline of a relationship which at other times an Elizabethan might have called friendship.[23]

This is not to say that they were always inventions. Homosexual relationships did indeed occur within social contexts which an Elizabethan would have called friendship, between masters and servants included. But accusations like those of William Reynolds are not evidence of it; and the ease with which he was able to make his case out of the most everyday of materials should make us wary. We see in them rather the unwelcome difficulty the Elizabethans had in drawing a dividing line between those gestures of closeness among men that they desired so much and those they feared.[24]

But to call someone a sodomite was to do more than invite public censure on what was thought of as a private vice. Its effect involved incomparably more than that. Let me give an illustration. In his autobiography Simonds D'Ewes gives a description of Francis Bacon, once lord chancellor to James I, in his disgrace and it contains an accusation which the reader may well now find familiar.

> For whereas presently upon his censure at this time his ambition was moderated, his pride humbled, and the means of his former injustice and corruption removed; yet would he not relinquish the practice of his most horrible and secret sin of sodomy, keeping still one Godrick a very effeminate faced youth to be his catamite and bedfellow,

although he had discharged the most of his other household servants: which was the more to be admired [wondered at] because men
generally after his fall began to discourse of that his unnatural crime
which he had practised many years; deserting the bed of his lady,
which he accounted as the italians and turks do, a poor and mean
pleasure in respect of the other; and it was thought by some that he
should have been tried at the bar of justice for it, and have satisfied
the law most severe against that horrible villainy with the price of his
blood; which caused some bold and forward man to write these
verses following in a whole sheet of paper, and to cast it down in
some part of York House in the Strand, where Viscount St Alban
yet lay.

> Within this sty a *hog doth
> lie that must be hanged
> for sodomy.
> *Alluding both to his surname
> of Bacon and to that swinish
> abominable sin.

But he never came to any public trial for this crime; nor did ever that
I could hear forbear his old custom of making his servants his
bedfellows so to avoid the scandal was raised of him, though he lived
many years after this his fall in his lodgings in Gray's Inn in Hol-
born, in great want and penury.[25]

Much of this plays over again the issues discussed in this essay. There is
the same social context for the charge of sodomy, here between a master
and his servant. There is the same inconsistency between the description
of his "secret" sin and the evident fact that many others (including the
author) were aware of it. There is also the same insidious detail: his old
custom was that he made his servants his bedfellows, and it worked to the
same end. Simonds D'Ewes in fact lacks any direct evidence of the sodomy he is accusing Francis Bacon of; but in the impropriety of this detail—for this was a menial servant, no gentleman companion—lay the
germ of a charge of sodomy and the suggestion that the common bed of a
master and his servant might suggest something much darker.

But this description is part of a larger description and only an incident in it. Its context in the manuscript is a broad indictment of the "injustice and corruption" D'Ewes mentions here, of the bribes that caused his downfall and of the support given him in his corruption. But there was a problem in this. What distinguished this corruption from the normal workings of friendship? What distinguished, in effect, the bribes of the one from the flow of gifts and the ready use of influence of the other? It is here that this small description has its effect, for if successful it necessarily changed the frame of reference in which the whole was to be viewed. If this man was a sodomite, then was he not likely in all his doings to be the enemy of God's good order, in society as well as in nature? That was the transubstantiation it brought about. It could turn what seemed like gifts into bribes and what seemed like patronage into the support of infamy; it revealed what they really were. If successful, it turned all to ruin, and it could work its alchemy by a manipulation of the signs of friendship which it found so ready to hand.

The Shadow in the Garden

Perhaps there is always a potential ambiguity about intimacy between men. It may be so. But in early modern England such intimacy was peculiarly ambivalent, for the protecting conventions that ensured that it was seen in an acceptable frame of reference were often absent by the end of the sixteenth century. It was a disturbing fact that the Elizabethans preferred not to acknowledge, but when it suited them it provided a weapon that lay close to hand; and it left this intimacy more open and less secure in its meaning than the formal Elizabethan essays on friendship would have us believe.

The ambiguity drew, though, on a tension in Elizabethan England we are not now accustomed to. The intimacy between men in Europe and in North America today is protected to a large extent by the notion of a quite distinct homosexual minority for whom alone homosexual desire is a possibility. This was a shield Elizabethan England did not have and we might well wonder if this cultural difference is the reason why later historians have been so blind to the fearsome weapon its absence provided.

I am inclined to think that it is, but whether or not this is so I would suggest that the study in this essay of the Elizabethan sin of Sodom places it outside a discrete history of sexuality; its shadow was never far from the flower-strewn world of Elizabethan friendship and it could never wholly be distinguished from it. A hard fact which those of power and influence in Elizabethan England preferred not to see; but they were willing, still, to make use of it.

Notes

This article first appeared in *History Workshop Journal* 29 (Spring 1990): 1–19; it is reprinted by permission. A shorter version was given at the conference "Homosexuality, Which Homosexuality?" at the Free University of Amsterdam in December 1987 and at the seminar "Society, Belief, and Culture in the Early Modern World" at the Institute of Historical Research; I am grateful to the participants there for their lively discussions of it, which have greatly influenced its final form. Jeremy Clarke, Anna Davin, and others also kindly read the first draft of the essay. I owe a particular debt also to Michel Rey, from whom over many years of discussions I have learned so much of the history of friendship.

1. Thomas Shepard, *The Works of Thomas Shepard* (Boston: Doctrinal Tract and Book Society, 1853), 1:28, included in the collection of documents of Jonathan Ned Katz, *Gay/Lesbian Almanac* (New York: Harper and Row, 1983), 82–84. "Sodomy" and "buggery" were overlapping (and equally vague). The first was the scholarly word, the second the vulgar, which Shepard is here using for emphasis. John Rainolds, *Th' Overthrow of Stage-Playes* (1599), 10 and 32. Alan Bray, *Homosexuality in Renaissance England* (London: Gay Men's Press and Gay Men's Press Publishers, 1982 and 1988), 16. This is cited below as Bray, *Homosexuality*; in each case the page references are the same to each edition. Arthur G. Kinder, *Casiodoro de Reina: Spanish Reformer of the Sixteenth Century* (London: Tamesis Books, 1975), 28, 29, 105, 107, 109. Quotations (here and elsewhere in this essay) are modernized and are given according to the rules in Bray, *Homosexuality*, p. 115; documents not in English are given in translation.

2. Public Record Office, State Papers, 12/151/100–102, 103–104v, 109–109v, 113–113v, 118–119v, and British Museum, Cotton MSS, Titus C VI/5ff. "Nature" here is the order of creation: that in "men's natural corruption" in the quotation from Rainolds is the nature given us by Adam's Fall. Edward Coke, *Twelfth Part of the Reports* (1656), 37. James VI (and I), Βασιλικὸν δῶρον (1887), 37–38. Buggery was usually excluded from a general pardon: J. A. Sharpe, *Crime in Seventeenth-Century England: A County Study* (Cambridge: Cambridge University Press, 1983), 147 and 257. The explanation given in this section of the nature of the "sodomite" in Elizabethan England is set out more fully in Bray, *Homosexuality*, 13–32. There is a criticism of the apparently functionalist form I gave to my analysis in chapter 4 of *Homosexuality*, in Eve Kosofsky Sedgwick, *Between Men: English Literature and Male Homosocial Desire* (New York: Columbia University Press, 1985), 83ff. There is also a careful criticism of my handling of Richard Barnfield's writings in Jonathan Goldberg, "Colin to Hobbinol: Spenser's Familiar Letters," *South Atlantic Quarterly* 88, no. 1 (1989): 107–26. Each of these anticipated in some ways the development in my thinking apparent in this essay, and I would warmly commend them.

3.   John K. Gruenfelder, "The Electoral Patronage of Sir Thomas Wentworth, Earl of Strafford, 1614–1640," *Journal of Modern History* 49, no. 4 (1977): 557. British Museum, Harl. MSS, 285/173, in John Bruce, ed., *Correspondence of Robert Dudley, Earl of Leycester* (1844), 33.

4.   Public Record Office, State Papers, 14/65/78 ("unrespectively": disrespectfully). Lambeth Palace Library, 653/318, in Gustav Ungerer, *A Spaniard in Elizabethan England: The Correspondence of Antonio Pérez's Exile* (London: Tamesis Books, 1974 and 1976), 1:219; he rightly corrects the transcription by James Spedding which I followed in *Homosexuality*, p. 49. James Bliss, ed., *The Works of . . . William Laud* (1853), 3:170. I have followed William Prynne's translation in *A Breviate of the Life of William Laud* (1644), 6; compare Charles Carlton, *Archbishop William Laud* (London and New York: Routledge and Kegan Paul, 1987), 152. Longleat House, Portland Papers, 2/44, in Historical Manuscripts Commission, *Calendar of the Manuscripts of the Marquis of Bath* (Dublin, 1907), 2:71; compare Roger Lockyer, *Buckingham: The Life and Political Career of George Villiers, First Duke of Buckingham, 1592–1628* (London: Longman, 1981), 22.

5.   Edwin Greenlaw and others, eds., *The Works of Edmund Spenser. A Variorum Edition: The Minor Poems* (Baltimore: Johns Hopkins University Press, 1943), 1:7. James Maidment and W. H. Logan, eds., *The Dramatic Works of Sir William Davenant* (Edinburgh, 1872), 1:119–20. Linda Levy Peck, *Northampton: Patronage and Policy at the Court of James I* (London: George Allen and Unwin, 1982), 30. Edward Arber, ed., *A Harmony of the Essays etc of Francis Bacon* (1871), 32–33. Peck, *Northampton*, 36.

6.   Ungerer, *A Spaniard in Elizabethan England*, especially the letters in the first volume, and Antonio Pérez, *Ant. Perezii ad Comitem Essexium . . . Epistolarvm. Centuria Vna* in *Cartas de A Perez* (Paris, n.d.); the reference here is to Epistola 75 in the latter. S. L. Adams, "The Gentry of North Wales and the Earl of Leicester's Expedition to the Netherlands, 1585–86," *Welsh History Review* 7, no. 2 (1974–75): 147. Ungerer, *A Spaniard in Elizabethan England*, 1:417 ("protection": patrocinium).

7.   British Museum, Lansdowne MSS, 12/217–217v and 23/179–179v; 107/168–168v; 61/170 (see also 31/40); 12/217–217v (see also 12/117–117v); 21/26; 36/212–213 (generally see also 25/135 and 107/170–170v). Discussed in Alan G. R. Smith, *Servant of the Cecils: The Life of Sir Michael Hickes, 1543–1612* (London: Jonathan Cape, 1977), 22, 70, 92–96.

8.   James Spedding, *The Letters and the Life of Francis Bacon*, vol. 4, 1868, pp. 139–40 and 144–45 and vol. 7, 1874, pp. 286–87, 428–31, and 542. Bacon helped him in his career and in the scandal that followed his conversion to catholicism; Matthew did the same for Bacon in his disgrace and acted both as a critic and translator of his writings. Kinder, *Casiodoro de Reina* (London: Tamesis Books, 1975), 25–26 and 95–97; see also William McFadden, *The Life and Works of Antonio del Corro, 1527–1591* (Ph.D. thesis, The Queen's University of Belfast, 1953), 165ff. and 392.

9.   R. W. Bond, ed., *The Complete Works of John Lyly*, vol. 1 (Oxford, 1902), 199. Arber, ed., *Essays of Francis Bacon*, 38–39. This is not to contrast literary with other sources. The same point could be made, in varying degrees, with all the images of friendship.

10. Prynne, *Breviate of the Life of Laud* (1644), 6; compare p. 29. *The Confessions of the Incomparable Doctor S. Augustine*, trans. Tobie Matthew (1620), 108–9. Bond, ed., *Works*

of John Lyly (1902), 1:280; this is an addition John Lyly made during his paraphrase of Plutarch (*Plutarch's Moralia*, with translation by F. C. Babbitt, vol. 1, 1927, pp. 54–55). One can see the expressions added to the biblical text in Corro's paraphrase of *Romans* 1:26–27 in Antonius Corranus, *Dialogvs Theologicvs*, 1574 (English translation Antonie Corranus, *A Theological Dialogve*, 1575) and in Antonius Corranus, *Dialogvs in Epistolam D Pauli ad Romanos*, Frankfurt, 1587, and Antonius Corranus, *Epistola Beati Pavli Apostoli ad Romanos*, 1581, in which Corro gathered his lectures together for publication.

11. Published by Pérez in *Ant. Perezii ad Comitem Essexium*, n.d., as Epistola 60. The original is given in Ungerer, *A Spaniard in Elizabethan England*, 1:424–25 (which probably would have circulated in manuscript as a literary exercise).

As often in Pérez's writings there is an obscurity here and more than one reading is possible, but the dangerous reading I have given it is certainly one of these possible readings. He was careful to avoid the charge that he was a heretic by the permission he obtained when he visited England to practice catholicism. Ungerer, *A Spaniard in Elizabethan England*, 1:145. Why would he have taken a different attitude to the charge that he was a sodomite? The one was the mere reflection of the other.

The Inquisition's charges of sodomy are set out in *Colección de Documentos Inéditos para la Historia de España*, vol. 12, D. Miguel Salvá and Pedro Sainz de Baranda, eds., *Documentos Relativos á Antonio Pérez* (Madrid, 1848), 224–36, 255–59, 400–401, and G. Marañón, *Antonio Pérez* (Madrid, 1948), 1:306–9 and vol. 2, appendix no. 26. See also 1:310–11. The independent nature of much of this evidence strongly suggests that in this case it was true.

12. Hatfield House, Cecil Papers, 83/62. The letters from Piers Edmonds at 90/76 and 90/77 contain more information about him. Calendared in Historical Manuscripts Commission, *Calendar of the Manuscripts of the Most Hon. the Marquis of Salisbury*, part 11, 1906, pp. 93–94 and 99. I have emended the "called Called" of the text and omitted the illegible (or deleted) word that follows.

13. Some critics have read the apparently homosexual relationship as an affirmation of humane values, for example Leonora L. Brodwin, "Edward II: Marlowe's Culminating Treatment of Love," *ELH* 31, no. 2 (1964): 139–55, or Purvis E. Boyette, "Wanton Humour and Wanton Poets: Homosexuality in Marlowe's Edward II," *Tulane Studies in English* 22 (1977): 33–50, or Ronald Huebert, "Tobacco and Boys and Marlowe," *Sewanee Review* 92, no. 2 (1984): 206–24. Others have read it as an obscenity, such as Wilbur Sanders, *The Dramatist and the Received Idea: Studies in the Plays of Marlowe and Shakespeare* (Cambridge: Cambridge University Press, 1968), 121–42, or William L. Godshalk, *The Marlovian World Picture* (The Hague: Mouton, 1974), 59ff. But the assumption is widespread in what has been written of the play that the play *does* deal with an openly homosexual relationship. The importance of L. J. Mills's early but neglected discussion of the role of friendship in the play has not been fully appreciated: "The Meaning of Edward II," *Modern Philology* 32, no. 1 (1934–35): 11–31; Mills missed the contemporary social and political meaning of "friendship" but he was on the right lines. Another neglected early clue was the importance of caricature in the writings of Marlowe that T. S. Eliot pointed to in his 1919 essay "Christopher

Marlowe" (*Selected Essays* [London: Faber and Faber, 1951], pp. 118–25). More recently Simon Shepherd and Jonathan Goldberg have discussed sensitively the language of sodomy in *Edward II* and the Baines note (Simon Shepherd, *Marlowe and the Politics of Elizabethan Theatre* [Brighton: Harvester Press, 1986], 197–207, and Jonathan Goldberg, "Sodomy and Society: The Case of Christopher Marlowe," *Southwest Review* 69, no. 4 [1984]: 371–78). And the sexual ambiguity in the play was referred to briefly but perceptively by Anne Barton in a review of Bray, *Homosexuality*, in *London Review of Books* 5, no. 15 (18–31 August 1983): 18.

14.   Fredson Bowers, ed., *The Complete Works of Christopher Marlowe* (Cambridge: Cambridge University Press, 1981), 56 etc. and 36–38, 46. Cambridge University Library MSS, Dd. 3.63/35; and see Peck, *Northampton*, 38–40.

15.   Bowers, ed., *Works of Christopher Marlowe*, 16–17. The opening is an epitome of the play as a whole. The depiction of the friendship between Edward and Gaveston with which it opens can be read as Edward, after the death of his father, building up a body of clients to secure his position, as we then see Gaveston doing in his turn and as Mortimer later says he will do: "Mine enemies will I plague, my friends advance" (Bowers, 88). In this familiar Elizabethan context we are then presented with the conventional expressions of such "friendship." It is this that accounts for the close similarity between the queen's description of Edward's intimacy with Gaveston (Bowers, 22) and Thomas Howard's of James I's with Robert Carr, which I quote in the third section of this essay. It is also why Gaveston's protestation of his love for Edward (Bowers, 20) is in the same form as that of the secretary of Antonio Pérez which I quote in section 5.

Gaveston's sexual image (Bowers, 15) and Edward's (Bowers, 40), of which much has been made, are part of these conventions; Antonio Pérez uses similarly sexual images in some of his letters to Anthony Bacon (Ungerer, *A Spaniard in Elizabethan England*, 1:490–93). The link is masculinity, expressed alike in sexual potency as in the bonds that bound men: "Clients love masculine men" wrote Pérez in one of his letters to the Earl of Essex "as wives their husbands": "amant enim clientes sicut vxores maritas viros viriles" (*Ant. Perezii ad Comitem Essexium*, Epistola 61, which is also given in Ungerer, *A Spaniard in Elizabethan England*, 1:475).

Ganymede: Bowers, 29. Giles Fletcher: Will T. Brooke, ed., *Christ's Victory and Triumph* (London: Griffin, Favian, Okeden and Welsh, n.d.), 117. Bray, *Homosexuality*, 16, 53, 66, 126. His Italian tastes are emphasized on pp. 16 and 35 and his foreign origins on pp. 21 and 22; on the assumed connection between these and sodomy, see pp. 75–76. Murder: pp. 90–93; I accept the arguments for the view that the murder of Edward as given in Holinshed was enacted in full view of the audience, but my point holds good even if Marlowe felt he could go no further than to allude to it in the references we see in the text.

16.   I. M., *A Health to the Gentlemanly Profession of Seruingmen*, 1598, C1–C1v. Cecil Papers 83/97v; calendared in Historical Manuscripts Commission, *Marquis of Salisbury*, part 11, 1906, pp. 107–8.

17.   Ungerer, *A Spaniard in Elizabethan England*, 2:47–48.

18.   Bowers, ed., *Works of Christopher Marlowe*, 20.

19. Jerónimo López and Laurence des Bouverie (Ungerer, *A Spaniard in Elizabethan England*, 1:327 and 472–73).

20. J. E. Neale, "The Elizabethan Political Scene," in *The Age of Catherine de Medici and Essays in Elizabethan History* (London: Jonathan Cape, 1963), 161.

21. I. M., *Seruingmen*, 1598. Muriel St. Clare Byrne, ed., *The Lisle Letters* (Chicago and London: University of Chicago Press, 1981), 3:1–35. Walter Darell, *A Short Discourse of the Life of Seruingmen*, 1578 (in *Studies in Philology* 31, no. 2 [1934]: 124).

22. Neale, *Age of Catherine de Medici*, 153, and Peck, *Northampton*, 59.

23. Bray, *Homosexuality*, 14–15, 72; Kinder, *Casiodoro de Reina*, 27–37, 58–59, 99–120; Bray, *Homosexuality*, 29–30, 49, 54, 121.

24. Bray, *Homosexuality*, 44–53 and 54–55. I would now be rather more cautious, though, in my comments on Francis Bacon on p. 49.

25. British Museum, Harleian MSS, 646/59–59v. There is a transcription in Thomas Hearne, *Vitae et Regni Ricardi II* (Oxford, 1729), 385–88 (Appendix).

The (In)Significance of "Lesbian" Desire in Early Modern England

VALERIE TRAUB

T HE "lesbian desire" of my title is a deliberate come-on. If this is the last you hear of it, it is because, enticing as it may sound, it doesn't exist. Not, at least, as such. For the conceptual framework within which was articulated an early modern discourse of female desire is radically different from that which governs our own modes of perception and experience. If, as David Halperin reminds us, we have witnessed only one hundred years of homosexuality,[1] then how is the even more recent discursive invention, the lesbian, to be related to sexual systems of four hundred years ago? The following discussion attempts to begin to answer that question by examining the asymmetrical representations of three early modern discursive figures: the French female sodomite, the English tribade, and the theatrical "femme." My intent is to keep alive our historical difference from early modern women and at the same time to show how historically distant representations of female desire *can* be correlated, though not in any simple or linear fashion, to modern systems of intelligibility and political efficacy. This essay is at once an act of historical recovery and a meditation on the difficulties inhering in such an act.

In *A View of Ancient Laws against Immorality and Profaneness*, published in 1729, John Disney reviews ancient vice laws from the perspective of a Protestant Englishman. Beginning his compendium of sexual sins with a chapter entitled "Of the Incentives to Vice, ill company, obscene Talk, and lewd Books or Pictures" and proceeding to such matters as "Of Polygamy," "Of Incestuous Lewdness," and "Of Rape," the ten chapters of

Section 1 exhaustively order people and behaviors according to their alleged deviations from "nature." What immediately strikes anyone who has read Michel Foucault's *The History of Sexuality* is the implicit shift as the volume progresses from categories of being—"Common Whores, and such that frequent them," "Bawds, Procurers, Pimps, &c"—to categories of acts—concubinage, adultery, sodomy, and bestiality. But something more peculiar than this division animates Disney's categories. In the final chapter, "Of Sodomy and Bestiality," not only are these two deviations linked, as they commonly were, in a rather strained narrative of causality,[2] but no mention is made of women. Defining sodomy as "the unnatural Conjunction of Men with Men or Boys" (180–81), Disney thwarts our modern expectation that all those engaged in same-gender erotic acts belong together. Used as we are to linking the identities and political fates of gay men and lesbians under the medico-scientific label of "homosexuality" or the political banner of "gay rights," Disney's silence about sexual "conjunction" among women seems odd, especially when we note that the only chapters focusing on women are "Of Common Whores" and "Of What the Roman laws called Stuprum; the Lewdnesse of (or with) unmarried Women, who are *not* Common Whores" (emphasis mine). This exacting division between those women who are lewd with men for money and those who are lewd with men for free provides a negative contrast against which must be measured any attempt to articulate a discourse of lewdness (pecuniary or not) between women.

A second curiosity arises when we note that in his discussion of prostitution, Disney conventionally cites Deuteronomy 23:17: "There shall be no Whore of the Daughters of Israel; nor a sodomite of the sons of Israel," parenthetically glossing "sodomite" as "whoremaster," and registering his incredulity that "How our [biblical] Translators came to think of a *Sodomite* here, is hard to say." For Disney, the biblical "sodomite," linked in Deuteronomy to female prostitution, must refer to a pimp, not to a male prostitute. Disney's dependence upon discrete, mutually exclusive categories of sexual sin gives his treatise an acute definitional clarity: not only can women not be sodomites; men cannot be whores.

We know, however, that men *could* be whores, not only because early modern plays employ the word and its variants to describe male characters, but because antitheatrical tracts obsessively articulate the anxiety that men will use their "feminized" bodies as loose women do.[3] Indeed, in the antitheatricalists' conflation of the male sodomite and the male whore we find precisely the interpenetration of categories that Disney's treatise, one hundred years later, so assiduously denies.[4]

If we recognize in Disney's tract not the idiosyncrasies of an individual but the discourse of a culture, we gain a point of access into the historical obscurity of early modern women's erotic desires for one another. For if the gender of the whore was not delimited in early modern culture, other categories of sexual sin may not have been as rigidly fixed as Disney would have us believe. Insofar as *A View of Ancient Laws against Immorality and Profaneness* demonstrates an Enlightenment attempt to stabilize, codify, and delimit those desires and practices which previously may have been unstable, resistant to codification, and defiant of limits, it suggests that what is at stake is the instability of gender within categories of sexuality.

Such anxiety about gender instability usefully illuminates and contextualizes the historical vacuum into which early modern women's erotic desires for one another seem to fall.[5] We know that prior to the codifications and normalizations initiated by eighteenth- and nineteenth-century criminology, sexology, and psychology, same-gender desire *in England* was, despite the apocalyptic talk about sodomy, hardly regulated at all.[6] We also know that theology and the law are only *two* social discourses, and not necessarily the most revealing of popular ideologies or practices. And yet, within our contemporary critical discussions, the theological and, more importantly, legal category of sodomy has functioned implicitly as a regulatory mechanism, preempting all possibility of analysis precisely because the discourse of law has stood as arbiter of social fact: if no Englishwoman was brought to trial under the sodomy statute, ipso facto no women practiced such behaviors.

If we look for the inscription of Englishwomen within the confines of the category of sodomy, we will find only absence, hear only silence. But if we shift our gaze slightly, away from exclusive attention to theological treatises, legal statutes, and court cases, and toward other discourses concerned with the representation and regulation of female sexuality—gynecology and stage plays, for instance—we discover a discourse of desires and acts that not only can be articulated but correlated with our modern understanding of diverse erotic practices among women. That discourse, of course, is not authored by women; it is highly mediated by the protocols of patriarchal control. At the same time, in its particular representations of female desire, and in its expression of anxiety (or, perhaps more significantly, *lack* of anxiety) about desire among women, it dramatizes particular conventions according to which such desire was culturally "staged." As critics and historians, the difficulty we face is not necessarily the lack of erotically desiring women, but our inability to crack the code organizing the conceptual categories of an earlier culture. Once that code is recognized, our task becomes not only detecting a discourse of such desire, but delineating that discourse's proper parameters and evaluating its various ideological effects.

Before I move to gynecological and theatrical discourses, however, it is necessary to point out that the conceptual categories and codes of different nations varied. Contrary to the experience of Englishwomen, Frenchwomen *were* prosecuted under sodomy statutes.[7] Consider the following anecdote with which Stephen Greenblatt begins his essay "Fiction and Friction":

> In September, 1580, as he passed through a small French town . . . Montaigne was told an unusual story that he duly recorded in his travel journal. It seems that seven or eight girls . . . plotted together "to dress up as males and thus continue their life in the world." One of them set up as a weaver . . . fell in love with a woman, courted her, and married. The couple lived together for four or five months, to the wife's satisfaction, "*so they say.*" But then, Montaigne reports, the transvestite was recognized . . . "the matter was brought to justice, and she was condemned to be hanged, which she said she would rather undergo than return to a girl's status; and she was hanged for using *illicit devices* to supply her *defect* in sex."[8]

I recall Greenblatt's use of Montaigne's anecdote in order to suggest that desire among women is revealed less in the discourse of the authorities— the trial and execution that took place just days before Montaigne's visit to the French town where the story was narrated to him—than in the discourse of the community, whose members were sifting the controversy through their own understandings of appropriate gender roles and their curiosity about the variety of erotic practices. That popular discourse is apparent in those ambivalently coded, anonymously referring words "so they say," which follow the widespread community affirmation of "the wife's satisfaction." People in that small French town were talking, and talking publicly enough for a stranger to overhear the details of the couple's conjugal relations, including their four or five months of apparently mutual erotic pleasure.

As this and other cases suggest, in the French context, sodomy for women is defined as the use of illicit sexual devices, devices which, Greenblatt later remarks, "enable a woman to take the part of a man."[9] Indeed, we possess a historical record of such cases not primarily because the women desired or seduced other women, but because of their prosthetic use of implements of penetration.[10] French sodomy, by definition, entails penetration; legal discourse demanded rigorous definitions of *proof*, and penetration seemed to meet that test. By means of this definition, an implicit distinction is set up between, on the one hand, sinful *desires* and criminal *acts* and, on the other hand, those sexual practices that do not involve penetration and those that do.[11] Neither a Frenchwoman's *desire* for another woman, nor any nonpenetrative acts she might commit were crimes, but the prosthetic supplementation of her body was grounds for execution.

This concern about the supplementation of women's bodies crosses the Channel in those French and English gynecological texts which repeatedly refer to female sexual organs growing beyond "normal" bounds.[12] An enlarged clitoris was believed to cause "unnatural" desires in a body already defined as sexually excessive. Writes Helkiah Crooke in the 1631 edition of *A Description of the Body of Man*:

> Sometimes [the clitoris] groweth to such a length that it hangeth without the cleft like a mans member, especially when it is fretted with the touch of the cloaths, and so strutteth and groweth to a rigiditie as doth the yarde [penis] of a man. And this part it is which those wicked women do abuse called Tribades (often mentioned by many authors, and in some states worthily punished) to their mutual and unnatural lusts.[13]

The reference to tribadism in the discourse of gynecology complicates the operation of sodomy as a legal if not moral category. Indeed, the asymmetrical prosecution of French and English "tribades" under sodomy statutes brings to light an irregular fracturing of the early modern conceptual terrain. Yet, when we shift our focus from legal categories, we find a previously undetected structural coherence unifying the French and English divide: both gynecological tribadism and statutory sodomy depend upon a logic of supplementarity for their condition of possibility, with tribadism functioning through anatomical rather than artificial supplementation. The discursive shift from a legal concern with prosthesis to a medical focus on clitoral hypertrophy enacts only a slight distinction within an overall economy of the supplement. Both discourses fail to distinguish between specific sexual acts: penetration, rubbing of clitoris on thigh or pudendum, and autoerotic or partnered masturbation. Instead, they employ vague analogies to male sexual practices, as in Jane Sharp's *The Midwives Book* (1671), which reports that sometimes the clitoris "grows so long that it hangs forth at the slit like a Yard, and will swell and stand stiff if it be provoked, and some lewd women have endeavoured to use it as men do theirs."[14] Whether employing a dildo or her enlarged clitoris, a sodomite's or tribade's "natural," "feminine" body becomes, in the gendered discourse of both nations, "masculine."

And yet . . . the terms by which such supplementation has been defined heretofore not only describe but *reproduce* gender ideology. In particular, in the passages cited above, Greenblatt's rhetorical style collapses any distance that might obtain between early modern ideology and a postmodern feminist understanding of female-centered erotic acts. His rigorous adherence to the replication of not only Renaissance discourses, but dominant discourses within the Renaissance, leads to a failure to articulate the multiple, sometimes contradictory meanings that erotic acts can express and, in particular, obscures whatever meanings the use of "illicit devices" signified for the women involved. Within Greenblatt's rhetoric, as within the rhetoric of early modern authorities, the commingling of two female bodies is subsumed by a heterosexual, male-oriented narrative: female penetration signifies an *imitation* of male (body and role-defined) *"parts."* Whatever independent agency obtains in the performance of such erotic acts is rendered invisible at the same time it is resecured into a patriarchal economy. Gaining no metacritical distance on the problems of representation and power posed by the "conjunction" of female bodies, Greenblatt implicitly, if unintentionally, preserves gender as an essence—it can be imitated, but not, ultimately, subverted.

The fact that the model of imitation was favored by early modern legal and medical authorities prompts my search for a more dynamic and heteronomous understanding of the ways erotic pleasure was achieved. Here, it seems necessary to employ a postmodern feminist analytic to create a conceptual space wherein erotic acts might be conceived differently than in the terms inscribed by the dominant ideology. Although we possess no first-person accounts written by "tribades" or female "sodomites," their actions were neither wholly imitative nor wholly autonomous. Taking place within a system of signification that precedes them, their erotic practice is molded by a set of conventions and contingencies for possible action—which does not, however, exhaust the meanings such practices signified to and for the women themselves.

If, as Judith Butler argues, gender is not only a representation but a performance staged within the enclosure of cultural coordinates;[15] and if masculinity is not an essential trait but a cultural production, then what these women perform is, in the words of Jonathan Dollimore, a "transgressive reinscription" of gender and erotic codes.[16] At once repetition *and* transgression, such reinscription displaces conventional understandings from *within* dominant systems of intelligibility. Indeed, by using the term *supplement*, I have been importing deliberately a Derridean instrument to break open the gender codes that have heretofore delimited the terms by which tribadism and sodomy are conceived. Derrida employs the notion of supplementarity as that which both adds to *and* replaces the original term; an instance of "differance," the supplement deconstructs the putative unity, integrity, and singularity of the subject, of its gender and its sexual desires, and registers them as always internally *different* from themselves.[17] Early modern women's prosthetic supplementation of their bodies is, I would argue, both additive and substitutive: as a material addition to the woman's body and as a replacement of the man's body *by* the woman's, it not only displaces male prerogatives, but exposes "man" as a simulacrum, and gender as a construction built on the faulty ground of exclusive, binary difference. Indeed, in the authorities' discourse, the enlarged clitoris and the dildo become objects of cultural *fantasy*. Which is not to imply that there did not exist real confusion about the status of and differentiation between male and female "yards"; but it is to suggest that the meanings attached to women's appendages exceed the biological. It is not scientifically established anatomical norms but gender expectations that manifest themselves in descriptions of "tribades." I would go so far as to argue that the enlarged clitoris and the dildo take on the quality of a fetish, a stand-in for a lost object of desire. The question is, whose desire is being represented in these accounts? What the authoritative discourse reveals is less the desire of the women than the authorities' desire for the (always already missing) phallus precisely at the moment of its literal displacement; and Greenblatt's account tacitly repeats this gesture by focusing on the replacement rather than the pleasures afforded by the performance of erotic supplementarity.

Primarily at issue, it seems to me, is not sexuality but gender. In England and in France, in gynecology and the law, it is not woman's desire for other women, but her usurpation of male prerogatives that incites writers to record and thus reveal the anxieties of their (and our) culture. What, then, of a female erotic practice that did not involve the use of a supplement? Although I have only a tentative response to this question, it seems worth noting that whereas such practices are *not* recorded by gynecology and the law, they *are* the subject of many early modern stage plays. From Shakespeare's *A Midsummer Night's Dream* (1594–95) to his collaboration with Fletcher on *The Two Noble Kinsmen* (1613), from Heywood's *The Golden Age* (1611) to Shirley's *The Bird in a Cage* (1632–33), what we might call, not a little anachronistically, "femme-femme" love is registered as a viable if ultimately untenable state.[18] By turning to early modern theatrical representations, I want to stress that although they do not function mimetically to reveal erotic practices, they indicate discursively a broader range of desires than those inscribed by gynecology and the law. Early modern drama does not express women's self-perceptions and experiences, but it does provide an index to how the male-authored culture imagined, impersonated, and regulated their desires.

In the absence of a historically accurate term for such desires, I will provisionally call them "homoerotic," in order to differentiate between, on the one hand, the early modern legal and medical discourses of sodomy and tribadism and, on the other hand, the modern identificatory classifications of "lesbian," "gay," and "homosexual." Neither a category of self nor normatively male, the term *homoerotic* retains both the necessary strangeness and historical contiguity between early modern and postmodern forms of desire.

Before I discuss female homoeroticism, it is important to note that when placed within the context of gynecological and legal discourses, the prominence of female cross-dressing on the English Renaissance stage takes on a very specific meaning. It is not just that transvestism accorded female characters the linguistic and social powers of men, nor that the phenomenon itself registered cultural anxieties about the instability of gender identity, but that male clothes worked as external projections, theatrical equivalents, of the cultural fantasy of the enlarged clitoris. The-

atrical transvestism, in short, was also prosthetic; the donning of masculine dress enacts the logic of the supplement through the displacement
of the body to the clothes. Signifying the independent use of a woman's
always possibly inordinately endowed clitoris, cross-dressing not only
masculinizes but eroticizes the female body. Such a displaced equivalence
gives a more situated, more *embodied* meaning to many critics' current
understanding of female transvestism as a strategic appropriation of the
phallus.[19]

The prosthetic logic of cross-dressing also enables us to achieve some
metacritical distance from our dependence on the transvestite heroine as
the privileged stage representative of early modern female desire. The
mutability of desire that infuses so many early modern plays tempts us to
depend on the changeability of dress as the originating instance of homoeroticism. But, I wonder whether we have not inadvertently brought the
"epistemology of the closet," to invoke Eve Kosofsky Sedgwick's phrase,
to bear on a world prior to closets.[20] Did homoeroticism have to be
physically disguised to be articulated? Or were there other ways of registering the expression of female homoeroticism while psychologically dispelling any anxieties such expression might elicit? The problem is not
only that female transvestism has seemed the only means of access into
homoeroticism, but that the result has been a privileging of Viola's self-
indictment in Shakespeare's *Twelfth Night* (1603):

> Disguise, I see, thou art a wickedness
> Wherein the pregnant enemy does much. . . .
> How will this fadge? My master loves her dearly,
> And I, poor monster, fond as much on him.
> (2.2.27–34)

Not only is cross-dressing presented as wicked, but a homoerotic position
to desire is implicitly monstrous. In contemporary critical practice, Viola's articulation of anxiety has implicitly served as the summation of
sixteenth- and seventeenth-century attitudes toward female homoeroticism, whereas it is more appropriately viewed as the expression of the
dominant discourse on *tribadism* and *sodomy.* In addition, however much a
fantasy of monstrosity underlies the discourse of tribadism, it hardly
sums up the self-perception and experience of women who were erotically
compelled by other women.

Shakespeare's *A Midsummer Night's Dream* and *As You Like It* both present two pairs of female characters whose initial erotic investment is in one another. The dialogues between Helena and Hermia, and Celia's speeches to Rosalind, are as erotically compelling as anything spoken in the heterosexual moments in these comedies. This eroticism, however, does not depend upon a cross-dressed figure like Rosalind who is not, in fact, the enunciator of homoerotic desire, but instead depends upon the "feminine" Celia, who urges Rosalind to "love no man in good earnest" (1.2.26) and later asserts, "We still have slept together, / Rose at an instant, learn'd, play'd, eat together, / And wheresoe'er we went, like Juno's swans, / Still we went coupled and inseparable" (1.3.71–74). Their love is presented as both exceptional in quantity and unexceptional in type: "never two ladies lov'd as they do" (1.1.107), says Charles, and Le Beau describes their love as "dearer than the natural bond of sisters" (1.2.265). Similarly, when Hermia compares the "primrose beds where" she and Helena "were wont to lie" (1.2.215) to the meeting place, and later the bedding place, of Hermia and Lysander, we are encouraged to notice a repetition and displacement of one bedmate for another. Indeed, *A Midsummer Night's Dream*, a play thoroughly concerned with the tension between unity and duality, merger and separation, oneness and twoness, presents Lysander's seductive come-on, "One heart, one bed, two bosoms, and one troth" (2.2.42) as no different—qualitatively, emotionally, physically—from Helena's pained admonition:

> We, Hermia, like two artificial gods,
> Have with our needles created both one flower,
> Both on one sampler, sitting on one cushion,
> Both warbling of one song, both in one key,
> As if our hands, our sides, voices, and minds,
> Had been incorporate. So we grew together,
> Like to a double cherry, seeming parted,
> But yet an union in partition;
> Two lovely berries molded on one stem;
> So, with two seeming bodies, but one heart.
> (3.2.203–12)

Helena concludes this passionate appeal with the question, "And will you rent our ancient love asunder . . . ?" (3.2.215), a motif repeated by Celia, who complains, "Rosalind lacks then the love / Which teacheth thee that thou and I am one. / Shall we be sund'red?" (1.3.94–96). That these texts formulate the divorce of female unity in such similar terms substantiates James Holstun's contention that female homoerotic desire was figured in seventeenth-century poetry primarily in an elegiac mode.[21] Likewise, in Fletcher and Shakespeare's *The Two Noble Kinsmen*, Emilia's love for her childhood friend Flavina is rendered elegiacally, even as the love of Theseus and Pirithous is allowed expression up to the eve of Theseus's marriage to Hippolyta (1.3.55–82). Presented as always already in the past, and hence irrecoverable, female homoerotic desire simultaneously was acknowledged *and mastered* by male poets. Or, in my reworking of Holstun's terms, symmetrical, "feminine" homoerotic desire was granted signification only *after* it was rendered insignificant.[22]

I am less interested in the male poets' containment of this desire, however, than in the implicit power asymmetry that seems to constitute the homoerotic pair: the relative power of each woman is aligned according to her *denial* of homoerotic bonds. It is the female rather than the male characters of these plays who, by their silent denial of the other woman's emotional claims, position homoerotic desire in the past. Female homoeroticism is thus figurable not only in terms of the always already lost, but the always about to be *betrayed*. And the incipient heterosexuality of the woman who is recipient rather than enunciator of homoerotic desire comes to stand as the telos of the play.

This staging of the eradication of homoerotic desire is replicated in the Titania-Oberon subplot of *A Midsummer Night's Dream*. Titania is psychologically threatening precisely to the degree she upsets the homosocial "traffic in women" formally negotiated by Egeus and Theseus in the opening scene, and implicitly played out by Demetrius and Lysander in the forest.[23] The changeling boy, child of Titania's votress and representative not only of her female order but of female-oriented erotic bonds, is an object of maternal exchange between women. In inverting the gendered relations of the homosocial triangle, Titania not only "effeminizes" the boy but usurps patriarchal power. The child is the manifest link of a prior, homoerotic affection between women that doesn't so much exclude Oberon as render him temporarily superfluous. This affront motivates Oberon's attempt to humiliate Titania *erotically*, capture the boy, and secure him for martial, exclusively masculine purposes.

The gendered and erotic scenarios enacted in these plays do not exemplify psychosexual *necessity*—that is, a developmental movement through progressive erotic stages—but an economic, political imperative: as each woman is resecured in the patriarchal, reproductive order, her desires are made to conform to her "place." Significantly, the homoerotic desires of these female characters existed comfortably within the patriarchal order until the onset of marriage; it is only with the cementing of male bonds through the exchange of women, or, in Titania's case, the usurpation of the right to formalize bonds through the bodies of others, that the independent desires of female bodies become a focus of male anxiety and heterosexual retribution.

In Shakespeare's plays, an originary, prior homoerotic desire is crossed, abandoned, betrayed; correlatively, a heterosexual desire is produced and inserted into the narrative in order to create a formal, "natural" mechanism of closure. The elegiac mode of Shakespearean drama, however, which renders "feminine" homoeroticism insignificant by situating it safely in the past, is supplanted in the history of the drama by a more immediate mode that not only locates such desire in the present tense but depicts it as explicitly erotic. Thomas Heywood's *The Golden Age* and James Shirley's *The Bird in a Cage* both momentarily stage the temptations of a female-oriented eroticism;[24] but they achieve temporal and psychological distance, not by the use of elegy but rather by employing mythological conceits and self-referential theatricality. Exuding homoerotic content within separatist female realms, the "Ladies Interlude" (act 4, scene 2) of Shirley's play and Diana's virgin circle in Heywood's repeat and extend the homoerotic pastoralism of *As You Like It* and *A Midsummer Night's Dream*.

The Golden Age is an episodic dramatization of the lives of Jupiter and Saturn, focusing, as does so much Greek and Roman myth, on military and erotic conquest. Act 2 of the play concerns Jupiter's attempted seduction and eventual rape of Calisto, daughter of his vanquished enemy, King Lycaon. Upon Calisto's refusal of Jupiter's offer of marriage, she flees her father's kingdom, joining Diana's virgin circle in the forest. Hot in pursuit, Jupiter disguises himself as a "virago," and successfully infiltrates Diana's pastoral cloister.

According to the rule of Diana's order, her "princesses" are paired off in a manner reminiscent of heterosexual, monogamous marriage. When Diana welcomes and prepares to accommodate Calisto, she asks Atlanta:

> *Diana.*   Is there no princess in our train,
> As yet unmatch'd, to be her cabin fellow,
> And sleep by her?

> *Atlanta.*   Madam, we are all coupled
> And twinn'd in love, and hardly is there any
> That will be won to change her bedfellow.
>
> *Diana.*   [To Calisto:] You must be single till the next arrive:
> She that is next admitted of our train,
> Must be her bed-companion; so 'tis 'lotted.
>
> (act 2, scene 1)

Jupiter, of course, is the "next admitted," who quickly vows Diana's oath of loyalty and chastity; the circle's definition of chastity, however, is explicitly defined as protection of one's hymen from *phallic* penetration:

> *Atlanta.*   You never shall with hated man atone,
> But lie with woman, or else lodge alone. . . .
> With ladies only you shall sport and play,
> And in their fellowship spend night and day . . .
> Consort with them at board and bed,
> And swear no man shall have your maidenhead.
>
> (act 2, scene 1)

To which Jupiter eagerly responds: "By all the powers, both early and divine, / If e'er I lose't, a woman shall have mine!" Not only is the double entendre spoken directly to Diana, and not as a secretive aside, but the huntress applauds Jupiter's vow—"You promise well; we like you, and will grace you"—and thereby grants Calisto as "her" bedmate.

The continual reiteration of the concept of women lying in bed, "consort"ing together as "bedfellows" and "bedcompanions" explicitly and matter-of-factly poses erotic "sport and play" between women as a "chaste" alternative to penetrative sex with "hated man." With their emphasis on being "match'd," "coupled," "twinn'd in love," Diana's "nymphs" pose monogamous, erotic "virginity" as the natural expression of love between women.

When Jupiter quickly attempts to sexually capitalize on his good fortune, however, Calisto resists. The play, however, takes no stand on whether her resistance is because of an aversion to passion between women, because of Jupiter's haste and aggressiveness, or because of some inchoate suspicion regarding Jupiter's coercive designs:

> *Jupiter.*   Oh, how I love thee: come, let's kiss and play.
> *Calisto.*   How?

Jupiter.	So a woman with a woman may.
Calisto.	I do not like this kissing.
Jupiter.	Sweet, sit still.
	Lend me thy lips, that I may taste my fill.
Calisto.	You kiss too wantonly.
Jupiter.	Thy bosom lend,
	And by thy soft paps let my hand descend.
Calisto.	Nay, fie what mean you?

(act 2, scene 1)

To which Jupiter offers the ambiguous response: "Prithee, let me toy. / I would the Gods would shape thee to a boy, / Or me into a man." That Calisto's transformation into a boy would help Jupiter's plight adds the further titillation of male homoeroticism to a plot already full of erotic possibilities. This enticing possibility, however, is foreclosed as Jupiter forcefully asserts his "rights" as a man, and carries Calisto offstage to be raped. The contrast between Jupiter's sexual assault and the loving ministrations of Diana's circle could not be more clear. And the ramifications for Calisto are tragic: eight months later, her pregnant evidence of heterosexual intercourse leads to banishment from Diana's society.

This theme of rape is doubled and complicated in *The Bird in a Cage*, as the Princess Eugenia is "threatened" not only by the sexual advances of her male beloved, but by those of one of her ladies. But, perhaps more importantly, the strategies that Heywood employs to distance his depiction of homoeroticism are in evidence in Shirley's play as well. Not only does *The Bird in a Cage* import into its subplot a mythological past, but that subplot also focuses on the exploits of Jupiter. In addition, Shirley's dramatic device of a play-within-a-play heightens the sense of theatricality to which Jupiter's cross-dressing in *The Golden Age* merely alludes.

At the same time, however, the social context of *The Bird in a Cage* works to obviate the efficacy of these distancing mechanisms, with the play's role in a contemporary controversy pushing its meaning toward a material referent and verisimilitude. Satirically dedicated to the Puritan polemicist William Prynne, who attacked women actors as "notorious whores" in *Histrio-mastix: The Players Scourge or Actors Tragedy* (1632–33), Shirley's play is implicitly a defense of Queen Henrietta, patroness of the Cockpit players for whom Shirley was principal dramatist. Just weeks before Prynne's publication, the queen and her ladies had performed speaking parts at court in Walter Montague's *The Shepherd's Paradise*. Prynne's alleged libel against the queen gave the authorities the chance they had been looking for to imprison him, inflict corporal punishment, and suppress his book. The gender and erotic consciousness expressed in *The Bird in a Cage* thus implicitly refers to the material reality of female royalty displaying and speaking her body not only in courtly but theatrical spectacle. A liminal moment in the history of the relation between theatricality and sexuality, Shirley's play thus renders problematic the use of those conventions that previously had largely governed depictions of female desire: the necessity of boy actors and the cross-dressing of homoerotically desiring female characters.

The "bird in a cage" refers extra-theatrically to Prynne languishing in prison, and within the play both to the princess Eugenia, confined with her ladies to a tower by her overzealous father, and to her beloved Philenzo, who secretly enters her chamber disguised as a bird in an enormous cage. During their confinement, the ladies decide to pass the time by staging an "interlude," the story of Jupiter's "seduction" of Danaë, which replicates in miniature the themes of the main plot, with Eugenia acting the part of Danaë, and her lady, Donella, playing Jupiter. Significantly, Donella's impersonation of the lustful god is not burdened with cross-dressing, which makes even more remarkable the extent to which she discovers and articulates her own desire through the course of playacting. As "Jupiter," her twenty-eight-line amorous speech to the sleeping "Danaë" ends with a self-admonition to forgo poeticizing and begin *acting*: "But I rob my selfe of Treasure, / This is but the Gate of Pleasure. / To dwell here, it were a sin, / When *Elizium* is within. / Leave off then this flattering Kisses, / To rifle other greater Blisses" (4.2. Sig H2v, 24–29). The threatened rape is interrupted by a bell announcing the surprise arrival of the bird cage, and, by means of this device, Philenzo's "rescue" of Eugenia. Donella's response to this interruption is explicit and confused disappointment: "Beshrew the Belman, and you had not wak'd as you did Madam, I should ha' forgot my selfe and play'd *Jupiter* indeed with you, my imaginations were strong upon me; and you lay so sweetly—how now?" (Sig H2v, 32–35).

In the context of Prynne's condemnation of the theatrical imagination and Shirley's implicit counterargument in favor of it, Donella's erotic "imaginations" are positively rendered. This affirmation of desire is voiced as well by the character Cassiana, who earlier remarked upon Jupiter's entrance: "now comes *Jupiter* to take my Lady napping, we'l sleep too, let the wanton have her swinge, would she were a man for her sake" (Sig H2v, 36–Sig H2v, 1). That the "wanton" *is* simultaneously Donella and "Jupiter" is suggested by Cassiana's retention of female pronouns, which helps to materialize the pun embedded in Donella's wish: to play Jupiter in *deed.* In light of this, it might not be stretching erotic allusion too far to see in Donella's earlier response to Cassiana's impromptu poeticizing a bawdy joke about female arousal. Cassiana begins: "Think Madame all is but a dream, / That we are in—Now I am out—beame, creame. / Help me *Katerina*, I can make no sence rime to't." To which Donella puns: "Creame is as good a Rime as your mouth can wish, / Ha, ha, ha" (Sig H1r, 34–38).

The two rapes with which Eugenia is threatened invert conventional expectations: whereas Donella's erotic approach first seems to exist only in the realm of her imagination, and conversely, the disguised Philenzo's erotic demands appear as a real threat to the princess's safety, it soon becomes clear that it is Donella who is actually so transported with desire as to force herself upon her mistress, and that Philenzo only adopted the guise of rapist as a manipulative ploy.[25] And whereas the stage directions tell us that Philenzo "discovers himselfe" to the princess (Sig. I1r, 11–12), Donella seems to have "forgot her selfe" (Sig. H2v, 33) in precisely the way Prynne and other antitheatricalists feared.

Despite the strength of Donella's "imaginations," the dramatic process of Heywood and Shirley is, like Shakespeare's, to pose eroticism between women as an option, only to displace it through the force of a seemingly "natural," ultimately more powerful heterosexual impulse. The final closure of these erotic incidents, and the dominant economy of desire that these plays endorse, however, do not cancel out the erotic attraction between some female characters which is represented as a legitimate, if ultimately futile, endeavor.

In all of these plays, the displacement of the homoerotic by the heterosexual happens so "naturally" that the *tension* between the two modes of desire is erased. But are these in fact *two separate* modes of desire? It would seem that for certain types of women such a contiguity existed between female homoeroticism and heterosexuality that the direction of object choice hardly figured at all. At least, for female characters who did not challenge conventional gender roles—who did *not* cross-dress, who did *not* wear swords, who were not anatomically "excessive," who did not use "illicit devices," and whose gendered "femininity" belied the possibility of "unnatural" behaviors—desire may have been allowed to flow rather more freely if less sensationally between homoerotic and heterosexual modes. That in these plays such desire is ultimately reduced and fixed within the institutional prerogatives of heterosexual marriage—that the eradication of the "feminine" homoerotic position to desire is precisely what must be *staged*—points to the political and economic use of women's erotic bodies within a patriarchal economy.

At issue here, it seems to me, is less sexuality or gender per se than reproduction. These women's desires are untenable not, as is the case with transvestism, tribadism, or sodomy, because they are viewed as implicitly imitative and hence monstrous, but because they are essentially nonreproductive; such desire becomes an issue—becomes significant—only when the time comes for the patriarchal imperative of reproduction to be enforced. Woman's social role within a system of reproduction relies not only on her biological capacity to give birth, but her willingness to perform that labor. It is only when women's erotic relations with one another threaten exclusivity, and thus endanger their reproductive "performance," that cultural injunctions are levied against them. And it is precisely the cultural anxiety that women will fail to comply with this role, a role that is violently forced upon Calisto, that the drama obsessively articulates and assuages. It is hardly incidental that such theatrical liaisons are articulated only within the context of heterosexual courtship plots, where the expulsion of female relationships from the dramatic terrain resecures the promise of husbandly authority. The drama also suggests, however, that *if* same-gender erotic practices *could* exist coterminously with the marriage contract, there would be little cause for alarm. Heywood's Jupiter, for instance, shows no distress upon learning of Diana's separatist "rule"; he merely tries to turn to his advantage the behavioral norms of a homoerotic environment. Although "tribades" and "sodomites" supplementing their bodies necessarily performed a certain amount of what Judith Butler terms "gender trouble," the absence of outcry against "feminine" homoeroticism suggests that it posed very little gender trouble at all. In the psychic landscape of the time, "femmes" would be assumed available to give birth; tribades and sodomites would not.[26] The "femme" involved with a tribade was seen as "abused," the not altogether innocent victim of another woman's lust; her crime was correspondingly more minor, her punishment less severe.

Conceptual problems, of course, exist with my account. Perhaps most importantly, my analysis extrapolates a cultural *presence* from a discursive *silence*; it therefore could be accused not only of applying illegitimately twentieth-century categories to an earlier time, but of creating something quite literally out of nothing. To this charge, I can only answer that I find it inconceivable that within the vast array of erotic choices reported by early modern culture, "feminine" bodies did not meet, touch, and pleasure one another.

Secondly, I presume that the erotic practices of "tribades" and "femmes" were radically discontinuous; that only "tribades," for instance, used dildoes on their partners. But here we stumble across a certain circularity of definition: it is, after all, the penetrative use of a dildo or an enlarged clitoris that *defines* the "sodomite" or "tribade." I confess ignorance as to the specific erotic acts in which early modern women may have engaged; but, in light of the fact that gynecological texts encouraged men to arouse their wives by caressing their breasts and genitals, it seems implausible that women's pleasure was exclusively centered on penetration.[27]

To what extent, then, can women's relationships with one another be perceived as "resistant," "oppositional," or "transgressive"? To the extent that they existed coterminously with patriarchal prerogatives, not at all. They only *became* oppositional when perceived as a threat to the reproductive designs of heterosexual marriage. Whereas the "tribade" and "sodomite" functioned as magnets for cultural fantasies and fears—about gender, reproduction, monstrosity, and the ultimate instability of all such cultural categories—the "femme" woman, who challenged neither gender roles nor reproductive imperatives, seems to have been so unworthy of notice that little note was taken of her at all.

In conclusion, there seems to have existed a radical discontinuity between, on the one hand, sodomy and tribadism and their theatrical correlative in cross-dressing plays, and, on the other hand, a theatricalized "feminine" homoeroticism that has no discernible material equivalent in the fantasized typologies in which early modern women were represented. Whereas the tribade and sodomite haunt essays, travel accounts, and gynecological texts, femme-femme love seems to exist discursively solely as a theatrical invention. However, perhaps we can extrapolate from the drama itself the reasons for this disjuncture, for the absence of animus against "femme-femme" love. For, if we have not interpreted the language of Helena, Hermia, Titania, Celia, Diana, and Donella as homoerotic, it is not only because of our internalized homophobia, or because of our formalistic inclinations to privilege the final heterosexual teleology of these comedies, but because the palpable "femininity" of these characters blinds us—and, I suspect, may have blinded many of their contemporaries as well—to the eroticism evident in their language of desire. Existing independently of the representational nexus of sodomy and tribadism, bodily supplementation and gender appropriation, these theatrical representations suggest that "feminine" homoerotic desires were dramatized precisely because they did not signify.

Notes

This essay originally appeared in *Erotic Politics*, ed. Susan Zimmerman (London: Routledge, 1992); reprinted by permission. I wish to acknowledge Brenda Marshall, Susan Zimmerman, Margaret Hunt, Richard Burt, Linda Gregerson, and Will Fisher for suggestions of where and how to look for female-centered desire. I would also like to thank the Gay and Lesbian Studies seminar participants at the Robert Penn Warren Center for the Humanities at Vanderbilt University for their insightful comments on an early draft. Finally, Misty Anderson provided timely research assistance and Kathy Cody gave invaluable help with the manuscript.

1. David Halperin, *One Hundred Years of Homosexuality, and Other Essays on Greek Love* (New York: Routledge, 1990).

2. The quotation in full is: "These lewdnesses are so detestable, that nothing needs be said to increase their Horror: for Nature suffers almost as great a violence in *hearing* of them, as in the perpetration. It is wonderful, indeed, how it ever came into the thoughts of *Men* to commit them: but, as the Apostle says, (Rom. I.20–28) when they gave them-selves up to Idolatry, God gave them up to vile affections; and the Devil put them upon going as much out of the way for wickedness, as he had brought them to do for their Religious Worship. They had changed the glory of the incorruptible God into Images of corruptible Men and Beasts, for Adoration: and therefore He left them to debase *themselves*; and turn the Channel of their Lusts, as well as their Devotions, from what was natural, to what was abhorrent from Nature; to their own Sex, and to brute beasts." John Disney, *A View of Ancient Laws against Immorality and Profaneness* (Nottingham: Vicar at St. Mary's, 1729), 180.

3. Arthur Kinney, ed., *Markets of Bawdrie: The Dramatic Criticism of Stephen Gossen* (Salzburg: Institut für Englische Sprache und Literatur, 1974); Philip Stubbes, *The Anatomie of Abuses* (London, 1583); William Prynne, *Histrio-mastix: The Player's Scourge or Actor's Tragedy* (1632–33; New York: Garland, 1974).

4. See, for instance, Thersites's labeling of Patroclus as "Achilles' male varlet, his masculine whore" in Shakespeare's *Troilus and Cressida* (5.1.15–17) and Hamlet's self-representation as a "drab, a stallion" in *Hamlet* (2.2.587–588). All references to Shakespeare are from *The Complete Works of William Shakespeare*, ed. David Bevington

(Glenview and London: Scott, Foresman, 1980), and will be cited parenthetically in the text.

5. With the exception of recent work by Katherine Park and Lorraine Daston, little historical, theoretical, or literary investigation has been attempted on early modern female same-gender pleasure. Lillian Faderman's encyclopedic historical overview of love between women devotes only two short chapters to the period prior to the eighteenth century, focusing mainly on Brantôme's *Lives of Fair and Gallant Ladies*. See Faderman, *Surpassing the Love of Man: Romantic Friendship and Love between Women from the Renaissance to the Present* (New York: William Morrow, 1981). Judith Brown's archival work on the life of Benedetta Carlini is helpful, but in many ways is more revealing of religious than erotic practices. See Judith Brown, *Immodest Acts: The Life of a Lesbian Nun in Renaissance Italy* (New York: Oxford University Press, 1986). The important work of James Holstun, Harriette Andreadis, and Elizabeth Harvey picks up the representation of Englishwomen's desires in the mid-seventeenth century, focusing primarily on the poetry of John Donne and Katherine Philips. And an important recent anthology, *Lesbian Texts and Contexts*, discusses only nineteenth- and twentieth-century texts. See James Holstun, " 'Will You Rent Our Ancient Love Asunder?': Lesbian Elegy in Donne, Marvell, and Milton," *ELH* 54 (1987): 835–67; Harriette Andreadis, "The Sapphic Platonics of Katherine Philips, 1632–1664," *Signs* 15 (1989): 34–60; Elizabeth Harvey, "Ventriloquizing Sappho: Ovid, Donne, and the Erotics of the Feminine Voice," *Criticism* 31 (1989): 115–38; Karla Jay and Joanne Glasgow, eds., *Lesbian Texts and Contexts: Radical Revisions* (New York: New York University Press, 1990).

6. Alan Bray, *Homosexuality in Renaissance England* (London: Gay Men's Press, 1982).

7. See Lorraine Daston and Katherine Park, "Hermaphrodites in Renaissance France," *Critical Matrix* 1 (1985): 1–19.

8. Stephen Greenblatt, "Fiction and Friction," in *Shakespearean Negotiations: The Circulation of Social Energy in Renaissance England* (Oxford: Clarendon Press, 1988), 66; emphasis mine. By means of this anecdote, Greenblatt positions his analysis of Shakespeare's *Twelfth Night*, which he views as a partial retelling of Montaigne's story, in relation to nontheatrical discourses; correlatively, he employs the play to support his claim that within the Renaissance imagination, transformations of identity occurred unidirectionally: from imperfect to perfect, from female to male.

9. Ibid., 67. Greenblatt retells another anecdote (originally recorded by the French physician Jacques Duval in *On Hermaphrodites, Childbirth, and the Medical Treatment of Mothers and Children* [Rouen, 1603]) of gender ambiguity, in this case occasioned not primarily by the adoption of clothes but by the confusions of the body. A female servant, Marie, revealed to the woman she loved, Jeane, that she was really a man. After consummating the vows they had made to the apparently mutual enjoyment of each, the couple sought public approval of their love. Marie changed her name to Marin, and began wearing masculine clothing. The two were subsequently arrested, tried, and condemned. The crime for which both were convicted was sodomy; despite Marin's claim that the terror of the trial had caused his penis to retract, the court maintained that Marie was a tribade who had used her unnaturally large

clitoris to abuse Jeane. It was only upon Marin's appeal to the Parlement of Rouen, which appointed a panel of doctors, surgeons, and midwives to repeat a medical examination, that Jacques Duval applied pressure to Marin's organs, and found there "a male organ," which on second examination "ejaculated" in a manner consistent not with woman's expulsion of seed, but man's (ibid., 73–75). These French cases are also discussed by Daston and Park, "Hermaphrodites in Renaissance France," and Ann Jones and Peter Stallybrass, "Fetishizing Gender: Constructing the Hermaphrodite in Renaissance Europe," in Julia Epstein and Kristina Straub, eds., *Body Guards: The Cultural Politics of Gender Ambiguity* (New York: Routledge, 1991), 80–111.

10.   In France (but not in England) cross-dressing was a punishable offense. In England only class transvestism was a crime (Jones and Stallybrass, "Fetishizing Gender").

11.   For the distinction between desires and acts, see Bruce Smith, *Homosexual Desire in Shakespeare's England: A Cultural Poetics* (Chicago: University of Chicago Press, 1991).

12.   See, for instance, Nicholas Culpepper: "Some are of opinion, and I could almost afford to side with them that such kind of Creatures they call Hermaphrodites, which they say bear the Genitals both of men and women, are nothing else but such women in whom the Clitoris hangs out externally, and so resembles the form of a Yard; leave the truth or falsehood of it to be judged by such who have seen them anatomized: however, this is agreeable both to reason and authority, that the bigger the Clitoris is in women, the more lustful they are" (*A Directory for Midwives* [London: 1684]). The uniformity of French and English gynecological texts is explained by their general dependence on previous authority, and especially their common inheritance of the Galenic model of heat.

13.   Helkiah Crooke, *A Description of the Body of Man* (London, 1615, 1681), p. 238. According to Audrey Eccles, Bartholin referred to such women as "Rubsters," and Dionis observed that "there are some lascivious Women, who by *Friction* of this Part, receive so great Pleasure, that they care not for Men" (*Obstetrics and Gynecology in Tudor and Stuart England* [Kent, Ohio: Kent State University Press, 1982], 34). Ambrose Paré included a section on such women in his original *Des Monstres et prodiges* (1573), but, according to his translator, Jean Ceard, he "was forced to eliminate a section on lesbianism, with a graphic description of the female genitals, before including *Des Monstres* in later editions of his collected works" (*Des Monstres*, trans. Ceard [Geneva: Droz, 1971], 26–27).

14.   Jane Sharp, *The Midwives Book* (1671; London and New York: Garland, 1985), 45. Sharp, however, takes care to minimize Englishwomen's culpability. In my edition she writes: "In the Indies, and Egypt [tribades] are frequent," and another editor of her work adds these words—"but I have never heard but of one in this Country" (p. 45). Sharp's displacement of the "unnatural" onto other nations and races is totally conventional within the context of medical discourses that regularly employed nationalist and racist paradigms of contamination and disease.

15.   Judith Butler, *Gender Trouble: Feminism and the Subversion of Identity* (New York: Routledge, 1991).

16. Jonathan Dollimore, *Sexual Dissonance: Augustine to Wilde, Freud to Foucault* (Oxford: Clarendon Press, 1991).

17. Jacques Derrida, *Of Grammatology*, trans. Gayatri Chakravorty Spivak (Baltimore: Johns Hopkins University Press, 1974).

18. Despite my use of the term *femme*, I want to encourage the reader to resist viewing these women as prototypes of modern erotic identities, and to emphasize instead the risk of collapsing *their* difference into *our* desire for continuity and similitude.

19. See my *Desire and Anxiety* for an analysis of the connection between early modern homoeroticism and theatrical cross-dressing (*Desire and Anxiety: Circulations of Sexuality in Shakespearean Drama* [London and New York: Routledge, 1992]).

20. Eve Kosofsky Sedgwick, *The Epistemology of the Closet* (Berkeley: University of California Press, 1990).

21. Holstun, " 'Will You Rent Our Ancient Love Asunder?' "

22. In using the term *feminine*, I do not mean to reinscribe arbitrary binary gender designations. However, it seems fruitful to differentiate between those women who were charged with appropriating masculine prerogatives and those who were not.

23. The phrase "traffic in women" was first coined by Emma Goldman in her critique of marriage as prostitution. It gained critical prominence through the work of Gayle Rubin. For the most powerful elucidation of homosocial triangles, see Sedgwick, *Between Men: English Literature and Male Homosocial Desire* (New York: Columbia University Press, 1985).

24. Thomas Heywood, *The Golden Age* (1611), in J. P. Collier, *The Golden and Silver Ages: Two Plays by Thomas Heywood* (London: Shakespeare Society, 1851); James Shirley, *The Bird in a Cage* (1633), in F. Senescu, *James Shirley's "The Bird in a Cage": A Critical Edition* (New York and London: Garland, 1980).

25. By conflating rape with seduction, I self-consciously reproduce the ideology of the play, and in no way mean to endorse such a view.

26. In arguing that "femme" women were not threatening because they did not disrupt the reproductive economy, I could be interpreted to mean that they were always sexually available to men. My point is merely that they were culturally *perceived* to be more available, more capable, more willing.

27. See Thomas Laqueur, *Making Sex: Body and Gender from the Greeks to Freud* (Cambridge and London: Harvard University Press, 1990); Th. Johnson, *The Works of that famous Chirurgion: Ambrose Parey, translated out of Latin and compared with the French* (London, 1634); Ambrose Paré, *Des Monstres et prodiges.*

Fraudomy: Reading Sexuality and Politics in Burchiello

ALAN K. SMITH

THIS essay considers sodomy in a particular historical context—early fifteenth-century Florence—under a number of guises: as a sexual practice, a subject position in the construction of gender identity, a literary *topos*, a legal and religious category, and a means of denouncing or defaming political practice. I propose to read sodomy in a way that has less to do with revealing a particular "truth" (or "truths") than with thinking about sodomy as a mode of knowledge, a way of reading the articulations between these various forms. As the title suggests, I am especially interested in the way sodomy works as an irreducible figure for sexual and political practices. I will argue that within this historical and cultural context sodomy enacts and masks a secret relationship between sexuality and politics, that it is the secret of another secret whose survival relies upon strategies of concealment and revelation, discretion and rumor.

From the broader perspective of its institutional genealogy in the Renaissance, this has been sodomy's precise role. It has served as an indispensable category of transgression linked with both the production of discourse and the enforcement of silence. Throughout the early modern period, sodomy, along with heresy, was officially classified in the category of the *nefandum*, crimes against "nature," the *unspeakable*. Yet, as Jacques Chiffoleau has shown, religious and political institutions worked tirelessly to produce its spoken and written testimony through torture and other means of coercion.[1] Although religious authorities (most notably the Inquisition) initially administered the punishment of sodomites and heretics (as well as the recording of their "confessions"), secular governments gradually assumed this responsibility. With the shift in European political structures toward absolutism, sodomy and heresy became in the last resort crimes of *lèse majesté*. Procedures for secret denunciation and torture were justified by defining sodomy and heresy as political rather than purely theological offenses.[2]

This antagonism between political order and sodomy raises a difficult question: in what way does sodomy menace political institutions, and, more specifically, the absolute monarchy? How does it accomplish *lèse majesté*, the wounding or infliction of a lesion upon the king's majesty as represented by his body or office? Explanations based on social relations, such as the anxiety over political friendships between the king and courtiers suspected of "unnatural" influences, define this problem in terms of access to power, embodied by the monarch's self. In such scenarios, real or imagined intimacy with the king's body threatens social order by circumventing the court's highly structured means of access. Chiffoleau's analysis confronts this question from a different perspective by emphasizing the discursive and phantasmatic construction of the figure of the absolute monarch. We may find the answer to this problem, he suggests, in sodomy's discursive classification as something that cannot be said, a secret and terrible knowledge. Its silence and mystery double and threaten another silence and another mystery, "the eminently respectable silence . . . that surrounds legitimate power, and which is one of the unmistakable signs of majesty itself."[3] In persecuting sodomy and heresy, the real task was to erect a prudent silence around the very concept of majesty by which these procedures were justified. The scandalous secret of "unspeakable" crimes like sodomy does not concern the formulaic confessions of thousands of burnt and mutilated victims, but rather the secret of political domination, the center of the institutions that vigilantly deflected indiscreet approaches to that center. In this historical configuration, the secret of sodomy works to regulate transactions between public and private spheres—between political institutions and marginalized sexualities—in a way that seals off the king's private person, in effect encrypting the most public and visible representative of political power.

In my conclusion, I will elaborate this theoretical framework by turning to psychoanalytic models of the secret.[4] These theories provide particular insight into the politicization of sexuality and/or the sexualization of politics meshed within "fraudomy": the nexus of poetry, politics, and sodomy in Quattrocento Florence.

The central figure in my discussion is the Florentine poet Domenico di Giovanni (1404–1449), better known as il Burchiello. Burchiello's verse belongs to a somewhat obscure tradition of Italian poetry known under a variety of names: the carnivalesque, the anti-Renaissance, the *comico-realistica* or *realistico-borghese* tradition, and so forth.[5] While literary scholars have recognized him as one of the most important poets both of this tradition and of the Quattrocento, his work has received little of the attention accorded to Lorenzo de' Medici, Poliziano, and Pulci, all of whom were influenced in various ways by Burchiello.[6] By the end of this essay, I think the reader will have some idea why Burchiello has been ignored. I would urge us to consider the relation between censorship and categories of transgressive sexuality in terms not only of moral and legal discourses, but also of the not-so-innocent processes of canon formation.

Burchiello led a colorful life. Born to a poverty-stricken family (next to their name, the 1427 *catasto*—the Florentine tax record—listed the one-word comment "miserabile"), he somehow acquired an education in literature.[7] His poetry reflects a thorough knowledge of Dante and Boccaccio, and makes interesting references to Latin authors as well.[8] He took up a trade as a barber and opened a *bottega* in the Calimala district, the center of the Florentine wool industry.

Even in his youth, the virtuosity of his sonnets won the admiration of humanists and poets who reportedly congregated in his shop to hear recitals of his verse. Burchiello exchanged a number of patterned sonnets (or *tenzoni*) with prominent literati such as Anselmo Calderoni and Leon Battista Alberti.[9] On the basis of these poems, which displayed exceptional inventiveness and ferocity even by Florentine standards, the anti-Medici political faction led by Rinaldo degli Albizzi apparently hired him as a propagandist.[10] He wrote a number of poems attacking the Medici and their allies, and when Cosimo de' Medici engineered a political takeover of Florence in 1434, Burchiello was among the opponents forced into exile. After a brief period of wandering about northern Italy, he moved to Siena. Chronically ill and unable to reestablish another *bottega*, he lived there for ten years in meager circumstances and at one point spent a few months in prison on the unlikely charge of stealing some sleeves (if we can believe his account of this incident, he was really caught climbing into the bedroom of another man's wife). He subsequently moved to Rome, where he died at the age of forty-five.

Critics usually divide Burchiello's sonnets into four categories: auto-biographical, the *tenzoni*, moral-political, and "non-sense" verse.[11] His literary fame derives from the latter poems, which constitute the vast majority of his work; they are also the least studied. These draw upon a range of semantic fields (economic, mythical, culinary, religious, and so forth), juxtaposing incongruent objects and figures to form surreal images. The following sonnet, one of the most frequently anthologized, presents an especially dazzling sequence of such forms:

> Nominativi fritti e mappamondi,
>> e l'arca di Noè fra due colonne
>> cantavan tutti *Chirieleisone*
>> per l'influenza di taglier mal tondi.
> La Luna mi dicea: "Ché non rispondi?"
>> Ed io risposi: "io temo di Giansonne,
>> però ch'i' odo, che il diaquilone
>> è buona cosa a fare i capei biondi."
> Per questo le testuggine e i tartufi
>> m'hanno posto l'assedio alla calcagna,
>> dicendo, noi vogliam, che tu ti stufi.
> E questo sanno tutte le castagne,
>> pei caldi d'oggi son sì grassi i gufi,
>> ch'ognun non vuol mostrar le sue magagne,
> E vidi le lasagne
>> andar a Prato a vedere il Sudario,
>> e ciascuna portava l'inventario.

> Fried nominatives and maps of the world,
>> And Noah's Ark between two columns
>> Were all singing "kyrie eleison"
>> Under the influence of misshapen plates.
> The Moon said to me: why don't you respond?
>> And I answered: I'm afraid of Jason,
>> Because I hear that ointment
>> Is good for turning hair blond.

> For this the war-machines and the truffles
>> Put my heel under siege,
>> Saying: we want you to warm yourself.
> And all of the chestnuts know this:
>> By the heat of the day, owls are so greased,
>> That not one wants to show its defects.
> And I saw the noodles
>> Going to Prato to see the Holy Shroud,
>> And each one was carrying the inventory.[12]

What—if anything—does this extraordinary collage of figures and objects mean? So far, most critics have concluded that the significance of such sonnets lies in their non-signification, that is, in their parodic manipulation of poetic forms. According to this view, the incoherent images, the mixture of quotidian and literary vocabularies, and the flagrant disregard of literary decorum express an opposition to cultural and poetic forms sanctioned by the ruling classes, such as the neoplatonic hermeneutics of courtly love. This polemic characterizes the entire *comico-realistica* tradition, tracing class differences and civic conflicts from the late Middle Ages to the Counter-Reformation.

In their more specific descriptions of Burchiello's poetics and its relation to dominant ideology, critics tend to diverge. Antonio Toscano argues that the breakdown of mimetic function in Burchiello's language reflects the working classes' political disempowerment and frustration before the rigid power structures of Florentine society.[13] Proposing metonymy as the essential trope in the "non-sense" poems, Domenico de Robertis suggests that Burchiello's deformation of poetic diction results from the explosion of new terms and expressions accompanying the massive influx of commodities into Florentine markets.[14] In contrast to de Robertis, Luisa Avellini claims that a kind of "regressive metaphor" is the crucial trope in Burchiello's work.[15] But despite their differences, these critics by and large share the opinion that the "non-sense" sonnets are not meant to be read as self-contained, coherent units of signification.

The important exception to these readings of Burchiello is the work of the French comparatist Jean Toscan. In 1981 he published *Le Carnaval du langage*, a four-volume study of the *comico-realistica* tradition (complete with a glossary of 2,250 entries).[16] His central thesis is that an entire tradition of Italian poetry throughout the early modern period employed a verifiable "equivocal code" that refers to transgressive sexual practices (especially sodomy) and homosexual culture. The obscurity of this tradition results in part from the marginal status of this culture and from the inventive, protean nature of its vocabulary (based on neologisms, dialect words, jargon, macaronic constructions, and borrowings from other languages).

Words or elements of the equivocal code refer to sexual organs or sexual acts, differentiated according to their orientation with either "normal" sexuality (vaginal intercourse) or sodomy (anal intercourse with either a man or a woman); for example, metaphors for the phallus may denote it as "normal" or "specialized" (that is, a sodomizing phallus).[17] Toscan argues that far from writing "non-sense" verse, Burchiello uses the code to refer in an encrypted form to "aberrant" sexual practices, and specifically to sodomy. To see how the code works in the sonnet "Nominativi fritti . . . ," one has to decipher the signifiers (with the help of Toscan and various dictionaries) into their sexual-anatomical signifieds, which in turn stage the operative "scene" of sodomy.[18]

"Nominativi fritti": the adjective "fritti" (fried) has a long tradition of pejorative associations.[19] In the Quattrocento, it designated victims of an *inganno*, or fraud, including passive partners in sodomy.[20] Translating "nominativi" literally—"nominatives"—recalls its grammatical context: the nominative case is the upright, or *retto* case, and thus is a phallic metaphor. Decoded into their equivocal meanings, the first two words consist of a noun, "phalluses," modified by an adjective, "sodomized." Although this sequence ("phallus-sodomized") seems nonsensical, it exemplifies a common grammatical procedure in Burchiello's verse. The active nature of the noun and the passive associations of the adjective obey a certain "logic" of equivocal poetics that aligns semantic and grammatical relations.[21] Since the adjective is grammatically dependent upon the noun that it modifies, their conjunction may be read as a figure for the act of sodomy itself, which privileges the "active" phallic trope over the "passive" one.

The lexemes "fried uprights" therefore signify either the specialized (sodomizing) phallus or the act of sodomy itself. One of the difficulties in deciphering the equivocal code is how to decide between the different meanings generated by shifts in textual focus. In this case, the rest of the phrase supports the first meaning. The obscene referent of "mappamondi" is well documented; the shape of the globe has lent this word a longstanding association with the posterior. By syntactically combining the "specialized" phallus with a metaphor for the buttocks, the first line juxtaposes the two organs and hence represents the act of sodomy.

For "arca di Noè," one has to keep in mind several equivocal connotations. First, the "arca," as a "box" or "square," is associated with the vulva and heterosexuality, as opposed to round things that connote the posterior and sodomy. Since we find this "ark" between two "columns" or "legs," one might say that this detail is "anatomically correct." Secondly, Noah is a figure of old age: "as old as Noah" was a common expression in the Italian Renaissance. This is consistent with a trope of heterosexuality, since sodomy was linked with newness and even with modernity itself, hence the euphemism "via moderna." Finally, Noah is famous for having survived the great flood. In the equivocal code, figures of floods, rain, water, and so forth signify the menstrual flow, always presented as a justification of sodomy. The typical scenario portrays a male subject, who, unwilling to engage in "normal" sexuality during his wife's menstruation, seeks sodomy (with a man or woman) as a "logical" alternative.

Together, these sexual organs sing a Greek hymn that signals the beginning of the mass and, in Rome, the entrance of the pope. The equivocal poets attributed varying reputations to different nationalities and social classes: Greeks, Italians, and especially Florentines were reckoned as notorious practitioners of sodomy. Furthermore, the higher his social standing, the more likely an individual (whether a hero, god, political or religious leader) was represented as a sodomite.[22] The pope embodies the vices of the clergy, and especially sodomy; as he who sits upright in the pulpit, he becomes a metaphor for the "specialized" phallus. "Kyrie" not only signals the "entrance" of this phallus, but also literally means "mercy."[23] The kind of mercy at issue is indicated by the phrase "taglier mal tondi," which combines "cutting" (implying an active, phallic intervention of a sodomizing agent) with "tondi," a metaphor for the buttocks. In the equivocal tradition, "mal" can refer to the injury or possibility of injury risked by the passive partner.[24] The first quatrain thus represents would-be passive partners of sodomy (both male and female) who, under the "influence" of this example, exhort the sodomizing agent(s) to exercise a degree of care.

Following Toscan's methodology, one can interpret most of the poem as a variation on this theme. The question posed by "la Luna" in the second quatrain is an invitation to sodomy: the moon is a common metaphor for the posterior, while speech acts—verbal intercourse—often rep-

resent sexual intercourse. I will discuss the speaker's reaction in greater detail below, but his observation that "ointment" is good for "dyeing
hair blond" may offer a solution to the risk of injury during sodomy.
"Blond" or "yellow" hair (or heads) signifies the "specialized" phallus,
and the ointment's usefulness for its deployment seems obvious. The
"war-machines" and "truffles" are tropes for the anus; their "assault" on
the speaker's "heel" (that is, his phallus) presents him in another (near-)
sodomizing situation.

The second tercet and the *congedo* represent women as potential partners in sodomy. "Chestnuts" and "noodles" are metaphors for the vulva.
The former hide their "defects" (that is, their anuses) from the "greased
owls," which signify the "specialized" phallus. The latter association
comes from the owl's reputation for trickery, since it supposedly preyed
upon other birds trapped by hunters' limed branches.

By now, most of the sonnet's equivocal tropes and motifs should be
fairly clear. Rather than continue a detailed exegesis of these obscene
referents, I would like to consider just what is at stake in this kind of
reading. While the reader's initial reaction may be skeptical (as my first
reaction was), we have to appreciate the strengths of Toscan's carefully
documented thesis concerning equivocal poetry. First of all, he demonstrates the clearly obscene meaning of similar figures and metaphors in
prose works; if in fact this poetry is truly "non-sense," then one would
have to explain such sharply divergent uses of equivocal language in different generic settings. Secondly, as Toscan points out, there is extensive
historical evidence of homosexuality in Quattrocento Florence.[25] The
crime of sodomy was sufficiently widespread in the eyes of civic authorities to warrant the creation of a "vice squad," the "ufficiali di notte," who
were assigned to patrol for sodomites.[26] San Bernardino of Siena and
Savaronola lashed out from the pulpit against sodomy, often labeling it as
a specifically Florentine vice. In the course of the century, approximately
ten thousand charges of sodomy were brought before Florentine courts.[27]
Finally, Toscan's thesis in no way contradicts the ideologically inflected
readings mentioned above; on the contrary, he sees the obscene referent of
these poems as strengthening that interpretation. Indeed, the celebration—or at least the description—of sodomy in lyric poetry would seem
to take an antagonistic stance toward poetic traditions like the *dolce stilno-
visiti* and Petrarchan love lyric.

These merits aside, Toscan's study is a philologically oriented decrypting of an entire tradition and should serve as a point of departure rather than the final word on Burchiello. While acknowledging that Burchiello's sexual metaphors are somehow ideologically charged, Toscan's thesis ignores their specific political dimensions and significance. Furthermore, like most modern readers, Toscan never considers Burchiello's complex allusions to Dante and Boccaccio.[28] In the next section, I will suggest ways of reading Burchiello's sonnet and its Dantean allusions in relation to the poem's particular historical and political context, beginning with a brief description of this context.[29]

Florentine political history in the Quattrocento involves a distinction between *political structures* designed to protect the Florentine republic from the threat of tyranny or domination by a single group, and *political practice*: the definition and actions of interest groups who actually controlled political power. The Florentine constitution allocated juridical, legislative, and executive authority to a hierarchy of political offices. At the top of this hierarchy were the eight "priors," the *Otto Priori delle Arti* (also known as the *Otto del Podestà* or simply the *Otto*), and the *gonfaloniere*, or presiding official, who were chosen, like all officers, from a pool of eligible citizens. This pool was based on pedigree, personal qualities (such as honesty and sobriety), and financial solvency, since debtors were automatically disqualified. The short tenure typical of most political offices was meant to promote power sharing and to avoid the entrenchment of one group or family. In addition to the structure of political offices, the Florentine constitution provided for the muster of provisional groups, the *Balìa* and the *Parlamento*, to safeguard the republic from extraordinary threats, whether external or internal.[30] In 1433 the faction led by Rinaldo degli Albizzi used such measures to force Cosimo de' Medici into exile under the charge that the Medici were plotting to control elections.

This was true—but the accusation applied to Albizzi and his followers as well; the Medici just happened to be better at it. The conflict between these factions marked a crucial point in the evolution of political and social struggle in early Renaissance Florence. Prior to the fifteenth century, political relations underwent crucial transformations as the city sought to resolve fundamental issues of participation, access to power, and citizenship rights. The continuous economic and social competition between the various classes—the aristocratic families, the wealthy mercantile and banking groups, the artisanate and workers' guilds—reached a crisis with the Ciompi revolt in 1381, during which the working classes and artisanate guilds for a brief time seized political control of the city. Following the overthrow of the Ciompi, the wealthier classes severely restricted the power and rights of the guilds. Earlier efforts to institute corporatism—active political participation based on egalitarian principles of guild membership—were eclipsed by a politics of consensus in which the control of political eligibility was placed in the hands of a powerful few, the oligarchy.[31]

From that point on, Florentine political practice evolved into a system of alliances based upon families, friends, and financial relations. The important difference between oligarchic factions such as the Albizzi and the Medici was the latter's masterful cultivation of such alliances. A typical mechanism consisted in paying off an individual's debts; this person would in turn both remain eligible for political office and be expected to reciprocate as a "friend" if elected. This kind of scheme might mean taking punitive actions against an opponent, putting that person into debt and thus rendering him ineligible for office.[32] After his triumphant return from exile in 1434, Cosimo de' Medici used such methods to consolidate his alliance into an internal clientele regime. In the striking formulation of one historian, Cosimo worked to maintain "the organized presence of a power-group within the central organs of the Republican State."[33]

Cast in the metaphors of the body politic, the language of this phrase suggests that sexuality—perhaps even sodomy—may be relevant to our understanding of the city's political history. It was to the Florentines. In 1426 an anonymous and controversial poem was found tacked upon the door of the palazzo della Signoria.[34] The poem rehashes a conventional topos made famous by Petrarch's *canzone* "Italia mia": Florence is personified as a "donna" who requires protection from "outsiders." The following lines advise Florentines to keep in mind the example of Maso degli Albizzi, who led the oligarchy during the crucial transition from corporatism to political control in the late Trecento:

> E' c'insegnò di far la buona via,
> La qual convien di far d'ogni dieci anni
> Sol una volta, et con piena balìa.
>
> Acciò che nuova gente sotto i panni
> Non faccin con le fave lor postierra
> Come più volte han fatto con inganni.

> And he taught us the right way to follow,
> That it is best every ten years
> To renew the vote with a full balìa.
>
> That way the new people under their cloaks
> Will not slip their votes in the door
> Like they have with trickery many times before.[35]

Referring to Maso degli Albizzi's historic support of the *balìa*, these lines exhort the aristocratic elite to "reform" election procedures, which in reality meant solidifying their control of elected offices. It reflects the anxiety felt by the oligarchic families whose hegemony was threatened by the rise of newer groups, lumped under the pejorative rubric *la gente nuova*. To anyone familiar with the equivocal tradition, especially in light of Toscan's work, the metaphors in the second tercet have a clearly sexual connotation: the fava bean was a metaphor both for the token used in voting procedures and for the glans of the penis. "Fave . . . sotto i panni" thus refer not only, as Dale Kent reads them, to "votes . . . under cover," but also to the phallic and illicit threat represented by the *gente nuova*.[36] The paronomasia of "postierra" and "posteriore" makes their activity even more suspect. These equivocal meanings reinforce the conventional figuration of Florence as a "donna" both by stressing the need to shield her from unwholesome advances and by linking the *gente nuova* to sodomy. Nor was this an unusual notion; readers of the poem could recall Dante's portrayal in *Inferno* XVI of the *gente nuova* in the circle of the sodomites. The fact that they were also associated with the Medici family ever since the Ciompi revolt underscores the topicality of this connotation.

In this overtly political poem, sexuality—sodomy—serves as a metaphor, a signifier, for *inganno*, or fraudulent political practice. But in the equivocal tradition, *inganno* (trickery or fraud) has a reversed figurative status: it functions as a metaphor for sodomy. This would seem to explain the complex allusion to "Giansonne" (Jason) in the second quatrain of Burchiello's sonnet. The speaker expresses an ambivalence in contrast with the univocity ("tutti cantavan") heard in the first quatrain. His refusal to "respond" to the "kyrie," an unwillingness to participate on a sexual level, is motivated by "fear of Jason."

It has been suggested that the allusion to Jason comes from Dante's *Inferno* XVIII, where Dante and Virgil see the Greek hero among the circle of the seducers.[37] In his retelling of Jason's seduction and abandonment of Isifille and Medea, Virgil uses the word *inganno* repeatedly:

> Ivi con segni e con parole ornate
>   Isifile ingannò, la giovinetta
>   che prima avea tutte l'altre ingannate.
> Lasciolla quivi, gravida, soletta;
>   tal colpa a tal martiro lui condanne;
>   e anche di Medea si fa vendetta.
> Con lui sen va chi da tal parte inganne . . .
> (*Inferno* XVIII: 91–97)

> There with gestures and ornate words
>   He deceived Hypsipyle, the young girl
>   Who had first beguiled all the other women.
> He abandoned her there, alone and pregnant;
>   Such a deed condemns him to such punishment;
>   And Medea too takes her vengeance upon him.
> With him go all those who use such fraud . . .[38]

Fear of Jason would seem to be a fear of *inganno*, and in turn of the seductive power of words and gestures, "segni e . . . parole ornate," analogous in some way to the collective activity of singing "kyrie eleison." If *inganno* is a metaphor for sodomy, this would support the reading of the first quatrain as referring to sodomy or its risks.

However, the reference to Jason may be an *inganno* itself, because there are two Jasons in Dante's *Inferno*. In the next canto (XIX), Dante the pilgrim encounters the pope Nicolas III among the simoniacs who are suspended upside down in barrels of fire. Dante holds a conversation with Nicolas while staring at the sinner's buttocks, or, using the equivocal metaphor, "la Luna." Nicolas makes a number of predictions concerning his successors, including Clement V, the notorious pope of the Babylonian Captivity:

> "Nuovo Iasòn sarà, di cui si legge
>   ne' Maccabei come a quel fu molle
>   suo re, così fia lui chi Francia regge."
> Io non so s'i' mi fui qui troppo folle,
>   ch'i' pur rispuosi lui a questo metro . . .
> (*Inferno* XIX: 85–89)

> "He will be a new Jason, like him we read of
>   In Maccabees who softened up
>   His king: thus he will be with the king of France."
> I do not know if I was too audacious,
>   But I answered him in this strain . . .

Nicolas compares Clement to the Old Testament Jason, a Hebrew priest who bought the highest religious office in Judea from the Roman administrator Antiochus.[39] After first hesitating out of respect for the office of the pope ("I' non so s'i' mi fui qui troppo folle"), Dante begins a long invective ("'i' pur rispuosi lui") against simony. This dramatic interaction is echoed by Burchiello's verse where the speaker, after hesitating to respond to the "kyrie," replies instead to the *Luna* ("Ed io risposi . . .").[40]

The sonnet's second quatrain thus restages a scene from Dante's *Commedia* endowed with a specific ethical and political meaning.[41] The strategic positioning of the citation of Dante—who was, after all, the authoritative critic of Florentine political practice—is a good reason to insist on the poem's relevance to Florentine political history. The sonnet's allusion most likely refers to the events surrounding Cosimo de' Medici's palace revolution in 1434. A turning point was the refusal of the pope, Eugene IV, to intervene on behalf of Rinaldo degli Albizzi's ruling faction. In fact, his audience with the pope spelled the moment of truth for Albizzi: Cosimo de' Medici's international prestige and wealth guaranteed the pope's full cooperation.[42] Without any hope of support from Eugene IV, Albizzi realized that continued resistance would only result in useless bloodshed and defeat. In the eyes of Cosimo's opponents, the pope's support of the Medici and of the bank that was the papacy's leading creditor must have represented a form of simony.

At this citational and "autobiographical" moment, interpretation of the sonnet becomes especially tricky. Just at the point where the speaker expresses ambivalence—where he apparently distances himself from sodomy—he introduces an allusion to a historical event as a way of condemning political practice: the Medici's fraudulent influence upon the papacy. Does this allusion constitute, within the overall sequence of obscene tropes, the poem's real or secret meaning? If so, then we have to read sexuality, or sodomy, as a signifier or figure for political practice, specified in this historical context as fraud. From this perspective, sodomy becomes a mode of knowledge, a way of revealing the truth about a historical event and political relationships.

However, the sonnet's rhetorical and strophic patterns complicate this conclusion. The first quatrain represents sodomy in terms of action and univocity: "tutti cantavan . . . per l'influenza"; "*everyone* was singing . . . under the influence," that is, *because of* the example of sodomy figured by the "badly shaped plates." Similarly, the first tercet begins with a causal explanation, "Per questo," for the assault upon the speaker's "heel." The "questo" refers either to the "medical" advice offered by the speaker on how to make "blond heads," or else to the scene described in the first quatrain. Each involves in some way the *techne* or practice of sodomy. Far from merely being a trope for something else, sodomy motivates and compels actions and events. On the other hand, the second quatrain and second tercet make statements of knowledge that express a certain ambivalence. Knowing something about sodomy implies a fear or withdrawal: the speaker refuses initially to respond, the knowing chestnuts hide their "defects" from the owls.[43] Expressed in terms of knowledge, sodomy seems to resist its own putting into action; yet paradoxically, sodomy is represented as the cause or justification for collective forms of activity. The oscillation between this form of action and the paralyzing effect of its knowledge (in psychoanalytic terms, the force of desire accompanied by its interdiction) unsettles the attempt to reduce the poem's configurations of sodomy to either a sexual or a political meaning. By encrypting sexual and political allusions together within its surreal procession of animated objects and literary references, Burchiello's sonnet recodes and interrogates the cultural logic that differentiates domains of the public and private, high and low. Alternately enlisting our confusion, laughter, and indignation, his verse disturbs protocols of interpretation dependent on this logic while thematizing our attraction to its signifiers and tropes, or, recalling Dante's formulation, "segni e . . . parole ornate." Burchiello's sly double allusion to Dante leaves the reader in the position of wondering if she or he has also been tricked or seduced in some way.

Beyond this interpretive impasse, other tropes and thematic configurations offer crucial possibilities for a further reading of the relationship between sexuality and politics in the sonnet. In this last section, it will be necessary to reconsider the historical record of the Medici dynasty as well as to introduce the psychoanalytic concepts of incorporation and the secret into the discussion. I will begin by focusing on the two moments where the speaker or lyric subject functions as a grammatical subject. The query posed by the "moon" in the second quatrain—"why don't you respond?"—interrogates the speaker's own sexual desire; the "moon" asks, in effect: "What is the secret of your desire?" The speaker replies by first introducing the allusion to Jason and then by confiding a "specialized" kind of information: "ch'i' odo"; "I hear that . . ." We can accordingly reformulate the question to read, "What is the secret of sodomy?" On the one hand, the speaker's practical advice concerns the "secret" of, or more accurately to, (good) sodomy. On the other hand, the disguised allusion to Eugene IV links the secret of sodomy to the secret of the Medici's political power. In the speaker's response (that explains his non-response), the foundation of a political order intersects with a prescription for fundaments.[44]

Civic and sexual topographies also coincide in the *congedo*, where the speaker reports that he saw the noodles going to Prato to see the holy shroud. Translated into its equivocal referents, this scenario depicts women (metonymically, the "noodles" or vaginas) who go to "Prato" or the "field" (the site of sexual activity in general) to "see the *Sudario*" (to enjoy anal sex).[45] The insinuation that women must leave Florence in order to seek sexual satisfaction in a neighboring and rival city imbues the *congedo* with a powerfully subversive message. But in at least one sense, this pilgrimage would be "endless" since the cathedral at Prato (a neighboring city that was part of the Florentine dominion) was famous for its relic of Christ's belt, not the shroud. This allusion also completes a series of references to discursive and graphic artifacts in the poem, beginning with the first three objects listed in the poem. The sequence of those objects delineates a politically charged telos; the transition from grammatical to geographical to religious artifacts ("nominatives" to "globes" to "Noah's Ark") marks a shift from linguistic realms to cosmography. As *topoi* associated with the foundation of political and religious orders, references to Noah, the Flood, and the pillars (or columns, as in v. 2) of Hercules were conventional *topoi* in fifteenth-century propagandistic literature written for popes and monarchs. A subgenre of this literature included *mappamondi*, sumptuously illuminated scrolls depicting dynastic genealogies and histories. The *congedo* seems to make a tantalizing reference to the material form of such manuscripts in the series *lasagne—Sudario—inventario*. These artifacts compose a hallucinatory surface whose metamorphic enfoldings refract their sexual and political connotations.

From the perspective of psychoanalytic theory, the sequence of these objects transcribes the psychic processes and phantasies underlying the foundation of linguistic order during the prehistory of the individual. According to Nicolas Abraham and Maria Torok, the child initiates linguistic activity in an originary situation of loss when he or she learns to substitute words for the missing breast.[46] The mother's visible presence allows the child to undertake the crucial process of introjection, for which ingestion remains the paradigmatic figure. Introjection enables the individual to internalize a psychic topography whose vocabulary of desires and fears traces his or her personal history. But faced with a loss that cannot be admitted or assimilated, as in situations of mourning, the individual may resort to incorporation, the failed double of introjection that mimics its relation to ingestion through a phantasmic "swallowing" of loss. In such cases of repressed mourning, the dead one is preserved or encrypted within a part of the ego sealed off and guarded from unwarranted intrusion or inspection.

Read in terms of this theory, the sequence *lasagne–Sudario–inventario* plays out a scenario of incorporation through its surreal concatenation of objects linked to food, mourning, and discourse. The noodles' futile pilgrimage to see the mis-placed shroud defers the end of their quest and thus emblematizes failed mourning. Their search for an image of the dead Christ in the wrong place doubles their sexual quest as they also seek pleasure in the "wrong" place. The *inventario* carried by the noodles may be read in a number of ways that turn on its antithetical meanings of an original discovery or creation and a mere catalog. This term also refers to the list of worldly goods that passed over to the Florentine state following the death of a political exile. The voracious appetite of such practices suggests the relevance of tropes of incorporation to political signification in Renaissance Florence.

The juxtaposition of incorporation in the context of repressed or aberrant mourning (often equated with melancholia) and "aberrant" sexuality in this reading opens an array of theoretical questions. Judith Butler, for example, makes the provocative claim that gender identity is a heterosexual melancholic structure whose development is accomplished through incorporation.[47] It would be difficult to assess the accuracy of this view for the historical context under study here. Since Burchiello and many poets in the equivocal tradition often claimed to be victims of melancholia, the relation of their melancholia to the homosexuality represented in their verse is not at all clear. In the conclusion that follows, I would like to pursue other political and discursive implications of incorporation in relation to the sonnet's historical situation.

As a discursive formation, sodomy not only functions as a trope of political practice (specifically fraud or *inganno*), but also maintains a secret relation to political institutions structured around an ideal or center. At the beginning of the essay, I referred to the crucial role sodomy played in strategies of repression and censorship in the early modern period. Jacques Chiffoleau's study suggests that, as a mysterious and secret kind of knowledge, sodomy mirrors the secret and mystery of the concept of majesty. The situation in Florence diverges from the model described by Chiffoleau, insofar as the city was, at least nominally, a republic. However, the Florentines wrote about their government using the same rhetoric of the sacralized State. The city ordinance written in 1433 that defines such sexual "crimes" specifically states that sodomy threatens the *divine majesty* of the government.[48]

The representation of sodomy in Burchiello's sonnet invites further comparison with the city's political structures. As the justification and explanation for collective activity, it functions rhetorically in the same manner that the idea of the "Republic" or "lo Stato" did for Florentine political structure. Even though, as Dale Kent notes, "the realities of power had ceased to correspond to the constitutional prescription for its distribution," the *sacred name* of the republic was vital to the production of Florentine political discourse throughout the entire century.[49] In this respect, the name of the state performs what Gilles Deleuze calls the "paradoxical instance": the "case vide," sliding signifier, or in Derridean terms, the center as a doubling and a rupture.[50]

However, in the course of the fifteenth century, the "center" of power in Florentine politics was shifting in a way that gradually hollowed out the concept of the Florentine republic. During the Medicean consolidation of power, the oligarchy continued to mouth the charter myths of the Florentine republic, even as the exercise of power was concentrated into one name, and with the advent of Lorenzo *il Magnifico*, into the person and body of an egocrat, the dictatorial embodiment of totalitarian power.[51] Indeed, as opponents to the Medici regime found out in 1458 to their chagrin, public acknowledgment of this fact was tantamount to treachery. They dared to name the Medici control as a tyranny—"tirannia"—in public, unmasking Cosimo de' Medici as the real powerbroker, the *pater-padrone* of the city.[52] In retaliation, they were denounced, arrested, tortured, exiled, and levied heavy financial penalties.[53] At that moment, the Medici name as a sign of political domination became something everyone "knew" but, within certain contexts, was relegated to the category of the unspeakable.

According to Abraham and Torok, an unspeakable secret betrays the uncanny work of incorporation and its encrypted terms of loss. "Inside" the crypt, the individual keeps both the lost figure and the memory (actual or phantasmatic) of a shared *jouissance*. The terms of this *jouissance* are "unspeakable"; it is always understood as an originary crime whose guilt is taken on by the survivor. Key words corresponding to its circumstances— names, a date, an action, its setting—cannot be said. They emerge instead as garbled, encoded pieces of language constructed from translations, interlinguistic puns, and hieroglyphic distortions.[54]

It might seem at first that this psychic process by which a name, practice, or word becomes "unspeakable" has little to do with the historical configuration I have just described. But it is likely that Florentine political culture was haunted by an original signing-on, an act of *incorporating*. The terms of loss became painfully clear to those opposed to the domination of consensual politics. The memory of its experiment with the democratic principles embodied by corporatism, that is, a sharing of civic responsibility among the corporations, remained even as first the oligarchic families and then the Medici gradually canceled the exercise of such principles. The utopian dream of brotherhood and civic cooperation surely resonated powerfully both with the transgressive *jouissance* of sodomy and with the sense of loss that accompanies the establishment of political order, which, in Freudian terms, always follows the murder of the Father by the Primal Horde and the advent of the regime of the Brother. Through its articulation of artifacts linked to the foundation of political order, the sonnet both transcribes and parodies the mourning for this failed dream. Within it also lies buried a reference to the repressed Father, the narcissistic tyrant whose memory authorizes sexual and political signification.[55] To find the visible mark or symptom of incorporation's secret pact with this figure, we must look in the "wrong" place, within the interstices of the text, that is, within its modulations between political and sexual registers. That is why I believe we can just barely distinguish the traces of Cosimo de' Medici's name in the sonnet's thematic shift from the cosmic-dynastic (*mappamondi*) to the medical (*diaquilone*). It is, of course, impossible to say whether this ephemeral signature is deliberate or the result of an unconscious impulse, political or otherwise.

Notes

1. "Dire l'indicible: remarques sur la catégorie du *nefandum* du XIIe au XVe siècles," *Annales* 45 (1990): 289–384.

2. Alan Bray's essay in this volume explores this same relationship in the setting of the English Renaissance while bringing out culturally specific differences with the situation I will describe.

3. See Chiffoleau, "Dire l'indicible," 294: "Le crime 'impossible à dire' est forcément le péril le plus grand aux yeux des juges puisqu'il reste innommé. Le silence qui le couvre, évidemment néfaste, s'approche en effet dangereusement, comme pour le menacer, d'un autre silence, celui-là éminemment respectable: le silence qui entoure toujours le pouvoir légitime, et qui est l'un des signes les plus clairs de la majesté. Les frontières de l'indicible dessinent donc en creux les contours, normalement insaissables, de cette zone de silence sacrée qui protège les arcanes, les mystères de l'Etat." Unless otherwise indicated, all translations are my own.

4. My understanding of the secret as an interpretive, historical, and psychoanalytic problem owes a great deal to Jacques Derrida's seminar on the secret conducted this past year (1991–92) at Paris.

5. For introductions to this tradition, see: Domenico Guerri, *La corrente popolare nel Rinascimento: berte, burle e baie nella Firenze del Brunellesco e del Burchiello* (Florence: Sansoni, 1931); and Mario Marti, ed., *Poeti giocosi nel tempo di Dante* (Milano: Rizzoli, 1956).

6. No critical, complete edition of his poetry exists; the two modern editions of his sonnets—*Antologia burchiellesca*, ed. E. Giovannetti (Rome: Colombo, 1949) and *I sonetti di Burchiello secondo l'edizione detta di "Londra,"* ed. Alberto Viviani, 2nd ed. (Milano: Bietti, 1954)—simply reprint the eighteenth-century "Londra" edition, *I Sonetti del Burchiello e altri poeti burchielleschi . . .* ("Londra"—but most likely Lucca or Venice—1757), along with a host of editorial problems. In his *Domenico di Giovanni detto il Burchiello* (Florence: Olschki, 1952), Michele Messina presents a number of previously unedited poems attributed to Burchiello along with a helpful discussion of the manuscripts and the historical background of Burchiello's critical fortunes.

7. For a review of his life, see Renée Watkins, "Il Burchiello (1404–1448)—Poverty, Politics, and Poetry," *Italian Quarterly* 14 (1970): 21–47, and Ann West Vivarelli, "On the Nickname Burchiello and Related Questions," *Modern Language Notes* 87 (January 1972): 123–34.

8. In a *tenzone* addressed to L. B. Alberti, Burchiello makes a complex and imaginative reference to a line from Virgil's *Georgics*; see L. B. Alberti, *Rime e versioni poetiche*, ed.

with commentary by Guiglielmo Gorni (Milano: Ricciardi, 1975), 3ff., and Giuliano Tanturli, "Note alle Rime dell'Alberti," *Metrica* 2 (1981): 104–6.

9. The *tenzone* form followed certain informal rules: one initiated an exchange by sending a sonnet to a friend, rival, or enemy. The latter responded (if he dared) to this challenge with another sonnet set in the same rhyme scheme. These poems usually featured extended wordplay and troping based on the addressee's proper name; the degree of insult and defamation reflected personal (and political) differences between the correspondents. Burchiello was recognized as a formidable opponent in this genre.

10. It is possible that Burchiello wrote these poems as an expression of his own political beliefs. But Albizzi and his followers were notorious for their low opinion of the working classes; Albizzi led the decision in 1426 to restrict and persecute guilds and associations of lower classes. The Medici, on the other hand, were more willing to cultivate alliances outside the restricted circle of the oligarchy. See n. 28 below.

11. See Antonio Lanza, *Polemiche e berte letterarie nella Firenze del primo rinascimento (1375–1449). Storia e testi*, 2nd rev. ed. (Rome: Bulzoni, 1991), and Gino Belloni, "Il Burchiello e la poesia burchiellesca," in *Dizionario critico della letterature italiana* (Turin: UTET, 1986), 1:439–47.

12. I have preferred Achille Tartaro's presentation of this sonnet over its version in the "Londra" edition; see Achille Tartaro and Francesco Tateo, *La letteratura italiana: Storia e testi. vol. III, t. 1. Il Quattrocento* (Bari: Edizione Laterza, 1971), 257. Almost all of the poems reliably attributed to Burchiello take the form of the *sonetto caudato*, a sonnet of hendecasyllabic lines to which a *congedo* (or additional concluding tercet) has been added with a heptasyllabic first line. The rhyme scheme generally follows a ABBA ABBA CDC DCD DEE pattern.

13. "Il Polisenso della parola nel Burchiello," *Forum Italicum* 10 (1976): 360–76.

14. "Una proposta per Burchiello," *Rinascimento* 8 (1968): 3–120. His article has probably been the most influential study to date. However, de Robertis does not account for Burchiello's remarkable range of allusions to classical authors and philosophers, mythological heroes, and historical figures, including contemporary references.

15. "Metafora 'regressiva' e degradazione comica nei sonnetti del Burchiello," *Lingua e Stile* 8 (1973): 291–319.

16. *Le Carnaval du langage. Le lexique érotique de Burchiello à Marino XVᵉ–XVIIᵉ siècles* (Lille: Presse de l'Université de Lille, 1981). Toscan's work, and in particular his analysis of Burchiello, extends Kurt Gutkind's original findings in "Burchelliana. Studien zur volkstümlichen Kehrseite der italienischen Renaissance," *Archivum Romanicum* 25 (1931): 1–34. In his later book, *Cosimo de' Medici* (Oxford University Press, 1938), Gutkind modifies his conclusions concerning the obscene nature of Burchiello's sonnets, suggesting that they may actually use a code created by secret societies of debtors (n. 1, pp. 58–59).

17. While retaining Toscan's narrowly defined terminology of "normal" sexuality (vaginal intercourse) and sodomy (anal intercourse with a man or woman), I have added quotation marks to indicate the relativistic value of terms like "normal."

18. Although Toscan does not discuss "Nominativi fritti e Mappamondi . . . ," he devotes a considerable portion of his analysis to Burchiello's poetry and considers Burchiello one of the two great representatives of this tradition, the other being Lorenzo de' Medici (!).

19. Unless otherwise indicated, the sources for semantic discussions are: the glossary in *Carnaval du langage* (vol. 4); the *Grande dizionario della lingua italiana*, directed by Salvatore Battaglia (Turin: UTET, 1961–present); and the *Nuovo dizionario della lingua italiana*, ed. Niccolò Tommaseo and Bernardo Bellini (Turin: UTET, 1865–1884).

20. Toscan (p. 1006) notes that in the equivocal tradition, *frodo* or *inganno* referred to sodomy, while *ragione* was linked with "normal" sexuality. In the realm of cooking, boiling was linked with heterosexuality, while "roasted" or "fried" foods usually denoted the sodomizing phallus.

21. For a review of Burchiello's innovational use of these procedures, see Toscan, 75–90.

22. Peasants, especially in the *canti carnescialeschi*, are generally represented as inflexible advocates of "normal" sexuality.

23. A slightly different reading results if one follows Toscan's definition of "cantare" (p. 362) as "to practice sodomy."

24. See Toscan, pp. 320–40. According to Toscan, "mal" usually signifies sexual desire and especially the desire of the active partner in sodomy. My reading of this phrase attempts to coordinate it with other thematic elements in the sonnet, most notably the expression of reticence or ambivalence in contrast with exhortations to sodomy.

25. For a summary of the juridical and historical evidence, see Toscan, 59–98; see also the sections: "Sodomie et classes sociales" (pp. 174–216) and "Extranéité" (pp. 229–39).

26. See David Herlihy, "Veillir à Florence au *Quattrocento*," *Annales* 24 (1969): 1338–52; and M. J. Roche, "Il controllo dell'omosessualità a Firenze nel XV secolo: gli *ufficiali di notte*," *Quaderni storici* 66 (1987): 706–23.

27. However, only two thousand individuals were found guilty, and the vast majority of convictions resulted in modest fines, making it hard to gauge the actual seriousness of the crime before public opinion.

28. The important exception to this rule is Luisa Avellini's excellent study.

29. My sources for Florentine political history in the Quattrocento include: J. Lucas-Dubreton, *La vie quotidienne à Florence au temps des Médicis* (Paris: Hachette, 1958); Nicolai Rubinstein, *The Government of Florence under the Medici, 1434–1494* (Oxford: Clarendon Press, 1966); Alberto Tenenti, *Florence à l'époque des Médicis: de la cité à l'état* (Paris: Flammarion, 1968); Anselmo d'Addario, *La formazione dello stato moderno in toscana da Cosimo il Vecchio a Cosimo I de' Medici* (Lecce: Adriatica ed. Salentina, 1976); Gene A. Brucker, *The Civic World of Early Renaissance Florence* (Princeton: Princeton University Press, 1977); J. R. Hale, *Florence and the Medici: the Pattern of Control* (London: Thames and Hudson, 1977); and Dale Kent, *The Rise of the Medici: Faction in Florence, 1426–1436* (Oxford: Oxford University Press, 1978).

30. These institutionally defined "legal means of revolution" (d'Addario) were meant to provide efficient decision-making apparatuses that would bypass the normal

chains of command and power invested in the *Otto*. The *Parlamento* consisted of an emergency convention of the "people"—*la gente*—in the Piazza della Signoria as a means to establish a new set of officials on the spot who, in due course, would set the reelection of the *Otto*. In reality, recourse to the *Parlamento* was often intended to mobilize as many of one's armed supporters as possible in a dramatic show of force. The *balìa* was an extraordinary committee elected by secret ballot and invested with the authority to make summary decisions, including the wholesale reconstitution of governmental groups; the suppression or creation of laws; and the condemnation of individual citizens and their families (often resulting in exile and/or the seizure of property). Without specifying the precise nature that would justify the convocation of the *balìa*, it was initially understood in the years before the Oligarchy took over as a means to counter potential abuses of the election and control of the *Signorìa*. Like the methods for the constitution of ordinary governmental groups, the procedure for election of the *balìa* was frequently contested and altered in the course of the century (1380–1490).

31. See John Najemy's important study of this transition: *Corporatism and Consensus in Florentine Electoral Politics, 1280–1400* (Chapel Hill: University of North Carolina Press, 1982).

32. The Medici held a double advantage over their opponents: they had both the enormous resources of their banks and a willingness to cultivate relations with the minor artisanate class, the so-called *gente nuova*, whom Albizzi and his aristocratic allies viewed as a dangerous class of parvenus and opportunists. In a sense, they were right, since the exiling *en masse* of the Medici's political enemies ensured many of the Medici allies access to the pool of citizens eligible for office.

33. D'Addario, *La formazione dello stato moderno* . . . , 35–36 (my translation).

34. G. Canestrini, "Nota ai Documenti che seguono," 285–91, and ibid., ed., "Versi fatti fa Niccolò da Uzzano," 297–300, both in *Archivio storico italiano* 4, part 1 (1843). This poem is also cited by Kent, *The Rise of the Medici*, 211–15.

35. Canestrini, ed., p. 299. Kent (p. 214) uses a variant in the fifth line: "postierla."

36. "So that the upstarts do not use their votes under cover as a back door, as they have often done so deceitfully," Kent, n. 10, p. 214.

37. Tartaro and Tateo, *La letteratura italiana*, 258. Demons punish them by whipping their heels, a detail echoed by the first tercet of the sonnet.

38. All quotations from Dante are from: *The Divine Comedy, v. 1: Inferno*, trans. and commentary by Charles S. Singleton (Princeton: Princeton University Press, 1970). I have slightly modified Singleton's translation.

39. II *Maccabees* 4:7–26.

40. The "taglier mal tondi" of v. 4 may be a distant allusion to the "piatti" (*Inferno* XIX) formed by the layers of simoniacal popes as they are stacked on top of each other.

41. Burchiello alludes elsewhere to *Inferno*, and especially to the circle of the barrators in cantos XXI and XXII; barratry is one way of characterizing Florentine political practice, including that of the Medici. See, for example, his sonnet "Parmi veder pur Dedalo che muova," Londra edition, 35.

42. See Kent, *The Rise of the Medici*, 334–36.

43. Translated from their equivocal terms, the women (i.e., vulvas) hide their anuses from ardent sodomizers.

44. As the speaker shares his information about the "diaquilone," the paronomasia of "chiodo" yields ways of hearing a different set of concerns related to the artifacts and ends of writing: *chiose*: gloss; *chiostro*: ink; *chiudo*: I close, end, or finish.

45. "Sudare" (to sweat) includes a range of sexual activities, and in particular, sodomy (see Toscan, vol. 4, s.v.).

46. *L'écorce et le noyau* (Paris: Aubier-Montaigne, 1978; rev. ed. Flammarion, 1987), 259–75 and passim.

47. While not entirely ruling out this possibility for homosexual gender identity, she suggests that cultural prohibitions against homosexuality reinforce heterosexual melancholia in significant ways. See *Gender Trouble: Feminism and the Subversion of Identity* (London: Routledge, Chapman, & Hall, 1990), 66–71.

48. Quoted in Chiffoleau, "Dire l'indicible," n. 91, p. 323.

49. Kent, *The Rise of the Medici*, 19.

50. Gilles Deleuze, *Logique du sens* (Paris: Editions de Minuit, 1969), 63–66, 83–89, and passim; Jacques Derrida, *L'écriture et la différence* (Paris: Editions de Seuil, 1967), 409ff.

51. See Claude Lefort's essay on the egocrat: "L'image du corps et le totalitarisme," in *L'invention démocratique. Les limites de la domination totalitaire* (Paris: Fayard, 1981), 166–86.

52. See Anthony Molho, "Cosimo de' Medici: *Pater Patriæ* or *Padrino?*" *Stanford Italian Review* 1 (1979): 5–31.

53. In order to strengthen their political hold, the Medici alliance "reformed" election procedures and renamed, with chilling cynicism, the Priors to the "Otto Priori della Libertà" (d'Addario, *La formazione dello stato moderno . . .* , 42).

54. See Abraham and Torok, "Sur le concept métapsychologique de la Réalité: notations sur le secret," in *L'écorce et le noyau*, 252–58.

55. The importance of mourning and melancholia to Freud's political theories is evident in both *Totem and Taboo* and *Group Psychology and Analysis of the Ego*.

Practicing Queer Philology with Marguerite de Navarre: Nationalism and the Castigation of Desire

CARLA FRECCERO

Every encounter with a representation of the rape of Lucretia is an encounter with a literary *topos* of Western civilization. And, as *topos*, the meaning of this rape is constructed as universal, transcending historical conditions: in every age and place, Lucretia had to be raped so that Rome could be liberated from tyranny.
—Stephanie Jed, *Chaste Thinking: The Rape of Lucretia and the Birth of Humanism*

AT the end of *The Heptameron*'s novella 42, Parlamente concludes her tale in characteristic exemplary moralistic fashion with the words, " 'Je vous prie que, à son exemple, nous demorions victorieuses de nous-mesmes, car c'est la plus louable victoire que nous puissions avoir,' " (294; "My appeal to you is that we should all follow her example, that we should be victorious over ourselves, for that is the most worthy conquest that we could hope to make," 389).[1] Oisille, the surprisingly feisty grandmother of the group, remarks, " 'Je ne voy que ung mal, . . . que les actes vertueux de ceste fille n'ont esté du temps des historiens, car ceulx qui ont tant loué leur Lucresse l'eussent laissé au bout de la plume, pour escripre bien au long les vertuz de ceste-cy' " (294; "There is only one thing I would regret . . . and that is that the virtuous actions of this young girl didn't take place in the time of the great [Roman] historians. The writers who praised Lucretia so much would have left her story aside, so that they could describe at length the virtue of the heroine of your story," 389). The name of Lucretia in such a context reminds us, as Stephanie Jed points out, of "the meaning of Lucretia's rape in the history of ideas: a prologue to republican freedom," presenting feminist scholars with a peculiar political (and ethical) dilemma: "To retell the story of the rape of Lucretia . . . is to enter into some sort of binding relationship with all of those readers and writers who somehow found the narrative of this rape edifying, pleasurable, or even titillating, and to be bound by the vision of those readers and writers to look at the rape as they did (and do)—as a paradigmatic component of all narratives of liberation."[2]

Thus it is with trepidation (and grief) that I confront the apotropaic power of this name as memorial to and icon of my entry into and complicity with humanism. But like Hélène Cixous, who argues against the phallogocentricity of horrifying myths of femininity and says, "You only have to look at the Medusa straight on to see her. And she's not deadly. She's beautiful and she's laughing," Oisille takes a skeptical view.[3] For what is already (and strikingly) apparent in Oisille's invocation of the *topos* of the rape of Lucretia is the way in which she first un-topics Lucretia by referring to the work of historians, thus historicizing the tale and its exemplary function, then dismisses "her," this emblem, this proper name, as "their" creation, "leur Lucresse." Lucretia lived, and should have been left, she says, at the tip of their pens, the point of contact or penetration that constitutes the humanist philological impulse to contaminate and violate in order, subsequently, to castigate and purge. To leave Lucretia there, "au bout de la plume," is to name her a patriarchal fantasm, the ventriloquizing automaton that permits what Alice Jardine has called gynesis.[4]

Jed argues that "only the description of textual experience can interrupt this tradition of imagining freedom in the context of sexual violence" (52), and she examines the relations between (masculinist) philology, the production of meaning, and the political ideologies of humanism. While her work makes possible the re-imagining of cross-historical philological relations, in this study she does not discuss what might arise from a textual encounter less clearly conceived of as adversarial. What else might obtain in the encounter between a feminist scholar and a woman writer of the past? In the case of Marguerite de Navarre, feminists have sought either to claim or to disavow a potentially sororal (af)filiation.[5] What if this sorority were also queer? While I cannot here propose to study the conditions of production of *The Heptameron*, I would like to describe disturbances produced by the intercalation of some of the castigated manuscripts and editions of this text as they relate, in part, to the interplay between the woman writer and the apparatus through which we may (wish to) read "her" text.

Editors argue that novella 42 deals with a family romance starring Marguerite's brother, the young prince François. Patricia Cholakian concurs, and devotes a chapter to it, aptly titled, "My Brother, My Hero."[6] In at least three places in the narrative and discussion of novella 42, the definitive edition A (*ms. français* 1512), reproduced by Michel François, and Adrien de Thou's 1553 manuscript (*ms. français* 1524) seem at war with the 1559 edition by Marguerite's first recognized and accredited editor, Claude Gruget, an edition commissioned by Marguerite's daughter Jeanne after her death.[7]

The struggle, what Bakhtin has called the dialogics of discourse, competing voices unharmoniously coexisting on different registers in a text, turns around, predictably, the person of the king, here described in terms that the editors and Cholakian attribute to Marguerite's enscripting of her sibling worship: "Des perfections, grace, beaulté et grandes vertuz de ce jeune prince, ne vous en diray aultre chose, sinon que en son temps ne trouva jamays son pareil" (*L'Heptaméron*, 286; "I shall say nothing of the perfections, of the grace and beauty of this young prince, except that in his day there was no one equal to him," 381).

In Longarine's speech praising the self-control of the female protagonist Françoise, manuscript A includes the passage "et celluy qu'elle aymoit plus qu'elle-mesmes avecq toutes perfections," referring to the young prince:

> Et voiant les occasions que ceste fille avoit d'oblier sa conscience et son honneur, et la vertu qu'elle eut de vaincre son cueur [;voyant les occasions et moyens qu'elle avoit, je dy qu'elle se povoit nommer la forte femme.] *et sa volunté et celluy qu'elle aymoit plus qu'elle-mesmes avecq toutes perfections* des occasions et moyens qu'elle en avoit, je dictz qu'elle se povoit nommer la forte femme. (295, with intercalated variant from Gruget; MS A "addition" in italics)

> Considering the opportunities which this girl had when she might have been tempted to override her conscience and forget her honour, considering her virtue in overcoming her heart and her desires, *and considering the way she resisted the man she loved above all else*, I declare that she was worthy to be truly called a woman of strength and honour. (390)

This "adding" of flattery is found also in Adrien de Thou's summary of the story:

> Un jeune prince meit son affection en une fille, de laquelle (combien qu'elle fut de bas et pauvre lieu) ne peut jamais obtenir ce qu'il en avoit esperé, quelque poursuyte qu'il en feit. Parquoy, le prince, congnoissant sa vertu et honnesteté, laissa son entreprinse, l'eut toute sa vie en bonne estime, et luy feit de grands biens, la maryant avec un sien serviteur. (286)

> A young prince falls in love with a girl whose favours in spite of her lowly station he fails to win, with the result that in recognition of her virtue the prince abandons the chase, holds her in great esteem for the rest of his days and marries her to a gentleman of his service. (54)[8]

The Gruget edition is far more terse, relegating (returning?—the relation between the first officially published edition and the "earlier" manuscript is in question here) the narrative to the genre of medieval *pastourelle* with its predictable, class-conditioned rape scenario that, in this case, has a happy ending: "Continence d'une jeune fille contre l'opiniastre poursuitte amoureuse d'un des grands seigneurs de France et l'heureux succez qu'en eut la damoiselle" (481; "Continence of a young girl in the face of persistent amourous pursuit by one of the great lords of France and the happy result obtained by the young lady," author's translation). As these variants and others suggest, what tears at the narrative is a gendering of heroic virtue at the site of nationalism, at the site of what also might be called a conflict between the people and their prince. Lucretia meets Marianne.[9]

Jed's study of the relation between the rape of Lucretia and the philological birth of humanism shows, in part, how a certain relation to "liberty" is established via a chastizing or castigating of a corrupted/violated body, which is in turn associated with the excessive passions of tyranny (27–28). Jed retells the narrative of Brutus the castigator, Lucretia's brother, who admonishes the Romans not to cry for the death of Lucretia but to take up arms against the Tarquins in order to found Republican Rome (15–17). Although she rightly marks Brutus's relation to Lucretia as a projective displacement, in other words, she points out that "Brutus finds in Lucretia's chastity the female version of his self-castigation" (15),

she does not explain why this narrative of masculine initiation into nationhood (into a being-for-the-state) should require passage through the
violated and castigated female body in order to erect itself. This narrative
of masculine accession to impassivity, to chaste thinking, to objectivity,
literally passes through the body of a woman; it founds itself upon the
bloody remains of a violated and excised femininity.[10]

Jean-Joseph Goux discusses masculine initiatory transitions in terms
of loss and compensation:

> In this transition it is, among other things, the sacrifice (the bloody
> loss necessary for the establishment of the phallus) that is recovered,
> forgotten, or rather changed in meaning to the point of becoming
> quite unrecognizable . . . That which the exercise of philosophy
> necessitates, is it not the cutting off of, the break with, sensible
> nature, the immediate, those things which alone allow elevation,
> ascension? It is in this movement of death to the sensible, indeed
> of the execration of bad matter, source of all evil, for the purpose
> of attaining the enjoyment of the idea, that the sacrificial motion
> would continue by interiorizing and sublimating itself. This resto-
> ration, this liberation, were archaically called phallic.[11]

In his account, the sacrifice of initiation is a symbolic castration, a movement from the penis (corruptible materiality, the body) to the phallus
(incorruptible ideality, the mind), a movement from the realm of the
mother (matter) to the father (idea), negotiated by and through the masculine initiate himself (56–61). As mythic antecedent to modern phallo-
centricity, the symbolic initiatory process haunts, as Jed's narrative of the
birth of humanism helps to show, the valorization of a chaste impassivity,
an adult masculine heroics of citizenship, won or restored at the cost of a
violent and "bloody renunciation," a cutting off:

> Access to the phallus is thus, in the initiation, the compensation, the
> symbolic reward for the loss that the masculine subject must suffer
> by the bloody renunciation of maternal ties, the sign of the tor-
> turous emancipation from an anterior bond, sealed by the first birth.
> The phallus has thus the role of a detachable value (it is detachment
> itself) which arises from the bloody cutting of a vital bond ("sym-
> bolic castration") and which rewards (by a second birth) the meta-

phoric joining of the paternal ancestors, even if they are only evoked by a name which continues the lineage and allows admission to the society of males. ("The Phallus," 61)

In the symbolic order that constitutes phallocratic modernity, this process inhabits, as representational remnant, the constitution of the citizen-subject, and a splitting off occurs whereby instead of the penis (body) of the masculine subject himself, the bloody matter that is excised, destroyed, castigated, is figured as the body, the mother, woman. This displacement must also, in some sense, constitute a disavowal of other libidinal matters, such that the price of admission into the society of males is a renunciation not only of incestuous heterosexual desire, but of other desires as well, though these remain implicit in Goux's account as well as in the cultural narrative it seeks to describe. For Marguerite, whose textual economy adopts this model, the excision required is, as we shall see, also potentially one that involves same-sex desire. In the narrative of the rape and death of Lucretia as the prelude to republican freedom, in the narrative whereby, mythically and eternally, "in every age and place, Lucretia had to be raped so that Rome could be liberated from tyranny," this (meaning of the) constitution of citizen-subjectry—as masculine and as "straight"—is reenacted.

Cholakian makes the point that novella 42 "develops the theme of the sentimental education . . . The question is how the hero will make the transition from boy to man (and from prince to king)" (*Rape and Writing*, 168), and thus is, in some sense, an initiatory narrative. But, as she also notes, the narrative shifts in point of view between a masculine perspective and a feminine one, for the moment the prince catches sight of the girl, a genealogy and a name, Françoise, is conferred upon her. If this is an encrypting of the hero's name, François (and for the purposes of my argument it will suit me well to go along with the belief that this is a story about Marguerite's brother, the king), then it is also a narrative about, at its simplest figural level, an accession to royal heroic virtue that passes through the (middle-class) body, person, of a woman. For what the story is designed in part to demonstrate is how the prince develops from a boy into a (worthy) king. From penis to phallus. From François, through Françoise, to France. Françoise, the feminine form of the nation for which François is the nominal icon, is thus somehow also France or French matter; and the French are, indeed, the people, the members of the body politic whose mind is their king. French matter, in its encounter with the royal imprint, is also, and not incidentally, the text.

This story is about Françoise too; indeed it is her heroic virtue which Parlamente and the other women praise at the end of the novella, heroic virtue defined in classic consonance with chaste thinking: " 'Je vous prie que, à son exemple, nous demorions victorieuses de nous-mesmes, car c'est la plus louable victoire que nous puissions avoir,' " says Parlamente (294; "My appeal to you is that we should all follow her example, that we should be victorious over ourselves, for that is the most worthy conquest that we could hope to make," 389); while Longarine adds, " 'Il fault estimer la vertu dont la plus grande est à vaincre son cueur' " (295; "One should always give due respect to virtue, and the greatest manifestation of virtue is to overcome one's emotions," 390).[12] Or is it? Chilton's English translation supplies the name of Saffredent as speaker in the passage that follows Longarine's remark above. In manuscript A (MS 1512), however, it is Longarine (and not Saffredent) who goes on to contradict herself by saying: " 'Puisque vous estimez la grandeur de la vertu par la mortiffication de soy-mesmes, je dictz que ce seigneur estoit plus louable qu'elle, veu l'amour qu'il luy portoit, la puissance, occasion et moien qu'il en avoit' " (295; "Since you take the degree of self-mortification as the measure of virtue I declare that the prince in the story was even more to be praised than the girl, because in spite of his love for her he still refrained from utilizing his power, although he had ample opportunity to do so," 390). Thus she nearly echoes the words [she?] used to praise Françoise.[13] Once again, textual variants manifest (or produce—the question of the philological production of a text is precisely what is at issue here) the symptoms of what Cholakian calls the problematic perspectival shifts between masculine and feminine points of view in these narratives. These variants suggest the possibility that what is occurring is, indeed, a splitting of the same (subject) into masculine and feminine subjects of heroic virtue. Whose story is this anyway?[14]

Aspects of the tale suggest that remnants of symbolic masculine initiatory transitions mythically haunt the accession to sovereign masculinity. There is, in novella 42, what has been called an "excessive" reference to kinship ties, most notably around Françoise:

> Ung jour, estant en une eglise, regarda une jeune fille, laquelle avoit aultresfois en son enffance esté nourrye au chasteau où il demeuroit.

Et, aprés la mort de sa mere, son pere se remaria; parquoy, elle se retira en Poictou, avecq son frere. Ceste fille, qui avoit nom Françoise, avoit une seur bastarde, que son pere aymoit très fort; et la maria en ung sommelier d'eschansonnerye de ce jeune prince, dont elle tint aussi grand estat que nul de sa maison. Le pere vint à morir et laissa pour le partage de Françoise ce qu'il tenoit auprès de ceste bonne ville; parquoy, après qu'il fut mort, elle se retira où estoit son bien. Et, à causequ'elle estoit à marier et jeune de seize ans, ne se vouloit tenir seule en sa maison, mais se mist en pension chez sa seur la sommeliere . . . elle sembloit mieulx gentil femme ou princesse, que bourgeoise . . . Et quant il fut retourné en sa chambre, s'enquist de celle qu'il avoit veu en l'eglise, et recongneut que aultresfois en sa jeunesse estoit-elle allée au chasteau jouer aux poupines avecq sa seur, à laquelle il la feit recongnoistre. (287)

But one day, when he was in a church, he caught sight of a young lady who had been brought up in the chateau which was his home. This girl was called Françoise. Her father had remarried after her mother's death and she had moved to Poitou with her brother. She also had an illegitimate half-sister, of whom her father was extremely fond, and who had been married to a butler in this young prince's household, with the result that she was as well-placed as anyone else in the family. The father died and left everything he possessed to Françoise, who went to live in her newly inherited property, just outside the town. But being marriageable, and only sixteen years old, she preferred not to remain alone in her house, and instead went to board with her sister, the butler's wife . . . she looked more like a noblewoman or a princess than a townswoman . . . When he returned to his chamber he made inquiries about the girl whom he had seen in church, and realized that when he had been small she had come to the chateau to play with her dolls with his sister, who, once reminded of her childhood friend, sent for her, gave her a warm welcome and invited her to come see them often. (381)[15]

The continuous reminder, throughout the narrative, that Françoise was raised in the household of the prince serves to impose the incest taboo on their relationship.[16] The kinship references in the tale are thus specific and overdetermined, for they function to mark the sororal relation of Françoise to the prince. "It is this sororal incest," Goux remarks, "which he must sacrifice in order to be able to enter into the exchange [of women]" (63).

Françoise, in the tale, both is and is not the prince's sister. The resemblance prevaricates so that she can be simultaneously circulating goods and prohibited sister. But the question of initiation and entry into a circuit of exchange applies as much to Françoise as it does to the prince. The narrative makes clear the dysfunctionality of her kin relative to their responsibility to circulate her properly (and to prohibit incest): her sister begs her to meet with the prince, while her brother-in-law arranges a tryst at his behest. The agent of accession to heroic virtue in the tale thus also becomes Françoise herself, for herself as much as for the prince.

Another element that marks the narrative as initiatory remnant is the determining presence of the prince's mother in the tale, she who recalls the prince to the household, or detains him there, who is his treasurer, and whose disapproval places constraints upon his actions; in short, she who controls his circulation. The family romance thus entails not the relation of the son and his desired, passive, and prohibited mother, to the father (or the law), but rather a relation between the son and his closest female kin. If the mother succeeds in keeping her son within the household, how does this young prince then accede to phallic sovereignty, for, Goux argues, "he must himself be able to enter into the ceremonial transaction as an available agent, and that presupposes, precisely, detachment, cutting off, the sacrifice of the mother which is the most obscure and the most torturous heart of the initiatory passage" (63–64)? Does the mother embody both maternal and paternal positions in the way that Françoise acts both as the prince's split subject (his abjected bodily self) and as resistance to the ideology of chaste thinking that would have her body as the castigated cost of its achievement? Here the narrative seems to militate against both heterosexual and phallocratic teleology by strengthening and rendering efficacious the maternal-filial relation and by installing the law as a maternal, rather than a paternal prohibition (291; 386; 292; 387). The place of sovereign phallic privilege is conserved, as we might expect it to be (Marguerite must have been a royalist, *n'est-ce pas?*), with an interesting twist: the phallic feminine—she who keeps her phallus and her son— rules. And yet, is this maternal (writer, queen) not herself a split subject, both sovereign and sororal (both Louise and Marguerite)?[17]

Female agency in Marguerite's tales frequently coincides with class difference, that is, with a nonaristocratic subject-position, and while this is a commonplace of more comic narratives of female agency (clever and/or lusty lower-class women) and a stereotype of the lower born in *The Heptameron* as elsewhere, it also works in this tale as a recognition of bourgeois resistance to aristocratic abrogation of privilege, where the Christian and courtly ideologies of "vraye amitié" (true friendship) equalize, as Longarine/Saffredent points out, "le prince et le pauvre" (295; "prince and pauper," 390). Françoise is French, after all, and a bourgeoise. Thus her resistance to inscription in the narrative of abjection, that is, as bloody, mutilated corpse that is defiled, reviled, castigated, etc., makes of her a revolutionary force. But this resistance is performed in the name of chaste thinking, that is, in the name of a self-castigation, a cutting off from desire and pleasure, for the good of the prince, the nation, honor. She is victorious in the tale, victorious over herself, as Parlamente points out, adding that this is the lesson that "nous," the female addressees of the moral exemplarity of the tale, must learn. Then our accession to honor would be achieved, like Lucretia's, through the self-castigating gesture of overcoming our emotions and desires, like Lucretia, for the good of the state.

Lucretia's self-castigation was suicidal, and the rebirth it produced was in her brother-citizens. Marguerite's narrative, with its split agency, its double rebirth into honor of both masculine prince and feminine pauper, suggests a more modern path toward the narrative of republican "freedom," one where the woman may live. The life into which one is reborn in this narrative is, as Goux notes, a phallic order; it is, indeed, phallocracy.[18] Marguerite's tale thus indicates one direction in which female subject-citizenry will be constituted, attested to by the advent of bourgeois nationalism in Europe and the documents of nineteenth-century liberal political philosophy.[19]

Goux argues that "in Western society, the masculine agent must consent to a sacrifice to which the returns (his entitled returns) correspond only virtually and abstractly," and that "what remains is subjection to a universal law, a symbolic order which is the same for all, and to which the subject must submit. This symbolic order arises from the interiorization of certain demands which are no longer experienced as social demands, and above all not as the demands of a *social exchange*" ("The Phallus," 67). His concern in this essay is to historicize and culturally delineate the phallus or symbolic order of contemporary (Lacanian) psychoanalysis and to show how an archaic and mythic initiatory configuration inhabits the unconscious of modern philosophical phallocentrism. In modernity, he argues,

> We see that the phallus must thus take on a new meaning. Rather than appearing as the immediately negotiable restitution of a loss, it becomes pure mediation, the mark of an integrity rediscovered after the sacrifice of the mother. With the phallus, the masculine subject affirms himself, but without any nuptial counterpart being necessary to ratify the function of renunciation. The phallus becomes a mediation in itself, an abstract opening which attests to the subject's accession to an order and a unity conceived of in their metaphysical elevation. Obtaining a woman surrendered by the group and thus the function of communication, is no longer the point. Erected for itself, the phallus is a monastic, celibate attestation of the detachment of "matter" and "nature" which guarantees integrity, identity, unity. (68)

The result is that "that which had been thought of as a procedure of gift-exchange, of giving and receiving between present and living partners maintaining a reciprocal relationship, is now broken into two acts which not only may be unaware of each other, but which no longer have any necessary relationship, either in social space or in social time, save the abstract subjection to a constraint which becomes law" (70). What remains implicit in Goux's description is that the subject, through his sacrifice, is initiated not only into "the exchange of women," but also into compulsory heterosexuality itself, through this process of renunciation. Thus, what is also permitted by the abstraction and interiorization of these social demands, as well as by the separation between sacrifice and entitled returns, is the abstraction and universalization of a law of heterosexuality. The occultation of this narrative of renunciation makes possible what Eve Kosofsky Sedgwick has called the "homosocial," a masculine affinity whose homoerotic boundaries are less clearly drawn for being less violently and definitively marked by excision or repudiation than the maternal bond.[20]

In his concern with the phallus as the "general equivalent for the objects of the drives," and thus for the inscription of the phallus within a Marxian economic logic, Goux overlooks or does not concern himself with what might be thought of as the intermediary historical stage of the symbolic or, to work against the notion of a progressive historical evolution of the phallus, what might be called another moment in the genealogy of phallocentrism, a moment that might also be said to mark Marguerite de Navarre's text as both early and modern. For in this text, it is true that the demands one must interiorize, the constraints to which one must submit, are not experienced as concretely (and entirely) social, as part of an immediate exchange, and do indeed become law. The order and unity to which the subject accedes are conceived of in their metaphysical elevation, as honor and virtue. Yet the biographical aura of the novella and the absent place of its paternal prohibition (and the present place of its maternal, royal, and phallic prohibition) suggest not quite a "pure" mediation; indeed, they suggest the presence of a nuptial counterpart in the nation, France her/itself. Nor is this symbolic order the same for all, though we might want to argue that the erection of the phallic sovereign subject of the nation-state produces the appearance of the godhead as guarantor of the universality of that symbolic order. Rather, what novella 42 delineates, in its tortured and (more or less) unconscious way, is the subject's submission to a law that is the nation-state, a place of phallocracy that is not quite yet phallocentrism. And that law is marked as heterosexual. Both François and Françoise, in the self-castigating movement that leaves behind emotion and desire, are reborn into honor and virtue, into France.

And it is here that we can witness one of the peculiarly modern inflections of Marguerite's text, in that it designates a future site not only for the masculine citizen-subject of the nation (whose sacrifice of incestuous desire is explicitly represented), but for the feminine one as well. In its most nationalistic version, we might read a directive to the nation's women to let their honor, virtue, and self-restraint be the civilizing force behind the nation's barbaric, appetite-driven, but nevertheless noble, virtuous, and heroic men, even as those men learn that women, as citizen-subjects, have the right (and the duty) to accede to honor and virtue, to be themselves citizens, *françoises.* Unlike the earlier narrative of republicanism, aptly illustrated in the fifteenth-century Italian wedding celebrations studied by Susanne Wofford, whereby "violence against women is figured as a necessary originary moment of male control and domination that makes possible the ensuing benefits of civilization which are brought by and symbolized by the women, but only after they are subjected to their husbands," novella 42 finds a way out of this sexual violence (homicidal or suicidal) by constructing a female subjectivity and the possibility of female citizenship on the model of the masculine renunciatory sacrifice.[21]

Yet this "equalizing" scenario, one that nevertheless firmly installs marriage as the foundation of the nation-state, also suggests traces of something other than the regimes of compulsory heterosexuality in this early modern narrative of nationalism. For, we might ask, what of the feminine force of the tale, its disdain for Lucretia, articulated by Oisille, the matriarch of *The Heptameron*'s storytelling group? And what of, on the other hand, the maternal phallus, the phallic feminine placed and displaced throughout *The Heptameron*'s conspicuously absented paternal/royal spaces? What of, finally, the absent narrative of (feminine) desire sacrificed; supplemented, ultimately, by the excessive love of the sovereign in manuscripts 1512 and 1524? An alternative heroic female figure haunts this narrative, haunts it because she appears only in the Gruget edition and substitutes for the name of Jambicque, whose story follows that of Françoise and the young prince. Jambicque is a woman who acts upon her desire, her pleasure, and gets away with it, as do many of the women in the tales of the fifth day (stories that deal with successful female agency).[22] Gruget replaces the name of Jambicque with Camilla throughout his edition. Camilla, amazon-like servant of Diana, chaste (lesbian?) warrior of Virgil's *Aeneid* and Aeneas's intratextual twin, assists Turnus against the ancestors of those whose historians will later celebrate the rape and death of Lucretia. Hers is a service to the state specifically marked by the absence of a sexual sacrifice, a refusal to assist in the construction of the masculine citizen-subject through self-castigation and the social exchange of marriage. Can we speak then of another archaic remnant in this text, the remains of what myth and anthropology, as well as radical lesbian feminism, might call matriarchy? A dream of another social order, a feudal one nevertheless, where women rule, where, in Luce Irigaray's formulation, the goods get together, where the traffic is among but not in women?

> . . . She is a warrior;
> her woman's hands have never grown accustomed
> to distaffs or the baskets of Minerva;
> a virgin, she was trained to face hard battle
> and to outrace the wind with speeding feet.

Across the tallest blades of standing grain
she flies—and never mars the tender ears;
or poised upon the swelling wave, she skims
the sea—her swift soles never touch the water.
And as Camilla passes, all the young
pour out from the field and house; the matrons crowd
and marvel, staring, in astonishment
at how proud royal purple veils Camilla's
smooth shoulders, how a clasp of gold entwines
her hair, at how she bears her Lycian quiver,
her shepherd's pike of myrtle tipped with steel.
(*Aeneid* VII: 1057–72)[23]

A guerrilla girl and not a Roman matron. And how might we understand this substitution in an edition commissioned by a mother's only daughter? Elsewhere I have discussed Jeanne's sacrificial role in acceding to the demands of the nation-state, the demands of a social exchange, the social exchange of marriage, imposed as law by Marguerite, her mother, and her mother's brother, the king of France.[24] Whose desires, and what kind, return to haunt a scene of excision, only to be castigated once again by future phallologists?

And what if Turnus, and not Rome? Is it a ruse of modern and Western phallocentrism, of the nation-state that France and elsewhere will become, that passion, emotion, lust, desire—incestuous, homosexual—cluster on the side of tyranny, to become the rapist designs of a Tarquin? That to be enfranchised citizens women must also excise these emotions from ourselves and ally with a Brute who would kill his own for the sake of the nation? "Marguerite" seems to suggest that yes, indeed, we must. And yet, in the disturbances of her texts, the texts we read as hers, shadows of a (utopian) doubt remain.

Notes

1. Marguerite de Navarre, *L'Heptaméron*, ed. Michel François (Paris: Garnier Frères, 1967); Marguerite de Navarre, *The Heptameron*, trans. P. A. Chilton (Middlesex: Penguin Books, 1984; rpt. 1986). All citations refer to these editions; page numbers to the French edition are given first.
2. Stephanie Jed, *Chaste Thinking: The Rape of Lucretia and the Birth of Humanism* (Bloomington: Indiana University Press, 1989), 54, 49. She also argues that feminist scholars

"become not only part of the scene of violation but agents in the reproduction of a violated body, a prod to prurience in a humanistic peep show" (49).

3.   Hélène Cixous, "The Laugh of the Medusa," in *New French Feminisms: An Anthology*, ed. E. Marks and I. de Courtivron (New York: Schocken Books, 1980), 245–64, 255.

4.   Alice Jardine, *Gynesis: Configurations of Women and Modernity* (Ithaca, N.Y.: Cornell University Press, 1985).

5.   Patricia Cholakian, in *Rape and Writing in the Heptaméron of Marguerite de Navarre* (Carbondale: Southern Illinois University Press, 1991), argues for Marguerite's feminism, as does Ann Rosalind Jones in "Assimilation with a Difference: Renaissance Women Poets and Literary Influence," *Yale French Studies* 62 (1981): 135–53; and Maïté Albistur and Daniel Armogathe, *L'Histoire du féminisme français*, vol. 1 (Paris: Editions des Femmes, 1977), 156. See also Deborah Losse, "Distortion as a Means of Reassessment: Marguerite de Navarre's *Heptameron* and the 'Querelle Des Femmes,'" *Journal of the Rocky Mountain Medieval and Renaissance Association* 3 (1982): 75–84; John Bernard, "Sexual Oppression and Social Justice in Marguerite de Navarre's *Heptaméron*," *Journal of Medieval and Renaissance Studies* 19, no. 2 (1989): 251–81. Colette Winn is less certain of Marguerite's sisterhood; see "La Dynamique appellative des femmes dans *L'Heptaméron* de Marguerite de Navarre," *Romantic Review* 77 (1986): 209–18, among other essays. I have also argued against a feminist reading of Marguerite; see "Rewriting the Rhetoric of Desire: Marguerite de Navarre's *Heptaméron*," in Marie Rose-Logan and Peter Rudnytsky, eds., *Contending Kingdoms: Historical, Psychological, and Feminist Approaches to the Literature of Sixteenth-Century England and France* (Detroit: Wayne State University Press, 1991), 454–73; and especially "Marguerite de Navarre and the Politics of Maternal Sovereignty," *Cosmos* 7 (1992): 132–49, Special Issue: *Women & Sovereignty*, ed. Louise Fradenburg.

6.   See Michel François, *L'Heptaméron*, 481: "Il n'est pas de doute que Marguerite veuille ainsi désigner son propre frère, le futur François Ier; on se souvient qu'elle a déjà usé de la même périphrase dans la vingt-cinquième nouvelle. La ville de Touraine est donc Amboise où résidait Louise de Savoie." Cholakian, *Rape and Writing*, 167–68: "All the evidence points to Marguerite's brother François as the hero/villain. The author's close emotional involvement with her male protagonist causes this tale to be split in focus between the heroine's and the hero's perspectives."

7.   Pierre Boaistuau's 1558 edition is banished by Michel François as corrupt because it "défigure par trop le texte de la Reine" (*L'Heptaméron*, xviii) and because "Le texte est incomplet; il ne compte que 67 nouvelles qui ne sont pas divisées en journées et ont été distribuées dans un ordre arbitraire" (p. xxv). For the question of the publication of the Gruget edition, and how it might relate to a feminist reading of Marguerite de Navarre, see Antoine Compagnon, "The Diminishing Canon of French Literature in America," *Stanford French Review* 15, nos. 1–2 (1991): 103–15, at 114, where he takes me to task for failing to include this fact in my discussion of the relation between Marguerite and Jeanne. This article is conceived, in part, as a playful response.

8.   Michel François, *L'Heptaméron*, 286; Chilton, *The Heptameron*, 54. François notes that the summaries provided for each story in the definitive edition come from Adrien de Thou's manuscript.

9.   See Neil Hertz, "Medusa's Head: Male Hysteria under Political Pressure," and the responses from C. Gallagher and J. Fineman, in *The End of the Line: Essays on Psychoanalysis and the Sublime* (New York: Columbia University Press, 1985), 161–217; also Kaja Silverman, "Liberty, Maternity, Commodification," *new formations* 5 (Summer 1988): 69–89.

10. See Elizabeth Pittenger's discussion, via Luce Irigaray and Gayatri Spivak, of a similar phenomenon as it relates to textuality, in "Dispatch Quickly: The Mechanical Reproduction of Pages," *Shakespeare Quarterly* 42, no. 4 (Winter 1991): 395: "The female body serves as symbolic site in which social meaning is concretized at the same time that any concrete, material specificity is emptied out of 'the female body' in order to insure its service as a pure and proper vehicle. The power of Irigaray's argument is the link she makes between sexuality and textuality. The formulation 'female as bearer of imprints' exposes the implications of a textuality figured as female." See also Luce Irigaray, "Women on the Market," in *This Sex Which Is Not One*, trans. C. Porter and C. Burke (Ithaca, N.Y.: Cornell University Press, 1985): 170–91; and Gayatri Spivak, "Displacement and the Discourse of Woman," in *Displacement: Derrida and After*, ed. M. Krupnick (Bloomington: Indiana University Press, 1983), 169–95.

11. Jean-Joseph Goux, "The Phallus: Masculine Identity and the 'Exchange of Women,'" in *differences* 4: *The Phallus Issue* (Spring 1992): 40–75.

12. That it is Parlamente who tells this story and provides its moral gloss is significant, marking the tale as a narrative of nationalism. Her name suggests her role as mediator and legislator of the group. She is also often believed to be the Marguerite persona of *The Heptameron*, which seems to reinforce the maternal, national, and biographical thematics of the narrative.

13. The differences are that *puissance* appears in this phrase, whereas desire and love appear in the first; honor and virtue are mentioned in the first but not the second, which takes a distance from chaste thinking by disparagingly calling it self-mortification.

14. Using the notion of split focalization, Cholakian argues that Marguerite deliberately encodes a "view from elsewhere" (20) to insert female agency and perspective into the conventional narrative plot of male desire. My argument differs in that I attribute the shifts in novella 42 to a phenomenon of twinning or splitting, whereby what is at work in the text is a (gendered) splitting or doubling of the subject of heroic virtue. Thus I am concerned less with authorial intentionality and agency and more with a psychoanalytics of the text.

15. Cholakian says of Françoise's genealogy that "although it does provide a kind of garrulous verisimilitude, this explanation seems at first glance to supply more information than the reader can possibly want or need" (*Rape and Writing*, 169).

16. Cholakian, *Rape and Writing*, 173.

17. This is another instance of the way in which *The Heptameron* can be called a maternal text, and Marguerite's praxis that of maternal sovereignty. See my "Marguerite de Navarre and the Politics of Maternal Sovereignty." See also Goux, "The Phallus," 63: "The phallus would thus be the more or less cryptic symbolic attestation that

the masculine subject (and it is this which makes him a subject) is entitled to enter as a taker into the circuit of the exchange of women: the sign, more precisely, that he has satisfied the differentiated requirements of a double sacrifice—maternal and sororal."

18. See Goux, "The Phallus," 64: "It would be archaically, as a *male subject*, and in a close relationship to the phallic simulacrum, that the subject would constitute itself."

19. See Cora Kaplan's discussion of Mary Wollstonecraft's "reply" to Rousseau in "Wild Nights: Pleasure/Sexuality/Feminism," in *Sea Changes: Essays on Culture and Feminism* (London: Verso, 1986), 31–56; see also Carla Freccero, "Notes of a Post-Sex Wars Theorizer," in *Conflicts in Feminism*, ed. Marianne Hirsch and Evelyn Fox Keller (London: Routledge, 1990), 305–25.

20. Eve Kosofsky Sedgwick, *Between Men: English Literature and Male Homosocial Desire* (New York: Columbia University Press, 1985), 2–3: "To draw the 'homosocial' back into the orbit of 'desire,' of the potentially erotic, then, is to hypothesize the potential unbrokenness of a continuum between homosocial and homosexual—a continuum whose visibility, for men, in our society, is radically disrupted." See also 25: "We can go further than that, to say that in any male-dominated society, there is a special relationship between male homosocial (*including* homosexual) desire and the structures for maintaining and transmitting patriarchal power: a relationship founded on an inherent and potentially active structural congruence. For historical reasons, this special relationship may take the form of ideological homophobia, ideological homosexuality, or some highly conflicted but intensively structured combination of the two."

21. See Susanne Wofford, "The Social Aesthetics of Rape: Closural Violence in Boccaccio and Botticelli," in D. Quint, M. Ferguson, G. W. Pigman III, W. Rebhorn, eds., *Creative Imitation: New Essays on Renaissance Literature in Honor of Thomas M. Greene* (Binghamton, N.Y.: MRTS, 1992), 189–238, 202.

22. I disagree with Colette Winn's view that "l'appellatif Jambicque dénonce ainsi la hardiesse de la femme qui affirme son désir d'aimer" ("La Dynamique appellative des femmes dans *L'Heptaméron*," 217). To argue that Jambicque is denounced for her desire is to accept only the moralizing judgments of some of the *devisants*. The narrative, in this case, contradicts their judgments, so that the question of Jambicque's desire is, at the very least, problematized.

23. *The Aeneid of Virgil*, trans. A. Mandelbaum (New York: Bantam Books, 1971), 189 (VII: 1057–72).

24. See Freccero, "Marguerite de Navarre and the Politics of Maternal Sovereignty"; also "1527: Margaret of Navarre," in *A New History of French Literature*, ed. Denis Hollier (Cambridge: Harvard University Press, 1989), 145–48.

Erasmus's "Tigress":
The Language of Friendship, Pleasure,
and the Renaissance Letter

FORREST TYLER STEVENS

SHORTLY after Desiderius Erasmus entered the monastery of Steyn in 1487, he met a young man, Servatius Rogerus, to whom he became particularly attached. Erasmus explains to his brother, Pieter Gerard, "He is, believe me, a youth of beautiful disposition and very agreeable personality and a devoted student . . . This young man is very anxious to meet you, and if you make your way here soon, as I hope you will, I am quite sure that you will not only think he deserves your friendship but readily prefer him to me, your brother, for I well know both your warmheartedness and his goodness."[1] We do not know whether Pieter Gerard got to know Servatius's goodness (or Servatius, Gerard's warm heart), nor do we know if Gerard preferred Servatius to Erasmus, but we do know that Erasmus himself became quite enamored of Servatius, and wrote a series of letters to him detailing the depth of his affection and attachment. Servatius seems to have responded to Erasmus's advances with equal ardor, then gradually pulled back from the relationship. Erasmus countered the withdrawal with rage and despair:

> So impossible is it, dear Servatius, that anything should suffice to wash away the cares of my spirit and cheer my heart when I am deprived of you, and you alone . . . But you, crueller than any tigress, can easily dissemble all this as if you had no care for your friend's well-being at all. Ah, heartless spirit! Alas, unnatural man! . . . *But you yourself are surely aware what it is I beg of you*, inasmuch as it was not for the sake of reward or out of a desire for any favour that I have wooed

you both unhappily and relentlessly. What is it then? Why, that you love him who loves you. (CWE 1 12, emphasis added)

Though Servatius seems to have known what it was that Erasmus begged of him—and Erasmus states it rather bluntly as "that you love him who loves you"—subsequent scholars have been embroiled in what has become a rather vehement controversy. Exactly what conclusions should we draw from the letters? Was Erasmus a homosexual? Worse still, was he a jilted homosexual pursuing an unwilling, straight acolyte? Were the monasteries refuge for those pleasures one dare not name among Christians? Most Erasmus scholars maintain an embarrassed silence about the letters, refusing to speculate about either Erasmus or the monasteries; a vocal minority maintain that letters are only epistolary exercises; and a small number talk of the love letters written by Erasmus as either a key to his latent homosexuality or another example of hidden homosexual history.

I realize that to frame the debate in terms of the "homosexual love letter" begs the question that, firstly, the letters to Servatius are love letters, and that, secondly, Erasmus was a homosexual. Even those who advocate a reading of the letters as epistolary exercises scrupulously avoid the word "homosexual"; of course, they also work doubly hard to let the reader know that "homosexuality" is precisely what is being avoided, not simply a conception of sentimental friendship. The operative assumption is that there was (and is) a blanket condemnation of same-sex sexual acts "among Christians," acts which at least since the nineteenth century are said to belong to a person called a "homosexual." Fingering Erasmus— Desiderius Erasmus, foremost humanist and church reformer of the Renaissance—as a practitioner of the crime which cannot be named among Christians is something little short of heresy. But deeper still, the controversy is about the nature of letters and literature as evidence. The first assumption, that the letters are "love" letters, is a question of genre, or perhaps a question of their status as literary artifacts: given that Erasmus was a master at what might be called with some trepidation "form letters," might it not be the case that the letters to Servatius Rogerus are, all in all, "simply" conventional? Erasmus wrote an important book on letter writing, *De conscribendis epistolis*, a book which is often cited to support the notion that all the letters are simply "epistolary exercises on simple themes."[2] The letters are certainly stylized, and perhaps more importantly, the words, expressions, sentences, quoted authors, and sentiments are similar to those of many, many letters written between men during the Renaissance. We might assume that Erasmus's letters to Servatius are only an instance of this wider category—a type of epistle which everyone wrote—and therefore could not properly be said to be evidence of anything, especially not sexuality.[3] To indict one letter would be, to one degree or another, to indict them all.

By way of addressing the complex relationship between literature and the ways in which gender and sexuality are deployed and negotiated in the Renaissance, this essay is a reading of the letters to Servatius alongside Erasmus's theoretical discussion of the purpose, substance, and style of the letter of friendship as expressed in *De conscribendis epistolis.* In part my essay is an attempt to draw attention to the sexual in a context which has been continually desexualized by a recourse to the "literary-ness" of much Renaissance writing—as if the "literary" were the agent which would police the propriety of sexual content and connotation. While we often think of the letter as having some purchase on the "real"—personal letters are thought to be indices to "history"—Erasmus's letters tend to be buried within the category of "literary" documentation (hence, imaginative or figurative) when the subject is his passionate relationships to other men in Renaissance Europe. By focusing a reading of the status of sexuality and gender within the prescriptions and proscriptions of "conventionality," I strive to rehistoricize the stories we tell about the sort of evidence "literary" and "historical" documents provide.

In the course of my study of the section of *De conscribendis epistolis* concerning the writing of "letters of friendship" I also wish to read past (and through) the "conventionality" of the Renaissance, exploring how gender, far from being the proscriber of sexuality and erotic possibility (as it is claimed to be in its modern ideological contexts), is an enabling trope for an early modern Europe in which the dyad of biological sex and the formations of sexuality are disconcertingly decoupled. As such, the understanding of love, friendship, propriety, and sexuality which appears in *De conscribendis epistolis*'s description of the letter of friendship documents a relationship in which the relative position of the sender and receiver of the letter—correspondingly, the wooer and wooed—determines "gender" and potential erotic responses. By now in sexuality studies it is a familiar point that "gender" and "sexuality" are not agents which reside in or make up the body natural; they more accurately describe sociostructural positions the body occupies and "convention" produces. My essay works to thread that observation back onto the grammar of social relations as they are encapsulated in a pedagogical work whose letters of friendship would teach the proper art of love-making and man-making.

Erasmus's handbook on the art of letter writing was published by Froben in 1522, and was among the most popular of all of Erasmus's writings on education, going through some twenty-two editions before his death in the summer of 1536, and exploding into nearly sixty or more editions by the end of the century. *De conscribendis epistolis,* "On the writing of letters," started out as a student study book for three pupils Erasmus taught in Paris of the early 1490s: Robert Fisher, William Blount (later Lord Mountjoy), and one Adolph van Veere. When the book was finally released in its definitive form, the positive response was overwhelming: the book was adopted by the supporters of the traditional church, the Jesuit colleges, and Lutheran educators who pushed for moral reform in both the church and its pedagogical institutions. "On the writing of letters" was even used in English grammar schools to teach upper formers the proper methods of "writing sundry epistles to sundry persons, of sundry matters, as of chiding, exhorting, comforting, counselling, praying, lamenting, some to friends, some to foes, some to strangers; of weighty matters or merry, as shooting, hunting, etc., of adversity, of prosperity, of war and peace, divine and profane, of all sciences and occupations, some long and some short" (CWE 25 lii).

Erasmus's "textbook" reworked and rewrote the medieval style of the *artes dictaminis,* teaching the art of writing in a lively, fluid manner (as opposed to the didactic and at times stodgy style of the popular medieval manuals); which is to say, the book was designed in that particular Erasmian way to hold the attention of the student while maintaining a requisite degree of precision, learnedness, and, above all, morality. Drawing examples from Roman and Greek literature—as well as his own letters to friends, acquaintances, and enemies (as the case required)—Erasmus extolled to the student the virtues of proper form and proper content, while exploring "what is by nature diverse and capable of almost infinite variation" (CWE 25 12).

One would suspect, however, that within a Christian context, the "infinite variation" of proper form and content would not include an amorous letter between men. The lines I quoted at the beginning of this essay are from one of the nine extant letters to Servatius Rogerus, the young acolyte and fellow Hollander at Steyn where Erasmus spent a number of years as an Augustinian canon. Within the confines of what was in institutional form and pedagogical curriculum a medieval monastery, the letters seem unseemly, perhaps compromisingly, passionate. Hardly the proper letter at all. Yet, to write such a letter to one's male friends was precisely proper: the epistles' propriety lay in their conventionality; the not unheard-of and even extremely popular practice of writing to "friends" in an ornate, intense, and passionate manner was encouraged by the monks teaching the acolytes of the monastery. A friend with whom you shared your feelings, prayers, dreams, bed, board, and books was, though in another body, the counterpart to your soul. In the language of the time, to have such a friend was to be "one soul in bodies twain."[4] Though the "cult of friendship" was mainly associated with court circles (and to many modern minds, court degeneration), it was found in the cloister as well, as Johan Huizinga explains:

> Each court had its pair of friends, who dressed alike, and shared room, bed, and heart. Nor was this cult of fervent friendship restricted to the sphere of aristocratic life. It was among the specific characteristics of the *devotio moderna*, as, for the rest, it seems from its very nature to be inseparably bound with pietism. To observe one another with sympathy, to watch and note each other's inner life, was the customary and approved occupation among the brethren of the Common Life and the Windesheim monks.[5]

The religious practices of the *devotio moderna* which Huizinga points to in this passage as an extension of the cult of "fervent friendship" were an integral part of a heavily sentimentalized religious fervor cultivated by the all-male communes. Steyn, like other fraterhouses devoted to the teaching of writing, cultivated the *devotio moderna*'s "constant ardor of religious emotion and thought."[6]

It would be difficult, I think, to characterize the letters which Erasmus wrote to Servatius as "religious"; however, each of the epistles does partake of the "constant ardor of emotion and thought" fostered by the religious community at Steyn. Given a survey of the secondary literature dealing with Erasmus's early life, this conclusion is not at all evident, or rather it would seem that what to *make* of that conclusion is not at all evident. The editors of the *Collected Works of Erasmus*, Wallace K. Ferguson, R. A. B. Mynors, and D. F. S. Thomson, explain: "The group of letters written to Servatius . . . may be no more than exercises in epistolary composition, like the formulae in *De conscribendis epistolis*. . . . Taken at their face value, though with considerable allowance for rhetorical exaggeration, the nine letters to Servatius indicate that Erasmus had become involved in an emotional attachment to his young friend" (CWE 1 6). The conclusions the editors wish to negotiate in this passage are a bit muddled or simply opaque: admittedly, they argue, the letters are emotional and fervent; yet one should make "allowances" for "rhetorical exaggeration" (or simply ignore the intensity of emotion); and one should remember that the letters might very well be "no more than exercises." But even if bled to that, they conclude, the letters evidence an "emotional attachment." D. F. S. Thomson, one of the two translators of Erasmus's correspondence, further argues that "literary imitation is the motivating force . . . and that the letters conform in style and content to a well-established tradition of monastic rhetorical letter-writing" (CWE 1 26). Thomson's recourse to "rhetorical" and "literary imitation" as epithets is meant to bleed the letters of any hint of sexual impropriety—in Erasmus as well as in the monasteries, lest the latter be seen as the breeding ground for a purple plague of homosexual corruption (which is not by any means an uncommon assertion of corruption to throw at the church); the terms deflect even the subtlest suggestion that the humanist icon was what we would consider to be a homosexual.

The assumption within the editors' gloss is, I think, that one must use caution to place the letters within the proper context. Instead of upbraiding the editors for their caution, I will commend it, and admonish that we haven't been cautious enough in explaining the meaning of the style, form, and content within its sociohistorical setting. The assumptions behind what constitutes the boundaries of style and propriety, the limits and limitations of form and content, are precisely what is under contention within a historical problem of the social negotiation of power and pleasure within the meanings and makeup of any given representation of sexuality. Accordingly, we need to examine more closely Erasmus's conceptions of the letter of friendship, since it is only by that route that we can assess the letters to Servatius and the questions of "homo"-sexuality which they entail.

The format of each section of *De conscribendis epistolis* is roughly similar. First, a general description of the type of letter being addressed is presented, along with its purpose(s) and proper execution, with thoughts on the form (each letter was itself a genre of sorts) and what is and is not successful as a means to carry out its intent. Sprinkled through each discussion are literary and classical antecedents of the type under scrutiny, antecedents from which the student might garner phrases, metaphors, and persuasive strategies. After the general comments, Erasmus gives an example which he feels exemplifies the genre, often from one of his own letters to a friend or acquaintance, but also examples from letters of the ancients: the epistles of Pliny, Cicero, and other writers of antiquity.[7]

Late in the body of the treatise, sandwiched between a discussion of "letters which give advice" and "letters of the demonstrative class" (a "demonstration" is an extensive description of something of interest) is a succinct exposition of "the letter of friendship" (CWE 25 203). The overall type of the letter of friendship is one of "persuasion," Erasmus explains; but laying out the theoretical groundwork for the friendship letter by breaking it into subtypes, he concludes, "Not all letters of friendship fall into the same class. For some contain a request, others a protest, or a complaint, or coaxing, or self-justification." Despite the disparate and seemingly endless categories into which the general class could be broken on the basis of specific content, he decides to follow previous thinkers and discuss the letter from a stance of moral classification. "I have noticed that some have divided this class into two sections, honourable and dishonourable," he observes; "I call the honourable kind 'conciliatory' and the other 'amatory.'" The basis for his divisions rests on the notion that the letter of friendship, like friendship itself, contains the sexual as well as the social. Which is to say, the taxonomy of "honourable" versus "dishonourable" rests on a distinction between gaining a new acquaintance through praise and persuasion versus sending a persuasive letter "of or pertaining to a lover, to love-making or to sexual love generally" (OED). It is important to note that the modern sense of a "love letter" per se is foreign to his schema. As will become clear from his description of the class, the love relationship and the erotic possibilities it entails fall together under the rubric "friendship." Both are seductions of sorts which the tool of the letter helps implement.

Erasmus first discusses the honorable section. "The conciliatory letter is that by which we insinuate ourselves into the good graces of a person previously unknown." The means of doing this consist of "convincingly set[ting] out the reasons that have led us to solicit his friendship," carefully devoid of "flattery" (though this is "hard to do"), followed by "anything in us which can induce him to reciprocate our affection" in a manner which would "indicate it without arrogance." Erasmus follows up the prescription with a rather dry example of the genre ("I am a frank admirer and honest partisan of the learned," "If in turn you can welcome such a friend," etc.). The honorable section is short, and he promptly advances to the "dishonorable" variety.

It is here, in the seamier half of the class of the letter of friendship (it contains just a taint of the "disgraceful"), that he deals with the relationship between pleasure and friendship. "But if we are seeking to arouse feelings of mutual love in a girl, we shall make use of two main instruments of persuasion, praise and compassion." Erasmus explains that the "instruments of persuasion," praise and compassion, are effective because "all human beings" find "delight in praise" (but "girls in particular"). To fan the fire of mutual love "we shall strive to be as supplicating as possible," bringing light to what merits we find, while "belittl[ing] our own, or at any rate mention[ing] them with great modesty."

> We shall demonstrate intense love joined to deep despair. We shall try by turns moaning, flattery, and despair; at other times we shall make skilful use of self-praise and promises; we shall employ precedents of famous and honorable women who showed favour to a pure, unfeigned love and to the devotion of youths far beneath them in social condition. We shall attempt to show that our love is very honorable. As a last resort, with great show of humility we shall beg that if she can in no way deign to give her love in return, she will at least resign herself to being loved without prejudice to herself; we shall add that if this request is not granted, we are resolved to cut short a cruel life by whatever means possible. (CWE 25 204)

The terms of the amatory letter are familiar. To coax, cry, complain, sigh, dream, "and all the rest" (204) are "things that are not so much disgraceful as rather foolish, giving the appearance of immorality, and therefore of doubtful propriety for setting before young men." Which, in the meantime, doesn't stop him from giving them as examples for an "honorable youth [who] is desirous to take an honorable and well brought up girl as his wife." Obviously, from the sentence just quoted, as well as the passage cited at length above, the "sexuality" in which the mechanics of arousing mutual love are framed is "heterosexual" if only because the sender is deemed masculine and the recipient is styled feminine. The mention of the wife is the first clue concerning the genders in which he casts his discussion. The treatise is written for young men such as William Blount, Lord Mountjoy. Like the "conciliatory" letter of friendship, the explication of the "amatory" version resides in a context of negotiations for social and economic position, the seduction to power as well as to pleasure. Making the connections explicit, Erasmus explains the ranging concerns of the letter of friendship: "More difficult and greater scope for the exercise of ingenuity is afforded in the case of a poor youth seeking marriage with a wealthy girl, one of humble birth with one nobly born, an ugly man with a beautiful girl, or finally an old man with a young girl." Thus, the machinery of the friendship letter is structured around axes of wealth, blood, beauty, and age—each brought to bear on securing a place in the sociopolitical contract of marriage.

But given the gender of the participants presented in the general discussion (poor youth, wealthy girl; masculine wooer, feminine wooed), the examples used to illustrate his points are surprising. The sample letters under the subsection entitled "Collection of Materials for Letters of Friendship" are all between men. For example, to illustrate the last set of binarisms (young/old, humble/noble, etc.), Erasmus presents "Virgil's Corydon" (205). Erasmus tells us that the relationship presented in Virgil's second eclogue is exemplary of the "persuasive class" mixed with the "demonstrative class": Corydon's plaint for Alexis illustrates "love [which] is chiefly obtained by praise." Erasmus cautions that the relationship itself is not all that exemplary—the principal wooer, Corydon, does give "an appearance" of "stupidity." Importantly, the latter comment echoes a caveat voiced in another pedagogical work, *De ratione studii*. In that work Erasmus hesitated to use the relationship between Corydon and Alexis as something to be emulated; the difference in age and class makes their relationship the paragon of "unstable friendship" and unlikely to succeed.[8] It is clear, however, that Erasmus's distaste for Corydon and Alexis as an example is not because of its male-male love relationship. By using the youth and shepherd to illustrate the mixed class of letters, the youth, the "beautiful Alexis, the master's favorite" for whom the "Shepherd Corydon burned,"[9] plays the role of the "young" or "beautiful girl," the body who stands in as recipient of the letter, just as the youth learning to write from *De conscribendis epistolis* is meant to stand in the stead of the shepherd himself. Masculine sender, feminine recipient; man Corydon, boy Alexis. No sodomitical taint of "immorality" of Corydon's love for Alexis makes the treatise "of doubtful propriety for setting before young men." Importantly, the gender of the recipient within the theoretical discussion does not restrict the gender of the players of "wooer" and "wooed" within the practice of letter writing. Although the discussion directs male writers to female recipients, amatory letters of friendship may be written between men too.[10]

Which is a less than intuitive point given the distance between the Renaissance and the present: but other examples from the "collection of materials" support such a proposition. Each of the remaining letters used to guide the practice of the student's writing is also from a man to a man, beginning with an epistle in Cicero's *Ad Atticum* ("Upon my life, my dear Atticus, neither my house at Tusculum, which otherwise is a favorite sojourn for me, nor even the Isles of the Blest mean so much to me that I can be without you for so many days") to "For, believe me, nothing is more beautiful, more fair, or more worthy to be loved than manly virtue. I have, as you know, felt affection for Marcus Brutus . . . yet on the ides of March my affection was so enhanced . . . Who would have thought that any addition could be made to the love I felt for you?" (CWE 25 205).

Though the skeleton of the theoretical discussion was cast in bi-gendered terms, as that discussion is put into practice, the "girl" of the original formulation drops out at the critical moment the practical examples are presented as scripts for the boy's own letter writing scenarios. All of the example letters are epistles between men. What might we then conclude about the theoretical discourse of Erasmus's thinking concerning friendship and its inextricable companion, love, and the specifically gendered attributes of power—wooer/wooed, pursuer/pursued, etc.—within these relationships? It is obviously not that the terms of the scenario automatically prescribe the gender of the objects they purport to adjudicate. That is, boy-girl rule book recipes for friendship/courtship do not ban boy-boy letters of equal intensity of affection, nor do they introduce a proper/improper, heterosexual/homosexual split between male-male and male-female love and courtship. Indeed, the genders of the subject and object within the grammar of social relations (in this case, the rules informing the practices of the sender and the recipient of the letter) become, in practice, orthogonal to the forms of position, power, and age which we recognize to be the quintessential Renaissance determinants of social and political relations from the prince on down through the human hierarchy. We have already seen this in Erasmus's explication of the binarisms which mediate the dialogue between the subject and object positions on either side of the letter of friendship.

To further illustrate the point, take, for example, his discussion of the general class of the "persuasive" letters (of which the letter of friendship is a subclass). Erasmus clumps together any "letters exchanged between young men, boon companions, and lovers" (CWE 25 37), and he delineates the decisive determinants in their composition as being not gender, but age, body, blood, and money.[11] The "letters exchanged between young men, boon companions, and lovers should be framed in a more winning manner," he points out. "In this way the person persuading will inspire more confidence . . . and he will evoke the memory of past sensual pleasures in such a way as to reveal that his mind shrinks from mere recollection." So, too, the letter writer

> will take advantage of the age of his correspondent. If this is greater than his own, he will say that it is proper for the one superior in years to have more wisdom . . . But if it is less, he will say that no time of life is more vigorous . . . He can argue from the person's appearance also . . . it is not right for a deformed mind to dwell in a beautiful body . . . Arguing from descent . . . he must be encouraged to acquire nobility by his own efforts . . . From the standpoint of wealth . . . he must devote himself with all the greater energy to the acquisition of learning, which produces both wealth and reputation. (CWE 25 38–39)

As a tool which negotiates the boundaries among "young men, boon companions, and lovers," the letter of friendship operates within and between the sexual relations promulgated by the alliance systems (marriage to secure property and family title, for instance) and other homosocial relations, sexual or not, but always sexualized, which existed to cement ties between men. The genders of the sender and recipient of the letter are equally—and indifferently—subject to the overall concerns of age, aesthetics, famous lineage, or family fortune.

Each line of courtship/seduction which Erasmus recommends to the young reader of *De conscribendis epistolis* is woven into his own letters to Servatius. In one of the first letters, he attempts to cheer his young friend, who is evidently greatly depressed, by resorting to the formula of moaning, flattery, and despair: "Although I who seek to give you consolation am rather myself in need of it . . . still it is my very special love for you, sweetest Servatius, that has caused me to forget my own pain and attempt to heal yours . . . For what has become of your usually delightfully gay expression and your former good looks and bright eye? . . . Alas for me; what more can I do to please you, my soul?" (cwe 1 7).

So, too, through every letter he "demonstrate[s] intense love joined to deep despair" ("as there is nothing on earth more pleasant or sweeter than loving and being loved, so there is, in my opinion, nothing more distressing or more miserable than loving without being loved in return"); shows that his love is very honorable (just as any amatory letter which drops such pick-up lines should); and "as a last resort" when he finds that Servatius "can in no way deign to give her [*sic*] love in return," asks that he resign himself to being loved, or else Erasmus would "cut short a cruel life": "So, my dearest Servatius, if I cannot acquire from you that friendship which hereafter I would most heartily desire, I request that at least the common intercourse of every day should exist between us. But if you think that I should be denied this also, there is no reason for me to wish to live further" (cwe 1 14).

The "her" in relation to the paragraph highlights one last important point. As recipient of the letter of friendship, Servatius steps into a role gendered female in the masculine-sender / feminine-recipient nexus, and the language Erasmus uses to describe him is inflected accordingly. "What am I to call it, dear Servatius—harshness or obstinacy or pride or arrogance? Can your nature be like that of a young girl so that my torments yield you pleasure, and your comrade's pain gives you happiness, his tears, laughter?" (cwe 1 9). Though exhorted by Erasmus to "play the man" (cwe 1 21) and "prove your manhood" (cwe 1 18), Servatius also operates within the role of "young girl" and "tigress" who refuses to move as Erasmus woos. Which is not to say Servatius is "passive," meaning "inactive," within the relationship. When Servatius does return his affection, Erasmus is overjoyed: "For as I was reading your very sweet letter, the effective proof of your love towards me which I long for, I wept as I rejoiced and in the same measure rejoiced as I wept" (cwe 1 14).

Of the topics that I have discussed—the language of the letter, the gender mechanics of wooing, and the sexualities put into play by those mechanics—I have not mentioned "sodomy." Sodomy within the Renaissance is an intractable topic, to say the least, but I do wish to touch on Erasmus's general view of that "horribly muddled category," *peccatum illude horrible, inter christanos non nominandum.* In *Paraphrases on Romans and Galatians* there are two features of Erasmus's gloss on the famous Pauline condemnation of sexual relations between men (read, "homosexuality"[12]) which should be noted. Erasmus is well aware of Paul's proscription and acknowledges that men "abandoned the natural use of women" and "burned for one another with a mutual desire to such an extent that the male committed foul acts with male" (CWE 42 18). What should be stressed, however, is that desire between men in and of itself is not the issue—amount or intensity is. Were it otherwise, Erasmus would surely have commented on the inappropriateness (to say the least) of Corydon's pining for Alexis, or Socrates' relationship with Alcibiades, something he never does. Indeed, sexual desire within the latter couple's relationship is used as a means to *amplify* the presence of virtue: "But the forms of amplification by reference to something else are innumerable, as when one magnifies the disasters suffered by the Greeks and Trojans to set off the extraordinary beauty of Helen . . . and as in Plato's Symposium the unusual sexual restraint of Socrates is inferred from the beauty of Alcibiades and the frequency of the occasions presented" (CWE 25 93).

Erasmus blithely presents Helen's beauty along with the beauty of Alcibiades (can you imagine someone like Jerry Falwell making such an analogy?), but more tellingly, comments upon Socrates' "unusual sexual restraint," a restraint magnified by the presence of a beautiful boy. The power of the amplification rests on the knowledge that an Alcibiades is, above all, desirable—and Socrates' being tempted by the goods more than once only increases the magnitude of his virtuous abstinence. After all, who wouldn't desire a beautiful youth? It would only be natural.[13]

Erasmus's discussion of sodomitical desire comes in the context of Paul's condemnation of paying tribute to God in improper ways. Erasmus refers to the impropriety as an "unnatural worship of God," stemming from their "foolish hearts" which were "darkened by a cloud of arrogance" (CWE 42 18). It is the "vapour of [their] empty glory" and "their vanity" which lead to God's allowing the miscreants to "rush headlong into the gratification of the desires of their own hearts." And the "desires of their own hearts" turn out to be, specifically, idol worship: "they worshipped a false statue fabricated by art in place of the true God, and absurdly venerated and worshipped created things and have honoured these more than him who created all things" (CWE 42 18). Such behavior was a crime against God and state: sodomy becomes the sign of sedition.[14] Sexual impropriety derives directly from the idol worship and their "bringing dishonour upon God who alone ought to be praised," not the other way around. Such "perverse worship of the known God" leads to becoming "steeped in every kind of wickedness": "fornication, covetousness, cunning, everywhere polluted with envy, murder, contention, deceit, malice, possessed of an evil character, gossips, backbiters, haters of the divine power, overbearing, . . . disobedient to parents, devoid of understanding, confused, lacking all sense of piety, ignorant of covenants, unmerciful." As Alan Bray points out in the context of Elizabethan England, sodomy is inextricable from other fantastic horrors and crimes against God and humanity.[15] The conceptual distance between what one does with one's friend and the acts committed by the sodomite is large, given a context of the persons involved and their relative relationship. To label one's own actions as sodomitical would be to identify oneself in league with "every kind of wickedness."

When Erasmus chides Servatius that the youth knows what it is that he wants, he also contrasts what he wants with other things which might be demanded from a friendship: the "sake of reward" or the "desire for any favour." It is when the sexualized friendship opens up into demands of reward and favor that the relationship comes precariously close to those representations of sodomitical friendship. The physical actions are the same; the language mediates the propriety:

> How sweet its language is and how pleasing its sentiments! Everything in it smacks of affection and of a very special love. And as often as I read it, which I do almost hourly, I think I am listening to the sweet tones of my Servatius' voice and gazing at his most friendly face. Since we are seldom permitted to talk face to face, your letter is my consolation; it brings me back to you when I am absent, and joins me with my friend though he be away. (CWE 1 14)

Erasmus doesn't shy away from imagining the relationship carried on through the language of the letter to be a substitute for the physical intercourse between the two. And if we cannot be together in person, which would of course be the most pleasant thing possible, Erasmus tells Servatius, why should we not come together, if not as often as might be, at least sometimes, by exchanging letters? And as the writing is the site of meeting and exchange of affection, so the body of the letter becomes the body of the lover: "As often as you look upon these and read them over you can believe that you see and hear your friend face to face. . . . Ah, 'half my soul' " (CWE 1 6).

A survey of the secondary literature concerned with Erasmus's early writings finds at one extreme the critic who argues that the letters are signs of a "young man of more than feminine sensitiveness; of a languishing need for sentimental friendship."[16] At the other end we find the facile, homophobic Freudian, making much of a "volatile neurotic, latent homosexual" Erasmus.[17] As I have attempted to show, the letters do not answer to the desexualizing move of the former; nor is the point to prove that Erasmus was a homosexual, and certainly not within the vituperative, pathological terms of "latent homosexuality." Rather, any approach to the question must work within the conceptual universe in which there is neither a state of gender boundary nor an absolute distinction between proper and improper sexual acts. Many critics of Renaissance friendship (L. J. Mills, for example) have read the varying elements of Renaissance writings of love and friendship as opposing factions, mutually exclusive elements in a conceptual universe governing affection. Were Erasmus or any other Renaissance thinker to have made distinctions between the two, it would not have been based on a supposedly naturalized sexuality mediated by genitalia or gender-roles: "My sweetest Servatius, though your letter was such that I was unable to read it without tears, still it not only removed the distress of mind which had already reduced me to an extremity of wretchedness, but even gave me an amazing and unexpected degree of pleasure" (CWE 1 14). Instead, the same language constitutes friendship, pleasure, and the Renaissance letter—and perhaps, for us as well, pleasure in the art to an amazing and unexpected degree.

Notes

I extend my appreciation and love to Alan Stephens and Joe Lazzaro for their friendship. Many thanks to Laura Yim for reading late drafts of this essay.

1. A note on notation: quotations from the *Collected Works of Erasmus*, 66 vols. (Toronto: University of Toronto Press, 1974) will be given in the form "CWE" followed by a volume number, followed by page number(s). This quotation from the letter to his brother appears at CWE 1 5. Further citations will be placed within parentheses within the text.

2. I am quoting P. S. Allen, the fin-de-siècle Oxford editor of Erasmus's Latin letters.

See *Opus Epistolarum Desiderius Erasmi Roterodami* (Oxford: Clarendon Press, 1906), Tom. I, p. 585.

3. As Eve Kosofsky Sedgwick puts it in *Epistemology of the Closet* (Berkeley: University of California Press, 1990), even the most liberal of academics have been willing to dismiss questions of sexuality between men, at least those posed by an antihomophobic gay studies movement, as meaningless. Take, for instance, the cult of friendship which I discuss in this paper: questions concerning the possibilities of sexuality are dismissed because, most would claim, "passionate language of same-sex attraction was extremely common during whatever period is under discussion—and therefore must have been completely meaningless. Or 2. Same-sex genital relations may have been perfectly common during the period under discussion—but since there was no language about them, they must have been completely meaningless" (52). If my supposition about the language in which these relationships was mediated proves to be correct, then to point to the popularity of a writing manual like *De conscribendis epistolis* is to point to the ubiquity of images, diction, and social functions which opened up spaces for relationships, even erotic ones, not only between men and women, but between men and men, and even, say, fathers and daughters (e.g., Thomas More's letters to Margaret More Roper). To rework the boundaries of possible sexual expression in early modern Europe is to dissolve the terms of the debate, the homo/hetero binarism—indeed, modern sexualities at all—and the psychological restrictions surrounding those categories (e.g., our [Freudian] understanding of incest and the network of its taboos—or even what makes up those taboos).

4. Lauren Mills's is (still) the most thorough discussion of the cult of friendship in Renaissance England. Mills examines both Renaissance and classical sources for the "repeated stress on friendship in Elizabethan and Stuart" England. See Lauren Joseph Mills, *One Soul in Bodies Twain* (Bloomington, Ind.: Principia Press, 1937). In one letter to Servatius, Erasmus quotes Pythagoras, saying "A friend is one soul in two bodies" (CWE 1 20), playing off of Cicero's definition in *De amicitia.*

5. Johan Huizinga, *Erasmus of Rotterdam* (London: Phaidon Press, 1952), 12. My discussion of Erasmus's early life at Steyn is drawn from Huizinga.

6. Ibid., 3.

7. "The lists of such lists [of the authors he quotes] is nearly endless. . . . There are, for example, over five hundred references to Cicero in *De conscribendis epistolis* and one hundred fifty to Pliny" (CWE 25 xv).

8. Jonathan Goldberg discusses literary propriety and Erasmus's use of Virgil's second eclogue to illustrate pedagogic method in "Colin to Hobbinol: Spenser's Familiar Letters," in *Displacing Homophobia: Gay Male Perspectives in Literature and Culture* (Durham: Duke University Press, 1989), 107–26. Goldberg concludes, "For Erasmus, Virgil's poem savors of disorderly love," which is to say that the relationship is, to use Erasmus's words, "a parable of unstable friendship": "Alexis cultivated, young, graceful; Corydon rude, crippled, his youth far behind him. Hence the impossibility of a true friendship" (110).

9. Virgil, *The Eclogues*, trans. Guy Lee (London: Penguin Books, 1984), 39.

10. Cf. Stephen Orgel, "Nobody's Perfect: Or Why Did the English Stage Take Boys for Women?" in *Displacing Homophobia: Gay Male Perspectives in Literature and Culture* (Durham: Duke University Press, 1989), 7–29. Indeeed, following Orgel's argument in "Nobody's Perfect," there is a certain substitutability of boys and women: they are both roughly analogous in that they are both sexual objects for men; gender doesn't count, inserter versus insertee does. A brilliant explication of the classical antecedents for this relationship appears in David M. Halperin's "One Hundred Years of Homosexuality," in *One Hundred Years of Homosexuality and Other Essays on Greek Love* (New York: Routledge, 1990), 15–40.

11. I mean to gesture toward Foucault's notion of *alliance* as explicated in *The History of Sexuality* (New York: Vintage Books, 1980). In that volume he explains "the relations of sex gave rise, in every society, to a *deployment of alliance*: a system of marriage, of fixation and development of kinship ties, of transmission of names and possessions" (106).

12. I wouldn't speculate on what Paul meant in Romans by the category of men having sexual relations with men. I would, however, stress that Erasmus's understanding was a fifteenth- and sixteenth-century one, not the post–nineteenth-century, naturalized category of the "homosexual."

13. And its "naturalness" is certainly one of its more distinguishing features. Several years earlier, at the time Erasmus was upbraiding Servatius for being "crueller than any tigress" and a "heartless spirit," what is marked as unnatural is an entire lack of mutual desire. "Alas unnatural man! Even the fiercest beasts are responsive to those who love them, forgetting their savage instincts" (CWE I 12).

14. As of this date, Alan Bray's discussion of sodomy in *Homosexuality in Renaissance England* (1988; London: Gay Men's Press, 1982) is the best handling of the social and political meanings making up that category. See especially pp. 20–30.

15. Bray notes this both in *Homosexuality in Renaissance England* and in "Homosexuality and the Signs of Male Friendship in Elizabethan England," elsewhere in this volume.

16. Huizinga, *Erasmus of Rotterdam*, 11.

17. Nelson H. Minnich and W. W. Meissner, "The Character of Erasmus," *American Historical Review* 83 (1978): 598–624.

John Bale and Early Tudor
Sodomy Discourse

DONALD N. MAGER

OME, kiss me sweet Soquette . . . Now purity defend me
from the sin of Sodom . . . This is a creature of the masculine
gender." These lines from Cyril Tourneur's *The Athiest's Tragedy*
(1611), spoken by the hypocritical Puritan clergyman Languebeau Snuffe, at first seem to carry one of the more common uses of the
word *sodomy*, namely foreplay prior to intercourse between men (4.3.193–
95).[1] Plucked from the play's full fabric of imagery and argument, the
word seems to have just such an unambiguous modern denotation. The
ahistoricist reader might well, therefore, miss the discursive site of these
spoken lines—a site which in rapid order seems to allude to adultery,
clerical sexual indulgence, necrophilia, prostitution, homosexuality, revenge, murder, and atheism. Admittedly, *necrophilia, homosexuality,* and *atheism,* as we use them, are modern categorical terms with social and discursive constructions that considerably postdate Tourneur; my point is not
to label unproblematically a particular series but to demonstrate a sweep
of terms. Such a sweep of vices huddled together in close proximity is a
kind of discursive praxis whose roots go back at least eighty years before
Tourneur wrote. It is also a catalog whose sweep does not ring with modern familiarity, although its lineaments will not be surprising to a reader
of Alan Bray's *Homosexuality in Renaissance England.* Part of the effort of this
essay is to further historicize the category of sodomy by exploring the
early Tudor practice of a specific sodomy discourse, similar but distinct
from Tourneur's; to do so, I contend, would identify epistemic differences, from period to period, as well as to identify continuities, borrow-

ings, and echoes such that they can be read without resort to transhistorical, universalist assumptions about the ways signification occurs.

The short parliament of 1533 was primarily concerned with the matrimonial issues surrounding Anne Boleyn, and the line of succession. The historic passage of the "Act of Restraint of Appeals to Rome" embodied in its preamble Thomas Cromwell's political theory which justified a sovereign national state, and marked the final split with Rome. The 1533 parliament also passed twenty-two other statutes ranging from weights and measures to the willful slaughter of fish spawn. Among these, 25 Henry VIII c.6 was the first civil regulation in England of unnatural sexual acts, variously called buggery or sodomy. The act designated sodomy was to be a felony with the punishment of forfeiture of property and death. Among the 72,000 executions which Holinshed claims took place during the reign of Henry VIII, none has been proved to have been under this statute, though some may have been. The statute seems to have been significant for ideological purposes, not judicial enforcement, and, as Montgomery Hyde states, "during the next twenty years the act was repealed twice and re-enacted four times, after which it was to remain undisturbed on the statute book for upward to three centuries."[2]

The text of 25 Henry VIII c.6 is worth being quoted in whole, because unlike many sodomy statutes in the United States, it does not use "crime against nature" language; instead, it simply announces that the civil authority in its assumption of roles previously performed by church courts will assume jurisdiction over the punishment of buggery.

Le Roy le veult

For asmoche as there is not yett sufficient and condigne punyshment appoynted and lymytted by the due course of the lawes of this Realme for the detestable and abhomynable vice of buggery commyttid with mankynde or beaste; It may therfore please the Kynges Hyghnes with the assent of his Lordes spirituall and temporall and the Commyns of this present parliament assembled, that it may be enacted by auctorytie of the same, that the same offence be henesforth adjudged felonye, and suche order & forme of proces therin to be used ayenst the offendours as in cases of felonye at the commen lawe; and that the offenders being herof convicte by verdicte confession or outlarye shall suffer suche peynes of dethe and losses and penalties of theire goods cattlis Dettes londes tenements and her-

ditaments as felons byn accustomed to doo accordynge to the order
of the comen lawes of this Realme, and that no person offendyng in
any such offence shalbe admyttid to hys clergie: And that Justice of
pease shall have power and auctoritie within the lymitts of their
commissions and jurrisdiccion, to here and determyne the seid offence as they do use to do in case of other felonyes: this acte to
endure to the last day of the next Parliamente.

Originally, the act of 1533 was part of Cromwell's larger program by
which Henry's parliaments systematically appropriated to the state domains of legislation hitherto controlled by the church courts, including
matrimony and sexuality. If we are struck by the connection between
Henry's impulse to appropriate authority for annulment to fit his personal policies and desires in a legislation which predates by less than five
years a statute which sets new limits on other people's desires, this is but a
modern irony, not a Tudor one, for the Henrician parliament was primarily concerned with appropriating to its sovereign king the property
and authority of the Roman church in England. The 1533 sodomy law in
its first instance is part of that program.

Hyde traces the history of its prosecution, and Alan Bray has added
new information; my concern, however, is not with the law and its enforcement—dreadful as that turned out in time to be.[3] I wish, rather, to
look at the radical reformation discourse about sodomy which lies behind
the statute's significance to some, if not all, of its original supporters.
There is no better place to tease out that discourse than in the remarkable
five-act morality play by John Bale "compyled" (his term) in 1538, *A Comedy Concernynge thre lawes, of Nature, Moses, & Christ, corrupted by the Sodomytes,
Pharysees and Papystes*. Bale's text naturalizes the statute by providing a full
deployment of the "crime against nature" theological argument—an argument whose legal formula can be traced back to the sixth century Theo-
docian and Justinian codes. Where the 1533 act is a legislation of civil
appropriation, Bale's play exposes a sexual system which seeks to ground
such legislation in a divinely authored nature.

John Bale's place in the history of English drama has been fixed upon
his mixed-genre play *King Johan*, which despite morality play features has
been seen as a prototype for the Elizabethan history play as written by
Shakespeare, dealing as it does with a particularly Tudor revisionist reading of an event from England's historical past. In this case the revision is

fiercely propagandistic, for John is imagined by Bale as the type of the anti-papal martyr. Bale was a prolific writer. No systematic edition of his moralities, polemics, pamphlets, and tracts on the history of writers in England has been attempted, nor will be, one suspects. As a result, readers of *King Johan* have no context for their reading of Bale other than the traditional one which sees the play as a step toward the teleological end achieved in the history cycles of Shakespeare. John N. King is almost alone in his scrutiny of other Bale works, in particular Bale's works in cataloging of and assigning authorship to ancient books in English and the tract *The Image of Both Churches* (c. 1541–47), a work produced during Bale's exile on the Continent after the fall of Cromwell, his patron.

I want to suggest that *Thre Lawes* along with his other four surviving moralities are significant also, but not because they point in any lineal fashion to later Tudor drama. In fact, I argue that *Thre Lawes* is worth attention because of the rigor of its pre-representational hermeneutic quite different from the narrative and representational impulses which typify the late Tudor-Stuart entrepreneurial stage. Its morality structure sets in motion a categorical system of distinctions so rigorously worked out that the sheer rationality of the scheme is dazzling.

To describe this machine as it processes the play's ideas through five scrupulously organized acts is to construct the text's signification as that text wishes itself to be read. To tease out epistemological slippages and categorical looseness within that rational design is to deconstruct it in order to read significances which the text does not seemingly wish to own. My aim is to do both, because parallel constructivist and deconstructivist readings of *Thre Lawes* provide valuable insight into the sodomy discourse which contextualizes the 1533 Henrician statute. Since the U.S. state laws (in the close to thirty states where they have not been repealed and are, as in Georgia, actively enforced) uniformly take both wording and precedent from the 1533 English law, this reading should be of use to legal scholars of those laws, even though it is not my purpose to offer such an analysis in this paper. As noted earlier, U.S. laws frequently include Justinean "crime against nature" references, absent from the English law, perhaps an inheritance from Blackstone and other post-Renaissance legal texts, which themselves might have derived their authority from the discourse deployed in Bale's play.

Thre Lawes, "compyled" as Bale says, begins with a prologue spoken by

Baleus Prolocutor. Bale the author/compiler is a site both inside and outside his text. This discrepant authorial position, as I will suggest later, offers some initial deconstructive leverage on the text. The authorial persona announces the play's message and, in the first line, places it in a legislative context.

> In ych commen welth   most hygh prehemynence
> Is due unto lawes   for soch commodyte
> As is had by them.
> (1–3)

Parliamentary appropriation of church-court functions is not a theme of the play; but the play's theme of divine-legalism is placed at the outset in a civic context, as if the argument to be explicated in the rest of the play has been mounted specifically to justify the commonwealth's right to legislate. The play shares Henrician concerns and comes close to being a propaganda instrument to serve Henry's reform project, for it was one of the widely performed moralities sponsored by Thomas Cromwell to be acted by his personal company of players.

A few lines later, Baleus Prolocutor names the three laws of the play's title as they will be explicated in the play.

> Our heavenly maker,   mannys lyvynge to dyrect,
> The lawes of Nature,   of Bondage, and of Grace,
> Sent into thys worlde   with vycyousnesse infect,
> In all ryghteousnesse   to walke before hys face.
> (15–18)

The prologue completes the initial statement of the play's theological and structural scheme by matching each of the three laws with the particular forces which have perverted them.

> The lawe of Nature   hys fylthy dysposycyon
> Corrupteth with ydolles   and stynkynge Sodometry,
> The law of Moses   with Avaryce and Ambycyon
> He also poluteth;   and even contynually
> Christes lawe he defyleth   with cursed hypocresy
> And with false doctryne   as wyll apere in presence
> To the edyfyenge   of thys Christen audyence.
> (22–28)

Confrontations of each law with its particular vicious opposite form the allegorical action of acts two, three, and four of the play.

Actus Primus states the thesis and outlines the plan of development. Deus Pater, like God Adonai in *Everyman*, summons an allegorical agent to appear on earth and perform his will. In this case, however, we have three agents: Naturae Lex, Moseh Lex, and Christi Lex. Bale relishes the significance of the number three, for Deus Pater announces a parallel set of trinitarian relationships. The act opens with his self-introduction:

> I am Deus Pater,   a substance invysyble,
> All one with the Sonne   and Holy Ghost in essence.
> To Angell and Man   I am incomprehensyble,
> A strength in infynyte,   a ryghteousnesses, a prudence,
> A mercy, a goodnesses,   a truth, a lyfe, a sapyence.
> (36–40)

After summoning his three laws, he explains their charge.

> Our lawes are all one,   though yow do thre apere,
> Lyke wyse as our wyll   is all one in effect.
> But bycause that Man   in hymself is not clere,
> To tyme and persone   as now we have respect;
> And as thre teachers   to hym we yow dyrect
> Through ye be but one,   in token that we are thre
> Dystyncte in persone   and one in the deyte.
> (62–69)

Bale's rational scheme establishes here at the outset two interrelated triads. The mystery of trinity in the deity's person is replicated in his tripartite law "in token" of God's nature, and is simultaneously necessary "bycause that Man in hymself is not clere, / To tyme and persone," just as men and angels cannot "comprehend" the one-in-three of God's person. God's laws are one with his person and his will; both person and will are revealed to man, but man is not "clere" in "comprehensyon" of them. For all its mystery of concept, this is a tight and rationally organized allegorical machine. But behind its scrupulous lucidity of design lies a slippage, for Bale now no longer announcing himself as the play's Prolocutor, stands modestly behind the text and its performance as what he calls its "compyler." This role, however, enacts behind the text the power to both comprehend and explain the very mysteries that Deus Pater in the foreground of the text and on the stage has explained are beyond human comprehension. This slippage points to a discrepant performance of Bale's authorial roles.

In this play, as with most of Bale's writings, he calls himself "compyler." John N. King, who reads Bale sympathetically, explicates this term as it would have been understood in Bale's day.

> The authorial role that Bale assigns to himself most often is that of "compiler" or "collector," terms that denote derivation from a variety of sources. "Compiler" designates a more active and creative role, as in the ascription for the plays . . . Bale associates himself with medieval commentary traditions that presuppose incremental accumulation and assimilation of the work of predecessors. In an age that defined rhetorical invention as the mastery of traditional commonplaces, "compilation" was a respectable literary activity.[4]

Surely King is correct that this is the authorial role Bale wishes us to see him construct for himself. As compiler, he lies outside the text, "incrementally" invisible, such that revelation through the tradition of commentary speaks to the text's audience without the imposition of a visible authorial bias. But, no sooner is this role declared, than Bale counters it by constructing a conspicuous voice for himself within the text, namely the persona Baleus Prolocutor, who speaks the play's prologue and announces its argument. This player-persona bearing Bale's name suggests an appropriation by Bale of some degree of authorial responsibility for the play's teaching beyond a tradition of incremental commentary. No sooner has Deus Pater declared his intention at the outset of the play, than he states, as already cited, "To angel and man I am incomprehensible" (4). The mystery of human knowledge of God is mentioned elsewhere as well, especially in relation to the trinity, as it is in this first instance. It also sets Bale as author in a strange relation with the congregations of angels and men who cannot comprehend God and the trinity, since his play itself by its rational clarity of design and detail suggests considerable levels of comprehension.

Bale's text invents space for a voice not at one with providential revelation. As explicator, this voice assumes a degree of knowing superior to that of a mere "compyler." This voice also stands in judgment, denounc-

ing and condemning particular human activities, while it apparently neither declares nor owns its judgmental role. It is from this discursive space
that a first-generation radical reformer such as Bale can denounce his
papal political foes, while apparently merely "compiling" the incremental
commentary of tradition.[5]

Actus Secundus is of central interest to this essay. Its design introduces
a pattern repeated in acts three and four. Therefore, I shall scrutinize it
only. Naturae Lex defines himself as the essential divinity within human
nature.

> The lawe in effect   is a teacher generall—
> What is to be done,   and what to be layed asyde:
> But as touchynge me,   the first lawe naturall,
> A knowledge I am   whom God in Man doth hyde,
> In hys whole workynge   to be to hym a gyde.
> (162–65)

Almost in the same breath, he laments that on account of man's "bryttle
nature" and "hys slyppernesse," "moch doth provoke" him (173–74). The
divinely implanted intuition of natural law in man must be asserted in
face of three vices which work to destroy it: Infidelitas, Sodomismus, and
Idololatria (who also appears in the guise of Idololatria Necromantic).
Infidelitas appears first, dressed as a singing pedlar, to ridicule and ha-
rangue Naturae Lex. In a lengthy exchange between the two, his infidelity
is shown to partake of both meanings of his name. Refusing to serve natural law, he is both disloyal and unbelieving. Finally, Infidelitas announces,

> I wyll cause ydolatrye,
> And most vyle sodomye
> To work so ongracyouslye
>   Ye shall of your purpose fayle.
> (357–60)

The three vices which oppose the law of nature are a kind of anti-trinity,
for both Idolatry and Sodomy seem to be aspects of Infidelity, not discrete entities. Infidelitas summons them onstage by an incantation of
Tetragrammaton (392), and Idololatria speaks first, in the guise of a woman—a point made several times as proof of idolatrous perversion of the
natural masculine hierarchy of the deity. Tellingly, Infidelitas links idolatry with the carnivals of Christmas and Lent.

> At Christmas and at Paske
> Ye maye daunce the devyll a maske
>   Whyls hys great cawdron plawe.
> (403–5)

Idolatry describes her habits of sumptuous feasting as part of holy days, of shrine worship, and of her own reversal of hierarchy in a female like-ness—a guise which is linked to the saying of the *"Ave Marye"* as a necro-mantic charm to "Ease mean of toth ake" (415) and to "helpe men of the ague and poxe" (418). She speaks a language of carnivalesque parody, ribaldry, folk superstition, perverse reversals of hierarchy, and assertions of transgressive female power; if she is not quite an allegorical icon for the Catholic church as is Spenser's Duessa, her imagery is fused with refer-ences to Roman abuses as perceived by the militant Reformation mind.

After much ranting along these lines, Sodomismus takes his turn at center stage. If Infedilitas combines disloyalty and disbelief, and Idolo-taria involves carnivalesque reversal of the divinity's essential sobriety and masculinity, Sodomismus is unchecked desire.

> My selfe I so behave,
> And am so vyle a knave
> As nature doth deprave
>   And utterlye abhorre.
> I am soche a vyce trulye
> As God in hys great furye
> Ded ponnysh most terryblye
>   In Sodome and in Gomorre.
>
> In the fleshe I am a fyre,
> And soch a vyle desyre,
> As brynge men to the myre
>   Of fowle concupyscence.
> We two togyther beganne
> To sprynge and to growe in manne,
> As Thomas of Aquyne scanne
>   In the fort boke of hys sentence.
> (555–70)

Bale's psychomachia goes something like this: disloyalty to and disbelief in one's divinely implanted human nature leads inevitably to worship of false

idols and reversal of natural hierarchies, and simultaneously to an un-
leashing of "vyle desyre" and "fowle concupyscence."

As Sodomismus expatiates upon his "desyres," I am impressed by two
features of his discourse. First is the obvious fact that for Bale (and one
assumes, therefore, for the Henrician parliamentarians), sodomy is not a
specific perversion but a large category—one which lumps together behaviors instead of drawing distinctions between them; the earlier distinction between lusts against nature and lusts of fornication no longer serves.
Second is the equally obvious fact that all of these perversions are viewed
as compellingly attractive to humans in their fallen state with little inherent tendency to be repugnant—especially this seems to be so in the case of
what we now call bestiality, a perversion to which Bale allots considerable
imaginative attention. The O.E.D. credits Bale with the first use of four
variants of "sodomy," including two usages of "sodomitical" (V.10, 366).[6]
These words crop up throughout his writings, and those Reformation
writers under Edward's patronage who follow him (especially Luke Shepherd and William Baldwin). They are not unique to this play; indeed, the
discursive habits which surround sodomy language in the Reformation
have traditions reaching back as far as Wyclif; the Reformation writers,
however, are more insistent and consistent in their displays of it.

To follow Bale's typical Reformation use of the word, the sodomitical
desires as displayed by Sodomismus include: one, priestly adultery in
place of lawful marriage (575–77); two, promiscuity (579–81); three, the
sin of Cham in "scorning" his father Noe's "dronkeness" (nakedness is
not mentioned) (584–85); four, Onanism (586–90); five, the mixing of
species, especially man with animals as practiced by Aristo, Fulvius, Semi-
ramis, and a number of others (591–618); six, "monkysh" abstinence which
"clean marryage they forbyd" (627–42); and finally, pederastic unions.

> In Rome to me they fall,
> Both byshopp and cardynall,
> Monke, fryre, prest and all,
>   More ranke they are than antes.
> Example in Pope Julye,
> Whych sought to have in hys furye
> Two laddes, and to use them beastlye,
>   From the Cardynall of Nantes.
>
> (643–50)

These are the "vyle desyres" and "fowl concupyscence" which rise from infidelity and idolatry. Although never stated, what they share is Aquinas's notion of seed planted in improper vessels.[7] (With Aquinas, a father of the Catholic church, Bale would typically repress the name.)

In any event, Bale's point is not primarily theological. Doctrine is not offered for deliberation and dispute; instead, it is the grounding which "naturalizes" Bale's rhetorical moves, for his is not a rhetoric of disputation and proof, but one of invective. Politics is his sphere. Bale's sodomy is not the name of a sexual activity, nor even an illicit desire. Instead, his sodomy is a highly charged anti-papal discourse. Encoded in that discourse is a set of presuppositions about natural sexuality, natural desire, and human nature itself. First, "clean marryage" is assumed to be a natural desire which, if one has not been perverted through infidelity and idolatry, will lead each human to fulfillment of his nature. I use the masculine pronoun exclusively because female subjects of God's purpose and law are absent from this play.[8] Second, all men if faithful believers will express the desire for "clean marryage" only. Abstinence and celibacy are just as perverse as are onanism, bestiality, and pederasty. Finally, despite glancing biblical and classical citations, Bale's attention turns again and again to the contemporary Roman church and its clergy as exemplars of those who most enthusiastically engage the sweep of sodomitical desires.

Bale's sodomitical discourse fosters a divinely ordained naturalized concept of marriage which displaces the ancient Pauline view that hierarchically set sexual renunciation as a perfection above marriage. Neither a cultural institution nor a sacrament, marriage for Bale is the natural end of human desire, and married coitus provides the only vessel for sanctioned procreative seed. King Henry's argument for annulment (and consequent bastardizing of the Princess Mary) as a cleansing of his own error in taking Catherine as an adulterous and incestuous wife is not specifically addressed in the marriage references in *Thre Lawes*, but the very generality and theological vagueness of Bale's categorical sweep assuredly leave room for Cromwell's arguments on the king's behalf. (By contrast, a carefully argued disputation in the theological tradition of Aquinas would make conspicuous the king's sinfulness, not unlike the "papysts" Bale excoriates.) Bale's rhetorical moves, therefore, may also be understood in terms of both the politics of denunciation which they support and the politics of royal protection which they conceal. What is stressed is not the institutional practice of marriage (how it is ordained and governed) but its

absolute naturalness. The Henrician case for divorce and Bale's psychology of providentially natural desire are discourses which complement and
nurture one another. But where marriage's naturalness is implicit and not
to be specifically argued, sodomitical desires are invested with two levels
of specificity, one theological and one historical. Theologically, they include all the perversions which subvert marriage, even though their common denominator is repressed: adultery, bestiality, masturbation, drunkenness, or nudity (whichever fits the Noe lines), interbreeding of species,
celibacy, abstinence, and pederasty. Historically, the sodomitical desires
are most manifest in the clergy of Rome. Thus Bale's discourse of sodomy
serves to enshrine a narrow notion of natural desire while at the same time
announcing its complicity in its historical moment by providing arguments which support the Cromwellian program on behalf of Henry's
marriage to Anne Boleyn, and his project to dissolve the monasteries and
drive the Roman clergy out of England. In the same breath, as it were, Bale
makes claims to a universal and transhistorical "nature" while simultaneously engaging in the most historically specific, local, and partisan
invective.

The universal and transhistorical "nature" that Bale assumes does not
exist in a symmetrical relation to the sodomy which he opposes, if only
because the latter is invested with considerable seductions, while the natural state of marriage is surprisingly fragile. Stephen Orgel, discussing
Renaissance notions and structures of gender difference, remarks, "It is
the fragility, the radical instability of our essence, that is assumed here [a
reference to antitheatrical tracts], and the metamorphic quality of our
sinful nature"[9] His comments might be applied to the marriage / sodomy
opposition as Bale displays it, for Bale's text reflects the same fragility,
radical instability, and metamorphic quality in human essence of a natural
desire to marry. Renaissance discourses of nature, grounded as they are in
a knowledge of resemblance, as Foucault has formulated it, are more
conspicuously metamorphic than discourses of nature from later historical situations. "This reversibility and this polyvalency endow analogy
with a universal field of application."[10] I do not mean to suggest that
those later discourses are any less signifying practices formed around
historically specific ways of structuring what is knowable and how that
knowability is structured at the level of the sign itself. The historical
differences are not that Renaissance "nature" is a discourse ill grounded in
empiricism, as commentators who believe in progressive knowledge might

wish to describe it in contrast, they believe, to later "natures" better reflective of "real nature" (whatever that might be); no, instead, the historical difference is the conspicuousness of the metamorphic effect—the instability of opposed categories—the semiotics of analogy. This effect must be fully engaged if we are to successfully read Renaissance texts which discuss sexuality, marriage, gender difference, and desire.

Except for its rewritten final speech, *Thre Lawes* stands as a central document of the Cromwell/Bales propaganda project under King Henry.[11] I argue that in part (particularly in act two) the play shares a discursive moment with the Sodomy Act of 1533, and that the Sodomy Act is part of a larger legislative project which included the king's annulment, the new law of succession which made Princess Mary a bastard, the dissolution of papal authority and institutions in England, and the decree that English clergy should take wives.

Thus, while I have offered a reading which foregrounds Bale's structured rationalism, I have done so in the intertextual context of the play's historical situation. Reading the play within the structure of its own scheme, indeed, gives insight into Bale's claims for rational design to God's order, and to the naturalness of a specific structure of desire which if obediently followed leads pious man to procreative marriage, however unstable and fragile the natural desire for that condition might be. Reading the play against its own logic reveals discrepant textual behaviors. I have already suggested the ambiguity of that authorial stance which, while claiming to be no more than a compiler, also claims to know the unknowable. I turn now to further instances of categorical slipperiness.

Given the degree of categorical rigor and design invested in every level of this text (the trinitarian parallels, the opposed matching of parallel vices and laws which simultaneously read diachronically as providential history and synchronically as an exposé of papal antichristism, and the five-act structure of the comedy itself), the slippages of category in this text are remarkable. Take, for instance, the moment in Actus Secundus when Infidelitas summons, in a parody of the trinity, his cohorts, Sodomismus and Idolatria Necromantic.

> By Tetragrammaton,
> I charge ye, apere anon
>   And come out of the darke.
> (392–94)

The unutterable Hebrew sacred name for God was utilized by Reformation iconographers as part of an iconoclastic program, in which Bale was deeply invested. Bale and his audience, therefore, would hear the oath to Tetragrammaton as a reverent iconoclastic speech-act.[12] The oath to Tetragrammaton is Infidelitas's summons of Sodomismus and Idolatria Necromantic in the name of God, without idolatrously naming that name. The oath would seem, therefore, to be devout and necessary, not ribald, irreverent, nor blasphemous. Because of the ritual of this oath as a potent act of "summoning" (a word that resonates with significance from earlier morality plays such as *Everyman*), I find no burlesque here; instead, Infidelitas's power to summon his cohorts is apparently a divinely ordained, or at least divinely sanctioned, power.

The irony is not that Infidelitas uses a sacred sign to empower his wicked summoning, but rather that his only power to make such a summoning is sanctioned by God. Bale's play does not analyze nor argue the problem of evil, but this moment would suggest that his view does not tolerate the Manichaean dialectic, positing evil, instead, as an aspect of the providential order as manifested in a fallen world. In turn, this means that sodomy, in all its categorical sweep, as that desire which is the exact opposite to the natural desire which is fulfilled in sanctioned marriage, is at the same time a providentially ordained, or at least providentially permitted, desire.

This slippage of categories perhaps in part explains the early Tudor discrepancies regarding where to locate sodomy, inside or outside of natural law, and sheds further light on why the 1533 statute repressed ancient Justinian references to "crimes against nature." Bale confidently (right from the play's title, *A Comedy Concernynge thre lawes, of Nature, Moses, & Christ, corrupted by the Sodomytes, Pharysees and Papystes*) draws a categorical opposition between nature and sodomy. At the same time, as his text unfolds, this opposition is not as rigorously sustained as the play's careful design leads one to expect, and a slippage like the oath by Tetragrammaton offers a counterreading of providence and nature. As a consequence, early Tudor sodomy discourse seems to want sodomitical desire to be simultaneously inside and outside nature, both inside and outside providential design—nature's opposite while still permitted by and necessary to God's plan.

The categorical slippage at the boundaries of nature is reflected more specifically in the denotative slippage which surrounds sodomy and the desire which fosters it. I have already listed the sweep of behaviors which Bale catches with the casting of this term's wide net. None of the historically later specificities of denotation for sodomy are fixed exclusively, or even predominantly, by Bale's usage. Such later denotations include two discrepant modern usages; in popular parlance, it commonly means anal intercourse (both homosexual and heterosexual), but in law, as interpreted by state and federal courts, it means as well any homosexual acts, including sex between women. By contrast, in the seventeenth century, based on the House of Lords' deliberations in the Castlehaven case, sodomy meant forced sex with status unequal partners such as a man with girls, boys, male or female servants, or unprotected women.[13] In place of either our or the seventeenth century's denotative specificity, categorical sweep is what characterizes Bale's use of the term. One might infer a similar indefiniteness of specificity for the parliamentarians who enacted the 1533 statute. The reason for Bale's usage has to do with the structure of his categories and the rationale that is displayed through those categories. Sodomy is not fixed to homosexuality, or to specific sexual acts, because the categorical opposition between homosexuality and heterosexuality did not exist at this time; it was not even thinkable. Likewise the later opposition between love and lust within sexual relations does not function for Bale— not even in marriage. Nor does he oppose marriage to adultery, concubinage, or other forms of potentially illicit procreative heterosexual union. The Victorian marriage / prostitution opposition would make no more sense to Bale than the modern gay / straight opposition. His categorical opposition is simply between procreative sexuality sanctioned by marriage on the one hand, and all nonsanctioned nonprocreative sexualities on the other. Sodomy means nonmarital nonprocreative desires and the behaviors which express those desires.

Nowhere, however, does Bale make this opposition explicit. And because there are no consistent distinctions between desire and behavior, a space for accusation is created, through which a righteous judge might designate almost anything sodomitical because even a desire within marriage cannot be proved exclusively to be the divinely implanted desire for procreation. This accusatory space can then be filled with politically charged attacks upon papists—or whatever other group one's politics opposes. In Actus Quartus, Evangelium replies to Infidelitas's charge that reformed priests have turned to sinful "wyvynge," because of the new policy of clerical marriages in England.

Infidelitas
   Marry, so they saye,   ye fellawes of the newe lernynge
   Forsake holy church,   and now fall fast to wyfynge.
Evangelium
   Naye, they forsake whoredome   with other dampnable usage,
   And lyve with their wyves   in lawfull marryage
   Whyls the Popes oyled swarme   raigne styll in their olde buggerage.
(1383–86)

One, I guess, should kindly overlook the inference that the reformed English priests, including Bale himself and his closet confederates, needed to forsake "whoredome" when they took wives under the "newe lernynge," and therefore gave up their own "olde buggerage."

   This is a particularly revealing passage, for it shows clearly that sodomy is attached to the act, not the person, and that its attractions are sufficiently potent that only the "newe lernynge" might be sufficiently powerful to dissuade one from both "whoredome" and the "olde buggerage." The natural law which is implanted in men to guide their desires seems surprisingly ineffective. At this early date, Bale already creates necessity both for the Puritan role of moral surveillance and the Puritan role for incessant teaching.

   My point is that looseness surrounding the denotative boundaries of Bale's usage of the concepts "nature," "sodomy" and "desire" creates a discursive space in which accusation and judgment can serve local political ends, at a level quite distinct from the universal providential rationalism of his wide design. Like the gaps within the authorial roles, these slippages lie in the cracks inside Bale's rigorous rationalist allegorical machine.

   Bale's text subverts its own best interest. The discrepancy in declared authorial stances brings into question both the authority of a "compyled," incremental tradition, and the declared unknowability of God's mysteries. The loose categories interrogate the nature of nature and its alignment within providential design. The text's own best interest which suffers most is therefore its claim to be revelation of a rational, providentially ordained design. As one teases out the slippages within Bale's text, his exquisite five-act design seems to be rhetorical imposition, not revelation. His textual behaviors belie his own anxiety with regard to that rationality, its manifest transparency, and the final success of its rhetorical practices, for throughout the play he lays on heavy swathes of traditional satire; the argumentative and structural clarity that his design claims for itself, therefore, cannot succeed without the counterweight of invective.

One cannot help but suspect that among original auditors the reasoned theological disputation won only those who were already reformed in their thinking—men of the "newe lernynge"—such as the Cromwellian party who may have attended the interlude-style performances in the hall of Bale's patron. But, at public performances at Hampshire, Kilkenny Cross, and elsewhere, where the play functioned as an iconoclastic displacement for annual performances of traditional morality plays such as *Mankind*, one suspects that the anti-papal invective, scurrilous language, and allegorical knock-about may have won applause from those in the audience who were not trained in the "newe lernynge" despite the intent that the play would teach them this theology. The displacement of reason by invective within the play's rhetorical practice may reflect irreconcilable audiences. A militant political agenda seems to be the play's major reason for being; propaganda wins over disputation; invective wins over reason. In drawing up a summary of Bale's sodomy discourse (for it is in the second act that some of the wildest invective is unleashed), we must not ignore the propagandistic obsession which accompanies and displaces a psychomachia of natural desire and its opposite, the nonprocreative sodomies.

With that said, I can now turn to just such a summary. The early Tudor sodomy discourse as displayed in Bale's *Thre Lawes* engages several aspects. It seeks to affirm a universal natural law to govern human sexual desires and behaviors. It maintains a categorical sweep, even looseness, regarding all that sodomy includes. In order to render sodomitical desire sufficiently potent of attraction to man, it leaves unsettled the epistemological boundaries of that which is divinely ordained as a part of or opposed to nature. Because of ambiguities in its working through of its own discursive practice, it creates interior spaces through which politically expedient accusations, denunciation, and invective can flourish, in a manner that implies that the judgment being made is by providence and nature, not the author and his political situation—a neat trick if one can bring it off! Finally, the rationalist impulse of this discourse self-subverts and at moments of persuasive climax gets displaced by invective at a loud, near hysterical level—"the Bilious Bale" of literary histories.

From Michel Foucault and his followers we have learned to attend to discursive practices within specifically located historical constructions.

The sodomy discourse of the early Tudor reformation is not the same as later periods in which sodomy discourses also flourished. At the same time, the particular practices I have just enumerated give to this early sodomy discourse a malleability which allows its appropriation into new epistemic constructions. In fact, its malleability is perhaps its most durable feature. To bring this feature under scrutiny adds to the analysis of other discourses, for by recognizing not only structural and denotative features, but the behaviors of a discourse within political and rhetorical situations, we extend our sensitivity of inquiry into discursive praxes. In the case of sodomy discourse, the less structural and denotative features of its early Tudor praxis are the very features which have made it so easy for later discursive moments to import the language of sodomy, particularly their ability to hide the denunciatory voice behind claims of nature, their potential for propagandistic demagoguery, and their almost inevitable tendency to self-subvert and move from rational systems to hysterical invective.

The history of sodomy discourses is an account of changing definitions of desires and behaviors, typically characterized by acute ambiguity and a taboo upon the speaking of specifics; it is also the record of newly invented political moments in which the denunciation of sodomy and sodomites serves the ends of "power"—ends which reach well beyond issues of morality and sexuality. It is a history of what Ed Cohen aptly calls "legislating the norm."

One such importation to a new ideological configuration is the late Tudor and early Stuart discourse of atheism. This discourse shows up among other places in the record of the heresy charges in the Star Chamber action against Marlowe, in the writings of King James, and in the lines from *The Atheist's Tragedy* which opened this essay. As noted earlier, Tourneur's sodomy speech falls within a climactic scene which sweeps across mention of a number of perversions outside procreative marriage: men lying with men, necrophilia, prostitution, and adultery. Indeed, Languebeau Snuffe is prototype of the Puritan hypocrite—the parodic paradigm of natural/normative piety. Tourneur's language wheels wildly from the macabre, to invective, to hysteria. The scene is redolent with the imagery of sterility, impotence, decadence, moral depravity, and death. But, here the object of Tourneur's tragic denunciation is not a papal antichrist, not a foreign religious imposition, but his own society's internal corruption— the atheism of early Stuart acquisitiveness, hypocrisy, and indulgence.

Tourneur's discursive moment and the politics it shares are aligned to the stage satire of Jonson and Middleton, but exactly how his language of atheism and sodomy takes part in Jacobean stage satire, on the one hand, and the denunciation of what that age called "athiesme," on the other, is another story—another episteme—another essay. Neither the theological argument nor the political purpose of Bale's sodomy discourse would be carried over to later contexts; but its discursive behaviors would continue to thrive: namely, a categorical sweep which opposes nature to its non-procreative opposite combined simultaneously with loose categories, authorial ambiguities which create spaces for denunciations that mask as the judgments of nature or providence, and epistemological slippages which create a space wherein invective displaces and even subverts ostensible claims to reason.

This was a discourse (and a discursive practice) which was constructed in the service of the newly empowered theocratic party which came to the fore during the last decade and a half of Henry's reign. Early Tudor sodomy language was both a part of the radical reformation's theological redefinition of marriage and its anti-papal politics. It served both the king's legislative ends in the affair of Anne Boleyn and the act of succession, and Cromwell's establishment of the English church.

Notes

1. *The Plays of Cyril Tourneur*, ed. George Parfitt (London: Cambridge University Press, 1978). Scrutiny of this climactic scene in Tourneur's play impresses one with the almost reflexive manner in which the playwright gathers these *topoi*.

2. H. Montgomery Hyde, *The Love That Dared Not Speak Its Name* (Boston: Little, Brown, 1970), 40.

3. Montgomery Hyde, a legal historian whose books included *The Love That Dared Not Speak Its Name* (1970), focused on public sodomy scandals and trials since 1533, in particular persons of public prominence such as Lord Castlehaven and Oscar Wilde. Alan Bray, by contrast (*Homosexuality in Renaissance England* [London: Gay Men's Press, 1982]) analyzes the impact of enforcement on the lives of obscure commoners. Ed Cohen's valuable historical survey, "Legislating the Norm: From Sodomy to Gross Indecency," *South Atlantic Quarterly* 88, no. 1 (1989): 181–217, reads legal discourses in the context of redefinitions of the individual body (and the sexual body). Cohen does not look at nonlegal texts; however, his brief but cogent remarks about the Tudor period (187–89) in no way contradict readings offered in this paper.

4. John N. King, *English Reformation Literature: The Tudor Origins of the Protestant Tradition* (Princeton: Princeton University Press, 1986), 69.

5. Bale's denunciations are in a style of invective which has received considerable critical attention. As early as the seventeenth century, commentators Thomas Fuller and Anthony à Wood identified a "bilious" style with Bale's own personality and Fuller's witticism. "Biliosus Balaeus" has had a long life in literary histories; but, Bale's "bilious" invective might as easily be fixed to an ideological function that his production of plays within a theocratic patronage system necessitated.

6. First citations credited to Bale are:

    1. "Sodometrous" as a synonym for "sodomitical." *The Acts of the Englysh Votarys*, II,A,ii (1550) "The Sodometrous vow of theyr simulate chastity."
    2. "Sodomitical" to mean "of the nature of, characterized by, consisting in, or involving sodomy." *The Acts of the Englysh Votarys*, II,21,b (1550) "Their sodomytycal chastyte agaynst Gods fre instytucyon."
    3. "Sodomitical" to mean "of places, institutions, etc.: Polluted or infected by sodomy." *The Apology of J. B. agaynste a Ranke Papyst*, 19 (1550) "Than were they allowed for a spyrytuall religion in that Sodomiticall churche of Antichrist."
    4. "Sodometry" as synonym for "sodomy." *Thre Laws*, Pref. 23 (1538) "Corrupteth with ydolles and stynkynge Sodometry."

7. Judith C. Brown provides a clear and insightful discussion of the theology of "the proper vessel" and its development through church history. Aquinas distinguished between lusts against nature and lusts of fornication. The former were those acts of coitus "outside of the natural place where children are made," whereas acts of fornication were those outside sanctified marriage (Judith C. Brown, *Immodest Acts: The Life of a Lesbian Nun in Renaissance Italy* [Oxford: Oxford University Press, 1986], 16–17). This distinction was difficult to maintain, and the degree of venial sinfulness accorded to different categories of lust varied from era to era and jurisdiction to jurisdiction, as reflected in penitentials.

8. In the last decade, much exciting work has been done on the constructions (medical, theological, epistemological, historical) of gender in the Renaissance. What has emerged from this inquiry is a double set of relationships between male and female gender as conceptualized in the Renaissance: first, as a powerfully organized set of homologies with the female understood to be a version of the male, not its bipolar opposite; second, as a powerfully structured hierarchy which sees masculinity as a fragile attainment, which at any point might fall back into femininity.

9. Stephen Orgel, "Nobody's Perfect: Or Why Did the English Stage Take Boys for Women?" *South Atlantic Quarterly* 88, no. 1 (1989): 16.

10. Michel Foucault, *The Order of Things: An Archaeology of the Human Sciences* (New York: Pantheon Books, 1971), 22.

11. By the time the play was printed, Bale had been in exile in Antwerp and sought to return under the Seymour patronage, Cromwell had long since fallen from power and been executed, and Henry had had six wives, not just two. The printed text rewrites the final speech to ask blessing for Edward, dowager Queen Katherine Parr (herself a center of a militant Protestant coterie) and the Lord Protector Seymour, the leader of the Protestant faction. Revision, with an eye to Seymour's or Edward's protection, seems to have occurred only in the final speech of the play.

12. John King (*English Reformation Literature*) has shown, with a number of plates taken from title pages of Edwardian books, that where papal iconography would have placed a bearded image of God often set in clouds, sun rays, or a pillar of fire, the Reformation iconographer would place the four Hebrew letters in the same visual space. The practice was instituted as part of Reformation iconoclasm, under Somerset's patronage.

13. Hyde, *The Love That Dared Not Speak Its Name*, 44–57.

"To Serve the Queere":
Nicholas Udall, Master of Revels

ELIZABETH PITTENGER

Thence for my voice, I must (no choice)
Away of forse, like posting horse,
For sundrie men, had plagards then,
    such childe to take:
The better brest, the lesser rest,
To serve the Queere, now there now heere,
For time so spent, I may repent,
    and sorrow make.
         .   .   .

From Paules I went, to Eaton sent,
To learne streight waies, the latin phraies,
Where fiftie three, stripes given to mee,
    at once I had:
For fault but small, or none at all,
It came to pas, thus beat I was,
See Udall see, the mercie of thee,
    to me poore lad.[1]

"T HE Authors life of his owne penning," written by Thomas Tusser for the introduction to his *Fiue hundred pointes of good Husbandrie* (1573), is a generic example of autobiographical writing that recalls the experiences of a schoolboy.[2] The conventional topics—being selected for the choir ("Queere"), going on from Petty school to higher forms (St. Paul's and Eton), the lessons in grammar ("the latin phraies") and discipline ("fiftie three stripes")—convey the boy's fraught relation to school and to his master, and go well beyond merely playing on the *topos* of "the best schoolmaster and the greatest beater." Moreover, *Fiue hundred pointes* was reprinted in nearly twenty editions up to 1638; it thereby enhanced and perpetuated the reputation of Tusser's teacher, Nicholas Udall, as a fierce flogger.[3] Udall (1504–56) was headmaster of Eton from 1534 until his dismissal in 1541. The obviously lasting impression he made on Tusser (and, presumably, on other pupils as well), is not my main concern in this essay.[4] Rather, I juxtapose the two stanzas from Tusser's poem in order to raise questions about the relation of the eruptive violence of the pedagogic scene to the quiet eroticism of the choice of boys "to serve the Queere." Illegitimate, anachronistic, irresponsible as it might be, if we hear a pun on "queer," it draws attention to the ways in which the lines acknowledge and displace the attractiveness of boys, encouraging us to treat with suspicion the assertion that men's interest in boys is due to their capacity to sing, "the better brest, the lesser rest." After all, it's hard to imagine what would happen in choir practice to provoke so much remorse: "For time so spent, I may repent, / and sorrow make." Or why being pressed into "Queere" service—"Thence for my voice, I must (no choice)"—registers simultaneously pride and shame, the need to be apologetic though victimized. In the pages that follow, I will be pursuing this nexus of guilt, repentance, and punishment in much of the material connected to Nicholas Udall. Through him, I will be exploring the relationship that Tusser's poem also displays: the relationship between what may and may not be said and the registers for occluding and acknowledging male-male desire.

Master of Revels

To begin, I turn to a curriculum vitae of sorts compiled by John S. Farmer, in his edition of Udall's comedy *Ralph Roister Doister* (1552): "Nicholas Udall . . . was a man of many parts in his time—public scholar, University man, heretic, recanter, Latin versifier, dictionary maker, potential monk, schoolmaster, suspect, Marshalsea man, theological translator and author, prebend, playwright, and Director of the Revels."[5] Amid the predictable and largely commendable activities of a Tudor humanist, two roles stand out: "suspect" and "Marshalsea man," oblique references to some crime or infraction beyond those that are named, "heretic" and "recanter."[6] Though Udall spent much time in litigation over debt and other financial problems, the crime Farmer does not name is the incident that brought Udall to the attention of the Privy Council. On March 14, 1541, one day after Thomas Cheyney confessed to robbing articles of silver, the record reads:

> Nic. Vuedale, Scoolmaster of Eton, beying sent for as suspect to be of councail of a robbery lately commited at Eton by Thomas Cheyney, John Hoorde, Scolers of the sayd scole, and . . . Gregory, seruant to the said scolemaster, and hauing certain interrogatoryes minis-tred vnto hym, toching the sayd fact and other felonious trespasses, wherof he was suspected, did confesse that he did commit buggery with the said cheney, sundry times heretofore, and of late the vjth day of this present moneth in the present yere at London, whervpon he was commited to the marshalsey.[7]

The record seems to leave little doubt: Udall confessed to committing buggery with his pupil, Thomas Cheyney, several times in the past and as recently as a week before the "interrogatoryes." Immediately following, Udall was dismissed as headmaster of Eton and committed to the Mar-shalsea prison. While this would seem to indicate his guilt, the resolution of the case is not that clear. Udall's punishment is a rather mild one considering that 25 Henry VIII c. 6 made the crime of buggery a felony punishable by death.[8] Indeed, as many scholars remark, the case hardly marked Udall's downfall, and in the decade following he enjoyed a distin-guished career, prominent publications, financial rewards, and even favor at court.

The perplexing nature of the case, even as it is represented in the records of the Privy Council, asks us to start again and raise the most basic kinds of questions: what crime, if any, was committed? What rela-tions obtain between the charges of burglary, debauchery, and buggery in the Privy Council record? How might these relate to the facts of the case, but also to the various representations of them that can be found in Udall's writing? Or indeed, in the explanations offered by modern scholars?

In his monograph on Udall, William Edgerton treats the case as a paradox.[9] He argues that there would be no doubt about the charges if Udall had disappeared from the map. But Udall went on to thrive, an oddity, according to Edgerton, given the "unsavory character" of the crime (38). Edgerton draws the "obvious conclusion" that Udall had powerful friends at court and on the Privy Council, who "kept his offenses and trial secret." Thomas Wriothesley, perhaps his patron, sat on the Privy Council and heard Udall's case. The situation was even more tangled because the Eton boy, Thomas Cheyney, was a relative by marriage to Wriothesley; thus there were other motivations for keeping the matter hushed. Plausible as this is, however, it will not explain why others in power would have had an interest in Udall. Nor will it account for the fact that even before the trial Udall's writing harps on being falsely accused and damaged by rumor.[10]

Udall's associations with well-connected men might explain why his career was left undamaged, but Edgerton argues that the "theory . . . leaves unexplained not only the Council's leaning over backward later to befriend Udall, but also why, if it was so anxious to keep the matter secret, it allowed his case to become a matter of record in the first place. Historians are only too aware that the Privy Council included in the register only matters it felt like recording" (38–39). Though it is not clear to me what Edgerton wants to claim about Udall's innocence or guilt, his language conveys an insinuating gesture: with the image of the Privy Council bending over backwards to help a sodomite out and then not too anxious about keeping the matter secret, Edgerton places both Udall and his Privy friends in compromising positions. Yet he continues oddly, coyly, to hedge "if the offense had really been buggery."

Edgerton throws up his hands and opts for an answer that would make a room of editors proud: "There is one solution, although it means cutting the Gordian knot, and that is to suppose that an error was made in recording Udall's confession in the register" (39). He cites an article by E. R. Adair, who argues that the record is full of mistakes.[11] The Clerk of the Council, William Paget, took rough notes and later transcribed them. His handwriting starts to deteriorate midway through the case. Thus "buggery" was accidentally confused with "burglary," which, Edgerton reiterates, are near enough orthographically to be mistaken (40). What does it mean that textual error can be used to explain (away) the problems raised by this case, that guilt is transferred from records that are supposed to be accurate to the "corruption" of a recorder, whose handwriting "deteriorates"?[12] And even if we entertain the textual emendation as a possibility, the correction still leaves questions unanswered; for how then do we understand the confession of repeated theft: "he did commit [burglary] with the said cheney, sundry times heretofore, and of late the vjth day of this present moneth in the present yere at London"?

One answer might be to note the way in which the questions surrounding Udall may belong to a more generalizable set of reactions stirred by legal cases that create the desire to know what really happened precisely because that knowledge is obscured or inaccessible. To operate within the problematic of these questions requires a constant negotiation of both historical and interpretive assumptions, a negotiation complicated in this case by sexual politics since the desire for evidence, both legal and historical, is exacerbated by the nature of the charges: the case insinuates but never openly pronounces that Udall was a pedagogue turned pederast. It suggests that any way of handling these oblique cases will have to be attentive to not only the circuitousness of the material but also the multiple ways that the material can and has been interpreted. Here, I would turn to the work of two readers of Renaissance "homosexuality," Alan Bray and Jonathan Goldberg.[13] Though they spend little if any time on Udall, I think they contribute the most to our historical and, in different ways, theoretical understanding of the elusive category of sodomy.

Alan Bray's account of the incident occurs during his sketch of the social structures that framed sodomy—households, pedagogy, prostitution, and theater.[14] He presents "evidence that homosexuality was institutionalised" in the educational system and that the "limited effect which complaints about this had" reveals how "deep-rooted the institution was."[15] This explanation accounts for why Udall seems to have escaped unscathed and goes much farther in "cutting the Gordian knot" than Edgerton's textual fudging. To paraphrase Bray, as long as hierarchic and patriarchal institutions surrounded sodomy, and as long as it didn't disturb the peace, there was little impetus to pursue it as a crime (76–77). Strangely enough, there may be something to that laughable emendation: there is no buggery until there's burglary in the sense that sodomy is rarely prosecuted on its own but follows in the wake of other crimes, to which it's added or which it symbolizes.[16]

Bray's analysis of Udall is brief, less than a paragraph, yet he draws a powerful conclusion from the case: "it is indicative of the degree to which homosexuality was effectively tolerated in the educational system" (52). But the word "tolerance" is tricky since what he means is a reluctance to recognize, what he calls "sluggishness" later (75–76). Bray's move to at-

tribute "tolerance" signals the framework of his own historically determined position in a post-Stonewall generation. Slippages resembling this
one are simultaneously productive and damaging for the case Bray makes.
For instance, notice that the particular way he words his account of Udall
actually moves it away from the institutionalized context of pedagogy: "In
1541 Nicholas Udall, who was headmaster of Eton at the time, was involved in a *scandal* because of the homosexual *relationship* he *had* had with
one of his *former* pupils. The events are somewhat *mysterious*, but the *affair*
seems to have come to light during an investigation by the Privy Council
into the theft of some school plate in which the boy had been involved"
(52; emphasis added). He distances Udall's contact with the boy, a "former" pupil whom the master "had had" an interest in. Bray's account
clashes with the Privy Council records, which make it clear that the boy
was currently a pupil and the "relationship" ongoing. More important,
since the Privy Council may not be the final word on the case, Bray's
description clashes with his own account of "homosexuality." He wants to
hold that pederastic relations occurred in school yet he simultaneously
fades out the image of a headmaster buggering a pupil by portraying a
more familiar scenario: the "somewhat mysterious" "events" of the "affair" involve the "scandal" of a "homosexual relationship." I hope I'm not
alone in thinking that this sounds much more like the case of Oscar
Wilde than it does that of an early sixteenth-century humanist.

The extent to which Bray operates out of a particular modern configuration is felt in the little ways he skews evidence, which are unavoidable
and not necessarily problematic, except as they point to something more
significant: Renaissance "homosexuality" is constructed on a model particular to the twentieth century. Two interconnected paradigms are deployed: Bray's historical method alternates between cruising and outing,
both involving larger assumptions. He brings them together in his advice
to others who might embark on the same itinerary: "In such circumstances historians should be *watchful for signs*, however difficult to detect,
that for someone involved in a homosexual relationship *the nature of that
relationship might not have been as obvious to him as it is to them*" (68). But the closet
this presupposes is curious: at some level he has to put them there first,
though he might argue that you don't always need an ID to get in.[17] The individuals who have been cruised and/or outed by Bray are "practically unconscious" that they are "involved in a homosexual relationship."[18] Even
though Bray's essay on friendship in this volume attempts to claim the

"open path" between the sodomite and male friend, he emphatically remains in the closeted world, frequently using the language of shadow and
darkness to indicate male intimacy: "the shadows on the edge of social life"
(40), "that hidden road" (47), "a darker interpretation" (51), and so on.

My point is not to Bray bash but to show, as others have, that the closet
model is collapsible. More important, that to place "homosexuality as the
dark secret at the heart of the symbolic world" (23) is also to place "sexuality" there, a problematic move given recent historical critiques of univer-
salism and feminist critiques of essentialism and identity. The glitches in
Bray's work raise two historical and theoretical issues, both centered on
the concept of misrecognition: on the one hand there's the claim that one
can see clearly through the misrecognitions of the early modern subject to
a real sexual identity, a displacement that is itself a misrecognition. On the
other hand, there's the claim that one can see clearly through the misrecognitions of the evidence to a real sexual practice.

The problem of identity, whether identity politics or essentialism, is
too large to go into for the simple point I want to make: indeed, that it is a
problem in Bray's work has already been pointed out by Goldberg in his
"Familiar Letters." To review briefly, Goldberg argues that Bray's account
of Renaissance "homosexuality" presupposes a "modern 'deployment of
sexuality' (in Foucault's term)" that "the deepest secret of the self is its
sexuality" (113). Goldberg radicalizes Bray's and other historicist readings
by arguing that "there were no homosexuals in Renaissance England"
(113). Rather, addressing homosexual acts, he argues: "Such acts do not
prove their actors homosexual; likewise, texts like . . . [Spenser's] *Januarye*
eclogue (or Barnfield's classical pastorals) will never tell us whether their
authors slept with boys. But they may, in the very exorbitancy that I have
been reading, tell us about the 'place' of homosexuality in Renaissance
England; not least if, as Bray contends, it had no place, was not a site
of recognition of sexual identity" (114). In fact, as Goldberg goes on to
point out about Bray's argument, recognition is systematically blocked by
the widespread circulation of stigmatized stereotypes that fostered an
effective dissociation ("disconnection," "cleavage," "disparity" 67–68) of
the "monstrous" image of a sodomite from the "everyday" practices that
involved sexual acts with other men or boys. But this and Goldberg's
emphasis on texts, on representation, leads us to the second problem of
misrecognition. In other words, the stereotypes work to enable the very

practices they mock or condemn because they provide the mechanism for systematic misrecognition, "a mechanism that required a certain amount of self-delusion" (66). However, because Bray valorizes "evidence" as traces of what really happened, what they really did, he slights most forms of representation, textual and cultural, as factually worthless, as exaggerations, "downright distortions," and "intensely frustrating."[19] Perhaps the conflict becomes clearer if we consider the double standard Bray applies to literary texts. For example, he cites John Marston frequently as one of the many satirists who built and perpetuated the distorted image of "the sodomite." Yet he reads other passages characterizing pederastic pedants at face value, as reflections and evidence of the real practices between masters and pupils.[20] The concept of misrecognition that he deploys (without using the term) does not presuppose a stable distinction between actual reality and mere representation, world and text; rather it presupposes that representation enables the world to go on as it does precisely because of the failure to translate text to world. And here I am using the language of Goldberg, who makes this argument elegantly:

> It has become commonplace in certain critical practices that are called "new historicist" to argue that "love is not love" or that pastoral otium is really negotium. This essay shares with such work the desire to read texts into the world. But in describing the trick mirror that the *Shepheardes Calender* holds up to the world . . . it seems to me important not to allegorize and thematize the text so entirely that its sole function is to read the world at the expense of the text, to decide beforehand that the world is real and that the only reality that a text might have would be its ability to translate the world in terms that need to be translated back into the social, historical, or political. (118)

Rather than engaging in a pursuit of sodomy, the untranslatable hidden behind the evidence, Goldberg pursues the "teasing play between revelation and reveiling" that "has the structure of the open secret" (115).[21] In refusing to privilege negotium over otium, in refusing the distinction, he entertains what he implies is an erotics of the letter. And this is to lead us out of the closet that encloses Bray and frustrates the political and sexual investments of his project. Goldberg's notion of the complicities of an open secret better accounts for the case of Udall even though it may put into play problems similar to those of Bray's model. But before I pursue that point, I would turn from the supposed hard evidence of the Privy Council to the world of letters.

Indictments: Doubtful Letters

Because interpretations of the case raise doubts about the nature of the charges and about the conclusion that Udall actually committed buggery, scholars turn to another piece of evidence that seems to reflect Udall's own point of view, a letter he wrote shortly after his dismissal in which he represents himself in need of pardon from the "singular good master" he addresses.[22] More than a dozen paragraphs long, the letter is a highly crafted piece of writing, maneuvering through appropriate *topoi* and anecdotes, peppered with Latin and Greek citations from highly regarded authors, and anchored by various expedient tropological figures.[23] The overall aim seems clear: it is a *mea culpa* performance that moves from confession to ask for pardon by promising to amend. But the letter doesn't follow this straightforward trajectory and instead introduces, in its many digressions, paths leading away from its purported destination.

For instance, though the presumption of the address is a profession of guilt, the letter never delivers a confession. Udall hedges: "I trust ye shall finde that this your correpcion shallbee a sufficient scourge to make me, during my lif, more wise and more ware utterly for ever to eschewe and avoid all kindes of all maner of excesses and abuses that *have been reported* to reigne in me" (3; emphasis added). Udall never actually confesses to anything in particular; furthermore, he takes it all back by insisting that the allegations are precisely that, rumor, report, talk and nothing more.

He combines his bracketed confessions with equally dubious promises to mend his ways: "if ever I shallbee *found* again to offend in any suche kind transgressions as at this tyme hath provoked and accended your indignacion against me, I shall not oonly *bee myn own judge* to bee accoumpted for ever moste unworthie the favor and good will either of your maistership or of any other honest frend, but also to bee *moste extremely punished* to theensample of all others" (3; emphasis added). The initial qualification not only secretes the matter of his initial guilt, but it also deviously dares to be caught again and then takes the high moral ground of remorse and promised self-punishment.

But the real trick to the letter is the way he implicates his master, indicts him in the complicities of the open secret. For example, he models the language of his master's disdain on that of penetration:

> Noo siknes, noo losse of worldly goodes, none ympresonyng, noo tormentes, no death, noo kind of other mysfortune could have *persed my herte*, or made in it soo *deepe a wound* as hath this your displeasure, whiche wound, if it might please your goodnes with the *salve* of your mercifull compassion to bryng for this oon tyme *ad cicatricem*, ye should not neede in all your life again to feare *ne quand mea culpa vitioque recrudesecret* [lest my fault and vice take root again]. (3; emphasis added)

In this economy of displeasure, one that provides undisguised rhetorical pleasure, for the master to withhold pardon is for him to become a partner in crime.[24] But yielding pardon, the response Udall wants and gets, means the master loses as well, not only because he gives in; in the circuitous language of the letter, for the crimes to be forgiven they cannot be forgotten. Indeed, to overlook them is to reinscribe them:

> All vices of which I have been noted or to your Maistership accused, being oons by the rootes extirped, and *in their places* the contrary vertues with counstaunt purpose of good contynuance in the same *depely planted*, I trust *ye wold become better maister unto me* aftir myn emendyng and reformacion then if I had never in suche wise transgressed. (4; emphasis added)

Udall sticks his master between a rock and a hard place. The language of piercing, wounds, and insemination registers sodomitical penetration that the master will further both by withholding his pardon and by delivering it. The complicities of the open secret force the master to entertain the vices of his servant in order to become a better master, the displeasure at the prodigal son acknowledged as an instrument for greater pleasure. The resonance of the scenario with more familiar practices of mastery comes from its heavy-handed moralized and scripted quality. The letter parades the prodigality of rhetorical moves available to the language of castigation:

> Accepte this myn honest chaunge from vice to vertue, from prodigalitee to frugall livyng, from negligence of teachyng to assiduitee, from playe to studie, from lightnes to gravitee . . . persuade yourself

> that the same repentaunce shall still remein within my brest as a
> *contynuall spurre* or *thorne to pricke* and *to quicken me* to goodnes from
> tyme to tyme *as often as neede shall require.* (7; emphasis added)

The letter is signed, "Your most bounden oratour and servaunte, Nicolas
Udall," and it comes, as he claims, "from the botom of my herte" (7).

If the bounds of the letter can be extended to include Udall's overall
position as a humanist, both teacher and writer, vis-à-vis influential members of Tudor society, the proper relation between master and servant
appears to be similar to an improper, sodomitical one. Whether patron,
pedagogue, or pater, the rules apply: straight service is marked by queerer
ways. The complicity, discussed by Bray in his "Signs of Male Friendship," points to "that network of subtle bonds amongst influential patrons and their clients, suitors, and friends at court . . . A concept so
necessary to social life was far removed from the 'uncivil' image of the
sodomite, yet there was still between them a surprising affinity, as in some
respects they occupied a similar terrain" (42). And later he asks impa-
tiently, "What distinguished this corruption from the normal workings
of friendship? What distinguished, in effect, the bribes of the one from
the flow of gifts and the ready use of influence of the other?" (56). Udall's
need to curry favor, throughout his career but especially at times of crisis,
kept him busy dangling a sense of secrecy about what was really at the bottom of his heart. The duplicity of his every move was felt so strongly that
he was also accused of being a "timeserver," that is, a flatterer, sycophant,
parasite, changing sails at every wind.[25] Of course it has to be pointed out
that if you consider the reigns of Henry VIII through Mary, Udall was
navigating in turbulent and treacherous waters.

It shouldn't be a surprise, then, that the letter of pardon brackets access
to evidence of sodomy and that if Udall plays at anything he plays at (not)
playing the sodomite.[26] The letter, with its rhetorical tricks, multilinguis-
tic play, and exemplary anecdotes, resists all the modes it seems to engage:
confession, sincerity, penance; it leaves little that can be traced as evidence. It doesn't deliver. However, if as Edgerton suggests, Udall's career
had ended here, we wouldn't have to search far to find ways to wrap up the
case. We might read the circumlocutions of the letter as testimony to
"things fearful to name" and to the unspoken recognition of the pedant
tutor's vice. However, just the opposite is the case: the very qualities of
Udall's writing that might deliver this evidence are the same ones ac-

knowledged as exemplary. More than ten years after Udall's dismissal, his former student Thomas Wilson (1523–81), in the third edition of his well-known handbook for logic, *Rule of Reason* (1553), singles out his master's writing as an example of writing letters that never seem to mean what they say. Wilson, that is, offers the letter for its exemplary dissimulation. Not the letter of remorse, to be sure, but another prevaricating text from Udall's hand, a literary love letter taken from Udall's comedy, *Ralph Roister Doister.* Two versions of a letter with nearly identical words yet nearly opposite meaning are reproduced as an "example of soche doubtful writing, whiche by reason of poincting maie haue double sense, and contrarie meaning, taken out of an entrelude made by Nicolas Vdal."[27] Wilson's textbook enjoyed a wide circulation; thus the mastery of "ambiguitie," imitated by later writers, most notably in the mechanicals' play of *A Midsummer Night's Dream*, was taught in the schools through the example of Udall's circumlocutions; his place as pedagogical master is restored by the techniques that he used to (not) play the pederast and by the devotion of Thomas Wilson, another Eton boy.[28] The master's desire is ultimately delivered by the pages of one of his boys.[29]

Thomas Wilson would testify on his behalf in another court case a few years after his master's dismissal.[30] Though much is known about Wilson's career and rise to power under Elizabeth, his relation to Udall puzzles scholars as much as the Privy Council record does. A. W. Reed concludes that "the association of the two men" that his study documents "argues an attitude on Wilson's part towards his old master that is not exactly reconciled with the charge alleged in the Acts of the Privy Council" (283). Reed may wish to insinuate that the disparity signals Udall's innocence; Bray would see in this "cleavage" yet another instance of "the sheer size of the mental adjustment they required" (67). But we might argue, along with Goldberg, that the "dehiscence" marks the complicities of an open secret, complicities between a pupil and his master all the more motivated in this instance since they are inscribed in the very same pedagogical space that brought Udall before the Council. When Udall was dismissed, Wilson chose to leave Eton with his master.[31]

The recognition that Udall was an exemplar for double and doubtful writing frustrates the project of "indicting" his letters in the sense of making public accusations and prosecuting formal charges. But "indict" has another sense, from Norman French, *enditer*, to dictate, a sense captured by an early Tudor spelling "endite." Letters are also "endited," dictated, composed, produced publicly. And it is in this sense that the letter of "ambiguitie" is produced in Udall's play.

The letter trick cited in Wilson's handbook involves two scenes of reading a love token penned by Ralph Roister Doister, a braggart soldier, and sent to Dame Christian Custance, a widow betrothed to Gawain Goodluck, whose absence leaves her open to advances. In what might be called a dalliance of the letter, she refuses to read it herself, which allows it to be deferred and eventually mishandled. The letter is delivered, in its entirety, not once but twice, in the course of the play (3.4.36–67 and 3.5.49–84).[32] The two versions read are meant to be exact opposites—the one a love letter intended to persuade Dame Custance to marry Roister Doister and the other an insulting, misogynist diatribe. The trick of the letter lies in its supposed punctuation. In the first reading, performed by the mischievous Matthew Merrygreek, Roister Doister's "parasite," it is "mispointed," mispunctuated so that its lines will be misunderstood by Custance as a scathing attack. Implicit in the double reading is the sense that the repetition of the letter yields different results, that the effects of the letter depend upon its reader and listener, including the possibility that the letter might be miscarried and mistaken.

When the letter backfires, Roister Doister takes his complaint to the source, the Scrivener, whom he thinks to be at fault. The discussion of the letter (3.5) by Roister Doister, Merrygreek, and the Scrivener reflects upon the process of writing and it articulates a theory (or possibly theories) of writing:

Roister Doister.	I say the letter thou madest me was not good.
Scrivener.	Then did ye wrong copy it, of likelihood.
Roister Doister.	Yes, out of thy copy word for word I it wrote.
Scrivener.	Then was it as ye prayed to have it, I wot,
	But in reading and pointing there was made some fault.

. . .

[The Scrivener recites the letter.]

Scrivener.	Now sir, what default can ye find in this letter?
Roister Doister.	Of truth, in my mind, there can not be a better.
Scrivener.	Then was the fault in reading and not in writing;
	No, nor, I daresay, in the form of enditing.
	But who read this letter, that it soundeth so nought?

(3.5.35–39, 84–88)

From the Scrivener's point of view, the letter has the kind of stability one might associate with a printed copy, an exact replica. The Scrivener, like Speed reading in *Two Gentlemen of Verona*, asserts that the letter's "in print," exact as it was in his copy book and could not be mistaken, unless it were corrupted in its delivery.[33] The Scrivener stands his ground on the letter's purity by staking everything on the exact reproduction of the original. He doesn't entertain the possibility that the very copy he wishes to secure might already be in question. We can see this if we ask where the letter originates and then factor in the many lines of transmission and the ambiguity these introduce. Roister Doister copies the letter so that it seems to be in his own hand. And this is confirmed by the exchange immediately following Merrygreek's misrepresentation:

Roister Doister.	Oh, I would I had him here, the which I did it endite!
Merrygreek.	Why, ye made it yourself, ye told me, by this light!
Roister Doister.	Yea, I meant I wrote it mine own self yesternight.
Dame Custance.	Iwis, sir, I would not have sent you such a mock!
Roister Doister.	Ye may so take it, but I meant it not so, by Cock!

(3.4.76–80)

It appears that however the letter was "endited," dictated, or composed, Roister Doister manually imitates a version in a copy book, as though he were in a marginal state of literacy with the manual dexterity to wield a pen but not the literacy to write out or make up his own speech. This insinuation is made by the Scrivener, who tells Roister Doister to look "on your own fist" (3.5.43).

But when the Scrivener says there was no fault in the "enditing," which scene of writing is meant? Roister Doister's copying or his own provision of the letter? The Scrivener seems to be the source of the original letter, which he apparently markets for prospective suitors. This is implied by Roister Doister's accusation: "Did you not make me a letter, brother?" To which the Scrivener responds, "Pay the like hire, I will make you such another!" (3.5.23–24). The letter in its original form was intended to be duplicated and intended for the duplicity of being signed by another. Though this might simplify the chain of transmission, it actually complicates the notion of both the original and the error. Roister Doister's love letter is not proper to him and he has no more access to its proper meaning than did Merrygreek or Custance (nor the Scrivener for that matter). So even though Merrygreek is blamed for the miscarriage of the letter, the potential for error in Roister Doister's imitation also is in play. Merrygreek suggests as much when he shows a suspicious interest as his master hands the letter to Madge Mumblecrust (Dame Custance's old nurse) to deliver:

Madge.	It shall be done.
Merrygreek.	Who made it?
Roister Doister.	I wrote it each whit.
Merrygreek.	Then needs it no mending?
Roister Doister.	No, no.
Merrygreek.	No, I know your wit.

. . .

Merrygreek.	But are you sure that your letter is well enough?
Roister Doister.	I wrote it myself!

(1.4.127–28, 139–40)

These suspicions ramify to the two versions of the letter delivered in the play (the two letters printed in Wilson's guide to "ambiguitie"). We might suppose that the two versions correspond to two distinct letters, that is, to two different pages:

Scrivener.	How say you, is this mine original or no?
Roister Doister.	The selfsame that I wrote out of, so mote I go!
Scrivener.	Look you on your own fist, and I will look on this,
	And let this man be judge whether I read amiss.

(3.5.41–44)

Although Roister Doister's page is clearly represented as distinct from the page in the Scrivener's copy book, the exchange between the parties nearly confuses the two. Although the printed texts of the two letters point them differently, there is nothing in this exchange to suggest that Roister Doister's copy and the Scrivener's are so differentiated. Rather, they appear to be "the selfsame," transferable; these copies always differ from themselves, and from the start. The "two" letters are there at once; the "selfsame" original letter is never one and the same; the same page read in two different scenes delivers two different letters. The letter is originally a duplicate and duplicitous. The letter Merrygreek (mis)delivers inhabits the same space as the "proper" letter.

Merrygreek reads according to rhymed line endings, following the dominant pattern of speech in the play. The Scrivener reads according to the idea of proper pointing, to a notion of inflection registered on the page by graphic marks and spacing. It is impossible to tell, however, which copy of the letter the Scrivener reads "properly," easier to suppose that both copies are unpointed, unmarked, unpunctuated, that each contains the other. True to his character type, Merrygreek delivers a letter that has a parasitical relation to the proper original, and he admits that he is at fault. But this verdict covers over the fact that the letter is duplicitous from the beginning. If the page that Merrygreek reads is graphically un-pointed, it's hard to resist claiming that Merrygreek makes no mistake in pointing, for he delivers the letter according to the strong marker of rhymed couplets; to read against these would violate deeply ingrained formal and poetic rules as well as the "normative" speech of the characters in the play. In order to deliver the "proper" scribal letter, Merrygreek would have to step out of character, off of the stage and into the text of the Scrivener's letter as represented in its pointed printing. Instead he delivers a letter proper to a parasite, staying within the lines of his charac-ter type and within the line endings of the play.

There are other reasons to think that Merrygreek's "mistaken" read-ing is not in error. First, he delivers the "unconscious" of the letter, the strongly misogynist undercurrent that is rendered invisible by the (per-haps imaginary) graphic marks. This "unconscious" might require a more elaborate argument about the insidious violence of letters written to win over, thus overtake, rich and defenseless widows, but we can observe that it is hardly out of character for Roister Doister to deliver a misogynist letter. Indeed, he moves without a blink from wooing to assaulting. Merry-greek's account of the letter to Dame Custance later registers both:

> Nay, Mistress Custance, I warrant you, our letter
> Is not as we read e'en now, but much better,
> And where ye half stomached this gentleman afore,
> For this same letter, ye will love him now therefore;
> Nor it is not this letter, though ye were a queen,
> That should break marriage between you twain, I ween.
> (4.3.30–35)

Second, Merrygreek's reading is true, in the ways that I've suggested, to the character of the play, in the sense that it corresponds to normative ex-pectations of the comedy, from the character types (parasite and braggart soldier) to the classical form of plotting and the English quality of the

verse.[34] Moreover, as a parasite he generates possibilities and alternatives by manipulating and inflecting the available material around him. In
this way, in his duplicity, he comes close to the Master of Eton, whose
"proper" reputation was based on his ability to translate material, to
appropriate the classics and find the appropriate English form, but he also
suggests the "other" Udall we have been pursuing through these letters.[35]
Thus Merrygreek resembles Udall in more ways than one. Merrygreek's
flair for generating alternatives produces a scene which bends Roister
Doister's desire for a wife back toward himself. The parasite, perhaps to
secure his position, suggests himself as the appropriate partner for his
master; he plays the woman's part to keep his master playing his own.

Playing the Man's Part

One scene separates the two that deliver the letters; Roister Doister has
heard that the love token caused his rejection and stands alone with his
parasite, who castigates him:

> *Merrygreek.*   What, weep? Fie, for shame! And blubber? For
> manhood's sake
> Never let your foe so much pleasure of you take!
> Rather play the man's part, and do love refrain.
> If she despise you, e'en dispise ye her again!
> *Roister Doister.*   By Gosse and for thy sake, I defy her indeed!
> (3.4.88–91)

That agreed, Merrygreek babbles baby talk to mock the woman and his
master:

> *Merrygreek.*   Canst thou not lub dis man, which could lub dee so well?
> Art thou so much thine own foe?
> *Roister Doister.*   Thou dost the truth tell.
> *Merrygreek.*   Well, I lament.
> *Roister Doister.*   So do I.
> *Merrygreek.*   Wherefore?
> *Roister Doister.*   For this thing:
> Because she is gone.
> *Merrygreek.*   I mourn for another thing.
> *Roister Doister.*   What is it, Merrygreek, wherefore thou dost grief take?

Merrygreek.	That I am not a woman myself for your sake;
	I would have you myself—and a straw for yon Gill!—
	And [make] much of you, though it were against my will.[36]

· · ·

Merrygreek.	And I were a woman—
Roister Doister.	Thou wouldest to me seek.
Merrygreek.	For though I say it, a goodly person ye be.

· · ·

Roister Doister.	I daresay thou wouldest have me to thy husband.
Merrygreek.	Yea, and I were the fairest lady in the shire,
	And knew you as I know you and see you now here—
	Well, I say no more.
Roister Doister.	Gramercies, with all my heart.
Merrygreek.	But since that cannot be, will ye play a wise part?

(3.4.99–106, 109–11, 116–20)

The scene borders on transgressions in many ways: first, because it replays a sodomitical exchange, it mocks the serious charges launched by the Privy Council. Second, the imagined marriage capitalizes on the perhaps submerged implications of a master's relation to his parasite. The possibility of sodomitical relations is registered in stereotypical depictions of "private parasites," servant boys for hire.[37] The model parasite in Terence is named Gnatho and inspired a range of dubious English characters named for their "insectuality" such as Moth in Shakespeare's *Love's Labour's Lost* or Butterflye in Michael Drayton's *Moone-Calfe*:

> And when himselfe he of his home can free,
> He to the Citie comes, where then if he,
> And the familiar Butterflye his Page,
> Can passe the Street, the Ord'nary, and Stage,
> It is enough, and he himselfe thinkes then,
> To be the onely, absolut'st of men . . .
> Yet, more than these, naught doth him so delight
> As doth his smooth-chinned, plump-thighed catamite.[38]

Merrygreek's tendency to appropriate any position for expedience accounts for the difficulty of pinning down his motivations, especially when he entertains the idea of being Roister Doister's wife. He plays the parasite's part, but that doesn't entail playing in an "honest fashion." "Scurrility" and scatology linger in his language, for instance, when he first appears and announces his role:

> For what he saith or doth cannot be amiss.
> Hold up his "yea" and "nay," be his nown white son;
> Praise and rouse him well, and ye have his heart won,
> For so well liketh he his own fond fashions,
> That he taketh pride of false commendations.
>
> . . .
>
> For exalt him, and have him as ye lust, indeed,
> Yea, to hold his finger in a hole for a need.
> (1.1.48–52, 55–56)

In this joking, he follows Udall's own translation of Terence's Gnatho, who characterizes the role of the parasite:

> Suche men do I folowe at the taile, and amonge suche persones I do not so fashon my selfe, that they may laugh at me, but contrarie wise, what so ever they say or do, I shew them a mery countenance of myn owne self, & also make a great mervailing at their high wittis. What so ever they say, I comende it, that if they denie the same ageyne, that also I comêde: if a man say nay, I say nay also: if he say ye, I say yea to. And for a conclusion to be short, I maister & rule myn owne selfe, to upholde his ye and his nay, and to say as he sayth, in al maner thinges, for that is the next way now a days to get money ynough.[39]

Udall's translation interpolates the physical description, "follow at the tail," in his effort to find the proper English character for the Latin (*consector*: follow, pursue, emulate). And in translating Gnatho into Merrygreek, he has his English parasite follow a similar bodily disposition.

In act 1, scene 4, Roister Doister leans over, "one word in thine ear," a gesture that involves imagining some physical humor that would spawn Merrygreek's response: "Back, sirs, from his tail!" (1.4.44–45). Modern editors insert a stage direction, partly to explain this, and partly because the speech prefixes in the early modern text are unclear. But they may be reacting to more than a textual anomaly or an elliptical gesture if we can gauge it by an odd joke of the next line. Roister Doister echoes Merrygreek with a twist: "Back, villains! Will ye be privy of my counsel?" (46). The joke works in a number of directions at once, including the innuendo about "privy," activated both by tail and by a possible set of gestures, but the most uncanny is the deliberately mocking evocation of the Privy Council. Not only is it brazen for Udall to make a joking reference to a case that could have meant his death, but that he would do so in the context of men bumping around a guy's tail, clamoring to get privy to his ears seems inconceivable. Or is it? Perhaps not: if we follow Bray's arguments about unacknowledged complicities or Goldberg on the "open secret," the "privy counsel" emerges right where we would expect it, in the midst of a sodomitical scene.

Similar jesting occurs in the seemingly gratuitous play later in the scene (1.4). Merrygreek takes the opportunity to pluck at Roister Doister's coat, reiterating "by your mastership's licence" and "by your leave" (1.4.94, 99). Finally Roister Doister erupts, "What is that?" (99). To which Merrygreek responds, "Your gown was foul spotted with the foot of a gnat" (100), the lousy parasite on whom Merrygreek's character is based. "Their master to offend they are nothing afeard" (101). Roister Doister speaks this line, but it speaks through him, saying more than he could possibly know, more both about Merrygreek's position and strangely about Udall's, if we think back on the letter to his master. And the next few lines enact a scenario analogous to the events ten years before:

> Merrygreek.   A lousy hair from your mastership's beard.
> All.   And sir, for nurse's sake, pardon this one offence.
>   We shall not after this show the like negligence.
> Roister Doister.   I pardon you this once; and come sing ne'er the worse.
> (1.4.102–5)

Though Udall may have never received his pardon with such ease, he did come to sing never the worse. Here we need only recall Tusser's generic autobiography or Udall's service to the queen as a master of Revels.

Udall's talent for the Revels envelopes his mastery at revealing and reveiling, dissembling moments in which his career surfaces as if hidden in the play. For example, when Dame Custance expresses disapproval toward her serving ladies, Tibet Talkapace says,

> If ever I offend again, do not me spare.
> But if ever I see that false boy any more,
> By your mistresship's license, I tell you afore,
> I will rather have my coat twenty times swinged
> Than on the naughty wag not be avenged!
> (2.4.24–28)

Once again, echoes of the letter, of appeals to the master, of the Eton boy, of promised self-punishment, of beating. Echoes then of Udall's career. "For fault but small, or none at all. / It came to pas, thus beat I was, / See Udall see, the mercie of thee, / to me poore lad." His reputation on the line, Udall is remembered as "the best schoolmaster and the greatest beater," pedagogue, and pedant but never pederast. The innuendo of "swinge," to beat and to fuck, is the word missing in Tusser's poem that would link the quiet eroticism and the eruptive violence noted in the Eton boy's tribute to his master.

Playing the Woman's Part

To end on this note would be not to recognize my own position. The economy of the open secret still indicts the letter, still translates text into evidence of the world, a world in this case between men. The open secret, more subtle in its procedures of revealing and reveiling, still opens and shuts like a closet. The erotic play of dangling a secret deploys the erotics of textuality as an instrument for the erotics of sexuality. And this is to play along with the revelling master, to follow him to the letter.

> The wise poets long time heretofore
> Under merry comedies wise secrets did declare,
> Wherein was contained very virtuous lore,
> With mysteries and forewarnings very rare.
> Such to write, neither Plautus nor Terence did spare,
> Which among the learned at this day bears the bell;
> These, with such other, therein did excel.
> (The Prologue, 15–21)

In finding the proper English translation of Plautus and Terence, Udall echoes the familiar theory of the spirit of the letter, the kernel and shell game played with classical texts in order to render them appropriate for Christian readers. The point of claiming that there are hidden "secrets" is to shuck off all improperness, in the words of the Prologue, "avoiding all blame," "scurrility," "abuse," mirth for health, the "honest fashion." But Udall can't keep a secret. All the jokes in the play are about the dishonest fashion, the pleasure of abuse, the appeal of scurrility, mirth for mirth's sake. The secret, in short, may be that there is no secret.

If Udall can't keep a secret it might be because he does not have one.

Even in the (non) place of early modern homosexuality, the open secret still assumes that there is a there there, a place not signaled yet signaling nevertheless. What happens when we pursue the secret, looking for signs that point to the bottom of Udall's heart, that confirm that he was a sodomite, and that he was brazen (or moved) enough to stage a scene between men? We might decide to continue to look for the words that might speak to his legal case. For instance, Christian Custance bemoans being accused unworthily, something repeated in Udall's letter and in his paraphrases of Terence:

> O Lord, how necessary it is now of days,
> That each body live uprightly all manner ways,
> For let never so little a gap be open,
> And be sure of this, the worst shall be spoken!
> How innocent stand I in this, for deed or thought,
> And yet see what mistrust towards me it hath wrought!
> (5.3.1– 6)

A little gap, a little pleasure, and it "hath stained my name forever, this is clear," says the Dame (4.3.66). Udall echoes this complaint in the work he did immediately after his dismissal from Eton, especially in a translation of Erasmus's *Apophthegmes*. In a passage (342) about Demosthenes not giving ten thousand drachmas to stay one night with Lais, "I will not buy repentance so dear," Erasmus writes, "Unto unhonest pleasure, repentance is a prest [ready] companion," and Udall adds, "Yea, and one property more it hath, that the pleasure is small and is gone in a moment; the repentance great, and still enduring as long as life continueth."[40] Or in the mouth of the Dame: "Gay love, God save it, so soon hot, so soon cold!" (4.3.38).[41]

But what does this reading perform? To put it in a manner that cuts both ways, what do we gain from another skeleton in the closet? I hope that I've pointed out enough of the problems to suggest that this would not be the way to go, though I concede that it has to be acknowledged as a constant temptation, one that recognizes our position as readers with particular sets of stakes and desires. In choosing another way, I don't want to minimize the importance of what the real person Nicholas Udall did. I honestly don't think there's any way to know. But I do wonder what more it would add if we did. Instead of indicting Udall, looking for evidence that proves he "played the man's part," that he swinged his Eton boys, we might look at the case as evidence itself of other things, of the different meanings—theatrical, sexual, and social—of playing the man's part and the woman's as well. One thing the play also enacts is production of misogyny at moments when the homosocial fabric is ruptured. Always the parasite, Merrygreek plays at playing the woman's part. He pretends to be the mouthpiece for Dame Custance in order to tell Roister Doister the thoughts he's kept secret:

> Now that the whole answer in my devise doth rest,
> I shall paint out our wooer in colours of the best.
> And all that I say shall be on Custance's mouth;
> She is author of all that I shall speak, forsooth.
> (3.3.1–4)

By putting the Dame in the authoring position, he de-authorizes her; she's just a cover, a shuck that can be scapegoated if necessary. His playing the woman's part allows him to dissimulate in speech, simultaneously saying nasty things directly to Roister Doister while avoiding the violence he would threaten against a man. Merrygreek has fun shoving it in his master's face, reporting to Roister Doister that he said to Custance: " 'Ye are happy,' ko I, 'that ye are a woman! / This would cost you your life in case ye were a man' " (3.3.37–38). Of course, this isn't true; he never said that to Custance because she never said the things he said she said. The only nugget of truth in it is that Merrygreek has in fact just performed the very act he makes up about the scene with the Dame: he has followed his own advice to her, happy that he plays the woman's part in teasing his master. The hypermasculine threat, like so many of Roister Doister's, is laughable since the joke behind the character of the braggart soldier is inability to play the man's part. If fear of retaliation doesn't work as a motivation, why then does Merrygreek play the woman's part? Even if the answer were that it's funny, we'd have to ask why. Merrygreek associates dissimulation with women: "O Jesus, will ye see / What dissembling creatures these same women be?" (3.2.39–40). And dissimulation is the dominant rule of his role as parasite. The relation of the parasite to the braggart can be differently gendered; what Merrygreek proposes to do to Roister Doister were he a woman (in the marriage scene), he's always already doing by virtue of the position he adopts toward Roister Doister. Parasites suck off their hosts.

More important than the homoerotic implications is that the parasitic relation he has to Roister Doister is structured around misogyny, on both of their parts, no matter what different things they do vis-à-vis Dame Custance. She carries all the culpability though she's never let a gap open. In the case of Merrygreek, the misogyny is often a displacement of his own parasitic relation. For Roister Doister, the play and the man, the misogyny is generated as a by-product of the circulation of homosocial energy, which at times, like that of the marriage scene, becomes homoerotic. Then it's no accident that the marriage scene occurs between the letters, for the joke of the letters is that gynophobia and gynophilia come from the same place: it just depends on how you point it. ("Ye may so take it, but I meant it not so, by Cock!") And it's no accident that Merrygreek is the one to reveal how a love letter could be taken as hate mail, since he has tried his hand at playing both parts. Playing the woman's part means recognizing that there is no "behind" behind the letter. The two letters in the play are hinged by a scene between men. And there's nothing between them.

Notes

1. Thomas Tusser, *Fiue hundred pointes of good Husbandrie* (London: Henrie Denham, 1580), 85r.
2. Tusser (1523–80) begins his verse "calendar of rural and domestic economy" with forty stanzas on his life, the sixth and eighth of which are quoted above.
3. William L. Edgerton brings up the issue of "the greatest schoolmaster and the greatest beater" in his discussion of the poem and Udall's reputation in his monograph *Nicholas Udall* (New York: Twayne Publishers, 1965), 32.
4. Edgerton cites a poem by John Parkurst, Bishop of Norwich, that praises Udall's command of Greek and Latin letters, his talent for teaching, and his inspiring "genuine love." Among the pupils at Eton, the two most notable are Richard Mulcaster, headmaster of the Merchant Taylor's School and author of two pedagogical works, and Thomas Wilson, secretary of state under Elizabeth and author of two rhetorical handbooks.
5. John S. Farmer, ed., *The Dramatic Writings of Nicholas Udall, Comprising Ralph Roister Doister, A Note on Udall's Lost Plays, Note-Book and Word-List* (London: Early English Drama Society, 1906), index. 151. In addition to the play, which some claim is the first successful reworking of Plautus and Terence into English, Udall translated Erasmus's *Apophthegmes* (1542) and *Paraphrases upon the New Testament* (1548) and Peter Martyr's *A Discourse Concerning the Sacrament of the Lordes Supper* (1550). His most important pedagogical contribution was a text that served as a textbook for Latin grammar and speech, *Floures for Latine Spekynge* (1533), line-by-line translations and glosses of Terence's *Andria, Eunuchus,* and *Heautontimorumenos.*

6.   In 1527 Udall may have been implicated in a heresy hunt at Oxford, where he was lecturing in Greek and logic. He was acquainted with a group circulating Lutheran works and the banned Tyndale translation of the New Testament. The incident is recounted in John Foxe's *Actes and Monuments*. For Udall's involvement, see Edgerton, 23–24.

7.   Harris Nicholas, *Proceedings and Ordinances of the Privy Council of England* (London: G. Eyre and A. Spottiswoode, 1834–37), 152, 155, 157. There is no record of the amount of time Udall spent in the Marshalsea prison. With the publication of his translation of Erasmus's *Apophthegmes* in 1542, one might wonder if he served any time at all. Edgerton implies that he fled to a friend or patron in the North (47–48).

8.   For further discussion, see Donald Mager's essay "John Bale and Early Tudor Sodomy Discourse," in this volume.

9.   Edgerton's chapter "A Turning Point" reviews the case and weighs the evidence, yet remains inconclusive. Half of the chapter is given over to a modernized reprint of a letter Udall wrote following his dismissal from Eton (41–45).

10. In his textbook *Floures for Latine Spekynge* the language is laden with a sense of the law. For example, he "translates" the line "*Quod illum insimulat durum, id non est*" as "Where as he accuseth hym, or sayeth to his charge, that he is harde or streyte, that is not so" and feels compelled to add a gloss: "*Insimulare* is proprely to lay to ones charge, a cryme that is not true, but a forged matter" (126v–127r). Spoken by Cremes to his son in *Heautontimorumenos* (2.1), the sentence concerns the harsh stance of fathers and the loose life of sons and is closer to "as to the boy pretending his father is hard, that's not so." Udall aims for paraphrase of the spirit rather than translation of the letter, but here as elsewhere he adds a sense of his own. See the facsimile edition, *Flowers For Latin Speaking, 1533* (Menston, England: Scolar Press, 1972).

11. E. R. Adair, "Rough Copies of the Privy Council Register," *English Historical Review* 37 (1923): 410–22.

12. For an analysis of the ways the materiality of handwriting serves various gendered and political agendas, see Stephanie Jed, *Chaste Thinking: The Rape of Lucretia and the Birth of Humanism* (Bloomington: Indiana University Press, 1989), and Jonathan Goldberg, *Writing Matter from the Hands of the English Renaissance* (Stanford: Stanford University Press, 1990).

13. I shall focus on Bray's *Homosexuality in Renaissance England* (London: Gay Men's Press, 1982), although his essay reprinted in this volume, "Homosexuality and the Signs of Male Friendship in Elizabethan England," is also useful and important. Jonathan Goldberg reviews Bray's argument in his "Colin to Hobbinol: Spenser's Familiar Letters," *South Atlantic Quarterly* 88 (1989):107–26, an essay included in his *Sodometries: Renaissance Texts, Modern Sexualities* (Stanford: Stanford University Press, 1992).

14. Beginning with "the land" and demographics, Bray describes the patriarchal household as the central institution on which others are modeled. He singles out the authority of the master over those who belong to the household, especially children

and servants, and suggests that the power differential similarly structures relations between teacher and pupil, client and prostitute, patron and actor (42–57). The power relations in pedagogy stand out as peculiar, though, since the position of power, the teacher or headmaster, is also one of service; the boys, or perhaps their fathers, are the clients of a school or tutor even if the boys register the lack of power (being "pressed" to perform lessons or plays, "to serve the Queere," and so on). A *paedagogus* was after all an educated slave.

15. His description of schools relies on pederastic jokes about pedant tutors (51–52). As he says of other satiric caricatures, these stereotypes circulated widely in forms so standard that it is difficult to know how they might be related to any specific context. The remarkable similarity of jokes about pederastic pedants, for instance, in fourteenth-century Florence (Boccaccio) or in medieval France (Alain de Lille), simultaneously flags attention for more investigation and a warning about assuming that they are straightforward "evidence."

16. Bray makes this point in his discussion of sodomy's relation to other "crimes" (heresy, atheism, blasphemy, sedition, drunkenness, lying) and concludes that as a sexual act it signified "hazily," closer to "an idea like debauchery" (2–3). A discussion of the "burglary" of this case with Jonathan Goldberg helped clarify this point.

17. He argues that "there was little or no social pressure for someone to define for himself *what* his sexuality *was*" (70), but as my italics indicate, this still presupposes that he has one.

18. "Practically unconscious" refers to a notion developed by Harry Berger, Jr., in an essay on psychoanalysis and discourse. Troping on the "practical conscious" of social theory, the practical unconscious is a strategy by which the subject remains ignorant of the effects of his acts in order to continue to perform them, a strategy of misrecognition. See Berger's "What Did the King Know and When Did He Know It? Shakespearean Discourses and Psychoanalysis," *South Atlantic Quarterly* 88 (1989): 811–62.

19. He begins his chapter "The Social Setting" with the problem of producing social history out of literary texts (33–38) and then moves on to similar problems with legal texts (38–42). His argument that court records are largely "convenient legal fictions" more concerned with "correct legal form" (38) adds even more reason to be suspicious of the Privy Council record, although he would take it in a direction opposite from that of Edgerton.

20. Immediately before the case of Udall, he quotes Marston on "some pedant-tutor in his bed / Should use my fry like Phrygian Ganymede" (52).

21. Goldberg reworks the notion of the "open secret" from D. A. Miller's *The Novel and the Police* (Berkeley: University of California Press, 1988), 192–220.

22. The addressee is unclear though it is assumed that he was a patron of some sort. Edgerton mentions three names: Robert Aldridge and Richard Cox, both Eton schoolmasters, and John Udall, high in court circles and possibly a relative (46).

23. A copy of the letter, Cotton MS Titus B VIII, is printed in Sir Henry Ellis's *Original Letters of Eminent Literary Men of the XVth through XVIIIth Century* (London: Camden Society, 1843), 1–7.

24. For this formulation, I am indebted to Jonathan Goldberg.
25. Such a debate was carried out in the pages of *Notes & Queries*: William Peery, "Udall as Timeserver," *Notes & Queries* 194 (1950): 119–21, 138–41, and William L. Edgerton, "The Apostasy of Nicholas Udall," *Notes & Queries* 195 (1950): 223–26.
26. For more on "playing the sodomite," see Goldberg's chapter entitled "The Transvestite Stage: More on the Case of Christopher Marlowe," in *Sodometries*, 105–43.
27. For a recent publication of Wilson's 1553 edition, see Richard S. Sprague, ed., *The Rule of Reason, Conteinying the Arte of Logique* (Northridge, Calif.: San Fernando Valley State College, 1972), 166–67. W. W. Greg discusses and reprints Wilson's citation of the two letters in a facsimile edition of *Ralph Roister Doister* (London: Malone Society Reprints, 1934), v–vii. Most critics now agree that this citation works to date the play to the early 1550s. Because of Wilson's close association with Udall, critics assume he would have quoted the play in earlier editions of *The Rule of Reason*, and therefore argue for a more precise date, 1552. Some argue that this date explains Udall's appointment to Court Revels in 1553–54, but this reasoning simplifies the matter. Udall was already involved with members of the court as tutor, translator, and writer; and while the records show the bestowing of praise and money for entertainments under Mary, Udall held no official position in the Revels.
28. The Prologue's "mispointed" speech insults the audience, though the aristocrats in the play are delighted rather than offended (6.1.108–17). Related tricks of misreading occur in Shakespeare's *Twelfth Night*, in Marlowe's *Edward II*, and in Kyd's *Spanish Tragedy*.
29. At work in the transmission of knowledge, through humanistic pedagogy, is the circulation of "pages," both letters and boys. The reproduction of mastery performed in school depends upon the imitation of the master and of master texts by the pupil, who then goes on to carry these letters, goes on, as Wilson did, to be imitated himself. This "master/page dialectic" is modeled on inscriptive practices, which in turn inscribe the subject. The close proximity of pedagogic inscription and pederastic insemination is a *topos* found especially in the Platonic dialogues.
30. A. W. Reed, "Nicholas Udall and Thomas Wilson," *Review of English Studies* I (1925): 275–83.
31. In his monograph *Thomas Wilson* (Boston: Twayne Publishers, 1986), Peter E. Medine suggests that there is "reason to suppose, furthermore, that something like an affectionate relationship developed between Wilson and the master, Nicholas Udall" (5).
32. The most accessible edition is an anthology in the New Mermaids' series, Charles Walters Whitworth, ed., *Three Sixteenth-Century Comedies: "Gammer Gurton's Needle," "Roister Doister,"* and *"The Old Wife's Tale"* (New York: W. W. Norton, 1984).
33. Though the letter Speed reads is handwritten, he claims "this I speak in print, for in print I found it" (2.1.159). The Scrivener subscribes to the promise of "mechanical reproduction," perhaps a fundamental assumption of his craft, but a promise never delivered by hand nor by the mechanical printing press. I argue this point in more detail in "Dispatch Quickly: The Mechanical Reproduction of Pages," *Shakespeare Quarterly* 42 (1991):389–408.

34. For a discussion of Udall as "the father of English comedy," see A. W. Plumstead, "Satirical Parody in *Roister Doister*: A Reinterpretation," *Studies in Philology* 60 (1963): 141–54.

35. On Udall's theory of translation, or paraphrase, as a step beyond the philology of early humanism, see T. W. Baldwin, "Schoolmaster Udall Writes the First Regular English Comedy," in *Shakespeare's Five-Act Structure* (Urbana: University of Illinois Press, 1947), 375–401.

36. There's a textual problem here: Whitworth prints "mock" while other editions have "make." The early modern text prints "mocke," which authorizes the Mermaid editor's choice. Since both are in the line, one heard through the other, depending on who is listening, I took the license to choose the one Roister Doister hears, the one that registers the sodomitical sense.

37. Bray, *Homosexuality*, 54.

38. The passage is cited in Bray, 33–34. See J. William Hebel's edition of Drayton, *Works* (Oxford: Basil Blackwell, 1961), 173–74, ll. 283–88, 315–16.

39. Udall's translation of Gnatho's speech in *Eunuchus* (2.2) in *Floures*, 67r–v.

40. For this point and the citations, I rely on Edgerton, 46.

41. The line, bracketed out of context, is a citation from another early English drama, *Wit and Science* (1540), which was a popular schoolboy play, cited and parodied in subsequent generations: "Hastye love is soone hot and soone cold." The large number of citational lines in *Roister Doister* pulls together proverbial sayings with morality plays and classical drama. The references to Terence are most important since the play is envisioned as a reworking, or reiteration, of Terentian subplots in an English inflection.

Into Other Arms: Amoret's Evasion

DOROTHY STEPHENS

I haue seldome seene an honest woman to haue many friends that wil take hir part . . . You may quickely ghesse a Strumpet by her multitude of friendes.
—Barnabe Riche

> A wind fane changabil huf puffe
> Always is a woomman.—Virgil (trans. Stanyhurst)[1]

I N a relatively minor passage from *The Faerie Queene*'s book 4, Spenser gives us a haunting description of Amoret as she recovers from a swoon to find herself in the "darknesse and dread horrour" of Lust's cave:

> She waked out of dread
> Streight into griefe, that her deare hart nigh swelt,
> And eft gan into tender teares to melt.
> Then when she lookt about, and nothing found
> But darknesse and dread horrour, where she dwelt,
> She almost fell againe into a swound,
> Ne wist whether aboue she were, or vnder ground.
>
> With that she heard some one close by her side
> Sighing and sobbing sore, as if the paine
> Her tender hart in peeces would diuide:
> Which she long listning, softly askt againe
> What mister wight it was that so did plaine?
> To whom thus aunswer'd was: Ah wretched wight

> That seekes to know anothers griefe in vaine,
> Vnweeting of thine owne like haplesse plight:
> Selfe to forget to mind another, is ouersight.
>
> Aye me (said she) where am I, or with whom?
> (4.7.9–11)[2]

We do not know at first who "some one" is, but her voice materializes so nearby as to take the place of Amoret's own thoughts, and because all of the gender-specific pronouns for several stanzas belong to Amoret, the clause "as if the paine / Her tender hart in peeces would diuide" pierces both women with the same pang of grief. It is as though the "tender teares" of one woman proceed from the other's "tender hart," so that when Amoret asks, "Where am I, or with whom?" her second phrase serves less as an additional question than as a reiteration of her first one. Unwittingly, she reveals the paradoxical nature of Aemylia's warning: rather than ignoring yourself in order to worry about me, Aemylia advises, you need to make yourself aware that your hapless plight is just like mine.

But why does the poem have Amoret exchange confidences with Aemylia in *this* particular cave? We usually think of lust as the sort of urge that requires the maintenance of ever more emotional distance as physical distance decreases. (Spenser makes it clear that this is no Cave of Pleasantly Naughty Dalliance; the monster Lust is gruesomely homicidal.) One readily available but incomplete answer is that this cave, like caves in many romances, figures the interior of woman's body, protected and protecting as long as man remains outside. When Aemylia makes her former life into a story for Amoret, we become conscious of other men besides Lust who hover at the cave's entrance:

> But what I was, it irkes me to reherse;
> Daughter vnto a Lord of high degree;
> That ioyd in happy peace
>
> · · ·
>
> It was my lot to loue a gentle swaine.
> (4.7.15)

We may also become conscious of a slight ambivalence—not in Aemylia, but in the narrative—toward her change from a state defined by these men to a state in which, although she is "of God and man forgot" (4.7.14), she can enter into close communion with another woman. Because *The Faerie*

Queene does not allow many such meetings between women to happen within its borders, however, the context as well as the contents of Lust's Cave deserves a closer look. This essay is about the space within that cave and about women's wandering to and from its enclosure. Although the second half of *The Faerie Queene* registers an intense anxiety about the forms of female power it presents, my premise is that Spenser's song to his aging queen also colludes with a feminine sexuality that has little to do with greatness.

The Lust episode's importance for the opening book of Spenser's second installment will become clearer if we circle back to the end of the poem's first installment, just after Amoret has escaped from another form of lustful coercion in the House of Busyrane. In order to weave Scudamour and Amoret's courtship and marriage into book 4, first published in 1596, Spenser unraveled the selvage of their story in book 3, by canceling the five final stanzas of the 1590 edition and replacing the lovers' blissful reunion with a painful continuation of their separation. Mistakenly convinced that Britomart (whom he believes to be a male knight instead of a woman in armor) has failed to rescue Amoret from the enchanter Busyrane, Scudamour in the 1596 revision wanders off in search of other assistance. Jonathan Goldberg has written that Scudamour and Amoret's hermaphroditic embrace in the original ending to book 3 represents a closure that the poem cannot allow itself or its readers to possess. Moreover, when Scudamour has the chance to "reclaim his wife" later in book 4, he chooses instead to tell his friends a story about how he originally won Amoret from Venus. "Rereading," Goldberg argues, "is his only prize. We are in Scudamour's place, left with our desire for an ending."[3] I would argue that Amoret strays from the confines of such a statement. Implicit in Goldberg's argument about books 3 and 4 is the idea that whereas Scudamour loses Amoret, Amoret loses herself; we cannot, however, dispense with Amoret simply by making her represent Scudamour's lack.

Otherwise astute criticism has run momentarily aground in these shallows. Judith Anderson describes Amoret's relationship to Timias and his beloved Belphoebe after the Lust episode in book 4:

> She is part of their story, and when she is simply abandoned by them in the middle of it, she becomes, both narratively and morally, a loose end waiting to be woven into the larger design. . . .
>   . . . In short, what befalls Amoret in the two cantos she shares

with Belphoebe and Timias looks very much like the other half of
their story, the half muted in Belphoebe's withdrawal from Timias
and suppressed in her return to him. What befalls Amoret unfolds
the "inburning wrath" of Belphoebe (8.17) and gives tongue to the
revilement and infamy that Ralegh's secret marriage incurred.[4]

Anderson's commentary provides excellent guidance within its own territory, but if Amoret does function as a textual register of other characters'
interiority, surely it is a mistake to treat her unproblematically as such.
What, for example, does her story mean for female or male readers who
do not desire the particular sort of closure that Scudamour or Timias
desires? And why should we believe that the poem expects us to desire this
particular closure?

When Amoret pours herself into Scudamour's waiting arms, her body
does become an "instrument of mutual pleasure," as Lauren Silberman
argues; nevertheless, the questions that various critics have raised about
the torturer Busyrane as a figure for the male artist and Petrarchan poet
should make us suspicious about this emblem's use of the female body as
an aesthetic instrument.[5] Glossing Busyrane as *"Busy-reign,"* Harry Berger
writes that the enchanter represents "the male imagination trying busily
(because unsuccessfully) to dominate and possess woman's will by art, by
magic, by sensory illusions and threats—by all the instruments of culture
except the normal means of persuasion."[6] After Amoret's escape from this
authorial manipulation, her joyful embrace with Scudamour is bound to
strike us at first as a direct contrast:

> Lightly he clipt her twixt his armes twaine,
>   And streightly did embrace her body bright,
>   Her body, late the prison of sad paine,
>   Now the sweet lodge of loue and deare delight:
>   But she faire Lady ouercommen quight
>   Of huge affection, did in pleasure melt,
>   And in sweete rauishment pourd out her spright:
>   No word they spake, nor earthly thing they felt,
>   But like two senceles stocks in long embracement dwelt.
>
> Had ye them seene, ye would haue surely thought,
>   That they had beene that faire *Hermaphrodite,*
>   Which that rich *Romane* of white marble wrought,

And in his costly Bath causd to bee site:
So seemd those two, as growne together quite.
(3.12.45a–46a)

Yet Busyrane is not dead, and the hermaphrodite analogy takes shape almost on his doorstep. If we gaze uncritically upon the bride while she "pour[s] out her spright," we risk the possibility of aligning ourselves with the proprietary voyeurism of the "rich *Romane*" who carved his own her-maphrodite.[7] Emblematic immobility is a new situation for Scudamour, but the image of Amoret melting into his welcoming arms oddly echoes a previous image of Amoret welded to Busyrane's cruelly phallic pillar of brass.[8] Subtly or not, the hermaphrodite begins to resemble Busyrane's own idea of a proper heterosexual relationship. Good women have often been admonished to keep still, of course, through happy times as well as adverse ones, and insofar as the hermaphrodite's ostensibly equal union of the sexes does recall Busyrane's brass pillar, we could say that it is all too normal in its social construction.

The Faerie Queene contains several hermaphroditic figures—notably the self-sufficient Venus, who "syre and mother is her selfe alone, / Begets and eke conceiues, ne needeth other none" and Dame Nature, who "whether she man or woman inly were, / That could not any creature well descry" (4.10.41; 7.7.5). But the hermaphrodite analogy at the end of book 3 in the 1590 edition differs from these others in representing the fusion of two distinctly sexed characters; the image is of a hermaphrodism something like Siamese twins, with two heads and four arms. The figure thus owes a great deal to Plato's *Symposium*, where Aristophanes speculates that hu-mans were once hermaphroditic, with "four ears and two organs of gener-ation and everything else to correspond."[9] Love, explains Aristophanes, is our impulse to return to the state before we were severed, "by attempting to weld two beings into one and to heal the wounds which humanity suffered."[10] Socrates modifies this simple picture later in the evening by saying that according to his teacher, Diotima, the object of love is to unite itself to beauty in order to procreate; nevertheless, Diotima's definition of love retains the hermaphroditic idea insofar as her emphasis on mutuality revises the traditional Greek notion that hierarchy is essential to a man's erotic experience.[11] Reminding us that the Greeks believed that only women could experience sex as a mutual act, David Halperin writes that when Socrates quotes the teachings of Diotima, a woman, Plato means to find in female eroticism "an image of the reciprocal erotic bond that unites philosophical lovers who are jointly engaged in conversation and the quest for truth."

As Halperin goes on to argue, however, this philosophy of mutual love ironically erases femininity altogether, given that the supposedly feminine views attributed to Diotima are actually predicated upon male physiology. (So, for example, Diotima teaches that the reproductive function is inseparable from erotic pleasure.)[12] "In other words, it looks as if what lies behind Plato's erotic doctrine is a double movement whereby men project their own sexual experience onto women only to reabsorb it themselves in the guise of a 'feminine' character."[13] But Halperin gives a word of caution:

> The radical *absence* of women's experience—and, thus, of the actual feminine—from the ostensibly feminocentric terms of Plato's erotic doctrine should warn us not to interpret Plato's strategy simplistically as a straightforward attempt to appropriate the feminine or as a symbolic theft of women's procreative authority. For Plato's appropriation of the Other works not only by misrecognizing the Other but by constructing "the other" as a masked version of the same.[14]

Or, in the words of Teresa de Lauretis, this Platonic appropriation of femininity "has also had the effect of securing the heterosexual social contract by which all sexualities, all bodies, and all 'others' are bonded to an ideal/ideological hierarchy of males."[15] Indeed, both Halperin and Philippa Berry show that *The Symposium* itself, as well as the critical tradition after Plato, codifies this elision of feminine desire by implying that Diotima must be merely a literary device invented by Socrates.[16]

Berry observes that the tradition of eliding Diotima informs the Renaissance neoplatonists' creation of their Petrarchan ladies, who wield moral, intellectual, and erotic powers precisely because they do not convincingly have existence apart from the men who write them.[17] In the House of Busyrane, which readers have long recognized as an allegory of a Petrarchan courtship, Busyrane concentrates all of his arts upon making Amoret fear her own wandering desires. More than that, however, in the process of turning Petrarchan *topoi* and tropes of sublimated desire (the burning passion, the Greek gods' visits to mortal women) into images of a particularly Petrarchan torture, he tries to make Amoret herself into a static emblem of sublimated pain when he shows Britomart a pageant in which Amoret "figures" the torments of love by being exhibited with a gaping wound in her breast, holding before her in a silver basin her bloody heart transfixed with a dart. This is what Amoret seems to escape when Britomart leads her to the waiting Scudamour in the 1590 edition of the poem. Yet the type of erotic bonding that we find in the neoplatonic tradition, where Diotima can only point toward masculinity, is precisely the danger that Spenser sets up for the 1590 Amoret who melts and pours her spirit into her husband's arms when she is overcome with "huge affection" (3.12.45a). The phrase refers to her love but also powerfully suggests his erection that overmasters and mysteriously transforms her, until it is his desire with which she is filled.

Maureen Quilligan argues persuasively that although the pen that Busyrane dips into Amoret's blood for ink makes him into a "sadistic sonneteer," Spenser "manages to correct this (male) art by viewing it from the opposite perspective of the lady, who usually merely peruses the lines of the poem."[18] She goes on to suggest that although Britomart forces Busyrane to close the gaping wound in Amoret's breast, his reversed charms cannot heal "the wound of desire—which Britomart shares with Amoret." By way of support for her suggestion, however, she quotes the hermaphrodite stanza, in which "*Britomart* halfe enuying their blesse, / Was much empassiond in her gentle sprite" (3.12.46a), explaining that "*Blesser*, in French, is to wound; such wounding, a real anatomical event in sexual consummation, is bliss." Whether or not Quilligan's irony is intended, this seems an odd way to conclude a discussion of the specifically female point of view, since wedding nights are not always blissful for wounded brides. Britomart's naiveté could certainly allow her to envy the wound without realizing its burden of pain, yet if we really wish to read the wound from the "perspective of the lady," we must take into account the irony of the lady's naive envy of this particular blessing. Most of Quilligan's chapter on "The Gender of the Reader" is extraordinarily insightful in its argument about the ways Spenser rewrites stories of masculine desire by viewing events from the perspective of the desired, desiring, or threatened woman; and Quilligan does go on to argue that in book 4, the rest of Amoret and Scudamour's story demonstrates "the tension between husbandly love and its implicit antagonism to women." This takes the form of a "conflict within the terms of chivalric love" between "ladies' undeniable rights, and those rights granted by conquest."[19] But for Quilligan, because the conflict does not taint the hermaphrodite itself, the hermaphrodite's disappearance cannot represent anything but loss. In a conclusion that recalls Goldberg's, Quilligan writes that "what we are left with is a desire for the canceled text of the 1590 ending, a desire that Spenser satisfies with illusory substitutions" and that, "like the cancellation of the happy ending to Amoret's story, the cancellation of the 'Letter to Ralegh' suggests an entire reorientation of Spenser's initial program in the face of hard political realities."[20]

Although my own argument runs in a different channel from these statements of Quilligan's, in making them she joins the company of other critics, and for a very good reason: we do desire closure of *some* sort, even if we are sophisticated enough to analyze and enjoy the frustration of our own literary desire, and the poem does clearly set up the hermaphrodite as an example of blissful closure in *some* sense. Nor should we necessarily disagree when Quilligan explains the cancellation of the hermaphrodite as Spenser's decision to "dismiss a male reader [Lord Burleigh], select a paradigmatic female one, and then reconstitute the canceled full-gendered readership (as imaged in the closing embrace of Amoret and Scudamour) within the 'androgynous' queen."[21] I do not so much want to contradict such readings as to select a different set of desires and relationships for our attention, with the conviction that just as there are other narrative positions possible besides ventriloquism on the one hand and subversion on the other, so are there other Amorets possible besides the Amoret whose meaning depends upon Scudamour at the same time that it validates him.

It is important to see, moreover, that if the hermaphrodite on Busyrane's doorstep resembles Busyrane's idea of the proper relationship between the sexes, it also begins to resemble his idea of the proper relationship between women. Signs in the House of Busyrane caution Britomart not to be too bold—lest, as the Bluebeard text behind this text puts it, her "heart's blood should run cold."[22] Because in the folk tale Mr. Fox (Bluebeard) commands Lady Mary not to look at his former wives, intending to make her join them if she does, Busyrane's own allusion to the tale implicitly warns his headstrong guest that it could be dangerously self-transforming or even lethal for her to attempt any sort of meeting with the woman who is his prisoner. Busyrane would like Britomart to think of Amoret as someone completely unlike herself at this point, completely subjected to Lust.

Like the epic's revised edition in 1596, Spenser's original edition has Britomart choose not to heed Busyrane's warning; she boldly enters and rescues Amoret. But Britomart's labor for Amoret's release has taken place on the prisoner's behalf rather than in her company. Only by canceling the hermaphroditic embrace between Scudamour and the freed Amoret can the poem emphasize just how thoroughly both Britomart and Amoret have ignored Busyrane's warning that they stay apart. By canceling the hermaphrodite, the poem not only gives these two women an additional quest, it gives them a quest together, as friends. The distance between "Amoret" as the sign of Scudamour's proprietary loss in book 3 and "Amoret" as the sign to Belphoebe of Timias's lust in book 4 constitutes a space for feminine desire, in which Amoret and Britomart may "wend at will" just as Scudamour does, and without his company. This is the promise—and the warning—with which the second version of book 3 ends.

I am arguing that the poem's replacement of the hermaphrodite revives and extends the implications of its disapproval of Busyrane's form of seduction. Busyrane insists that Amoret confine her thoughts and speech to his claustrophobic system of meanings—and if the other demands that he makes are immoral, they nevertheless exert pressure upon his prisoner because his initial demand for her rapt attention resembles similar demands made by moral men.[23] Both the House of Busyrane and Amoret's subsequent journey in search of her husband, who has left in despair, problematize the complex distribution of blame and punishment that occurred in the sixteenth century whenever a wife wandered. The wronged husband deserved the shame of a cuckold's horns because he was assumed to have given too little correction to his wife, leaving her too much to her own devices. He was culpable precisely because every woman left unsupervised was considered perilously on the verge of becoming morally wayward.[24] Yet the requirement that women remain sexually constant—immovably fixed—was irreconcilable with the requirement that they always adapt to masculine social and literary structures. Britomart must wander to find Artegall, and Amoret, to find Scudamour, but their wandering exposes them to lustful men. When Scudamour and Amoret are separated in an unfamiliar territory, she becomes the stray by definition—but this condition also makes her the one who must adapt quickly if she wishes to remain "perfect hole" (3.12.38).

Obviously, a woman's ability to adapt herself to the men around her would have dubious social value when it extended to her evil abductor, whatever his prerogatives as a man. Curiously enough, *The Faerie Queene* experiments with this ambiguity most explicitly in a passage that involves only women. I am thinking of the beginning of book 4, where Amoret does not yet realize that her flirtatious rescuer is female. Amoret trembles:

> For well she wist, as true it was indeed,
> > That her liues Lord and patrone of her health
> > Right well deserued as his duefull meed,
> > Her loue, her seruice, and her vtmost wealth.
> > All is his iustly, that all freely dealth:
> > Nathlesse her honor dearer then her life,
> > She sought to saue, as thing reseru'd from stealth;
> > Die had she leuer with Enchanters knife,
> > Then to be false in loue, profest a virgine wife.
>
>   .   .   .
>
> His will she feard; for him she surely thought
> > To be a man, such as indeed he seemed,
> > And much the more, by that he lately wrought,
> > When her from deadly thraldome he redeemed,
> > For which no seruice she too much esteemed,
> > Yet dread of shame, and doubt of fowle dishonor
> > Made her not yeeld so much, as due she deemed.
>
> (4.1.6–8)

Within the story, Britomart's duplicity reflects a benign strategem, since she believes that her male disguise will make her and her timid charge appear less vulnerable to outsiders. What Amoret doesn't know, she can't betray to anyone else. At the same time, however, Britomart's armor allows this passage to do double service as a commentary on the relationships between the sexes by converting some of our laughter at the transvestite comedy into a sense of irony about glitches in the patriarchal system. Here, as in the original conclusion for book 3, Amoret acts in dutiful accordance with cultural expectations pressing upon her from two sides: she should be resolutely self-contained; she should be pliantly grateful. (The final two lines of stanza eight do not say that "doubt of fowle dishonor / Made her not yeeld so much, as due *he* deemed.") In book 3, Amoret's positive and negative obligations are divided between two male characters—Busyrane and Scudamour—who merge into each other allegorically only when it suits our particular critical agendas for them to do so. Amoret's momentary uneasiness with Britomart here in book 4 clearly tags these competing obligations as a cultural paradox: the notion that every man of miscellaneous goodness who saves a woman from torture "right well deserue[s] as his duefull meed, / Her loue, her seruice, and her vtmost wealth" cannot seem anything but misguided in this comedic context; by indicating that strong bonds do not assure sexual parity, the poem tacitly underscores its mistrust of the absolute fusion represented earlier by the hermaphrodite (4.1.6).[25]

If we collapse the two readings in the above paragraph, fusing the poem's commentary on women's friendships (where Britomart must protect the two of them from possible marauders by pretending to be male) with its commentary on heterosexual relationships (where Britomart represents actual men), we arrive at a third reading: if women's unavoidable inconstancy exposes them to lustful or otherwise demanding men, it also may expose them to other women. This possibility often generates anxiety in Renaissance texts, bound up as it is with the suspicion that women's friendships may supply goods and services over and above those supplied by husbands or lovers.[26] Without registering much anxiety at this point, however, Spenser's text heads directly toward this question of what one woman renders another. The two stanzas quoted above, in which Amoret tries to render the same service to her male rescuer that she withholds from him, enclose a stanza about the way that Amoret's serviceable nature allows her rescuer to tease her:

> Thereto her feare was made so much the greater
>   Through fine abusion of that Briton mayd:
>   Who for to hide her fained sex the better,
>   And maske her wounded mind, both did and sayd
>   Full many things so doubtfull to be wayd,
>   That well she wist not what by them to gesse,
>   For other whiles to her she purpos made
>   Of loue, and otherwhiles of lustfulnesse,
> That much she feard his mind would grow to some excesse.
> (4.1.7)

Nothing in Britomart's history of comical aggression toward strange knights (as when she and Paridell crash like bump-cars in book 3) has quite prepared us for her infliction of gratuitous anxiety upon a waif who cannot defend herself. The motives we are given for Britomart's teasing are that she wishes both "to hide her fained sex" and to "maske her wounded mind." Yet each of these phrases encloses two opposing ideas. In Spenser's grammar, where two negatives make a deeper negative and where redundant intensifiers—"fowle euill," "greedy *Auarice*," "equall peares"—defy our accusations of superfluity, hiding one's fained sex means that one does an awfully good job of hiding it. But of course the phrase also means, illogically, that Britomart manages to hide her pretense of being male. And if she "maske[s]" her painfully frustrated desires the way that Busyrane masques his, she is not concealing but displaying, putting on a show of signs meant to be deciphered. (Remember that in Busyrane's house, the "wounded mind" is Amoret's, masqued publicly as a heart in a silver basin.) These two phrases' duplicity about Britomart's duplicity suggests that her flirtation is more than just a private antidote for tedium and that she halfway intends Amoret to guess what her armor hides. If Amoret hesitates in the face of this riddle, still believing in her rescuer's specifically masculine seductiveness, our own partiality for the other half of the answer (that this knight is really a woman who flirts only in order to feign) may excuse her.

But Britomart dallies more with Amoret than she ever does with Artegall, and it is tempting to say that at this stage of the game, she feigns only in order to flirt. By keeping her helmet on, Britomart can afford to raise the dialogue to a higher erotic pitch, engaging in a closer intimacy than would otherwise be allowable.[27] Although the text thereby betrays a male fascination with eroticism between women, it also demonstrates concern for the two characters and an unwillingness to carry its farcical use of them beyond a certain point. Britomart's public unhelmeting when she and Amoret do reach a castle transfers the humor of Amoret's nervous sense that her rescuer's conversation is "doubtfull to be wayd" onto lords and ladies who can hardly believe their eyes when a fierce knight turns out to have floor-length tresses: "All were with amazement smit, / And euery one gan grow in secret dout / Of this and that, according to each wit" (4.1.14). Her traveling companion's vast relief at this new turn of events could have been treated comically but is not:

> And eke fayre *Amoret* now freed from feare,
> More franke affection did to her afford,
> And to her bed, which she was wont forbeare,
> Now freely drew, and found right safe assurance theare.

> Where all that night they of their loues did treat,
>   And hard aduentures twixt themselues alone,
>   That each the other gan with passion great,
>   And griefull pittie priuately bemone.
> (4.1.15–16)

These stanzas have an erotic subtext; the double entendres of "passion," "bemone," and "hard aduentures" reinforce one's initial sense that the phrase "their loues" not only points outward to two male objects but encloses a more private exchange between the two women. They speak "twixt themselues alone" of their previous "hard aduentures," while at the same time, they speak of "hard aduentures" that happen "twixt themselues alone."[28]

Like the water that half-covers Sir Guyon's dripping bathers in book 2, this enclosure may titillate outsiders, but because book 3 has already given us an investment in Britomart's and Amoret's individual griefs, the stanzas above do not request primarily that we "see and know, and yet abstain."[29] Instead, we are asked to see, know, and sympathize—perhaps even to envy this friendship which provides such a telling commentary on book 4. Stanza 16 shows both the narrator's indulgence and something like respect in refraining from laying the two women's conversation bare to us. It may seem as though Spenser has repeated the time-honored riddle about what women discuss when men aren't around (of which the time-honored answer is: "As it happens, thank God, they always talk about us"), except that the imprecision of "their loues" allows eavesdroppers no assured answer.[30]

These two women do find "right safe assurance" with each other, banishing their own doubts precisely at the moment when ours enter. It is wonderfully puzzling that the one happy bed scene in the whole poem appears here. This is the closest *The Faerie Queene* gets to the *Epithalamion*'s joyful, nocturnal union of two heretofore separate persons, and because Spenser refers to Britomart and Amoret indistinguishably in the stanza describing their nocturnal conversation, the absence of mastery that the *Epithalamion* both asserts and undercuts seems here in book 4 actually a present condition for one night. While the text declares literally that each of the women longs to complete herself in her absent mate, the subtext at least momentarily believes in the self-sufficiency of their interaction with each other.

This interaction moves out of its safe enclosure the next day when

Britomart and Amoret meet Blandamour, whose name "descrie[s] / His
fickle mind full of inconstancie," as if to heighten by contrast the example
of female constancy that the poem has just shown us (4.1.32). As soon as
Blandamour spies the two women, naturally believing one a "knight ad-
uenturous" and the other "his faire paragon, his conquests part," his immediate reaction is to attempt to steal the strange knight's lady. Britomart
has other ideas:

> The warlike Britonesse her soone addrest,
>   And with such vncouth welcome did receaue
> Her fayned Paramour, her forced guest,
>   That being forst his saddle soone to leaue,
>   Him selfe he did of his new loue deceaue.
>
> (4.1.36)

"Her fayned Paramour" and "his new loue" ought to refer to the same
ironically frustrated relationship, but they do not. Blandamour sees in
Britomart only an armored knight; if he had won the joust, "his new loue"
would have been Amoret.[31] The humor of Spenser's reference to Britomart's "fayned Paramour" depends upon our knowing, as Britomart and
Amoret do, that both of them are equally appropriate targets for Blandamour's lust—and equally inappropriate, of course. And so when they
gallop off, the man who has crassly attempted interference lies in the dust,
"Well warned to beware with whom he dar'd to dallie" (4.1.36). Just who *is*
"whom," anyway? Given the slippage inherent in Spenser's word "dallie"
(which wanders uncontrollably between eroticism and violence, perhaps
translated most aptly in our phrase "mess around with"), and given the
skirmish of grammatical references in previous lines, this "whom" means
both women. Blandamour would separate them by distinctions of gender;
they demur.

   Although the relationships that develop between women and men in
this poem do not prohibit friendships among men, they often exclude or
put pressure on those among women. Yet the authorial voice that asks us
to take pleasure in Britomart and Amoret's exchange of confidences clearly
is not asking us to believe along with Barnabe Riche that one can tell a
strumpet by her multitude of friends. Granted, Spenser does not argue coherently against this position, and in fact, he provides much support for it
in characters such as Duessa and Ate, or Serena (who meets a rapist when
she wanders away from Calepine in search of flowers). I suggest that it is

precisely because of the overwhelmingly negative cultural pressure upon women's friendships—superadded to the pressure of romance narrative structure, which tends to deflect and defer the desires of both sexes—that the few female alliances allowed in the poem take on such importance. While some of the poem's voices attempt to circumscribe or constrict relationships among women, other narrative voices seem on the point of acknowledging that these socially marginal alliances provide the poem with a kind of energy found nowhere else.

Blandamour's divisive and coercive impulses resurface so often in other men who meet the two women that these male characters begin to reflect badly upon the whole patriarchal enterprise (an enterprise conscientious-ly promoted by much of the rest of the poem). After having disarmed Blandamour, Britomart and Amoret next appear at the tournament for the False Florimell, another exercise in the acquisition of female property. Humorously enough, Britomart wins the prize, but she does not explain her refusal to accept the False Florimell by unhelmeting and revealing her own sex, as on other occasions. Nor does the narrator give the explanation for her. Instead, we are asked to compare the admirable nature of her and Amoret's existing relationship to what *would* be the questionable nature of the False Florimell's relationship to any of the knights who have jousted for her, including some of the poem's most illustrious heroes:

> *Britomart* would not thereto assent,
> Ne her owne *Amoret* forgoe so light
> For that strange Dame, whose beauties wonderment
> She lesse esteem'd, then th'others vertuous gouernment.
> (4.5.20)

The critique of the traffic in female property takes another turn when Satyrane decides to let the False Florimell choose her own mate. His method is not to ask her preferences but to set her in the middle of a circle of men in order to observe "to whom she voluntarie came" (4.5.25). These are the tactics we use with puppies or small children when we ourselves are feeling childish enough to want to know their favorites. Childishly, then, the False Florimell moves "of her accord" to the buffoon Braggadochio. General indignation takes the field, and when Braggadochio removes him-self and his prize that night by stealth, all of the men trot off in droll pursuit. Britomart remains behind with "*Amoret*, companion of her care" (4.5.30).

Before Britomart reappears in the following canto, her relationship with Amoret has already brewed further discord, as we learn when Artegall and Scudamour meet companionably "vnder a forrest side" to swap grudges (4.6.2). Artegall, who has no idea that his destiny is to marry the strange knight who unseated him at the tournament, feels bitter over having been deprived of his chance to win the False Florimell. The stranger, he says, "hauing me all wearie earst, downe feld, / The fayrest Ladie reft, and euer since withheld" 4.6.6). Meanwhile, Scudamour has been tricked by Ate into believing that this same unknown knight, who rescued his bride from Busyrane's house, has been having an affair with her ever since. Though we know he is wrong about the affair, one of Britomart's functions in the poem is in fact to withhold female prizes the way some of Spenser's women withhold sexual favors; it is her aggressive substitute for coyness. And so the two men have reason to grumble:

> Whiles thus they communed, lo farre away
>   A Knight soft ryding towards them they spyde,
>   Attyr'd in forraine armes and straunge aray:
>   Whom when they nigh approcht, they plaine descryde
>   To be the same, for whom they did abyde.
> (4.6.9)

Plainly, "communed" means "conversed," but when Britomart sends both Scudamour and his horse to the ground in the following stanza, the narrator's wry observation that "neither [man nor horse] greatly hasted to arise, / But on their common harmes together did deuise" (4.6.10) links the men's conversation with the holding of certain experiences and attitudes in common (at the same time that it establishes community between a man and the beast who serves him). Artegall and Scudamour's version of community centers upon their "common harmes," while their anger brings them together precisely because they know that they do not hold *things* in common. Britomart, their common enemy, is the one who has perversely drawn their female property back into circulation.

I would argue, then, that Britomart's tenacious refusal to "forgoe" Amoret "so light" bears only superficial resemblance to the male knights' attempts to keep hold of female property, and that by the same token, Britomart and Amoret's wandering in each other's company while searching for their lovers bears only superficial resemblance to the knightly rush for Florimell's look-alike. Spenser sets the stage for the latter contrast in his argument for this same canto, which has to be one of the funniest and most profound moments in the poem: "Both Scudamour and Arthegall / Doe fight with Britomart, / He sees her face; doth fall in loue, / and soone from her depart" (4.6.arg.).

Despite Britomart's tenacity, however, Amoret goes "astray" while her friend lies sleeping outdoors (4.6.36). Carelessness on Britomart's part? Perhaps so, since Spenser often uses naps to represent the temptation to let down one's guard. But if we move from the chronology of the plot to the order of the poem, we see that the more immediate reason for us to read in stanza 36 about Amoret's straying is that in stanzas 20 through 33 Britomart and Artegall have seen each other without armor for the first time and have fallen in love. If the plot does not directly say that this heterosexual union will put extra pressure upon the two women's story, the poem's ordering does suggest such a possibility. Squeezed between the stanzas in which Britomart tells of Amoret's earlier disappearance and those in which she and Artegall first become allies are two stanzas that take one last look at the odd negotiations the two women have been making with the world's view of them: in stanza 34, Scudamour interrupts Britomart's and Artegall's pleasurably embarrassed murmurs because of his own, less pleasant anxieties about his absent bride. Obviously, Amoret cannot have been having an affair with this strange knight, after all, given that the knight has turned out to be a maiden. But where *is* Amoret, if not in this knight's arms? Confused and unhappy, but polite, Scudamour begins his request for an explanation from the delicately golden-haired Britomart, "But Sir . . ." (4.6.34). In the following stanza, Britomart herself inscribes a kind of epitaph upon the monument of her and Amoret's friendship: "Ne euer was there wight to me more deare / Then she, ne vnto whom I more true loue did beare" (4.6.35). There is not room among the living for this "true loue" and Artegall, too.

The coincidence of Scudamour's confused perception of Britomart's gender (even as he clearly perceives her actual sex) and Britomart's declaration of love for Amoret in the same passage in which the poem supplants Amoret with Artegall may throw some light on the Cave of Lust, which is where Amoret lies at this narrative moment. But my metaphor is misleading, because I do not propose to light up the Cave's dark interior, only to point out its obscure internal contradictions: first, although the monster Lust is extravagantly male, Amoret loses herself to Lust—becomes lustful—while in the company of the sleeping Britomart. Second, unlike the

House of Busyrane, the Cave of Lust enacts the opposite of violation's wound, when the darkness enables Amoret and Aemylia to develop a sense of community by emptying out their painful life stories. The cave protects these women's intimate conversation even as it imprisons their bodies.

"Community" may seem a broad label for just two people, but of course there is a third prisoner in the cave, to whom Aemylia owes her life. We learn of this debt when Amoret asks Aemylia about survival:

> Thy ruefull plight I pitty as mine owne.
> But read to me, by what deuise or wit,
> Hast thou in all this time, from him vnknowne
> Thine honor sau'd, though into thraldome throwne.
> Through helpe (quoth she) of this old woman here
> I haue so done, as she to me hath showne.
> For euer when he burnt in lustfull fire,
> She in my stead supplide his bestiall desire.
>
> (4.7.19)

The old woman who supplies her own body appears genuinely selfless here; if we follow the allegory, we may conclude that lust as well as Lust acts upon this unnamed woman, but the stanza's tone and the narrative situation give more occasion for our admiration than for our censure. Aemylia expresses gratitude for help rather than horror at the woman's wickedness, and the "lustfull fire" and "bestiall desire" are "his."

After Amoret escapes, Belphoebe peers into the cave's shadows to ask who remains. With eerie spareness, Spenser tells us that she sees nothing and hears only "some little whispering, and soft groning sound" (4.7.33). Griefs shared within the cave have prepared us for pathos here, but the light of moral day requires that our sympathy make distinctions among women:

> Then forth the sad *Æmylia* issewed,
>   Yet trembling euery ioynt through former feare;
>   And after her the Hag, there with her mewed,
>   A foule and lothsome creature did appeare;
>   A leman fit for such a louer deare.
>   That mou'd *Belphebe* her no lesse to hate,
>   Then for to rue the others heauy cheare.
>
> (4.7.34)

As long as the women remained inside Lust's cave, the poem asked us to sympathize with their fear of male invasion from without. Now, however, when the cave empties itself out, a female character absorbs and re-emits that element of threat. Daylight transforms the unnamed "old woman" into a "Hag" who incurs both Belphoebe's and the narrator's contempt. The burden of disgust has moved from a male rapist to one of his captives. No one defends her; the poem does not refer to her again.

Just what distinguishes the old woman's surrender of her body in the cave from Amoret's self-"ouersight" in worrying about a stranger's sobs— or from Aemylia's own captivity to Lust? Daylight declares our questions moot by bidding us to believe its loathsome picture of the old woman's true nature and to compare this picture with Aemylia's purity. Yet Aemylia and Amoret emerge from the cave's immoral influences into a confusingly immoral world, where dashing young rescuers give sexual wounds and then more or less accidentally leave their rescued maidens to famish, as Timias does.

The relationships constructed by women who are hedged with threats of violence—Britomart and Amoret, Amoret and Aemylia, Aemylia and the old woman—differ markedly from Amoret's relationships with men after her rescue, and Spenser takes pains to underscore the difference. After Arthur has cured Amoret's wounds with herbs and restored Aemylia to her lover, he escorts Amoret onward in search of her husband. At this point, the poem carefully echoes and intensifies its earlier account of Amoret's discomfort at finding herself alone with a knight who might, within the poem's terms, justly claim a debt of gratitude from her:

> But now in feare of shame she more did stond,
> Seeing her selfe all soly succourlesse,
> Left in the victors powre, like vassall bond;
> Whose will her weakenesse could no way represse,
> In case his burning lust should breake into excesse.
> (4.9.18)

As with Britomart in canto 1, here Amoret remains unknowingly safe in Arthur's care, and as earlier, the knight with whom she travels has a romantic quest of his own. There is just one difference:

> Thus many miles they two together wore,
> To seeke their loues dispersed diuersly,
> Yet neither shewed to other their hearts priuity.
>
> (4.9.19)

Whereas Britomart and Amoret break their silence and soon become close confidantes when Britomart takes off her helmet, good breeding will not allow Arthur and Amoret to speak more than a few courteous words while circumstances dictate that they sit closely together on a horse. Or rather, Spenser calls good breeding to mind here, though he chooses not to do so in other outwardly similar situations.

The phrase "Yet neither shewed to other their hearts priuity" retroactively deepens the value of that earlier relationship with Britomart. It also retroactively makes Amoret's and Aemylia's mingled, shadowy voices all the more important in that their tenuous response to divisive violence has given the poem a means of questioning the restrictions placed upon women's public—and private—expression. In fact, the statement that neither Arthur nor his charge "shewed to other their hearts priuity" marks the end of Amoret's conversations in the entire poem, since this is the last line that brings her before our eyes. From here on, she remains silent and invisible, existing only in the mouths of other characters, who refer to her as if she were present but who never speak directly to her. In one sense, a chaste woman's silence can never be mysterious, since it is so completely expected, but Spenserian critics have long felt the necessity of imagining a lost or unwritten interpolation that would cancel the narrator's silence on the subject of Arthur's merely implicit presentation of Amoret to her voluble husband. (See 4.9.38–41, where a stanza could be inserted.)

After book 4 sets up a reunion between Scudamour and his bride, it inexplicably replaces the bride's presence with the bridegroom's story of their courtship. To paraphrase Aemylia's warning in the cave, the text apparently forgets Amoret's self to mind another. But the oddest maneuver of all in the silent presentation of the bride is simply that Scudamour does not refuse to take Amoret back. After all of her wandering and sexual wounding, she remains unproblematically blameless when she comes home to the husband whom she left on their wedding day. Scudamour need not swallow his pride or debate whether to strangle his wife in her bed, because in his account, she is still a virgin. I propose that we consider Amoret's silence in the face of Scudamour's story about her chastity and his loss of it as a type of resistance—not so much from a female character to a male one as from one of the poem's narrative voices to another. If Scudamour attempts through his oral reminiscences to reconstitute Amoret as the perfectly whole sign of his proprietary loss, crying up her value within a masculine system of meanings, then rather than interpreting her failure to reappear as her own loss of self, we can read her absence as a successful resistance to mere contextualization. The coercion of discourse joins that of desire here, and if we read this scene back into the passage about Lust's cave, the masculine forces just outside the cave's entrance pose semantic dangers as well as sexual ones. Within the story, of course, Amoret does want to return to her heterosexual context. Nevertheless, Spenser renders the cave's interior perfectly ambiguous for the poem's own set of desires. Just as a wife's body is and is not her own territory, the cave is and is not woman's context.

So it is with Amoret's body. Because Scudamour, Busyrane, Lust, and Timias are in one sense representations of the same person, Amoret's wounds become various representations of one attempt to possess her. Thus the continual retelling of Amoret's violation and reconstitution of virginity places the story of her wandering into other women's arms both before and after that of her rape, effectively allowing her straying from Scudamour not only to invite the damage that men do to her—as the traditional moral would run—but also to cure it. Nor does her husband repossess her healed body.

Even well-educated Englishwomen of the Renaissance tended to believe much of what they were told about their need for masculine protection in view of the intellectual and physical weakness of their own sex; nevertheless, their diaries, letters, and published writings give little indication of their accepting the charge of inconstancy that men routinely leveled against them. Some seventeenth-century writers, such as Elizabeth Tanfield Cary and Lady Mary Wroth, questioned the Petrarchism of previous decades for having attempted to ascertain women's interior purity by deciphering arbitrary emblems: white hands, starry eyes, golden hair.[32] One of Petrarch's most devoted followers in *The Faerie Queene* is the enchanter Busyrane, who surrounds himself and his prisoner with emblems of cruel inconstancy that carry no less power for all their unpleasantness. Busyrane misreads Amoret as someone susceptible to his rewriting, someone whose heart's blood he can make into his ink. I would argue that Spenser counteracts Busyrane's authorial misreading not so much by providing correct readings elsewhere in the poem as by testing the limits of women's power to resist the standard definitions that would bond them always to men.

What does this say about Spenser's relationship to his chief reader, a female prince? In response to recent critics' tendency to emphasize Elizabeth Tudor's participation in an androcentric social order, Philippa Berry argues that the courtly cult of Elizabeth often represents Elizabeth as a Diana surrounded by women, or as an inaccessible, feminine moon. "In order to understand her contradictory historical position *as a woman,*" Berry writes, "we have to consider the potentially subversive representation of Elizabeth as a Petrarchan or Neoplatonic beloved who also had both worldly and spiritual power."[33] Berry goes on to speculate that although Spenser begins his career by praising the cult of Elizabeth in the *Shepheardes Calender,* where Eliza is a shepherdess queen among shepherdesses, the final books of *The Faerie Queene* testify to Spenser's growing dissatisfaction with the courtly cult. Yet although I agree with Berry that Spenser begins to decenter Elizabeth as his epic progresses, it does not therefore follow that he represents all feminine power as becoming progressively weaker. On the contrary, some of the voices in his poem turn toward another sort of femininity—a femininity just as secretive as the Eliza of the cult, but far less committed to the masculine good. If Elizabeth's male courtiers and poets feel sometimes barred from the feminine interior of her circle of power, they can nevertheless participate by declaring themselves her servants and her body politic. But Amoret is not the politically powerful queen, nor is she the Petrarchan mistress whom Scudamour paints when he narrates the story of the day he stole Amoret from Venus's temple. She is, finally, no one to whom any man can bond himself.

In this way, *The Faerie Queene* puts itself in the delicate position of sympathizing with a type of feminine error that does not always benefit men. Spenser differs from more single-minded moralists of his day in the degree to which he opens his text to the very powers that threaten it— specifically to a female world not entirely controlled by male expectations. Doing this, he allows women's alliances to trouble some of the poem's most resolutely trod paths, including those that lead toward matrimony and a propertied empire, yet these glimpses from inside the female world continue to gain poetic strength after various other motivating energies of the poem have dissipated. It is true that Amoret resembles Plato's Diotima in her ability to confer poetic power. Yet Amoret's silent disappearance differs from that of Diotima in that Spenser's text, unlike Plato's, registers its own inability to speak for the woman who has vanished.

In 1615, Joseph Swetnam warned "vnmarried wantons" that their way-wardness had made them lose their very identities, leaving them without definition: "You haue . . . made your selues neither maidens, widowes, nor wiues."[34] Two years later, the pseudonymous Ester Sowernam retaliated with a pamphlet in which she described herself, with an air of defiant mystery, as "neither Maide, Wife nor Widdowe, yet really all, and there-fore experienced to defend all."[35] Amoret—who leaves her husband's side before they have consummated their marriage, undergoes a series of rapes that leave her "perfect hole," and bereaves Scudamour at the very moment of their reunion—is unreasonably neither maid, wife, nor widow. Yet she is really all, and therefore experienced to defend her particular brand of evasion and error.

Notes

An earlier version of this essay appeared in *ELH* 58 (1991):523–44; it is reprinted by kind permission of *ELH* and the Johns Hopkins University Press.

1.   Barnabe Riche, *Favltes favltes, and nothing else but favltes* (1606, STC 20983), G4v–r; Virgil, *Thee First Fovre Bookes of Virgil His Aeneis Translated intoo English heroical verse by Richard Stanyhurst, wyth oother Poëtical diuises theretoo annexed* (Leiden, 1582, STC 24806), 81.

2.   This and all further parenthetical citations are to Spenser's *Poetical Works*, ed. J. C. Smith and E. de Selincourt, Oxford Standard Authors Series (Oxford: Oxford University Press, 1912).

3.   Jonathan Goldberg, *Endlesse Worke: Spenser and the Structures of Discourse* (Baltimore: Johns Hopkins University Press, 1981), 66.

4.   Judith H. Anderson, "'In liuing colours and right hew': The Queen of Spenser's Central Books," in *Poetic Traditions of the English Renaissance*, ed. Maynard Mack and George de Forest Lord (New Haven: Yale University Press, 1982), 59–60.

5.   Lauren Silberman, "The Hermaphrodite and the Metamorphosis of Spenserian Allegory," *ELR* 17 (1987):223.

6.   Harry Berger, Jr., "Busirane and the War between the Sexes: An Interpretation of *The Faerie Queene* III.xi–xii," *ELR* 1 (1971):99–121.

7.   I am indebted to Janet Adelman for pointing out to me the Roman artist's possible sleaziness.

8.   The image of Busyrane's pillar appears in the final canto of book 3, where Spenser elaborately schematizes the violent potential of sexual desire. Spenser leaves his readers to decide whether this violence represents fear or fantasy and whether it is

filtered through Amoret's consciousness as a bride, Scudamour's as a groom, Busyrane's as an artist, or Britomart's as an onlooker:

> Ne liuing wight [Britomart] saw in all that roome,
> Saue that same woefull Ladie, both whose hands
> Were bounden fast, that did her ill become,
> And her small wast girt round with yron bands,
> Vnto a brasen pillour, by the which she stands.
>
> And her before the vile Enchaunter sate,
>   Figuring straunge characters of his art,
>   With liuing bloud he those characters wrate,
>   Dreadfully dropping from her dying hart,
>   Seeming transfixed with a cruell dart,
>   And all perforce to make her him to loue.
>   Ah who can loue the worker of her smart?
>
> (3.12.30–31)

9. Plato, *Symposium*, trans. Walter Hamilton (Harmondsworth: Penguin, 1981), 190b.

10. Ibid., 191c.

11. David Halperin, *One Hundred Years of Homosexuality, and Other Essays on Greek Love* (New York: Routledge, 1990), 131–36.

12. Ibid., 140–42.

13. Ibid., 142.

14. Ibid., 145.

15. Teresa de Lauretis, "Sexual Indifference and Lesbian Representation," in *Performing Feminisms: Feminist Critical Theory and Theatre*, ed. Sue-Elle Case (Baltimore: Johns Hopkins University Press, 1990), 20.

16. See Halperin, *One Hundred Years of Homosexuality*, 147. "Naturally," writes Berry ironi-cally, "Diotima must be fictitious, an hallucination of the otherwise impeccably rational Master. For were she not to be a figure of fantasy, behind the text of *The Symposium* would loom the disturbing shadow of woman both as mystic and as original possessor of the Socratic *logos*. And how could a search for masculine identity through sublimated desire be reconcilable with a maternal, rather than a paternal source for this system?" *Of Chastity and Power: Elizabethan Literature and the Unmarried Queen* (London: Routledge, 1989), 36.

17. Berry, *Of Chastity and Power*, 36–37.

18. Maureen Quilligan, *Milton's Spenser: The Politics of Reading* (Ithaca: Cornell University Press, 1983), 198.

19. Ibid., 206–7.

20. Ibid., 207–8.

21. Ibid., 201.

22. Though we do not know what version of the Bluebeard story Spenser would have read, we do know from *Much Ado* 1.1.186 that the story was already considered old and familiar. A. C. Hamilton makes this point, citing Earle Broadus Fowler, who takes his version of the tale from Robert Chambers. My perhaps erroneous as-sumption is that because Spenser's quotation of the jingle's first line is an exact

match, he probably knew a similar version of the rest of the tale. See A[lbert] C. Hamilton, ed., *The Faerie Queene*, by Edmund Spenser, Annotated English Poets Series (London: Longman, 1977; rev. 1980), 3.11.54n); Earle Broadus Fowler, *Spenser and the Courts of Love* (Menasha: George Banta, 1921), 56; and R[obert] Chambers, *The Book of Days: A Miscellany of Popular Antiquities* (London: W. & R. Chambers, 1862–64; rpt. 1906), 291.

23. Whereas Busyrane plies his arts to confine a woman, Barnabe Riche (*Favltes favltes*) claims it is men whose freedom of intellectual movement love curtails. These seemingly opposite arguments complement rather than cancel each other: "In loue, what seeth the eie? lasciuiousnes; what heareth the eare? lasciuiousnesse; what vttereth the tongue? lasciuiousnesse; what thinketh the heart? lasciuiousnesse; what in[c]ureth the bodie? lasciuiousnesse" (20v). For Riche, the male lover's senses do not serve as windows to the world but as claustrophobic walls. The only thing a man in love can apprehend is lasciviousness—which is to say, woman, since the surrounding text makes it clear that love's contamination proceeds from her innate impurity rather than simply from the impropriety of a particular relationship. We could pronounce Riche's cultural anatomy a rationalization, a blind for the social fact that it was women rather than men who were exhorted to confine their thoughts and speech to what the opposite sex wanted of them. On the other hand, Riche's rationalization is precisely the sort of discourse that reifies itself. Undoubtedly, men could and did sometimes feel claustrophobic in the presence of their own erotic responses to women. Spenser addresses this phenomenon early on: Red Crosse breaks out of *The Faerie Queene*'s first canto by charging from Archimago's little hermitage into the open air, terrified by a conviction that Una has begun to wander sexually. In book 2, Phaedria, whose lack of moral purpose achieves a sort of purity in its thoroughness, laughs when her perversely wandering boat restricts the choices open to each man who embarks with her in the mistaken belief that she will ferry him to his destination. Aside from all of the complex concerns for property and legitimate succession, an errant wife, fiancée, or daughter disconcerted a man by robbing him of a safe haven, while someone else's errant wife, fiancée, or daughter provided the same man with a false haven that turned into confinement (in the manner of Acrasian or of Circean islands). This was a zero-sum sexual economy; enlarged scope for her necessarily meant narrowed sights for him.

24. The courts could hold a husband legally responsible for his wife's debts. Unless he were convicted of being a pimp, a husband could not be legally punished for his wife's sexual misconduct; nevertheless, popular punishment outside the courts often took the form of skimmingtons—rough music—that could be almost as severe on the cuckold as on his wife. A husband's subjection to either legal or popular punishment proceeded from the idea that wives had no legal status separate from that of their husbands. For the husband's legal responsibility and the wife's legal duty to submit, see J. H. Baker, *An Introduction to English Legal History*, 2nd ed. (London: Butterworths, 1979), 391–99; Martin Ingram, *Church Courts, Sex and Marriage in England, 1570–1640* (Cambridge: Cambridge University Press, 1987),

143–44, 163–65, and 283; Dorothy M. Stetson, *A Woman's Issue: The Politics of Family Law Reform in England* (Westport, Conn.: Greenwood Press, 1982), 3–6; Ian Maclean, *The Renaissance Notion of Woman: A Study in the Fortunes of Scholasticism and Medical Science in European Intellectual Life* (Cambridge: Cambridge University Press, 1980), 58, 72–81; and *The Lavves Resolvtions of Womens Rights: or, The Lavves Provision for Woemen* (1632, STC 7437), passim. Maclean also gives ample evidence for philosophical, religious, medical, political, and social notions of women's essentially wayward and unstable nature (*Renaissance Notion*, passim, but especially 42, 72), and Linda Woodbridge lists pamphlets that contain both popular and learned opinions of husbands who abdicate their authority, *Women and the English Renaissance: Literature and the Nature of Womankind, 1540–1620* (Urbana: University of Illinois Press, 1984), 190–95. A. L. Beier shows that magistrates often assumed a connection between women's geographical wandering and their sexual appetites in *Masterless Men: The Vagrancy Problem in England: 1560–1640* (London: Methuen, 1985), 7, 25, 55–57. David Underdown discusses the fears enacted in skimmingtons; see "The Taming of the Scold: The Enforcement of Patriarchal Authority in Early Modern England," in *Order and Disorder in Early Modern England*, ed. Anthony Fletcher and John Stevenson (Cambridge: Cambridge University Press, 1985), ch. 4. Karen Newman gives one example of a rough music directed at a cuckold and his erring wife in "Renaissance Family Politics and Shakespeare's *The Taming of the Shrew*," *ELR* 16 (1986):86–87.

25. At the end of the second book of *Il Cortegiano*, when Castiglione's female characters rebel against several disparaging remarks made about women, they call upon a sympathetic man, Lord Julian, to defend them. In Sir Thomas Hoby's 1561 translation, Lady Emilia teases Julian, "You are counted the protector of the honour of women, therefore it is now high time to shew that you come not by this name for nothing, and . . . now must you thinke that in putting to flight so bitter an enimie, you shall binde all women to you much more, and so much, that where they shall doe nothing els but reward you, yet shall the bondage still remaine fresh, and never cease to be recompensed." A few moments later, she declares roguishly that women are not only as virtuous as men but "a great deale more, and that it is so, ye may see, vertue is the female, and vice the male" (Baldassare Castiglione, *The Book of the Courtier* [1528], trans. Sir Thomas Hoby [1561], intro. J. H. Whitfield [London: J. M. Dent & Sons, 1975], 182–83). Yet her humor has already undercut itself in the subtext of her first request, which amounts to a promise that Julian's defense of the ladies' virtue will prompt them to give it to him. As with Spenser's hermaphrodite, the metaphor of emotional and social bonding points toward a metaphor of emotional and social bondage.

26. Three standard *topoi* of the literature of anxiety about women's friendships are the Amazons, the gossips' meeting, and Diana's encounter with Actaeon. Defenders of women praised the Amazons for their courage, but even this praise was sometimes mixed with a repugnance for the Amazons' self-sufficiency. And just as often, writers used the Amazons to represent all that was wrong in interactions among women. One thinks, for example, of *Epicoene*, where the epicene is accused of being an Amazon and reviled for encouraging "her" female friends to meet and plot

against the men. Linda Woodbridge cites many examples of uneasiness about the Amazons in Shakespeare's and Jonson's plays and in pamphlets about women; see *Women and the English Renaissance: Literature and the Nature of Womankind, 1540–1620* (Urbana: University of Illinois Press, 1984), 117, 128, 142, 160, 164–65, 181, and 277. Gossips' meetings were a favorite target for misogynist pamphleteers, who represented women as meeting at one another's houses to plot against their husbands and to deride their husbands' lack of prowess with scornful descriptions of the men's sexual equipment. For selections of these pamphlets, see Katherine Usher Henderson and Barbara F. McManus, eds., *Half Humankind: Contexts and Texts of the Controversy about Women in England, 1540–1640* (Urbana: University of Illinois Press, 1985), and also Woodbridge, "The Gossips' Meeting," chapter 9 of *Women and the English Renaissance.* The story of Diana and Actaeon has served critics as a model for the Petrarchan lover's fears about his mistress, but it is worth noting that whereas the Petrarchan mistress often seems to float in a vacuum, Diana is emphatically surrounded by her protective nymphs, and it is Actaeon's breaking of this circle that earns him his horrific punishment.

27. While shopping for a valentine for my grandparents one year, I noticed a valentine that depicted a beautiful medieval woman fervently kissing the hand of a knight who had apparently just slain a dragon. Because something about the card seemed out of kilter, I took it down and looked inside. No surprises there: "You're My Knight in Shining Armour. Happy Valentine's Day." The problem was that in the picture, which was a photographic reproduction of a pre-Raphaelite painting, the knight was gazing quietly over his lady's shoulder, as though at some invisible complication or heaviness. Only when I looked at the back of the card did I learn that the painting, completed by Mary F. Raphael in 1898, was titled *Britomart and Amoret.* Whose armored dalliance is this? Britomart's? The painter's? The card writer's? Mine? Some other unsuspecting purchaser's? Which two figures does this masque pair for the dance? (Fairfield, Calif.: Marcel Schurman Company, Inc., 1988; original in the Bridgeman Art Library, London).

28. Jonathan Goldberg (*Endlesse Worke*) sees Britomart and Amoret's "embrace of friendship" as an opportunity for them to "fall into each other's arms and reveal their mutual desire to each other, sharing one another's wound" (95). Camille Paglia considers the passage more clearly homoerotic; see "The Apollonian Androgyne and *The Faerie Queene,*" *ELR* 9 (1979):51–52.

29. This often-quoted remark about Sir Guyon's form of temperance appears in Milton's *Areopagitica.* See *John Milton: Complete Poems and Major Prose,* ed. Merritt Hughes (Indianapolis: Bobbs-Merrill, 1957), 729.

30. I am indebted to James Turner for the idea cited in parentheses, which he contributed to an informal conversation about various seventeenth- and eighteenth-century texts, at the University of California, Berkeley, 10 March 1989.

31. Judith Anderson makes essentially the same point about these pronouns, but in the service of a different argument: "It is not at all clear whose 'fayned Paramour' or whose 'forced guest' Blandamour is or with whom he dares 'to dallie.' Do the pronouns in stanza 36 refer to Britomart or to Amoret? And does this sudden

blurring of referents arise from a shift in point of view—essentially a narrative or dramatic technique—from Blandamour's to Britomart's? Or is it, perhaps, meant to suggest an identification of Britomart and Amoret which, therefore, involves a sudden vaporizing of the narrative or story level? Perhaps it is worth making the point that these are precisely the interpretive choices which pertain to cantos x and xi. . . . By the end of canto i it is clear that the narrative and figurative realms are neutralizing and undermining one another." Judith Anderson, "Whatever Happened to Amoret? The Poet's Role in Book IV of *The Faerie Queene*," *Criticism* 13 (1971): 191–92.

32. In Cary's play about Mariam, Herod laments the necessity of ordering his wife's execution, since he finds that he still loves her despite his belief that she has been unfaithful. When he soliloquizes on the nature of this love, however, we see just what he will miss when Mariam is gone: her hands, her eyes, and her forehead. This Petrarchan dismembering becomes crazily appropriate in the mouth of a man who is having his wife beheaded. See Elizabeth Tanfield Cary, Lady Falkland, *The Tragedie of Mariam, the Faire Queene of Iewry* (1613; rpt. Oxford: Malone Society, 1914), act 4, scene 7. Wroth's ideas about earlier Petrarchan poetry, especially about that of her uncle, Philip Sidney, inform almost every poem in *The Countesse of Montgomery's Urania* and *Pamphilia to Amphilanthus* (1621; excerpts rpt. in *The Poems of Lady Mary Wroth*, ed. Josephine A. Roberts [Baton Rouge: Louisiana State University Press, 1983], 85–210).

33. Berry, *Chastity and Power*, 5.

34. Joseph Swetnam, *The Araignment of Lewde, idle, froward, and vnconstant women* (1615, STC 23533), 27; modern-spelling rpt. in Henderson and McManus, eds., *Half Humankind*, 204.

35. Ester Sowernam (pseud.), *Ester hath hang'd Haman; or, An Answere to a lewd Pamphlet, entituled, The Arraignment of women. With the arraignment of lewd, idle, froward, and vnconstant men, and Hvsbands* (1617; rpt. in Henderson and McManus, eds., *Half Humankind*, 217).

ROMEO AND JULIET's
Open Rs

JONATHAN GOLDBERG

O
VER the past twenty years, *Romeo and Juliet* has become the Shakespeare play assigned to more U.S. high school students than any other. *Julius Caesar* has been usurped; the sexual revolution has replaced the civics lesson. Yet, given the conservative nature of most high school curricula, one can only assume that the play is taught in formalist terms (the young vs. the old, night vs. day, love vs. society, etc.) and toward a valuation of a kind not limited to high school lesson plans. Typical in this regard might be these sentences from Brian Gibbons's "Introduction" to his Arden edition of the play (1980): "The lovers are from the outset withdrawn in an experience of sublime purity and intense suffering which renders them spiritually remote from other characters and the concerns of the ordinary world. The single clear line of ideal aspiration in love is set against the diversified complex intrigues which proliferate in the ordinary world, and contact between the two has tragic consequences."[1] In such an estimation (it recurs as the thesis in the thirty-five pages of his "Introduction" given over to—ominously—"The Play"), Gibbons would seem to be doing little more than echoing the closing lines of the play, in which the prince intones, "never was a story of more woe / Than this of Juliet and her Romeo" (5.3.308–9) as his response to the offer of Montague and Capulet to raise a monument to the dead pair of lovers:

> *Mont.* For I will raise her statue in pure gold,
> That whiles Verona by that name is known,

> There shall no figure at such rate be set
> As that of true and faithful Juliet.
>
> *Cap.*   As rich shall Romeo's by his lady's lie,
> Poor sacrifices of our enmity.
>
> (298–303)

Predictably enough, Gibbons finds in this moment that the "artifice of eternity" (74) is being erected, the statues symbolizing for him "the alchemical transmutation of worldly wealth, property, earth, into the spiritual riches of the heart and the imagination" (76).

In such estimations of the "purity" and transcendentality of their love, and, by extension, of Shakespeare's art, mystifications are set up to obscure what can as easily be read in the lines: that the corpses of Romeo and Juliet continue to have a social function, indeed that they make possible the union of the two opposing houses; moreover, this is as long lasting as the name of the city in which their monument is erected, while the material value of the statues, insisted upon as Montague and Capulet vie in their offers, is tied to that contingent temporality, to a future that cannot be predicted or controlled however much these grasping and still rivalrous fathers would do so. Reading the lines this way, one can hear them echoing against the concerns in the play, voiced over and again, about the possibility that names and words might be unmoored and uncontrollable, subject to accidents and to determinations that no artifice of eternity can secure. One could also see that the three men speaking at the end of the play are bent upon securing the social through the dead couple, and one could extend this back to the entire play, reading the love of Romeo and Juliet as imbricated in rather than separated off from "ordinary" life. The idealization of the lovers, to be brief, serves an ideological function. The marriage of their corpses in the eternal monuments of "pure gold" attempts to perform what marriage normally aims at in comedy: to provide the bedrock of the social order. Or, to speak somewhat more exactly, the heterosexual order.

Yet, what is solidified in this final set of gestures is indicated just before, when Capulet offers his hand to Montague and calls him "brother" (295). For, to speak more exactly, what the ending of the play secures is a homosocial order,[2] and it is that configuration that continually triangulates the relation of Romeo and Juliet, adding in every instance a third term that gives the lie to the shelter of their love. Romeo and Paris as possible husbands, still fighting over the body of Juliet in the final scene of the play; Capulet and Paris as the patriarchal couple trading Juliet between them; Romeo and Tybalt as enemies and yet as lovers, joined and divided by Juliet. The functioning of the patriarchy (the "brotherhood" of Montague and Capulet at the end of the play, the surrogate sonship that extends from Capulet to Paris), as well as its misfunctioning (if rivalry and enmity are that—an easily disputed point), is tied to the love of Romeo and Juliet. Indeed, what makes their love so valuable is that it serves as a nexus for the social and can be mystified as outside the social. The sexual revolution replaces the civics lesson indeed: with the myth of love as a private experience the personal is disconnected from the political.

One would think, therefore, that feminist criticism that has engaged the play would speak against the formalist project that I have conveniently fetched from the account offered by Gibbons; to a certain extent it has, and valuably, by excoriating patriarchal violence in the play. But it too dreams of the ideal world that Gibbons imagines. I take as typical the opening sentences of Coppélia Kahn's discussion of the play: "*Romeo and Juliet* is about a pair of adolescents trying to grow up. Growing up requires that they separate themselves from their parents by forming with a member of the opposite sex an intimate bond which supersedes filial bonds."[3] This seems ready for high school use; the play is translated effortlessly into modern (at any rate 1950s) terms. The tragedy of the play implied in these opening sentences has to do with the failure of Romeo and Juliet to grow up into the mature couple that has separated itself from parental bonds. Mystified, thereby, is the fact that at the end of this ideal trajectory lies the transformation of the couple into its parents; what they rebel against is also what they become. These blandly descriptive sentences reek of prescriptiveness, most notably when growing up is allowed, indeed required to have, a single heterosexual trajectory. How far this might be from *Romeo and Juliet* the term "homosocial" has already begun to suggest, and Kahn's rewriting of the play to suit her normalizing plot couldn't be clearer. For rather than breaking the filial bond, Romeo and Juliet reensure it; it is the brotherhood of Montague and Capulet that they secure. And such would have been the case too had the play been the comedy Kahn desires, in which boys would arrive at manhood free of the phallic aggression and fear of women that deform the patriarchy, for even in this benign state they would not leave behind the institutional site of marriage upon which patriarchy rests. Were the social order to work properly, Kahn implies, it would effortlessly produce heterosexuality. Shakespeare, she believes, critiques patriarchy because it does not make growing up easy; his art is on her side.

In the pages that follow, I do not seek to enlist Shakespeare for the projects of a formalist and heterosexist agenda, but rather, following Eve Kosofsky Sedgwick, to suggest that the homosocial order in the play cannot simply be reduced to a compulsive and prescriptive heterosexuality; that sexuality in the play cannot be sheltered from sociality; that sexuality in the play cannot be found enshrined in an artifice of eternity because neither the social work that the play performs nor the play itself (a formalist phantasm) can be thought of in those terms.

Accounts of the sort that I have been invoking rest upon the value of the love between Romeo and Juliet, treating it as a unique manifestation, the locus of all kinds of intensities and transcendentalities (the perfection of the individual and, concomitantly, of the work of art). So doing, critical estimations could be said to follow a path that the play itself marks out, for, at the opening of the play, Romeo is in love, but not, as it happens, with Juliet, rather with Rosaline, and from the opening of the play, Romeo is being solicited to forget her and pass on to some more responsive object. The critics, that is, manage to do what Romeo is told to do. "Forget to think of her" (1.1.223), the peace-mongering Benvolio counsels his friend—his "fair coz" (1.1.205)—a lesson he reiterates in less than exalted terms: "Tut man, one fire burns out another's burning" (1.2.45). It is a lesson Romeo learns; to Friar Laurence's worried query, "Wast thou with Rosaline?" Romeo replies, "I have forgot that name, and that name's woe." "That's my good son" his "ghostly father" returns (2.3.40–43): Benvolio and Friar Laurence have been preaching Romeo the same sermon, a lesson in forgetting that, at least in the first scene of the play, Romeo protests that he cannot learn, a lesson when, once accomplished, involves, arguably, the very transformation that Benvolio counsels, not so much a forgetting as a replacing, a substitution. Seen in that light, Juliet as replacement object is inserted within a seriality rather than as the locus of uniqueness and singularity. The play offers reasons to think about the relationship in these terms, not least when Juliet on the balcony ponders Romeo's name and likens it to the rose that remains itself whatever it is called (2.2.38–49). Is Juliet that rose, and, thereby, Rosaline renamed?

What would the consequences be of thinking of her as the newest avatar of Rosaline in the play? What, moreover, would follow from the other identification implied in Juliet's lines, one which locates Romeo in the place of the rose, and thus also in Rosaline's place? At the very least, a recognition that desire might not be determined by the gender of its object, that the coupling of Romeo and Juliet is not a unique moment of heterosexual perfection and privacy but part of a series whose substitutions do not respect either the uniqueness of individuals or the boundaries of gender difference.

These implications can be read from the start, in Benvolio's gentle solicitations of his "fair coz"; as the play opens, Benvolio knows where to find Romeo because he shares with him a like condition, "measuring his affections by my own" (1.1.124), keeping his distance as Romeo keeps his, weeping at his sorrows, displaying thereby a "love . . . that . . . / Doth add more grief to too much of mine own" (186–87); one heart vibrates to the other's:

> Romeo.   Dost thou not laugh?
> Ben.   No coz, I rather weep.
> Romeo.   Good heart, at what?
> Ben.   At thy good heart's oppression.
> Romeo.   Why such is love's transgression.
> (1.1.181–83)

"Love's transgression" here refers indifferently to the effects of Rosaline upon Romeo, dividing him from himself, and the affection, the love of Benvolio for him, marked as it is, at once, by the strongest indications of identification and distance. His counsel, that Romeo forget Rosaline, is tantamount to a desire for him to remember himself and his friend; his counsel to replace Rosaline with some other flame is undertaken in the belief that a happy Romeo would be a happier companion.

The situation with Rosaline can't help but recall the initial sequence in Shakespeare's sonnets, where the sonneteer urges the young man to marry in order to further solidify bonds between men. In those poems, as Sedgwick astutely observes, the woman is barely present, no more than the conduit for firming up the patriarchy and guaranteeing the young man's place within a social order in which all the most heavily invested relations are those between men. The woman in these poems is no one in particular, simply anyone whom the young man would marry, and she poses no threat to the men or to the love that the sonneteer proffers. Rosaline would seem to be in much the same situation; she has no lines in the play and if she ever is onstage—at the ball at the Capulet's to which she has been invited, for example—her presence is unmarked and unremarked. Benvolio's desire that Romeo replace Rosaline with some more willing young woman seems to operate within the assumption that such a woman could occupy the position of the woman in sonnets 1–17, a nonentity that would guarantee that Romeo fulfilled his debt to society and yet remained available for the comforts of friendly solicitations. Such assumptions, it might be supposed, are at play too when Friar Laurence breathes a sigh of relief that his "son" has not transgressed with Rosaline, and he hastens to legitimate the relation with Juliet by arranging their marriage. If these plans presume a smooth transition from one love to another, they also make clear that from the start Romeo's condition is not one in which love exists in the privatized domain to which commentators assign it. Romeo's absence is remarked by his parents as the play begins; his friend's counsels make clear that love affects their relation too; and Friar Laurence moves quickly to legitimize the relationship through the institution of marriage.

In this context it is worth noting that Romeo's initial oxymoronic descriptions of love are occasioned by the signs of the street fight that opens the play; that is, he reads his emotional state as the reflection of the public brawl. This is only to say from another vantage point that love, from the start of the play, is implicated in the social, not separate from it. Thus if, from one vantage point, it might appear that in moving from Rosaline to Juliet, Romeo moves from an unproblematic love to a disruptive one, the plot of replacement would seem rather in either case to recognize the sociality of desire. The difference between Romeo's two loves—of comfort and despair?—is crossed from the start, and both loves work to secure and to disrupt the social; both loves are "transgressive." Both loves are forbidden, a fact made clear when we recall the moment when Rosaline is first named in the play; her name appears on the list that Romeo reads of those invited to the Capulets' ball; she is Capulet's "fair niece" (1.2.70). "My only love sprung from my only hate" (1.5.137): Romeo may be, for Juliet, her first transgressive desire, but she is, for Romeo, the second in his pursuit of forbidden loves. When Juliet delivers her speech about Romeo and the name of the rose, she inserts him into the series in which she already participates as Romeo's substitute love, a new Rosaline with a different name (it is worth noting that the Rosaline figure in Shakespeare's source has no name).

Placing him in her place, however, Juliet follows a textual track marked out earlier. For while it is arguable, as I have argued, that the negotiations around Rosaline resemble those in the initial sequence of Shakespeare's sonnets, one moment in which those poems are recalled might suggest that the configuration is not quite the one I have already described. Romeo's complaint about Rosaline is that she is unresponsive, chaste as the moon; refusing to be "hit / With Cupid's arrow" (1.1.206–7), she is armed against love, even against "saint-seducing gold" (211): "O she is rich in beauty, only poor / That when she dies, with beauty dies her store" (213–14). These are recognizable complaints from the initial sonnets, but there they are directed at the young man who threatens by a kind of usury to make waste. These charges are laid at Rosaline as well in the lines immediately following those quoted above, when to Benvolio's query, "Then she hath sworn that she will still live chaste," Romeo replies, "She hath, and in that sparing makes huge waste." In these respects Rosaline duplicates the young man who seems to have a patent on a beauty that the sonneteer cannot imagine located anywhere but in him and a progeny of young men who will duplicate and keep forever in circulation his unmatchable beauty.

> Looke what an unthrift in the world doth spend
> Shifts but his place, for still the world injoyes it
> But beauties waste hath in the world an end,
> And kept unusde the user so destroyes it.[4]

If Rosaline is, in this respect, in the place of the young man of the sonnets, the connection is furthered by her name, for it is possible to suspect that in the sonnets her name is his; in the very first poem he is named "beauties *Rose*" (1.2). Hence, when Juliet ponders the name of the rose—a name that might as well be hers or his—her lines operate in this sphere of gender exchange too.

On the one hand this could explain why the figure of Rosaline is so unthreatening in the play, how easily Romeo's grief over her can be incorporated in homosocial relations; she is so little a woman that she might as well be a man, so little a woman that all she does is to consolidate relations between men and serve as a conduit for them. Yet before one endorses this reading, one would also have to add: she is a forbidden love, as much as Juliet is, and as threatening too. If, that is, Rosaline, and the infinite replaceability of the rose, intimate the smooth workings of a homosocial order that gives women a place only in order to erase them, the transgressive danger spied in this love—even if it is between men and so secured—is what the period might call *sodomy*. Moreover, that transgression—of alliance, of the ties of the patriarchal organization and distribution of property and entitlements—while usually thought to occur between men, can also take place between a man and a woman. Locating Rosaline as the young man, in short, might as easily place her in the sphere of the homosocial as in the space of less containable and less socially approved desires. It's here that one might suspect that the name of the rose—like the name Rosaline as it travels in Shakespeare's plays to characters in *Love's Labours Lost* and *As You Like It*, where Rosalind's other name, of course, is Ganymede—plots a trajectory from the fair young man to the dark lady. For it is of course the case that the threatening sexuality that the dark lady represents—outside marriage and promiscuous and dangerous to the homosocial order—is closer to sodomy than almost anything suggested in the poems to the young man. Yet one must think of these sets of poems in a complementary and displaced relationship rather than, as in Joel Fineman's account, as marked by the uncrossable diacritical markings homo and hetero.[5] Just as the threat to Romeo's masculinity that Juliet represents when he declares himself effeminized by her—valor's steel gone soft (3.1.111–13)—might be read not only within the dynamics of the dark lady sonnets (Juliet assuming Rosaline's guise in that transformation), but also as suggesting another movement across gender: if Romeo is feminized by her, she perhaps is masculinized. Hence, at the moment when Romeo spies Juliet on the balcony, he declares that the sun has replaced the moon; the moon earlier is Rosaline's celestial counterpart, mythically allying her to Diana. Is the sun, then, male, and is Juliet Romeo's Apollo? Such a question returns us to the position of Rosaline as fair young man and to the possibility that Juliet's gender is equally destabilized, and thereby leads us to ponder desires that are not governed by the gender of objects and which are not allied to the formations of gender difference as the homo/hetero divide imagines them.[6]

Such a way of reading the play is anathema to heterosexualizing readings of *Romeo and Juliet* and of Shakespeare in general. Thus, when Janet Adelman, for example, declares that the tragedy begins at the moment in which Romeo announces his effeminization ("O sweet Juliet, / Thy beauty hath made me effeminate / And in my temper soften'd valour's steel" [3.1.115–17]) because it signals the breakup of male-male relations in the play, solidified by their aggression toward and fear of women, this marks a tragedy that she regards as inevitable when comedy takes the form of male bonding or, worse, as it seems in Adelman's account, when male bonding can extend itself to the transvestite actor.[7] In those instances, Adelman opines, Shakespeare's plays indulge in the supposition "that one need not choose between a homosexual and a heterosexual bond" (91), a belief that she terms a fantasy that stands in the way of maturity and male development, which must culminate in heterosexuality. Otherwise, the plays might suggest "the fantasy that the relationships [with transvestite actors] are simultaneously homosexual and heterosexual—a simultaneity that threatens to become uncomfortable when, for example, in *As You Like It* we hear that Orlando has kissed Ganymede-Rosalind" (86). We, it is presumed, don't like it, and the reason seems to be that anything other than heterosexuality is repellent.

However much arguments like Kahn's or Adelman's expose the misogyny of Shakespeare's plays, their enforcement of heterosexuality and gender difference belies energies in the plays that cannot be reduced to the erasure of women. For if one thinks of Rosaline or of Juliet assuming the place of men, or of Romeo taking up a feminine position, those differences only read invidiously within the logic of a compulsory heterosexuality. When Rosaline is imagined as hoarding herself, and refusing to open her lap to gold, she is, like the young man and like the dark lady, imagined as sexually autonomous and sexually self-fulfilling. Insofar as Juliet takes up the position of Rosaline, their difference is marked by a single word. The woman who says no has become the woman who says yes; "Ay" is Juliet's first reported word (1.3.43), her first word in the balcony scene (2.2.25), and the locus of her subjectivity is her assent to desire, her active solicitation of sexual experience (see, in this respect, her play on "Ay" and "I" in 3.2.45–51). When she thinks about having sex with Romeo, she imagines cutting him up into little pieces (3.2.21–25); whether this marks her as (in the favored terms of Kahn's analysis) phallically aggressive or not, it suggests that the diacritical markings of gender are transgressed in the play, something to be seen as well earlier in the same soliloquy, in which the solicitation of night, a maternal figure, is transformed into the scene of an enactment of a "strange love" (3.2.15) in which Romeo first is night and then lies "upon the wings of night / Whiter than new snow upon a raven's back" (18–19). In this "purification" and masculinization of her beloved not only has he become—as she was—the brightness of day, but he also takes Night from behind; strange sex indeed.

It is, of course, arguable that the transgressions of gender that masculinize Juliet (or Rosaline) participate in misogyny (either by way of erasure or by excoriating active sexuality, as occurs most often in the play through attacks on the nurse), but this move across gender also allows a subject position for women that is not confined within patriarchal boundaries. That is to say, it is only by seeing the energies in the plays that are not dictated by a compulsory heterosexuality and gender binarism that one can begin to mark their productive energies. In the case of *Romeo and Juliet*, as I have been suggesting, this means to put pressure on the heterosexualizing idealization of the play and on the magical solution it arrives at over the corpses of the young lovers. It is, in short, to make them available for forbidden desires that really do call patriarchal arrangements into question. Readings of the plays, written from whatever position, that seek to enforce a compulsory heterosexuality must be complicit with the domestication of women and with the scapegoating of men (often by palming off the ills of heterosexuality on homosexuality). Such readings need to be opposed, and not merely on ideological grounds; hetero- and homosexuality are profound misnomers for the organization of sexuality in Shakespeare's time. As this essay has been suggesting, gender and sexuality in *Romeo and Juliet* do not subscribe to the compulsions of modern critics of the play.

So much Juliet's lines on the name of the rose prompt us to think, especially, as I have been suggesting, in the identifications across gender that they allow, and for the ways in which they open trajectories of desire that cross gender difference. If the rose is most literally Rosaline's name respelled, it is, with only the slightest metaphorical force, Juliet's as well, since she is not only Romeo's newest rose, but is herself locked within "orchard walls . . . high and hard to climb, / And the place death" (2.2.63–64), a dangerous flower to be plucked, dangerous, as I have been suggesting, and as this description does too, because the desires she represents are closely allied to forbidden sexual acts more usually thought of as taking place between men. Juliet is most explicitly a flower when she has apparently been taken by death. "The roses in thy lips and cheeks shall fade" (4.1.99), Friar Laurence tells her, and this is what her father sees; "the sweetest flower of the field" (4.5.29), he tells her husband-to-be, has been taken already, not, as is the case, by Romeo, but by death: Death has "lain with thy wife. There she lies / Flower as she was, deflowered by him" (36–37). Such imaginings of the sexual act as taking place in the wrong place ("the place death") and with the wrong partner only further the sense that the sexual field in which desire operates in the play is the forbidden desire named sodomy. The ungenerative locus of death allies the sexual act to the supposedly sterile and unreproductive practice of usury associated with the young man and with Rosaline's self-hoarding and waste, themselves as suggestive of sodomy as they are of masturbatory activities as well.

If the living-dead Juliet is the flower deflowered, the usual deformations of the signifier that works to make these connections in the play—the name of the rose—find a further point of transformation (of nominal difference and identification) at her funeral. Friar Laurence orders rosemary to be strewn on her supposed corpse (4.5.79) and the stage direction at line 96 suggests that it is done: *"Exeunt all but the Nurse and musicians, casting rosemary on Juliet."* Juliet's living-dead status could be taken to prevaricate in bodily terms between the generative and ungenerative desires whose paths cross each other in the play; much as she has and has not been deflowered by death, her union with Romeo is, from the end of the second act of the play, legitimated by marriage and continues to summon its allure from the unspeakable terrain of sodomy. If, in her balcony speech, Juliet joins herself to Romeo through the name of the rose—the name that connects them both through the cross-gendered figure of Rosaline as well—at her funeral the name has been transformed to rosemary. But this too has been anticipated by the vagaries of the signifier, or so the nurse reports in lines that seem to have misheard the balcony declaration and to send those lines about the rose along the route to the rosemary cast upon Juliet:

Nurse.   Doth not rosemary and Romeo begin both with a letter?
Romeo.   Ay, Nurse, what of that? Both with an 'R'.
Nurse.   Ah, mocker! That's the dog's name, 'R' is for the—No, I know it begins with some other letter; and she hath the prettiest sententious of it, of you, and rosemary, that it would do you good to hear it.

(2.4.202–8)

The circuit of desire moves through the letter R, linking Romeo, the rose, Rosaline, rosemary, and Juliet, whose name begins with some other letter but is not misspelled in this sequence, proper and improper at once like the name Rosemary attached by her to Romeo and through the rosemary to her living-dead body, or like the forbidden fruit (whose other proper name we will, in a moment, confront) that can be domesticated behind the orchard walls.

The nurse's lines deform the lovely alliteration of the letter R; she hears in it not only the growling of a desire that is less than transcendentally human—the bestial bark—but also something else. In his note on lines 205–6, Brian Gibbons allows Phillip Williams to complete the nurse's unfinished sentence: "the Nurse just stops herself from saying the word *arse*—'with a somewhat unlooked-for show of modesty.' "[8] Another name for alliteration, apt here: assonance; another name for the movement of the letter R and the cross-couplings it allows, the *open Rs*. Gibbons goes where the nurse does not, immodestly allowing the unspeakable, and not just in the margins; the word is pronounced outside the garden walls as well:

> *Mer.* If love be blind, love cannot hit the mark.
> Now will he sit under a medlar tree
> And wish his mistress were that kind of fruit
> As maids call medlars when they laugh alone.
> O Romeo, that she were, O that she were
> An open-arse and thou a poperin pear!
>
> (2.1.33–38)

The medlar, whose other name, open-arse, is this secret now pronounced, is a member of the rose family (check Webster's if you don't believe me).[9] Gibbons allows the open-arse into his text (it appears in no quarto nor in any early edition of the play), an instance, in which, as he puts it in the textual introduction of his edition, he has "retained" an "archaic" form (25) unwarranted by his copytext.[10]

I don't want to be detained here by the textual crux of 2.1.38, much as it would communicate with the other moment that has animated this discussion—the passage on the rose, which also has a famous textual problem around the very issue of the proper name or word which makes possible the open Rs of this text; or the nurse's assonance, available only in Q2, a text of the play remarkable for its self-remarking textuality.[11] Rather, I would simply notice that in this scene Mercutio begins by conjuring Romeo, naming him by his proper—which is to say, entirely generic— names: "Romeo! Humours! Madman! Passion! Lover!" (2.1.7), and that when these (im)proper names fail to raise him, Mercutio tries a more (in)direct approach, naming him by calling him up in the name of Rosaline: "In his mistress' name / I conjure only but to raise up him" (28–29). If the lines imagine Romeo rising to occupy this place, they deal at once in an identification between Romeo and Rosaline and with Romeo's desire for Rosaline. These meet in that conveniently open place that the Rs mark, the open-arse that also hits and deflects the mark (much as both Q1 and Q2 fail to deliver what Gibbons and most modern editions now allow Mercutio to say). Mercutio's lines about a blind love that does and does not hit the mark recall Benvolio's counsels earlier about the deflection of Romeo's desires from Rosaline (1.1.203–5), and they too suggest that the path of the deformations of desire away from her never leaves the spot that she marks, which is precisely the unnameable crossing here (in the modern text) not left blank or marked out or marked over. The locus of anal penetration, of course, is available on any body, male or female. Mercutio's conjuring also conjures him into the magic circle, an O that is not, as most commentators would have it be, the vaginal opening, for this is how Mercutio voices—through Rosaline—his desire for Romeo, his version, that is, of Benvolio's more benign voicing of the place she can occupy between men.[12] Mercutio is calling Romeo up for him, as he does throughout the opening acts of the play, a deflection of Romeo's desire from the unresponsive beloved, to one who, as much as Juliet later, wants to share a bed with Romeo (where Mercutio would lie is suggested by the solitary bed he goes home to, the "truckle-bed" [2.1.39] that lies under one placed above it).

As Mercutio conjures up Romeo in his generic names, and then deflects those names through the name of Rosaline, he calls up his relationship to Romeo. The secret name of Romeo in the play, as Joseph Porter has convincingly argued, is Valentine, the otherwise nonexistent brother of Mercutio named only in the list of those invited to the Capulet ball that the illiterate servant cannot read, and that Romeo does: "*Mercutio and his brother Valentine*" (1.2.68).[13] It resonates (assonates) with another name down the list, "*Signior Valentio and his cousin Tybalt*" (71). This second Valentine, as invisible elsewhere in the play as the first, participates in a cousinship that, like the brotherhood of Mercutio and Valentine, may name properly what cannot be said. This male couple resounds when Tybalt charges Mercutio with being Romeo's "consort" ("Mercutio, thou consortest with Romeo. / *Mer.* Consort?" 3.1.44–45), and to Mercutio's dismay at Romeo's declaration a few lines later that he would rather make love than fight with Tybalt. Tybalt, after all, is someone that Mercutio characterizes as ill-equipped to handle a sword; if Romeo is his man, as he declares (3.1.55), then, Mercutio opines, Romeo will follow him, taking him, it would seem, from behind. If Mercutio counsels Romeo to prick love for pricking (1.4.28), it is, it appears, because he fears that his Valentine has received the "butt-shaft" (2.4.16) of love, that Rosaline, armed like Diana, has hit his mark, that the boy love has come to the depth of his tail and buried his bauble in that hole rather than in his (see 2.4.90–100). To return to the scene of conjuring, then, is to register Mercutio's rivalry for a place that anyone might occupy and to recognize his projection into Rosaline's place as his own, as his way, that is, of occupying the magic circle or owning, to vary the metaphor slightly, the desires named by the open Rs in the text.

That these desires can be named variously, and never properly, Mercutio's lines further intimate when the secret name is one that maids trade among themselves in private. Female secrecy is broached in those lines, and appropriated to a secret about transgression that does not respect gender difference. If there is, in this context, something to be said about the textual crux at 2.1.38, it is perhaps best suggested by J. Dover Wilson's gloss in the Cambridge edition of the play (1955) on the reading that is adopted by Gibbons (and by a number of other editions, most recently by Stanley Wells and Gary Taylor in their 1986 Oxford *Complete Shakespeare*). Q1, as noted above, has "open *Et caetera*" at this point while Q2 prints "An open, or thou" (D1v). Wilson argues that a compositor or scribal error is responsible for "or" (as a misreading of manuscript "ers," the presumption that leads Gibbons to "retain" a reading not found in any printed text but assumed to have been in Shakespeare's hand). In writing his note on the crux, Wilson conveniently ignores the comma in Q2 which might, like the unfinished sentence of the nurse's, indicate that Mercutio leaves unsaid what needs not be said (the alternative name for the medlar is about as available as anything, an open secret not to be said more openly). This allows him to dispose of the possibility that "or" means "or" rather than being a misread arse. "He speaks," Wilson opines, "of the fruits [the ripely rotten apple and the popping pear] as complementary not alternative so that 'and' not 'or' is required" (151). "And" introduces, anglice, the "bad" Q1 evasion of the more forthrightly named Rs. For Wilson, this is what is proper and required at this spot, that her arse and his poperin complement each other. In other words, Wilson reads "and" to mean "or" (inserts "and" in his text so that it does so) since "or" might mean "and"; "or," were it to be there, might offer an "alternative" that Wilson will not allow, the possibility that either member of the couple could assume either position. This is perhaps the scandal that the whispering of the maids is about, or that can be heard as Juliet swallows the potion in order to get Romeo in the grave before Tybalt does ("O look, methinks I see my cousin's ghost / Seeking out Romeo that did spit his body / Upon a rapier's point! Stay, Tybalt, stay" 4.3.55–57). In those lines Juliet assumes Mercutio's rivalrous position, while Tybalt functions for her—as he had for Romeo, and as he does earlier for Juliet in a scene that prevaricates over and also enforces the identity of her cousin and her lover (3.5.65–125)—as the switching point for an identification that breaches love and enmity, friend and villain, death and life, the open arse and the open grave of transgressively (un)productive desires. What these moments share—and they structure the trajectories of desire imagined in the play—is the recognition that anyone—man or woman—might be in the place marked by the open Rs of *Romeo and Juliet*.

Notes

1. Brian Gibbons, ed., *Romeo and Juliet* (London: Methuen, 1980), 70. All citations are from this edition. For further evaluations of this edition, see my review of it in *Shakespeare Studies* 16 (1983):343–48 and Stanley Wells's review in *TLS* 4030 (20 June 1980):710. G. Blakemore Evans in his New Cambridge edition of the play (Cambridge University Press, 1984) devotes pp. 16–20 to "language, style and imagery" in familiar formalist terms.

2. I take the term from its usage by Eve Kosofsky Sedgwick, *Between Men* (New York: Columbia University Press, 1985), and in the pages that follow depend upon her arguments throughout the book as well as their particular application to Shakespeare in the chapter "Swan in Love."

3. "Coming of Age in Verona," reprinted from *Modern Language Studies* 8 (1977–78):5–22 in Carolyn Ruth Swift Lenz, Gayle Greene, and Carol Thomas Neely, eds., *The Woman's Part* (Urbana: University of Illinois Press, 1980), 171–93.

4. 1609 text quoted from *Shakespeare's Sonnets*, ed. Stephen Booth (New Haven: Yale University Press, 1978), 9.9–12.

5. Fineman's account in *Shakespeare's Perjured Eye* (Berkeley: University of California

Press, 1986) compulsively reproduces this distinction—even claiming for Shakespeare nothing less than the invention of "the poetics of heterosexuality" (18), yet, as he moves to take up the issue of cross-coupling, and with it the phenomena of the pricked prick and the cut cunt (see, e.g., pp. 275 ff.), as he terms them, the difference between hetero- and homosexuality is breached. Nonetheless, the mode of breaching is by the route of castration and thus operates under the aegis of the oedipal and thereby within the heterosexualizing argument that allows for difference only under that rubric.

6. Work on the historicity of gender that would lend support to these suppositions would include Stephen Greenblatt's "Fiction and Friction," in *Shakespearean Negotiations: The Circulation of Social Energy in Renaissance England* (Oxford: Clarendon Press, 1988), esp. pp. 73–86; Thomas Laqueur's *Making Sex* (Cambridge: Harvard University Press, 1990); and Ann Rosalind Jones and Peter Stallybrass, "Fetishizing Gender: Constructing the Hermaphrodite in Renaissance Europe," in Julia Epstein and Kristina Straub, eds., *Body Guards* (New York: Routledge, 1991).

7. See Janet Adelman, "Male Bonding in Shakespeare's Comedies," in Peter Erickson and Coppélia Kahn, eds., *Shakespeare's Rough Magic* (Newark: University of Delaware Press, 1985); pp. 80–81 are on *Romeo and Juliet*.

8. G. Blakemore Evans also cites Williams at this point in his New Cambridge edition, but then misunderstands the implications of the nurse's speech: "Obviously she can't read or spell, and because of its rude associations she decides that 'Romeo' and 'rosemary' must begin with some other letter" (p. 115). The nurse, however, registers that she stops herself from saying a word that sounds like it begins with an R but doesn't; Evans's swipe at the nurse's illiteracy displaces, one suspects, his discomfort at the associations implicated in the nurse's assonance.

9. I'm grateful to Natasha Korda for pointing this out to me as well as to a set of notes she prepared on the crux in Mercutio's lines which has helped me think through the points argued here.

10. For a glance at this "retention" (anal?) and its supposed restoration of an original unavailable in any text that might claim to be close to a Shakespearean original, see Random Cloud, "The Marriage of Good and Bad Quartos," *Shakespeare Quarterly* 33 (1982):430–31. For a defense of the properness of this scandalous reading by the modern editor who first printed it in his 1954 Yale edition of the play, see Richard Hosley, "The Corrupting Influence of the Bad Quarto on the Received Text of *Romeo and Juliet*," *Shakespeare Quarterly* 4 (1953):21. Hosley would rather have *open-arse* than allow his text to be "contaminated" by the "bad quarto," Q1, which reads "open *Et caetera*" (D1r) at this spot.

11. For pursuit of the crux about the name of the rose, up to the point engaged in this essay, I refer the reader to an earlier essay of mine, " 'What? in a names that which we call a Rose': The Desired Texts of *Romeo and Juliet*," written for and delivered at the 1988 session of an annual conference at the University of Toronto on editorial and textual matters and forthcoming in the volume of papers from that meeting, *Crisis in Editing: Texts of the English Renaissance*, ed. Randall McLeod. In that essay I call into question the usual supposition that of the two quarto editions of the play, Q1

(1597) is simply a "bad quarto" (shaped by the memories of actors and the imposition of nonauthorial materials), while Q2 (1599) is authoritative and derived from Shakespeare's hand; rather, I suggest, both texts arise from a theatrical milieu of continual revision and rewriting, and no modern text of the play can fail to consult both or can easily adjudicate differences between the two texts or, as often happens, when Q2 offers more than one version of the same set of lines, in the hope of arriving at final or original authorial intention. I argue that intentionality was never so limited.

The crux involved in 2.1.38 will be unraveled in the discussion that follows; in Q1 the line alludes to an "open *Et caetera*" (D1r), which, were one to take that script as depending solely on stage performance, would mean that this reports the line as spoken (i.e., as speaking and possibly evading speaking more forthrightly), though it is also possible to regard the *Et caetera* either as a way of naming otherwise what need not be named any more forthrightly or as an evasion of more direct naming supplied by the printer and not following what the actor actually said.

At this point, Q2 reads "open, or," (D1v), and, it is assumed, as I discuss below, that "or" represents a misreading by the compositor of Shakespeare's hand ("ers" is assumed to have been in the manuscript); the notion that "arse" was once really in the text or spoken on stage is not quite so easily made, however, since the comma in Q2 might indicate that a pause, and not a word, was offered at this spot. Again, one faces the dilemma of whether an unsaying said more than the more forthright reading offered by Gibbons; whether the lines in each earlier text have been censored, and if so, by whom; what, if anything, was actually spoken by the actor at this point; or, indeed, whether there was one way in which this line ever was delivered. Or, finally, whether this massive textual problem does not also correspond to the very nexus of the utterly unspeakable / absolutely commonplace nature of anal sex, in this instance dictated by all the proprieties surrounded by the supposed unbreachable difference between the allowable spheres of male-male intimacy and the excoriated one called sodomy, or between the supposition that the only "good" sex performed by male-female couples is procreative and conducted under the auspices of marriage, everything else being capable of being called, once again, sodomy.

12.   I follow Joseph Porter here, who argues in *Shakespeare's Mercutio* (Chapel Hill: University of North Carolina Press, 1988) that the lines "involve the idea of Mercutio's taking Rosaline's place not only as conjurer but also as container of Romeo's phallus" though I do not follow him in wishing to make this the "fleeting apparently subliminal trace of sexual desire on Mercutio's part" (157) since that assumption implies that homoerotic desire must operate within the regimes of a closet that, I think, more appropriately might be seen as part of the modern apparatus of sexuality with its markers of homo- and heterosexuality. Since these desires are not distinguished and their boundaries are more fluid in Shakespeare's time, there is no need to make them unavailable, which locating homoeroticism as subliminal does. On pp. 160–62, Porter ably dismantles the heterosexualizing readings of this moment, in which even an open-arse is read as a figure for female genitalia, the most extraordinary of such instances perhaps being that of Eric Partridge, *Shakespeare's*

Bawdy (London: Routledge, 1990 [1947]): "'An open *et-caetera*' must here mean 'an open arse'. Yet my interpretation of Shakespeare's 'open *et-caetera*' as 'pudend' is correct, for the opening clearly refers to the female cleft, not the human anus. With the human bottom regarded as involving and connoting the primary sexual area, compare the slangy use of *tail* for the human bottom in general and for the female pudend in particular" (101–2). While Porter valuably insists that Mercutio's lines are about sodomy, his concession that "of course the sodomy is heterosexual" (161) could be seen as complicit with the heterosexualizing of Partridge and other commentators on the line precisely because it differentiates homo- and heterosexual sodomy. The acts are not so distinguishable; moreover, the conceptual range of the term sodomy in the period does not heed the hetero/homo distinction, as Alan Bray makes clear as a starting point in his discussion in *Homosexuality in Renaissance England* (London: Gay Men's Press, 1982), 14. My arguments above about a transgressive sodomy, and its link to cross-gender relations, seek to void this diacritical marker, and the move seems to me important both because it takes account of the history of sexuality but also insofar as it opposes the ways in which the distinction of homo- and heterosexual sodomy was mobilized in the U.S. Supreme Court decision in *Bowers v. Hardwick*, which denied any fundamental constitutional right for acts of so-called "homosexual sodomy" while guaranteeing the legality of the act for heterosexuals.

13.   See Joseph A. Porter, "Mercutio's Brother," *South Atlantic Review* 49 (1984):31–41, and the fuller development of the argument in *Shakespeare's Mercutio*, 1–10, 145–63.

The Epistemology of Expurgation:
Bacon and THE MASCULINE BIRTH
OF TIME

GRAHAM HAMMILL

> *Bacon:* I have persuaded men, and shall persuade
> them for ages, that I possess a wide range of
> thought unexplored by others, and first opened
> by me. Few subjects that occurred to me have
> I myself left untouched or untried: one
> however, hath almost escaped me, and surely
> one worth the trouble.
> *Hooker:* Pray me Lord, if I am guilty of no
> indiscretion, what may it be?
> *Bacon:* Francis Bacon.
> —Walter Savage Landor, *Imaginary Conversations*

Ask any writer about the anxiety that he experiences when faced by a blank sheet of paper, and he will tell you who *is* the turd of his fantasy [qui *est* l'etron de son fantasme]. —Jacques Lacan, "Subversion of the Subject and the Dialectic of Desire"

FRANCIS Bacon's unpublished fragment *Temporis Partus Masculus*, or *The Masculine Birth of Time*, written in either 1602 or 1603, is one of the first elaborations of his new epistemology. It is a failed experiment whose subsequent, almost compulsive revision in Bacon's later and more monumental attempts to write a new epistemology points to the Baconian corpus as a kind of palimpsest upon which *The Masculine Birth* and following texts are written, and from which *The Masculine Birth* is expurgated. More to the point, the expurgation of this fragment establishes the receptive surface of Bacon's corpus as a palimpsest—a surface punctuated by purgings most legible in their insistent repetition when Bacon theorizes the epistemological relationship between himself and his readers.

Finding a mode of writing that effectively transmits knowledge is fundamental to Bacon's epistemological project, to be sure, and Bacon is especially sensitive to the difficulties due to stylistic complexities and misunderstandings—due to, as Bacon writes in *The Advancement of Learning*, "a kind of contract of error between the deliverer and the receiver: for he that delivereth knowledge desireth to deliver it in such form as may be best believed, and not as may be best examined; and he that receiveth knowledge desireth rather present satisfaction than expectant inquiry; and so rather not to doubt than not to err."[1] Bacon's stylistic strategy is not to unravel this contract of error. Even though this mode of delivery "seemeth to be a way that is abandoned and stopped up," nonetheless Bacon makes this contract of error central to both his style of writing and to his epistemology. He manipulates this contract by deferring the promised "present satisfaction" of understanding in favor of a temporally protracted "expectant inquiry," thus forcing his readers to recast the experience of recognition, however satisfying or jubilant it may seem at first, as an experience of *mis*recognition. To the former, "Magistral" method of presentation, Bacon adds a method that he calls "Probation"—a method that allows "a man" to "revisit and descend into the foundation of knowledge" (6:290) because it delivers knowledge "*in the same method wherein it was invented*" (6:289, Bacon's emphasis).

In *The Masculine Birth of Time* Bacon uses the metaphor of the palimpsest to characterize this temporally protracted "expectant inquiry." Specifically, he uses the metaphor of the palimpsest to theorize a model of pedagogical writing and reception that establishes a particular temporal relation between teacher-writers and student-readers, a temporality dependent on the act of purging. Without the experience of purging, there can be no understanding. "To grapple immediately with the bewildering complexities of experimental science before your mind has been purged of its idols" ("Ego vero (fili) si te jamjam animo ab idolis non repurgato vertiginosis experientiae ambagibus committerem")[2]—this would amount to readerly confusion and, even worse, would prompt a reader to desert or abandon the lesson at hand. Confused and potentially mutinous, Bacon's reader must be purged to be able to accept the "complexities of experimental science" as something familiar. The experience of purging, however, while it can be enacted, cannot be represented per se. "On waxen tablet you cannot write anything new until you rub out the old. With the mind it is not so; there you cannot rub out the old till you have written the new" (72). ("In tabulis nisi piora deleveris, non alia inscripseris. In mente contra: nisi alia inscripseris, non priora deleveris" [7:32].) Bacon uses the example of the waxen tablet to explain how it differs from the mind. According to Bacon, the mind, unlike a waxen tablet, can sustain no blank moments. While with a waxen tablet the new can be written only after the old has been erased, with the mind the *experience* of the new must precede the *understanding* of the new for it to succeed in replacing the old. Thus, neither simply rubbing out the old nor writing in the new will suffice: "Nor, even if you were inclined to do so, would you rid yourself of idols by simply asking any advice without familiarizing yourself with Nature" (72). ("Idola autem exuere simplici praecepto meo sine rerum notitia, ne, si velles maxime, posses" [7:32].) For Bacon, no simple replacement will suffice. Rather, Bacon's student-reader needs an experience, analogous to the rubbing out of the old, that will prepare his mind for an understanding of the new, an experience situated between understanding of the new and riddance of the old—an experience cast most generally as purging.

To say that this relationship between Bacon and his readers is solely epistemological is not enough, however, since purging also defines the sexuality of the Baconian corpus. As much as the Baconian corpus insists on an epistemology of expurgation to prepare the reader's mind for the reception of a new science, the Baconian corpus also insists on a sexuality of purging, the experience of which creates an erotic link between men. In effect, I want to argue, this slippage from an epistemology of expurgation to a sexuality of purging depends on a sense of self, or subjectivity, created by Bacon's representation of truth. Put most tersely: Bacon's search for truth produces a sense of self, a subjectivity, in which what is *not known*, what remains *un*represented, defines what counts as sexuality.

Probing, opening up, purging the intellect, expurgating the mind, and making the intellect clean and pure—this is how Bacon variously describes the effects of his epistemological project on his readers throughout his writings. "Do you suppose," Bacon asks his reader, "when all the approaches and entrances to men's minds are beset and blocked by the most obscure idols—idols deeply implanted and, as it were, burned in—that any clean and polished surface remains in the mirror of the mind on which the genuine natural light of things can fall?" (*MBT*, 62). ("An tu censes, cum

omnes omnium mentium aditus ac meatus obscurissimis idolis, iisque alte
haerentibus et inustis, obsessi et obstructi sint, veris rerum et nativis radiis
sinceras et politas areas adesse?" [7:17].) In *The Masculine Birth of Time*, the
mind, because it is blocked by idols, "exacerbated by violent oppositions,"
not only acts out the difference between "genuine natural light" and its
resemblance reflected in the unpolished mirror of the mind; more important, the mind internalizes that difference, so that Bacon's search, at least in
The Masculine Birth of Time, is for "a new method" that purges this difference
by allowing "for quiet entry into minds so choked and overgrown" (62).

We can see this strategy at work in Bacon's *Essays*, to be sure; however,
instead of calming a reader frenzied by violent oppositions, Bacon exacerbates that exacerbation. Somewhat like jesting Pilate who asks "What is
Truth?" (12:81) and does not stay for an answer, Bacon, too, asks the
question and refuses to stay put. Bacon defines truth through the necessity
of "a mixture of a lie": "Doth any man doubt that if there were taken out
of man's minds vain opinions, flattering hope, false valuations, imaginations as one would, and the like, but it would leave the minds of a number
of men poor shrunken things, full of melancholy and indisposition, and
unpleasing to themselves?" For the Bacon of the *Essays*, since truth is
expressed through lies and "doth judge itself," it is never singular, but
always double. Truth is never a matter of similitude for Bacon, but a
matter of dissimilitude—truth differing from itself to judge itself. Thus,
the crucial issue for Bacon is not so much how to achieve or dis-cover the
truth as it is truth's effects on the mind. "It is not the lie that passeth
through the mind," Bacon writes, "but the lie that sinketh in and settleth
in it, that doth the hurt" (12:82). In Bacon's epistemological search, this
latter lie, the one that sinks in, must be forced to pass through; it must be
purged. This purging does not guarantee a sense of psychological wholeness, however. Because the truth is split, so too is the sense of self that it
assumes. In "Of Simulation and Dissimulation," Bacon elaborates three
versions of this split sense of self:

> The first: closeness, reservation, and secrecy, when a man leaveth
> himself without observation or without hold to be taken what he is.
> The second: dissimulation, in the negative, when a man lets fall signs
> and arguments that he is not that he is. And the third: simulation, in
> the affirmative, when a man industriously and expressly feigns and
> pretends to be that he is not. (12:96)

The first, which assumes a politic and moral "habit of secrecy," and the second, which assumes a cunning "secrecy by necessity" (12:97), expose the self to others as a dissembling self. The third, however, what Bacon calls simulation, ends up being psychological dissimulation, not only being not what one is, but also exposing this dissimulation to no one. Bacon's point is not that one can control the truth by speaking it, but rather that one cannot help speaking the truth by lying: "Tell a lie and find a troth" (12:98).

Thus, Stanley Fish argues that the experience of the Baconian essay is the experience of deception, one that tricks the reader into rejecting "a too easy acceptance" of generalizations, into "an awareness of the unresolved complexity of the matter under discussion," and, most importantly, into "an open and inquiring mind."[3] For Fish, Bacon is *the* dissembler par excellence. If Bacon's essays are scientific, Fish argues, then they are in no way objective. Rather, according to Fish, Bacon moves from the materials of the essays to "the *experience* that form provides" (12:81). This form, I am arguing, depends on Bacon's representation of truth as split. According to Fish, there are two steps in Bacon's stylistic program: first, a recognition of the necessity of misrecognition whenever language is concerned, and second, an effacement of that necessity. "If the 'cautions' Bacon institutes are successful, the mind may once again be a 'clear glass,' unclouded by errors and misconceptions; and then (but only then), when understanding no longer distorts what is presented to it, will the transparent effortless style of the Royal Society ideal be proper for the transmission of truth."[4] While the second step—a transparent, effortless style—may be the articulated, ideal goal of Bacon's epistemology, nonetheless the first step—a recognition of the necessity of misrecognition—makes the second step impossible, because the experience of Bacon's form invents not only a subject split from itself, but also an object that expresses or embodies that difference—the object "whereby the imagery doth appear in figure," as Bacon puts it most tersely (12:171).[5] Bacon's *Essays* do not so much move away from the material of their content as they focus on the effects of that object that expresses formal duplicity. For instance, in "Of Friendship" Bacon explains both a man's need for a friend, since "many things there are which a man cannot do himself" (12:173), and the dangers of having a friend, since, as Fish points out, all of Bacon's examples of good friends—Pompey and Sylla, Brutus and Caesar, Augustus and Agrippa, Tiberius and Sejanus, Comineus and Duke Charles the Hardy—involve one friend's betrayal or murder of the other.[6] While the simultaneous need for and danger of friendship create in "a man . . . two lives in his desires" (12:173), a life based on the self-sufficiency of the body, which friendship destroys, and a life in a cultural and historical order, which friendship sustains, this need and danger finds its support in an object which is the "principal fruit of friendship," the "ease and discharge of the fullness and swellings of the heart" (12:166). These two desires are literally embodied by the purged heart, since, on the one hand friendship "openeth the heart" so that one may "impart griefs, joys, fears, hopes, suspicions, counsels, and whatsoever lieth upon the heart to oppress it" (12: 167), on the other hand, in the examples that Bacon gives, friendship results quite literally in the heart cut open by the murderer who murders his friend.[7]

The Masculine Birth of Time produces this object that expresses difference as a psychological effect of misinterpretation. Bacon presents a version of bad reader-response, one based on an epistemology of mimesis:

> Take a man who understands only his own vernacular. Put into his hands a writing in an unknown tongue. He picks out a few words here and there which sound like, or are spelled like, words in his own tongue. With complete confidence he jumps to the conclusion that their meaning is the same, though as a rule this is very far from true. Then, on the basis of this resemblance, he proceeds to guess the sense of the rest of the document with great mental exertion and equal license. This is a true image of these interpreters of nature. For each man brings his own idols—I am not now speaking of those of the stage, but particularly those of the market-place and those of the cave—and applies them, like his own vernacular, to the interpretation of nature, snatching at any facts which fit in with his preconceptions and forcing everything into harmony with them. (69–70)

> (Prorsus ita et in universalibus theoriis fit. Nam veluti si quis lingua tantum vernacula uti sciens [adverte, fili, nam simile est admodum] scripturam ignoti sermonis capiat, ubi paucula quaedam verba sparsim observans suae linguae vocabulis sono et literis finitima, illa quidem statim ac fidenter ejusdem esse significationis ponit [licet ab ea saepius longissime recedant], postea ex iis invicem collatis reliquum orationis sensum multo ingenii labore, sed et multa libertate, divinat; omnino tales et isti naturae interpretes inveniutus. Nam

idola quisque sua [non jam scenae dico, sed praecipue fori et spe-
cus], veluti linguas vernaculas diversas, ad historiam afferentes, con-
festim quae simile aliquid sonant arripiunt; caetera ex horum sym-
metria interpretantur. [7:27–28])

By interpreting nature based on a model of resemblance or correspondence, this interpreter experiences "with complete confidence" the satisfaction of recognition. However, instead of presenting a true interpretation of nature, this interpreter forces his interpretation of nature to
conform to his own idols. He thus internalizes the difference between his
interpretation and the nature that he interprets, the effect of which is his
alienation both from nature as well as from truth. Bacon's project fails for
the same reason that this interpretation of nature fails. It announces an
impossible epistemological project, the satisfactory performance of "the
legitimate mode of handing on the torch of science" (61)—a "vital principle which will stand up against the ravishes of time" (62)—("ut vim
quandam insitam et innatam habeat tum ad fidem conciliandam, tum ad
pellendas injurias temporis" [7:17]); a hot, phallic, "bright and radiant
light of truth, shedding its beams in all directions and dispelling all error
in a moment" (70)—("veritatis lumen clarum et radiosum, quod omnia
collustret, et errores universos momento dispellat" [7:29]). Bacon's hope is
to hand over a vital principle that dispels error by filling out the difference
between a thing and its resemblance; the problem, however, is that this
vital principle does not exist—or more precisely, it exists only in its differentiation from itself: "Genuine truth is uniform and self-reproducing"
(71). It is both one thing, "uniform," and divided from itself in its own
self-production, "self-reproducing." There is no vital principle, no "radiant light of truth," that can dispel all error "in a moment," that can fill out
the difference between a thing and its resemblant without also forcing a
division of the subject. Thus, the failure of this fragment is the failure to
produce the *kind* of object that Bacon announces. Even so, Bacon's fragment does produce an object, one whose rhetorical impact is to differentiate itself from itself in its failure to achieve what the Baconian program
promises. If Bacon's reader takes this object to be "genuine truth," then
that object becomes yet another idol of the mind that must in turn be
purged.

It is perhaps this quality that led Benjamin Farrington to assume that
Bacon's inability to complete *The Masculine Birth of Time* was due to its

abusive style. Farrington writes that toward the end of this monologue "Bacon [had] begun to suspect that the style of abuse he [had] adopted [was] likely both to cause confusion and to give offense."[8] However, as my discussion above of the essays suggests, Bacon never stopped performing this "style of abuse." In his subsequent writings, Bacon demands and enacts the probing and purging of the intellect, whereas in *The Masculine Birth of Time* he addresses a *specific* intellect to be purged, a young man whom he calls "fili," "my son." In *The Masculine Birth of Time*, when Bacon refutes and abuses Aristotle, Plato, Galen, Paracelsus, and Hippocrates, he does so specifically for the young man—not to make him understand ("You very likely do not understand my refutation of them" [70], Bacon writes), but rather to prepare him for understanding. Bacon explains himself:

> It is bad luck for me that, for lack of men, I must compare myself with brute beasts. But when you have had time to reflect you will see things differently. You will admire beneath the veil of abuse the spirit that has animated my attack. You will observe the skill with which I have packed every word with meaning and the accuracy with which I have launched my shafts straight into their hidden sores. (70)
>
> (Verum sub velo maledicti miras accusationum animas, et singulari artificio in singula fere verba contractas et reductas, et exquisitissima oculi acie in ipsa criminum ulcera, directas et vibratas, postmodum respiciens videbis. [7:28–29])

Bacon performs the new for the young man by attacking the old, all the while banking on the young man's recognition of his own inability to understand the skill that Bacon has just performed. All Bacon needs is for the young man to become interested in this skill, in the promised new, so that he can perform *on* the young man what he performs *for* the young man—so that he can purge the young man's idols by exposing and launching shafts into the young man's hidden sores. Thus Bacon's seductive plea and promise at the end of *The Masculine Birth*: "Take heart, then, my son, and give yourself to me so that I may restore you to yourself" (72). ("Confide [fili], et da te mihi, ut te tibi reddam" [7:32].) One hand purges and launches shafts while the other offers to restore—more than restore: it offers to pass on Bacon's generous gift, the burning torch of science.

If, as I have claimed, Bacon fails in handing on the torch of science, this failure also necessitates the repeated purgings of Bacon's readers, to prepare them for the torch that they end up never quite receiving. Instead of handing on the phallic torch of science, Bacon repeatedly enacts the purging of his readers, forcing the rubbing out of the old through the experience of purging. To be more precise, purging locates a temporal moment between riddance of the old and understanding of the new, one that produces Bacon's generous gift not as a "vital principle," but as an object already at least partly insufficient, though perhaps not yet understood as such. Purging, in other words, looks like palimpsest revision. The insufficiency of this object continually rewrites the Baconian reader, including the young man, as formally divided: to be united "with things in themselves in a chaste, holy, and legal wedlock" (72), the young man, like "self-reproducing truth," must be split; he must give himself over to Bacon so that Bacon can give him the gift of restoration.[9]

Bacon was a notoriously generous gift giver, and he was especially generous to his male servants, which prompted his mother to complain in a letter to his brother that he kept a particular servant "as a coach companion and as a bed companion,"[10] and which caused Aubrey to speculate in his *Brief Lives* that "he was a [pederast]" and that "his Ganimeds and favourites took bribes."[11] According to Alan Bray, the giving of gifts is what lets Bacon be recognized as what we might (retroactively) call homosexual: "Francis Bacon was apparently in the habit of having sexual relations with his male servants; this would probably have gone unnoticed had it not been for his prodigal generosity to them, which was the subject of a good deal of disapproving comment."[12] Although these scenes of Bacon's generosity plausibly entail a male-male erotics infused by eroticized differences of class and of age, if we stay attuned to the language of purging in Bacon's *Masculine Birth* and to its sites of transmission, we can glimpse another figuration of erotic attachment, one whose amazing, somewhat compulsive regularity is indelibly marked with writerly anxiety. In his diary Bacon meticulously elaborates a regime of enemas that he hoped would cure him of painful body heat and gas. He took what he called his "familiar cooling glyster [clyster]" twice a day four or five days in a row, one at four o'clock in the afternoon and the other before going to bed, "for that the one styrreth the more viscous humour and the other carry it away."[13] Besides enemas, Bacon also took purging pills—the problem with either method being that after "certen inward pleasure" Bacon "found great vapourousnesse and disposicion *ad Motu mentis,* much wynd, great and glowing and sensible heat sub hypochondrus, wth some burnyng and payne more than usuall, besides wyndynes and rasping" (80). Bacon complains that "after a good purge or purge repeted the 5th and sometymes 4th day," his farting and heat only worsen. "The more ease I fynd for the tyme, the woorse I fynd upon ye return" (80). Like the structure of temporality to which Bacon attempts to subject the young man in *The Masculine Birth,* this temporality of the enema promises a new ease that only returns Bacon to the old burning. Moreover, like the anticipated purging of the young man that is repeated in the expurgation of *The Masculine Birth of Time* from the Baconian corpus, this section of Bacon's diary is crossed out and purged, though not made so unreadable that it cannot be included in James Spedding's voluminous *Letters and Life of Francis Bacon.* Neither erased nor completely expurgated, only crossed out and marked through, Bacon's experience of purging is made readable *as* writerly anxiety.

Thus, in the Baconian corpus, not only is the epistemology of expurgation repeated between writer and reader, teacher and student, older man and younger man, but it is also repeated as physical expurgation. Both the physical and the epistemological establish an impossible, though promised restoration, be it "genuine truth" or "ease" and "inward pleasure," that also assumes a split subject, a "frenzied" reader split in the "violent opposition" that Bacon's prose demands, the "burnyng" and anxious Bacon split between past ease and future pain. As I have shown, this split is both necessary to and a product of the epistemological restoration that Bacon promises both at the end of *The Masculine Birth of Time* and elsewhere in his prose, and it is both necessary to and a product of the "certen inward pleasure" that enemas offer as well. Because of the promised restoration, Bacon produces a formal structure of restoration or revision whose net epistemological effect is to place knowledge in the seat of truth—that is to say, whose net epistemological effect is to purge the idea of stable truth and replace it with a notion of reconstructed and reconstructible knowledge. And because of the promised "ease," Bacon produces a formal structure of health or cure whose net physical effect is to place purging quite literally in Bacon's seat.

It is the overlapping of the physical and the epistemological that makes for a sexuality of expurgation. Sexuality appears to the subject not in and of itself, but rather, as Lacan puts it, as "deduced from something other than sexuality itself":

> Sexuality is established in the field of the subject by a way that is that of a lack.
>
> Two lacks overlap here. The first emerges from the central defect around which the dialectic of the advent of the subject to his own being in relation to the Other turns—by the fact that the subject depends on the signifier and that the signifier is first of all in the field of the Other. This lack takes up the other lack, which is the real, earlier lack, to be situated at the advent of the living being, that is to say, at sexed reproduction. The real lack is what the living being loses, that part of himself *qua* living being, in reproducing himself through the way of sex. This lack is real because it related to something real, namely, that the living being, by being subject to sex, has fallen under the blow of individual death.[14]

While the epistemology of purging that Bacon elaborates in *The Masculine Birth of Time* both exposes the young man's inadequacies, his "hidden sores," and reproduces the young man as split, while the physical enema both exposes Bacon's purged anus and reproduces him as split between the old burning and a fleeting "inward pleasure," the sexuality of Bacon's corpus depends on equivocations that embody this split, above all on the equivocations that define expurgation. The repetition of expurgation speaks to Bacon's purged, incomplete *Masculine Birth*; to his purged readers, still left without truth; and to his purged anus, still burning. Purging is the site of a misrecognition or "contract of error" that connects them all. Despite the equivocations that surround its locus, the act of purging produces a formal structure whose most critical, epistemological effect is the revision and reconstruction of knowledge, and whose most critical sexual effect is the cathexis and eroticization of the purged male anus.

The experience of purging supersedes what at least one critic, Evelyn Fox Keller, finds oxymoronic about Bacon's *Masculine Birth*: Bacon's masculine co-optation of a feminine reproductive function. Keller argues that Baconian epistemology and, subsequently, Baconian science promote a simultaneous appropriation and denial of the feminine. To be a scientist in the Baconian sense, one must enact a masculine domination over feminine Nature; also, though, to be a Baconian scientist, one must become receptive (for Keller, a particularly feminine quality) to empirical data. In Keller's reading of *The Masculine Birth of Time*, Bacon plays the part of the father whose paternal function is to hand his son over to Nature in marriage, so that the son can reproduce himself in a fashion increasingly viviparous. What is troubling about Keller's reading is not her powerful feminist observation that Baconian science carries with it the "lawful sexual domination" of a feminized Nature, but rather that her highly oedipalizing reading concludes that the young man whom Bacon addresses ends up bisexual—i.e., hermaphroditic, identifying with both genders.[15] Reading through the lens of hermaphroditism, Keller ignores precisely what I have argued is the process by which this birth happens: anal purging. Bacon's relentless and pointed abuse does not in fact enact the same woman-hating panic as does the tightly woven and highly resisted network of male-male eroticism that infuses, say, Shakespeare's *Othello*.[16] Even when he promises a "lawful marriage"[17] between his readers and Nature, even when he cleans and expurgates the "strewing and decoration of the bridal chamber of the mind" (*NO*, 23), and even when he invites his reader "to penetrate further . . . that passing by the outer courts of nature, we may find a way at length into her inner chambers" (*NO*, 36), Bacon imagines these not as an odyssey into the vagina but rather as wanderlusts into the anus: "And if that ordinary mode of judgment practiced by logicians was so laborious, and found exercise for such great wits, how much more labor must we be prepared to bestow upon this other, which is extracted not merely out of the depths of the mind, but out of the very bowels of nature" (*NO*, 20–21).

If the slippage that counts the most in Bacon's writing is not between anus and vagina, but rather between epistemology and sexuality, then the Baconian corpus does offer an important equivocation, the de-differentiating *energia* of heat—both the body heat that Bacon obsessively attempts to cool with enemas and pills, as well as with ointments, oils, and creams, with spoonfuls of vinegar and lemon syrup, and with regimented abstinence and dieting; and the heat that the second book of *The New Organon* obsessively probes, refracts, dissects, and assays after the first book effects the purging of the mind. For Bacon, heat leads to his regime of enemas as well as to an analysis and schematization of methodological instances—instances of analogy, of power, of divorce, of the door, and of the fingerposts, to name a few of the twenty-seven that Bacon lists. For one reader of the Baconian corpus, Simon D'Ewes, Bacon's heat recalls another instance, one that he "should rather bury in silence than mention it, were it not a most admirable instance how men are inflamed by wickedness, and held captive by the devil."[18] In D'Ewes's reading, Bacon serves as *exemplar extraordinaire* of captivating and inflammatory wickedness: the "most abominable and darling sin" of sodomy—an "abominable sin," according to the legalist and Bacon's foremost enemy Edward Coke, "amongst Christians not to be named, committed by carnal knowledge against the ordinances of the creator."[19] We know that D'Ewes means sodomy because to name the unnameable he quotes a particularly phobic poem, one thrown into Bacon's rooms when he lodged at York House and at Gray's Inn: "Within this sty a *hog* doth lie, / That must be hanged for villany." The poem's unspoken joke is that the sizzling heat produced by sodomitical rubbing rewrites the hog as Bacon. As Bacon himself noted, with the mind—even with his own—"you cannot rub out the old till you have written in the new." Might we then say that Bacon's writing in the new rubs out the old epistemological search for the hot and burning phallic torch of science in *The Masculine Birth of Time* and replaces it not with a new organ, but with a new *organon?* This new instrument, whose ability both to purge and to join men together "as true sons of knowledge" (*NO*, 36), sounds perhaps not so coincidentally like the clyster pipes that join Bacon and his servants together in his various bedrooms. Even so, Baconian heat foregrounds the refusal to answer questions—like what exactly happens in Bacon's bedrooms and what are the acts that satisfy Bacon's anal eroticism—by giving a wide and varied set of associations: the transmission of the hot torch of science, the cooling clysters after which the heat gets hotter, the heating and purging of Bacon's readers, the inflammatory heat of sodomy. It is the undecidability of these heated moments that determines the experience of purging as the site of sexuality in the Baconian corpus.

Notes

1. From *The Works of Francis Bacon*, ed. James Spedding, Robert Leslie Ellis, and Douglas Denon Heath (Boston: Taggard and Thompson, 1857–74), 6:289. All Bacon quotations are from this collection, unless otherwise noted. Subsequent references to Bacon's works are included in the text.

2. All quotations from *The Masculine Birth of Time* are from Benjamin Farrington's translation in *The Philosophy of Francis Bacon* (Liverpool: Liverpool University Press, 1951), 72. I also include the Latin origin, from *The Works of Francis Bacon*, 7:31.

3. Stanley Fish, *Self-Consuming Artifacts: The Experience of Seventeenth-Century Literature* (Berkeley: University of California Press, 1972), 91.

4. Ibid., 89.

5. In his essay "Bacon's Hieroglyphics and the Separation of Words and Things," Martin Elsky argues that because of his scientific views, Bacon separated the order of language from the order of reality, only to join them again through the force of conventionality. Bacon abandons the notion of correspondence and analogy and replaces it with a fundamental difference between word and thing: "The Baconian linguistic sign mirrors the world by fiat"—but *only* by fiat; "the task of maintaining the correspondence of word and thing was therefore to be a never ending task (a task the royal Society would later take upon itself), since the artificially devised word always threatens to split asunder from the thing it represents." In *Philological Quarterly* 63 (Fall 1984):457. Thus, according to Elsky, when Bacon writes in *Valerius Terminus* that the goal of scientific knowledge "is a restitution and reinvesting (in great part) of man to that sovereignty and power (for whensoever he shall be able to call creatures by their true names he shall command them) which he had in his first state of creation" (3:222), we should understand this restitution not so much as a return to Adamic language nor as a *Cratylitic* fantasy of the *etymon* that speaks origins and truth, but rather as a reconstruction of that first state—a palimpsest revision that, instead of effacing the difference between word and thing, in its return or reconstruction exacerbates that difference.

   The crucial question is where to locate correspondence or mimesis in this version of language. At times, Bacon represents a language in which "words are but images of matter" (3:284), and at other times, Bacon represents a language in which words refer to things *via* the mediation of the mind. Bacon quotations from *The Works of Francis Bacon*, rpt. New York: Garrett Press, 1968. This latter, psychological understanding is the one that Bacon enacts in his *Essays*, and it is the one that he presents, negatively, in *The Masculine Birth of Time*.

6. Fish, *Self-Consuming Artifacts*, 141–43.

7. One might think of this object whose effects express formal duplicity in terms of what Gottlob Frege theorizes as the concept "not identical with itself." Gottlob Frege, *The Foundations of Arithmetic*, trans. J. L. Austin (Oxford: Basil Blackwell, 1950), 87. According to Frege, this concept is signified by the number zero, a number that signifies the absence of numbers, and, in the process, makes an object of nothing. As Brian Rotman points out, once the number zero gets introduced into Western civilization in the Renaissance, it changes the way that subjectivity can be thought out. For a subject to identify in language with any particular signifier, it must also assume as a "necessary residue" its own extinction:

   > Zero marks the theoretical limit of this sort of one to one correspondence; the point at which a counting subject, instead of tallying idealised marks to objects, must signal the complete absence of any such corresponding mark. If counting is interpreted ordinally, the proto-numbers I, II, III, etc. appear as records which mark out by iconic repetition the sequence of stages occupied by a counting subject. Zero then represents the starting point of the process;

indicating the virtual presence of the *counting subject* at the place where that subject begins the whole activity of traversing what will become a sequence of counted positions.

Brian Rotman, *Signifying Nothing: The Semiotics of Zero* (New York: St. Martin's Press, 1987), 13; see also Jacques-Alain Miller, "Suture (elements of the logic of the signifier)," *Screen* 18 (Winter 1977–78): 24–34. When Fish argues that "the essays advocate nothing (except perhaps a certain openness and alertness of mind)," he is in a very particular sense correct. Rather than expressing a particular perspective, the essays, and I would argue *The Masculine Birth of Time* as well, are motivated by an object not identical with itself whose subjective effect is an openness, or to use a more Baconian term, purging, of the mind. Fish, *Self-Consuming Artifacts*, 94.

8. Farrington, *The Philosophy of Francis Bacon*, 37.

9. In a comparison between a Sidneyan or Spenserian model of reading and a Baconian one, Julie Robin Solomon proposes that while the former two "admit desire in order to exploit and channel it, Bacon virtually eradicates it as an instrumental force." She goes on to argue that while desire defines the reading process for the two poets, for Bacon, the reader is "self-divested or 'objective.'" "To Know, To Fly, To Conjure: Situating Baconian Science at the Junction of Early Modern Modes of Reading," *Renaissance Quarterly* 44 (Autumn 1991):519. If Bacon does attempt to eradicate desire by alienating the reader from the reading process into a stance of objectivity, nonetheless, the Baconian object returns as an image of the very desire that Bacon hopes to eradicate.

10. Quoted in Alan Bray, *Homosexuality in Renaissance England* (London: Gay Men's Press, 1982), 49.

11. John Aubrey, *Brief Lives* (Oxford: Clarendon Press, 1898), 1:71.

12. Bray, *Homosexuality in Renaissance England*, 49.

13. *Letters and Life of Francis Bacon*, ed. James Spedding (London: Longman, Green, Longman, Roberts, 1861–74), 4:78. Subsequent citations in text.

14. Jacques Lacan, *The Four Fundamentals of Psychoanalysis*, ed. Jacques-Alain Miller, trans. Alan Sheridan (New York: Norton, 1981), 203–5. Lacan's very important point here is that sexuality is not named by any particular signifier, say "homosexual" or "heterosexual," but rather is produced as excessive to signification. Lacan situates this excess at the junction between one's relationship to the social, or to the Other, and one's relationship to oneself, at the point where social representation or reproduction meets up with one's representation or reproduction of oneself. This definition of sexuality is very much like the one Foucault offers in *The Use of Pleasure*, when he turns from the legal and medical consolidation of the signifier "homosexual" in the nineteenth century to the Greek ethics of sexuality. Because the Greeks incarnate the receptive element of force as female and the active element of force as male, and because the Greeks link this gendered representation of force to one's ethical relation to oneself, the Greeks lay the foundation for an unavoidable encounter between being, representation, and sexuality . See Michel Foucault, *The Use of Pleasure: The History of Sexuality, Volume Two*, trans. Robert Hurley (New York: Vintage,

1986), 46–62. For some very useful pages on Foucault, see Gilles Deleuze, *Foucault*, trans. and ed. Sean Hand (Minneapolis: University of Minnesota Press, 1988), 94–123.

15. Evelyn Fox Keller, *Reflections on Gender and Science* (New Haven: Yale University Press, 1985), 33–42.

16. The violence of jealousy in *Othello* establishes, as Freud pointed out in 1922, erotic gender conventions dependent on a desire *not* to know. Freud uses the lines "I called my love false love; but what said he then? / If I court moe women, you'll couch with moe men" from Desdemona's Willow Song to illustrate a kind of projected jealousy and unconscious desire between men at the root of male love for women. Sigmund Freud, "Certain Neurotic Mechanisms in Jealousy, Paranoia, and Homosexuality," in *Sexuality and the Psychology of Love*, trans. Philip Rieff (New York: Collier Books, 1963), 161. More important, these energies intensify as the locus of jealousy slips away from Freud's gendered social conventions to ignored and eroticized body parts. For instance, Iago claims a love for Desdemona that ignores not only a homosexual love for Othello, but more explicitly an obsessive concern with anal eroticism: "For that I do suspect the lusty Moor / Hath leaped into my seat," he says, "And nothing can or shall content my soul / Till I am evened with him, wife for wife." *William Shakespeare: The Complete Works* (New York: Penguin, 1969), 2.1.295–96, 298–99. The misogyny underlying Iago's jealous equation "wife for wife" protects the language of anal sex in which Iago's jealousy is pronounced, "The lusty Moor / Hath leaped into my seat," a language that reappears when Iago imagines what his revenge will look like. "I'll . . . Make the Moor thank me, love me, and reward me / For making him egregiously an ass / And practicing upon his peace and quiet, / Even to madness" (305–10). Iago's misogynistic and jealous love for Desdemona, a love not advanced elsewhere in the play, is in part a refusal to recognize that the equivocation victimizing and being loved and its flip-side equivocation loving and being victimized both depend on a language of anal sex that devalues the penetrated male anus. In *Othello*, the anus becomes the locus of both death and derision in the scene between the clown and the musician, a scene whose noise quite significantly interrupts the already delayed wedding night between Othello and Desdemona:

> *Clown.* Why, masters, have your instruments been in Naples,
> that they speak i' the nose thus?
> *Musician.* How, sir, how?
> *Clown.* Are these, I pray you, wind instruments?
> *Musician.* Ay, marry, are they sir.
> *Clown.* O thereby hangs a tail.
> *Musician.* Whereby hangs a tale, sir?
> *Clown.* Marry, sir, by many a wind instrument that I know.
> (3.1.20)

While the equivocation between "tail" and "tale" in Shakespeare's play secures the anus as the butt of a particularly phobic joke about sex and syphilis, for Bacon the anus becomes more properly the seat of knowledge.

17.   Quotations from *The Great Instauration* are in *The New Organon*, ed. Fulton H. Anderson (Indianapolis: Bobbs-Merrill, 1960), 14.

18.   *The Autobiography of Simon D'Ewes*, ed. James O. Halliwell (London: R. Bentley, 1845), 1:192.

19.   Quoted in Ed Cohen, "Legislating the Norm: From Sodomy to Gross Indecency," *South Atlantic Quarterly* 88 (Winter 1989): 187.

Pleasure and Devotion: The Body of Jesus and Seventeenth-Century Religious Lyric

RICHARD RAMBUSS

That our sensuality by vertue of Christ's Passion, be brought up into the substance.—Hugh Cressy, *Revelations of Divine Love* (1670)

I N "On our crucified Lord Naked, and bloody," one of Richard Crashaw's many devotional poems whose proprieties (poetic and otherwise) have been questioned and even assailed as perverse, the poet laments that Christ's unclothed body wasn't rendered even more fully naked:

> Th' have left thee naked Lord, O that they had;
> This Garment too I would they had deny'd.
> Thee with thy selfe they have too richly clad,
> Opening the purple wardrobe of thy side.
> O never could bee found Garments too good
> For thee to weare, but these, of thine owne blood.[1]

Ubiquitous images of the unclothed body of Jesus on the cross—the scene evocatively termed Christ's "Passion"—occupy, as Eve Kosofsky Sedgwick has recently noted, a privileged, perhaps even necessary, but nonetheless disjunctive place within the ostensibly homophobic libidinal scheme of Christianity. What are we to make of a cultural formation whose investment in men's desire for the male body is pronouncedly phobic and prohibitive, yet features at its core an iconic display of an unclothed male body in a state of ecstasy, rendered as such to be looked at ("*Ecce homo*"), adored, desired? Christianity, that is, offers us the spectacle of the naked male body rendered, in the adoring terms of one of John Donne's Holy Sonnets, as "This beauteous form."[2] "The scandal of such a figure within a homophobic economy of the male gaze," Sedgwick remarks, "doesn't seem to abate: efforts to disembody this body, for instance, by attenuating, Europeanizing, or feminizing it, only entangle it the more compromisingly among various modern figurations of the homosexual."[3] The lyrics of Crashaw, Donne, George Herbert, and other seventeenth-century religious poets offer one place (admittedly an extravagant one) from which to begin tracing such compromising entanglements of male same-sex desire as they are spun out from and around Christ's body—entanglements that have been, we shall see, much resisted and obscured in prevailing accounts of the erotics of Renaissance devotional poetry.

Crashaw's Orifices

Probably no other English Renaissance poet was as rapt as Crashaw by the spectacle of the unclothed body of Christ on the cross. Not at all given to "efforts to disembody this body," Crashaw writes, and obsessively rewrites, numerous epigrams, lyrics, hymns, and devotional offices that rhapsodically hold in view Christ's body and its various iconic figurations *in extremis.* Along with the dozens of poems he composed on the crucifixion, Crashaw was similarly prolix on such markedly corporeal events in the life of Christ as the complicated technicalities of his virgin conception, development in utero (*"The mighty Son . . . /* (believe it) *is cramped by the fragile tissues"*[4]), and easy parturition; his circumcision in the temple (the "first fruits of my growing death" ["Our Lord in his Circumcision to his Father," line 1]); the various physical tortures he underwent on the road to Calvary; the preparation of his body for burial; and the manipulation of his wounds after his resurrection from the dead. The locus of interest in these poems, indeed the fulcrum of their swooningly sentimental devotion, however, is not merely the display of Christ's body, but the display of that body as penetrable and penetrated.[5] "But o thy side! thy deepe dig'd side," Crashaw rhapsodizes in one version of his "On the bleeding wounds of our crucified Lord" (line 13). Crashaw, in fact, writes a number of divine epigrams devoted chiefly to the various implements—the priest's circumcising blade, the soldier's whip, the thorns, nails, and the Roman lance at Calvary—which pierce or open up the body of Jesus: "And now th'art set wide ope, The Speare's sad Art, / Lo! hath unlockt thee at the very Heart"

("I am the Doore," lines 1–2). Even the Roman proctor's dismissal of Christ to his fate at the hands of the Jews is refigured by Crashaw as an act of bodily penetration through a collocation of the crimes of murder and rape. "Is murther no sin? or a sin so cheape, / That thou need'st heape / A Rape upon't?" the poet wonders in a curious epigram "To Pontius washing his blood-stained hands" (lines 1–3).[6]

Not unexpectedly, included by Crashaw among the implements that render the body of Christ penetrable is the poet's own instrument, the pen. "Are NAILES blunt pens of superficiall smart?" he asks in his englishing of the "Office of the Holy Crosse" ("Sixth Houre," line 19). In "Adoro Te. The Hymn of St. Thomas in Adoration of the Blessed Sacrament," we learn of Christ that it was his "wounds [that] writt thee man" (line 22).[7] Crashaw's extended version of the Marian hymn "Sancta Maria Dolorum" gives the Passion a more complicated textuality as a scene of dual inscription between Christ and the Blessed Virgin, in which "son and mother / Discourse alternate wounds to one another" (stanza 3). Here Christ's "Nailes write words in her, which soon her heart / Payes back, with more than their own smart"—a "costly intercourse / Of deaths, and worse, / Divided loves." Their reciprocating wounds eventually compose what the poet terms "This book of loves" (stanza 6). From here the "Sancta Maria Dolorum" unfolds with Crashaw looking to inscribe himself into what has now become a triangulated scene of mystical wounding / writing / wooing, hoping that by placing himself "in loves way" his "brest may catch the kisse of some kind dart, / Though as at second hand, from either heart" (stanza 7). Thus the end of the poem finds him courting the Blessed Virgin, routing through her his desire for Christ, his wish to "mix wounds" and "become one crucifix" with the savior's / lover's body. In terms which themselves mix spiritual and erotic desire, Crashaw implores Mary to act as Mediatrix in facilitating this blissful *imitatio crucis*:

> Rich Queen, lend some reliefe;
> At least an almes of grief
> To'a heart who by sad right of sin
> Could prove the whole summe (too sure) due to him.
> By all those stings
> Of loue, sweet bitter things,
> Which these torn hands transcrib'd on thy true heart
> O teach mine too the art

> To study him so, till we mix
> Wounds; and become one crucifix.
> (stanza 10)

That very "art" of wounding transcription is evident in yet another epigram entitled "On the still surviving markes of our Saviours wounds." Here the imprinting which "Naile, or Thorne, or Speare have writ in Thee" remains "Still legible" (lines 2,4) because the poet's own implement of penetration "did spell / Every red letter / A wound of thine" (lines 6–8) in the very act of writing the poem. Each of Crashaw's many poems on Christ's beautiful macerated body, in other words, ritually renders it open once again.

It would seem, then, that for Crashaw to display, to make "legible," the body of Christ is to display its permeability, its openings for penetration. In the poem with which I began, "On our crucified Lord Naked, and Bloody," Christ's body is rendered (and rent) to produce a "wardrobe," a sort of clothes-closet, out of which is secreted a royal, viscid garment of blood, the only garment too rich to clothe a body the poet would prefer to think of as wholly naked. Similarly, in his swelling "Hymn to the Name of Jesus," Crashaw first corporealizes, gives a body to, that name ("the wealthy Brest / Of This vnbounded NAME . . ." [lines 11–12]), and then he implores the now incarnate name to "Vnlock" in itself "thy Cabinet of DAY" (line 127). As George Walton Williams has cataloged, it is a habit of Crashaw's poetics to imagine bodies and various body parts as cabinets, as secret spaces, as closets to be opened.[8] In the first version of his verse "Letter to the Countess of Denbigh," Crashaw thus entreats Christ to take aim at "The self-shutt cabinet of an unsearcht soul" (line 36),

> And 'mongst thy shafts of soveraign light
> Choose out that sure decisive dart
> Which has the Key of this close heart.
> (lines 32–34)

In this teasingly erotic conversion poem Crashaw now figures Christ not as the penetrated body but as the penetrating one. Moreover, we are told at the end of the poem that the "Dart of love" (line 49) that Christ has let fly into the Countess's "self-shutt cabinet" is a kind of liquid bolt: "hast to drink the wholsome dart. / That healing shaft, which heaven till now / Hath in love's quiver hid for you" (lines 46–48). A similar invitation is extended by Christ in another of Crashaw's extraordinary sacred epigrams: "Tast this," the spurting infant Jesus enjoins in "Our Lord in his Circumcision to his Father"—"this" being "this seed of the purple font," as the poet names it in another of his numerous epigrams on the subject ("*Ah ferus, ah culter!*" line 6).

Robert Martin Adams remarked a while ago in an essay on taste and bad taste in metaphysical poetry that Crashaw "has a sometimes disturbing way of dealing with orifices, which he likes to dwell upon."[9] As I have been suggesting, Crashaw is especially given to dwelling upon the orifices opened up in the wounded body of Jesus. And what is particularly disturbing—or at any rate remarkable—in Crashaw's treatment of that body is his tendency to portray it as nothing but orifices. Here is, for example, Crashaw's fantasmatic, eerie rapture "*In vulnera pendentis Domini*" ("On the wounds of the Lord hanging [on the cross]"):

> Whether I call your wounds *eyes* or *mouths*—
> surely everywhere are mouths—alas!—everywhere are eyes.
>
> > Behold the mouths! o blooming with lips too red!
> > Behold the eyes! ah wet with cruel tears!
>
> Magdala, you who were accustomed to bring tears and kisses
> to the sacred foot, take yours in turn from the sacred foot.
>
> > The foot has its own *mouths*, to give your kisses back:
> > This clearly is the *eye* by which it returns your tears.

With characteristic overflowing sentimentality, Crashaw conceives of the wounds of Jesus as so many mouths to kiss and so many eyes to shed tears. What excites adoration here is the conceit that the body of Christ on the cross is uncovered to be all openings; no surface on it is sealed. Everywhere penetrable, this body presents no fixed boundaries of permeability and impermeability. Consider in these terms a stanza from Crashaw's own English rewriting of this epigram "On the wounds of our crucified Lord":

> O these wakefull wounds of thine!
> > Are they Mouthes? or are they eyes?
> Be they Mouthes, or be they eyne,
> > Each bleeding part some one supplies.
>
> (lines 1–4)

The sanguinary openings in Christ's body are portrayed as "wakefull eyes": that is, his body won't ever be closed up, won't ever be rendered impermeable. Instead, Christ's "love sees us with these eyes" ("Joann. 20:20. *In vulnerum vestigia*" ["On the marks of the wounds"], line 3). Although the conceit of wounds as open eyes and kissing mouths may strike us as rather grotesque, Crashaw clearly intended its valences to be erotically charged ones. For in the Latin version of "Luc. 24. *In cicatrices Domini adhuc superstites*" ("On the wounds of the Master still present"), we are told of those wounds that "by whatever name—the soldier was Love" who inflicted them, and the instruments he used—"the bows, the quiver and the light darts" (lines 1–2)—are those of Cupid.

In refiguring Christ's body as a surface of numerous, erotically suffused openings, Crashaw moreover reconstitutes that displayed male body as a multiplicity of secretionary sites.

> "*In vulnera Dei pendentis*"
> ("On the wounds of God hanging [on the cross]")

> O streams of blood from head, side, hands, and feet!
>   O what rivers rise from the purple fountain!

> His foot is not strong enough to walk for our safety (as once it was)
>   but it swims; ah—it swims in its own streams.
> His hand is held fast; *but it gives, though held fast*: his good right hand
>   gives holy dews, and it is dissolved into its own gift.

>   O side, o torrent! for what Nile goes forth in greater
> flood where it is carried headlong by the rushing waters?
> His head drips and drips with thousands and thousands of drops
>   at once: do you see how the cruel shame reddens his cheeks?

>   The thorns cruelly watered by this rain flourish
>   and hope forthwith to change into new roses.

>   Each hair is a slender channel for a tiny rill,
>   a little stream, from this *red sea*, as it were.

> O too much *alive* [are] the *waters* in those precious streams!
>   Never was he more truly the *fountain of life*.

This poem, which is itself built up out of an accretion of reiterating ejaculations ("O streams"; "O what rivers"; "ah—it swims"; "O side, o torrent!"), presents the opened and penetrated male body as liquescent, as a source of generativity.

Crashaw's verse is, of course, well known for its abundant and extreme images of liquefaction, as well as for the extraordinary transitivity of the fluids that flow therein.[10] In "The Weeper," to take no doubt the most famous example, Mary Magdalen's copious tears transmogrify to "milky rivers" and then shoot upwards to provide the "cream" (stanza 4) upon which "Every morn from hence / A brisk Cherub somthing sippes" (stanza 5).[11] In "On the Still Surviving marks of our Saviours Wounds" Christ's blood is changed, we have seen, into ink for the poet's pen. In "*Vexilla Regis.* The Hymn of the Holy Crosse" we find "the streames of life, from that full nest / Of loves" pouring out "in an amorous floud / Of WATER wedding BLOOD" (stanza 2). Still more spectacularly, "*In vulnera Dei pendentis*," the chromatic, unrestrainedly effusive poem cited in the previous paragraph, portrays Christ's body on the verge of being entirely dissolved "in its own streams." Those "rushing waters" are streams of blood and perhaps tears, but they are also "holy dews," an effluvia that is "the fountain of life." These images and terms recur in Crashaw's translation of the first book of the *Sospetto d'Herode*, one of his most highly wrought poems. In a stanza that enthusiastically eroticizes the devotional convention of Christ as honey, Crashaw compounds those "holy dews" and "the fountain of life" into a "deaw of life" which becomes suggestive of fructifying sexual emissions that are to be drunk in, made part of the body:

> Nor needs my Muse a blush, or these bright Flowers
> Other then what their owne blest beauties bring.
> They were the *smiling sons* of those sweet Bowers,
> *That drink the deaw of Life*, whose deathlesse spring,
> Nor Sirian flame, nor Borean frost deflowers:
> From whence Heav'n-labouring Bees with busie wing,
>   Suck hidden sweets, which well digested proves
>   Immortall Hony for the Hive of Loves.
> (stanza 3; emphasis added)

In this all-male "Hive of Loves" Christ offers "hidden sweets," a fecund discharge Crashaw casts as "the deaw of Life," to be ingested by his "smiling sons." The sucking depicted in Christ's "Hive of Loves" mixes eating and the erotic (specifically the homoerotic), but the poet, we are told, has no need to be coy, no need to apologize for what he frankly acknowledges as the arousing nimbus of this scene. That is because the kind of ravishing enacted here on Christ's "smiling sons" does not involve the mortal "deflowering" of the seasons; instead these "smiling sons" and "labouring Bees" imbibe the exudings of Christ himself as an "immortal Hony," an inseminating dew that leads to a "deathlesse spring."

Crashaw's rapturous, insistently erotic poems about Jesus' crucifixion and his wounds are ecstatic meditations on the permeabilities of male bodies. They are rhapsodies rung on what is outside Christ's body that can be made to enter it (whips, thorns, nails, spears, even the poet's own pen), as well as on what is inside Christ's body that can be made to flow out from it (blood, tears, waters, wine, ink, an inseminating "deaw of Life"). The effect of turning Christ's whole body into wounds, mouths, eyes, orifices is to render his body open—or to render open that body—to all sorts of heightened emotive, even erotic possibilities for bringing together that body and the body of the worshipper.[12] Crashaw's emphatically corporealized devotional poetry expresses no desire to triumph over or to transcend the flesh; rather it seems intent on realizing and extending the flesh's many possibilities, including its homoerotic ones. And presiding over the whole is the naked body of Jesus. Around this body accrue a sensuous, even sexy thematics of ecstatic rupture, of penetration and its attendant spurting streams. Such are Crashaw's privileged vehicles for expressing the desired joining with Christ, for making the suffering and the bliss of Christ physically commutable. The fluid permeabilities of Christ's own body become so many openings for identification with his passion and for a passionate, pleasurable union with his saving flesh. The wound, the site of bodily penetrability, becomes a conduit for uniting with Christ, so that in being "drunk of the dear wounds," Crashaw might "Fold up my life in loue; and lay't beneath / My dear lord's vitall death" ("Sancta Maria Dolorum," stanza 11).

Devotional Homoerotics

In his recent treatment of sexuality and spirituality in George Herbert's *The Temple*, Michael C. Schoenfeldt attends to a number of poems related to those we have been examining by Herbert's most admiring follower Crashaw, that portray Christ naked on the cross and envision piercing his body. *Passio Discerpta 4*, "*In latus perfossum*," for instance, "depicts the 'remorseless steel . . . open[ing] up a path' in Christ, a path the speaker hopes his heart will follow." Similarly, *Lucus* 30, "*In Thomam Didymum*" begins, Schoenfeldt remarks, "with a striking image of a mortal penetrating the divine body—'The servant put his fingers in you'—and sees Jesus' allowance of such penetration as a manifestation of his love."[13] However, despite the fact that what Herbert has so viscerally figured here is a scene of penetration involving a *male* "mortal" and a *male* "divine body," Schoenfeldt no sooner begins discussing the penetrable body of Jesus than he also begins discussing what he wants to see as "the possibility of a feminized Christ."[14]

Schoenfeldt likewise peremptorily recasts Christ's gender as female in his discussion of "The Bag"—"Herbert's uncharacteristically grotesque portrait [that is, more like Crashaw's usual doings] of the wounded Christ"—as a poem about "the mystery of Christ's descent into vulnerable flesh as an adoption of tacitly feminine traits."[15] Herbert's poem imagines the wound opened up by the soldier's spear as transforming Christ's side into the bag of the title, a pouch for carrying letters—"any thing to send or write"—up to heaven and "Unto my Fathers hands and sight" (lines 31, 33).[16] Christ thus invites his torturers, Schoenfeldt comments,

> to follow the spear in penetrating his body so they may "put [their messages] very neare my heart," and enticingly reminds them that "the doore shall still be open." . . . The poem's details—the action of "undressing," the placement of an "inne," the emphasis on pregnability, the seductive promise that "the doore / Shall still be open"— all connote a sexual scenario which never fully surfaces, but which suffuses the process by which the almighty God of power becomes a vulnerable and compassionate deity. The wound of "The Bag" functions as a kind of vaginal orifice, feminizing a traditionally masculine Christ.[17]

I concur with Schoenfeldt's sense that "The Bag" is enticingly evocative of a "sexual scenario," but I don't see why the "traditionally masculine Christ" ought to be refigured here as female. Is it simply because his body is a penetrated one? Don't male bodies have openings as well? In Crashaw's poetry, we have seen, Christ's body is covered with them. Moreover, in Crashaw's own English version of his "*In cicatrices Domini* Jesu," an elaboration of the conceit of Christ as Cupid, the poet portrays Jesus' body as penetrated and penetrating in the same representation: "In [his wounded side] there sate but one sole dart; / A peircing one, his peirced heart" (lines 9–10). Crashaw's Latin version of this epigram similarly figures Christ's wounded body as "both his dart and he himself the quiver for his darts" ("*suumque / Et jaculum, & jaculis ipse pharetra suis*" ["Luc. 24," lines 3–4]). Herbert's "Artillerie" likewise enticingly renders God and the poet who "wooe[s]" him with "tears and prayers night and day" (line 19) as "shooters both" (line 25).[18]

To return to "The Bag" and Schoenfeldt's reading of it, certainly Herbert never stops referring to Christ as "he" in this poem, never really blurs gender or presents Christ's wounded body as anything but a male one. Indeed, the world of the poem appears to be another all-male one, populated by the Son of Man, his Father, the spear-wielding Roman soldier, and the spectators Christ addresses as "brethren" (line 30).[19] Consequently, the "sexual scenario" suggested in "The Bag" is, despite Schoenfeldt's attempt to heterosexualize it, a markedly same-sex one. Where is, we might furthermore ask, "the emphasis on pregnability" Schoenfeldt ascertains in "The Bag"? For Christ's body to be penetrated "upon his side" (line 29) doesn't necessarily imply that his body is also impregnated. And finally if one is meant to think of Christ's "bag" as genitalic, as Schoenfeldt suggests we should, why does it have to be as "a kind of vaginal orifice"? Is it going too far to think of that pouch as instead something more like a kind of scrotum: "I have no bag, but here is room / Unto my Fathers hands and sight / Beleeve me, it shall safely come" (lines 32–34)?[20]

The detection of "Jesus as mother" figurations seems to me to take up more convincing grounds when Schoenfeldt turns to Herbert's Latin verses "To John leaning on the Lord's breast (*Lucus 34*)," which he interprets as depicting "an overtly female Christ, nourishing with milk and blood his mortal disciples."[21] "Ah now, glutton, let me suck too!" Herbert's speaker insists, as though he were John's rival younger brother:

> You won't really hoard the whole
> Breast for yourself! Do you thieve
> Away from everyone that common well?
> He also shed his blood for me,
> And thus, having rightful
> Access to the breast, I claim the milk
> Mingled with the blood.

Crashaw, too, follows suit in addressing a Latin epigram to the beloved disciple, "*Sancto Joanni, dilecto discipulo*": "Enjoy yourself: hide your head in his majestic bosom, for then it / would never wish to be placed on a bed of everlasting roses." No less erotic than Herbert's version, Crashaw's poem, however, bypasses the opportunity to frame in maternal terms this sensuous encounter between Christ and the "dilecto discipulo" reposing at his breast. Nor does Crashaw's speaker demand, like Herbert's does, his own turn at the bosom of Christ. "Enjoy yourself," he instead repeatedly encourages John, "and while he carries you in his holy *bosom* thus / o it will be enough for me to have been able to ride on his *back.*" No trace of sibling rivalry here. Instead Crashaw puts forth another, but equally arresting metaphor for union with his savior—one of riding on Christ's back, of mounting him: "*O sat erit tergo me potuisse vehi.*" Like the "smiling sons" sucking "hidden sweets" from Christ in *Sospetto d'Herode*, Crashaw once again posits an erotics that is homoerotic for the male worshipper's desired merging with the adorable male body of Jesus.

I am by no means suggesting that Crashaw is incapable of conceiving bodies, even Christ's indicatively male body, across genders. His notorious epigram "Luke ii. *Blessed be the paps which Thou hast sucked*" testifies to his ability to render gender as stunningly labile:

> Suppose he had been Tabled at thy Teates,
>   Thy hunger feels not what he eates:
> Hee'l have his Teat e're long (a bloody one)
>   The Mother then must suck the Son.

Characteristically, what Crashaw presents here is, I think, not so much an image of androgyny as it is a figuration of a more radical gender undecidability. The operations of Christ's body in this epigram are neither determinately male nor determinately female. For that body is first imagined as that of a son feeding at his mother's breast and then it is provided with its own to suckle her; that body is split open with a wound that somehow manages to function as a protrusion; that body is given a "Teat" that is mammary and phallic at the same time.[22]

The readings of Crashaw and Herbert that I have been advancing are thus by no means directed against the transitivity of gender effects that are often part of the extravagant bodily performances and figurations everywhere on display in seventeenth-century devotional poetry, of which Crashaw's "*Blessed be the paps*" is a striking, but by no means unprecedented, example. I am suggesting rather that we resist the going tendency to encode unproblematically every figuration of the penetrable and penetrated male body—whether that body is Christ's or, as I will treat in a later section of this essay, the worshipper's—as somehow feminized. Accounts that purport to give us a paradoxically "female" Jesus or a "bisexed" Jesus often do so at the cost of too quickly effacing the primary maleness of his body and its operations. Consequently, it seems to me that the androgynous maneuverings now favored in recent critical treatments of Renaissance religious poetry are unable to head in the more interesting direction of really problematizing gender, sex, and the body, of thinking of these performative constructs outside an imposed "natural" binarism—of taking them in the direction, that is, of what Judith Butler has termed "gender trouble."[23] "This feminization of Christ"; "the vision of a bisexual or female Christ"; the conception of "a relationship to the body of Jesus which is at once erotic and maternal"; "to enter into Christ is to return to the womb": such formulations work essentially to render the poetry's metaphorics of highly affective, erotically charged scenarios of (male) penetration of the male body (regularly accompanied by streaming discharges) as more familiarly, more comfortably heteroerotic.[24] The male body penetrates; the body that is penetrated is "female," even if it is male. But I would argue that if we can impute to these poems a transitivity across genders, we should also be willing to admit that their envisioned couplings of God and worshipper are sometimes expressed in erotic languages that, if I may use an anachronism, cut across "sexualities" as well.[25] In short, any investigation of an erotics of devotional literature and experience must also entail an elaboration of its attendant homoerotics. Turning on the spectacle of the naked, beautiful, and (literally) vulnerable body of Christ, the voluptuously corporealized devotional poetics of Richard Crashaw (arguably the queerest poet of the period) requires as much, as do the usually, but not always, less extravagant lyric performances of his poetic forefather, George Herbert. And we haven't even broached Donne yet.

"This is my body. Take and eat it."

I would suggest that one of the reasons why current critical treatments of seventeenth-century religious poetry have been so disinclined to engage the homoerotics of Christian devotion is genealogical, having to do with its adoption of interpretive models and investments now being advanced in historical and iconographic work on the medieval devout body. The pathbreaking scholarship of Caroline Walker Bynum deservedly holds an especially influential position within this project. *Holy Feast and Holy Fast*, her learned and luminous treatment of the pronouncedly somatic dimensions of medieval spirituality, demonstrates at length that "the extravagant penitential practices of the thirteenth to fifteenth centuries . . . are . . . not primarily an attempt to escape from the body. . . . Rather, late medieval asceticism was an effort to plumb and to realize all the possibilities of the flesh."[26] Bynum's *Holy Feast and Holy Fast*, as well as her earlier study *Jesus as Mother*, provides an enabling guide to any study of the central role occupied by the body and the bodily in the often bizarre performances of Christian devotion. But what makes a consideration of Bynum's work on medieval mysticism particularly germane for the concerns of this essay is its recent emergence as a favored gloss on seventeenth-century religious verse as well.[27] Moreover, in her essay "The Body of Christ in the Later Middle Ages: A Reply to Leo Steinberg," a largely critical review of Steinberg's *The Sexuality of Christ*, Bynum herself extends the interpretive agenda of her work on the Middle Ages in the direction of Renaissance cultural materials.[28]

Interestingly, unlike the Renaissance literary critics now adapting her work in their own mappings of the erotics of seventeenth-century religious poetry, Bynum is herself reluctant to admit the sexual as a constitutive component of the extreme physicality everywhere on display in the medieval devotional texts and experiences she studies. "The recent outpouring of work on the history of the body, especially the female body, has largely equated body with sexuality," she remarks. "We must wipe away such assumptions before we come to medieval source material. Medieval images of the body have less to do with sexuality than with fertility and decay."[29] Bynum thus contests what she takes to be Steinberg's anachronistic imputation of the sexual to the startlingly numerous pictorial representations his book gathers in which the focal point of the image is the display and sometimes even the manipulation of Christ's penis.[30] It is chiefly the suspicion of the modern reader, Bynum insists, that imports narratives of sexual yearning and expression to such images or to any artifact of the highly corporealized devotional experiences of the late Middle Ages and the Renaissance: "Twentieth-century readers and viewers tend to eroticize the body and define themselves by the nature of their sexuality. But did medieval viewers? For several reasons, I think we should be cautious about assuming that they did." "Nor," she continues, "did medieval people understand as erotic or sexual a number of bodily sensations which we interpret that way."[31]

Bynum's interpretive strictures against reading the body sexually are surprising, given that her work purports to be invested in the task of bringing back into view the spectacular efforts in Christian devotional literature and practice "to plumb and to realize *all the possibilities* of the flesh" (emphasis added). But before turning to a consideration of just what sort of flesh or body Bynum has seen fit to restore to the Middle Ages and the Renaissance, I would like to comment briefly on her usage of Steinberg's book to make a case against "suspecting" the sexual whenever the body or the bodily is present. For Bynum's polemic against Steinberg seems to me to be something of a misdirected volley. Despite its alluring title, *The Sexuality of Christ* is actually far less concerned with any notion of the "sexuality" of Christ than it is with his genitality.[32] Furthermore, Steinberg carefully and consistently hedges with doctrinal explanation the possibility that the multitude of images his book uncovers of Christ's naked body and his not infrequently erect penis could ever have anything at all to do with sexuality or sexual desire—be it Christ's or the artists' who rendered it as such. For Steinberg, the depiction of Christ's naked body and the rendering of his sexual member as an object of *ostentatio* are always only emblems of the Son of God's incarnation, of his thoroughgoing descent into human form and all its weaknesses: "The sexual member exhibited by the Christ Child, so far from asserting aggressive virility, concedes instead God's assumption of human weakness; it is an affirmation not of superior prowess but of condescension to kinship, a sign of the Creator's abasement to his creature's condition."[33] This account may suffice for depictions of the naked infant Jesus, but it hardly does so for an image like Michelangelo's brazenly nude, beautifully muscled statue of the "Risen Christ," which also appears in Steinberg's book. Scrupulously left unexplored by Steinberg is any notion that such a display of the beautiful male body could also function as an erotic icon—as it so unembarrassedly does in the writings of Richard Crashaw, incidentally the poet most frequently cited in *The Sexuality of Christ*. Indeed, Bynum's critique to the contrary, what is most remarkable about Steinberg's book (apart from its fabulous illustrations) is how little concerned it is with questions of gender and sexuality.

Ironically, Bynum herself does on occasion concede an erotics to the devotional experiences of the female mystics she details in all their extravagances. Even so, when it comes to sexuality and the sexualized body, what her discussion allows on one hand, it seems to take away with the other. Exemplary of this practice is Bynum's exegesis of Catherine of Siena's remarkable vision of wedding Christ, not with a band of gold and jewels as we find depicted in a number of early modern paintings, but instead with the ring of his circumcised foreskin. "When Catherine of Siena received the foreskin of Christ from him in a vision and put it on as a wedding ring," Bynum asserts, "she associated that piece of bleeding flesh with the eucharistic host and saw herself appropriating the pain of Christ. It is we who suspect sexual yearnings in a medieval virgin who found sex the least of the world's temptations."[34] Perhaps so, but I feel tempted to wonder whether, if indeed Catherine found "sex the least of the *world's* temptations," it wasn't more a matter of her otherworldly "sexual orientation" (so to speak) and its object choice in Christ, than it was a function of the kind of absolute abrogation of the sexual insisted upon in Bynum's account.

Bynum's method for treating materials like Catherine's fantasy of marrying Jesus with the wedding band of his foreskin seems to unfold according to an almost pedagogical pattern: first we are enticed with an image of desire for union with Christ that of course strikes us as erotic, and then we are issued a requisite chastisement for succumbing to the temptation to take such expressions "that way." In *Holy Feast and Holy Fast*, Bynum returns to the example of Catherine of Siena, this time citing the saint's ecstatic exhortation to other women about "putting on the nuptial garment" of Jesus and "climbing up Christ's body from foot to side to mouth."[35] But, Bynum warns, we are not to see such an expression as "erotic" or "nuptial" in the least. Why? Because, first of all, Catherine equates this kind of communion with suffering and pain. That, Bynum determines, is "extremely unerotic." Secondly, and perhaps more interestingly, Catherine's spirituality cannot be eroticized, we are told, because she sees Christ as "either a female body that nurses or a piece of flesh that one puts on oneself or sinks into":

> Catherine understood union with Christ not as an erotic fusing with a male figure but as a taking in and taking on—a becoming—of Christ's flesh itself.
>
> In fact, Catherine clearly associated Christ's physicality with the female body, underlying thereby both her capacity for assimilation to Christ and her capacity, like him, for service.[36]

Not unlike what we have already seen in Crashaw's poems on Christ's Passion, Catherine desires a union with the exposed and wounded body of Christ, a union imagined and enjoyed in the most graphically physical terms. Yet whereas Crashaw usually regards Jesus' body as indicatively male, Catherine, Bynum shows persuasively, can regender that body as female. In fusing with the body of Christ and its exquisite suffering and bliss, Catherine sees herself intimately engaging with another female body. What is similar to Crashaw's devotional poetics, however, is that the erotic fusion with Christ envisioned by Catherine is still a same-sex one: in surrendering to Christ Catherine sees herself sharing the "nuptial garment" with a desired and desiring female body. But for Bynum this is precisely the reason why we must not think of as sexual Catherine's intense yearnings to embrace, kiss, mount, take in, put on the body of Christ. This union cannot be erotic, the unspoken supposition of Bynum's argument dictates, because then we would have to recognize it as homoerotic.

Bynum claims that she aims to extend the cultural significations of bodies, bodily parts, and bodily processes, reminding us that "medieval symbols were far more complex—polysemic as anthropologists say—than modern people are aware."[37] On the other hand, we have seen that she is often quick to delimit the erotic—and especially the homoerotic—potentialities of her medieval polysemy of the body. Thus it seems to me that although Bynum's work, along with that of Leo Steinberg, Peter Brown, and others, has enabled a revival of interest in the vivid corporealities of pre- and early modern devotional practices, we need to consider carefully at what cost the body and the bodily are here being restored to us. Bynum, in fact, broaches her agenda for the reembodiment of the Middle Ages and the Renaissance at the end of "The Body of Christ in the Later Middle Ages": "If we want to express the significance of Jesus in both male and female images, if we want to turn from seeing body as sexual to seeing body as generative. . . ."[38] But let us stop here. Why does this argument need to be structured in terms of an opposition? Indeed, why should we turn away from regarding the body as always at least potentially sexualized, as a truly polysemous surface where various significances and expressions—including a variety of erotic ones—compete and collude with each other in making the body *meaningful*? And even granting the opposition Bynum desires between the "generative" body and the sexual and sexualized body, why should we want to prioritize the former? Evidently, that is what Bynum would direct us to do, not only in our study of medieval piety but also, it would seem from the oddly nostalgic lament that concludes *Holy Feast and Holy Fast* concerning "the impoverishment of twentieth-century images," in the experience of our own histories.[39] It is striking and perhaps telling how the sexual is linked here to a notion of cultural impoverishment. For one form of cultural impoverishment that Bynum's work on the devotional body and its desires fails to treat, and regrettably may even have contributed to, is the obfuscating turn away from devotional envisionings of the body's homoerotic possibilities, possibilities as richly present in the medieval religious materials she studies as they are in seventeenth-century devotional verse to which we now return.

Christ's Ganymede

Crashaw, a midlife convert to Roman Catholicism, may be the English Renaissance poet most directly in line with the tropes and traditions of female mysticism discussed by Bynum. Like the medieval writing she treats in *Holy Feast and Holy Fast*, Crashaw's poetry is emphatically corporealized in its presentation of extreme devotional states and desires, undecidably gendered bodies, images of liquefaction, and the conflation of wounds, breasts, and bodily orifices and valves as sites of spiritual and sensuous ecstasy. Himself a hanger-on of that "Arminian Nunnery" Little Gidding, Crashaw moreover directed most of his poems to female patrons and remained especially interested in female conversion, female saints, and female piety.[40] Unlike the versions of female mysticism Bynum presents, however, Crashaw's saints and devotees appear less interested in a eucharistic feeding on Christ's body. Crashaw does compose a few eucharist poems and does on occasion represent Jesus as food or (even more often) as drink that can be sucked, tasted, consumed, incorporated as part of the self. But on the whole the desire physically to draw close to Christ is more often styled in Crashaw's verse, as we have seen, in terms of a thematics of bodily permeability and penetration. One merges with Christ, becomes "one crucifix" with him, through his wounds and what proceeds from out of them—by entering him or being entered by him, and then being engulfed by the salvific streams that flow from the multiple openings in his body.

Such expressions and enactments of spiritual desire are never gender-bound in Crashaw's poetry. Male and female bodies alike can penetrate or be penetrated by, can possess or be possessed by, Crashaw's fully human, fully embodied Christ. Moreover, whereas Donne and Herbert tend to rely on the device of the first-person speaker—a by turns imperious and abject male "I"—for recording their devotional apostrophes, Crashaw is just as likely to speak across gender in narrating or even ventriloquizing the struggles and raptures of female saints. In this context let us briefly consider his extraordinary sequence of poems on the ecstasy of St. Teresa. In "A Hymn to Sainte Teresa," Crashaw tells how the saint was rescued from the Moors and a "barbarous knife" that threatened to break open her "Brest's chast cabinet" (64–72), only to be made "love's victim," a martyr to another kind of death when "thy spouse's" (Christ's) "DART" pierced her willing heart (lines 75–82). The result is spiritual impregnation and the eventual delivery of disciples—"Sons of thy vowes, / The virgin-births with which thy soveraign spouse / Made fruitful thy fair soul" (lines 167–69). But what is so startling about Crashaw's portrayal of Teresa's ecstasy is not the unblushingly orgasmic quality with which he imbues it; rather it is Crashaw's presentation of that ecstasy as the ecstasy of a *male* body being penetrated and possessed by its male lover, Jesus:

> O how oft shalt thou complain
> Of a sweet and subtle PAIN.
> Of intolerable JOYES;
> Of a DEATH in which who dyes
> Loves *his* death, and dyes again.
> And would for ever so be slain.
> And lives, and dyes; and knowes not why
> To live, But that *he* thus may never leave to DY.
>   How kindly will thy gentle HEART
> Kisse the sweetly-killing DART!
> And close in *his* embraces keep
> Those delicious Wounds that weep
> Balsom to heal themselves with. . . .
> (lines 96–108; emphasis added)

In "The Flaming Heart," the final poem in the sequence, Crashaw continues to envision Teresa's body as male, though now he feminizes the male angel who is Christ's proxy in the scene. "Read HIM for her, and her for him" (line 11) the poet instructs us at the onset of the poem. Accordingly, we are then told to reverse the standard iconography of Teresa's transverberation and "Give HIM the vail, give her the dart" for "it is she / . . . [that] shootes both thy shaft and THEE" (lines 42, 48–49). The end of the poem finally restores the angel's shaft to him and makes Teresa's heart "Bigge alike with wounds" (line 76), but not before we are informed that "Love's passives are his activ'st parts" (line 73)—a declaration which once again bottoms up the poem's hierarchy of sexual positions.

In Crashaw's poetry, then, gender never really poses a limit to what the devout body can perform or what can be performed on it. The subject positions of penetrator and penetrated, possessor and possessed, can variously and successively be assumed by both the male and female bodies depicted in Crashaw's lyric performances, which themselves regularly speak back and forth across genders. Add to these habits such matters as the ejaculatory, creamy tears of Mary Magdalen in "The Weeper," or the desire of the speaker in the epigram to the beloved disciple St. John to mount the body of Jesus, or the constant probing of Christ's wounds, and we have, as I suggested earlier, a strong case for Crashaw as the queerest poet of the seventeenth century. Indeed, critics such as T. S. Eliot, William Empson, and Robert Martin Adams long ago posited as much, admittedly in different contexts but not in unfavorable terms.[41]

Yet in conclusion I also want to insist that it would be seriously misleading to bracket off Crashaw and his queer poetics completely from the practices of the other, generally more esteemed religious poets of the period. Earlier we noted that Herbert scores many of the same erotic effects as Crashaw on the naked and penetrable body of Jesus. And for homoerotic incendiariness, little in Crashaw's baroque excesses can surmount Donne's Holy Sonnet "Batter my heart":

> Batter my heart, three-personed God; for, you
> As yet but knock, breathe, shine, and seek to mend;
> That I may rise, and stand, o'erthrow me, and bend
> Your force, to break, blow, burn, and make me new.
> I, like an usurped town, to another due,
> Labour to admit you, but oh, to no end,
> Reason your viceroy in me, me should defend,
> But is captived, and proves weak or untrue,
> Yet dearly'I love you, and would be loved fain,
> But am betrothed unto your enemy,
> Divorce me, untie, or break that knot again,
> Take me to you, imprison me, for I

> Except you enthral me, never shall be free,
> Nor ever chaste, except you ravish me.

Expressing sheer impatience with divine measures to date, Donne metaphorically aligns the extremity of his longing for redemption and spiritual satisfaction with the desire to be taken and ravished by God in what amounts to a kind of trinitarian gang-bang. It isn't enough for him to be ravished, raped by Jesus alone, that is; Donne aggressively demands that the whole Godhead be enlisted in the task: "Batter my heart, *three-personed God.*"

In his essay "The Fearful Accommodations of John Donne," William Kerrigan usefully places "Batter my heart" in the context of a Donnean theology of accommodation, which entails the poet working out fully and eagerly "the most anthropomorphic consequences of anthropomorphism—in short, to imagine with some detail the sexuality of God."[42] Regrettably, as by now we might have come to expect, Kerrigan himself works out those consequences and that sexuality only so far as they can be made to accommodate a heterosexual coupling between God and worshipper. "If the good man weds God, then the sinful man weds God's 'enimie,'" Kerrigan argues, "and if God would claim this recalcitrant soul, then he must grant divorce and possess her by force."[43] Note the modulation in gender here as the sentence slides from the "good man" and the "sinful man" to God's efforts to recapture the sinner and "possess *her* by force." From this point on, Kerrigan's discussion mandates a female speaker for Donne's sonnet, recasting its "battered heart" as "the ravished vagina."[44] Gender switching remains the standard practice in criticism concerned with this poem, as evidenced by Stanley Fish's "Masculine Force: Donne and Verbal Power," his contribution to a recent state-of-the-art collection of essays on seventeenth-century poetry. Though the reading of "Batter my heart" he suggests is kinkier than Kerrigan's, Fish follows suit in performing another sex-change on Donne's desiring speaker remarking, "The fact that Donne now assumes the posture of a woman and like the church of 'Show me deare Christ thy spouse' spreads his legs (or cheeks) is worthy of note."[45]

But Donne's astonishing poem, to return to Kerrigan's terms, actually reaches for an accommodation rather more fearful even than this. Reminiscent of Shakespeare's unsettling hypothesis in *The Merchant of Venice* that the most compelling human bond is an S/M same-sex one (I'm thinking here of Shylock's undeterrable desire to literalize the romantic cliché and win a piece of Antonio's heart, along with Antonio's apparent resolve in the trial scene to let him have it), we find Donne imagining and embracing a limit experience with his God in terms of a homosexual bondage and rape fantasy. But far from thinking himself a woman in this scenario, Donne remains aggressively priapic throughout: "That I may rise, and stand, o'erthrow me." At the same time, he bawdily calls up the suggestion of anal penetration ("I . . . / Labour to admit you, but oh, to no end"). It is as though Donne wants to be enthralled and ravished so that he can remain potent and erect. Thus I see Donne, rather than trying out the woman's place in "Batter my heart," casting himself in something closer to the position Thomas Traherne assumes in a poem entitled "Love." Drinking in Christ's "delicious stream" (line 1), Traherne, like Donne in his longing for ravishment, is rapt at the prospect of Christ selecting him as

> His Ganymede! His life! His joy!
> Or he comes down to me, or takes me up
> That I might be His boy
> And fill, and taste, and give, and drink the cup.
> (lines 31–34)[46]

Of course by Traherne's time the rapture of Ganymede had long since been widely spiritualized as a Christian allegory of the devout soul's ascent to God. Indeed, as Leonard Barkan notes, Claude Mignault, the commentator on Alciati, goes so far as to align Jupiter's love for Ganymede and Christ's invitation to "Suffer little children to come unto me."[47] Moreover, Alan Bradford suggests that the figure of Ganymede as cupbearer to the gods would also have appealed to Traherne in terms of his own vocation as bearer of the Communion chalice.[48] Nonetheless, Traherne's poem makes it abundantly clear that it is not interested in the figure of Ganymede as a wholly de-eroticized emblem. Writing with the same swooning sentimentality and unblushing cupidity we find in Crashaw, Traherne makes it clear that he wants to see himself as Christ's "boy"—"His son, bride, glory, temple, end"—in other words, as his boy-bride.

My argument is thus that the canonical religious poetry of the seventeenth century—devoutly fixated on the incarnation of its deity as fully human and indicatively male—is fundamentally queer in ways recent criticism has refused to acknowledge or has obscured. The rhapsodic pinings of Donne, Crashaw, Herbert, and Traherne for union with Christ are, among other things, a form of love poetry written by men that revels in its desire for the male body—the naked male body of Jesus, "that beauteous form," rendered by turns penetrable and penetrating, ravished and ravishing. And as such, the verse of these poets is full of queer excitations to pleasure and devotion.

Notes

1. *The Poems English, Latin, and Greek of Richard Crashaw*, ed. L. C. Martin, 2nd ed. (Oxford: Clarendon Press, 1957). All citations of Crashaw's English poetry are according to this edition, though I have silently modernized typographical conventions.

2. "What if this present were the world's last night?" cited from *John Donne*, The Oxford Authors series, ed. John Carey (Oxford: Oxford University Press, 1990). All citations of Donne's poetry are according to this edition.

3. Eve Kosofsky Sedgwick, *Epistemology of the Closet* (Berkeley and Los Angeles: University of California Press, 1990), 140. See also pp. 136–50.

4. These lines are taken from Crashaw's Latin epigram *"Deus sub utero virginis,"* lines 3–4. For Crashaw's Latin verse I rely on the translations of George Walton Williams in his edition of *The Complete Poetry of Richard Crashaw* (Garden City, N.Y.: Anchor Books, 1970).

5. Suggesting that sentimentality is not so much a particular "thematic or a particular subject matter, but a structure of relation, typically one involving the author-or-audience-relations of spectacle," Eve Sedgwick calls attention in *Epistemology of the Closet* to a never abating proliferation of deeply sentimentalized depictions of the exposed body of Jesus on the cross—in his pain and his passion—and links them to what she terms a "vast national wash of masculine self-pity" expressed in such genre writing directed to men as the *New York Times* "About Men" column, country music, and the sports pages (pp. 142–45). "If the sentimental, as we have been taught, coincides topically with the feminine, with the place of women," Sedgwick asks, "then why should the foregrounded *male* physique be in an indicative relation to it?" Noting how feminist criticism has successfully reversed the negative valuation of the category of "the sentimental," Sedgwick calls for further work in the "somewhat similar" rehabilitation of "the sentimental" as an important gay male project as well (pp. 144–45). I would like to push this project back beyond the nineteenth-century novel, its usual starting point, to the enticing vagaries of Renaissance devotional materials and especially to Crashaw, who has regularly been derided for what is seen to be the effeminizing sentimental excesses of his devotional poetry.

6. What Crashaw imagines as being raped here is the water that washes Pilate's hands. Revisiting and rewriting the story of Niobe, the epigram enacts a second metamorphosis on the unfortunate nymph. Having already once been changed from maiden to "well-fam'd Fountaine," Pilate's culpable hand-washing is an "Adult'rous touch" that alters her yet again from water to "Nothing but Teares."

7. See also Crashaw's "*In cicatrices quas Christus*": "Whatever the spiked *thorn*, or the sharp-pointed *nail*, / or the *spear* had written with crimson letters, / still lives with you" (lines 1–3).

8. George Walton Williams, *Image and Symbol in the Sacred Poetry of Richard Crashaw* (Columbia: University of South Carolina Press, 1963), 119–23. Leah Sinanoglou Marcus notes a similar thematic in Crashaw's verse in her *Childhood and Cultural Despair: A Theme and Its Variations in Seventeenth-Century Literature* (Pittsburgh: University of Pittsburgh Press, 1978), 148. I discuss the formative, often eroticized, relations in Renaissance literature and culture between, on the one hand, hiding places and enclosures such as cabinets and closets (or bodies imagined as such), and, on the other, writing and subjectivity in *Spenser's Secret Career* (Cambridge: Cambridge University Press, 1993).

9. Robert Martin Adams, "Taste and Bad Taste in Metaphysical Poetry: Richard Crashaw and Dylan Thomas," *Hudson Review* 8 (1955): 67.

10. See Williams, *Image and Symbol*, 84–104. See also Austin Warren, *Richard Crashaw: A Study in Baroque Sensibility* (Baton Rouge: Louisiana State University Press, 1939): "All things flow. Crashaw's imagery runs in streams; the streams run together; image turns into image. His metaphors are sometimes so rapidly juxtaposed as to mix— they occur, that is, in a succession so swift as to prevent the reader from focusing separately upon each. The effect is often that of phantasmagoria" (p. 192). Crashaw's verse is so liquescent that the poet himself has become mingled with his poetics: "a religious pourer forth of his divine Raptures and Meditations" is, for instance, how Crashaw is described by William Winstanley in *The Lives of the Most Famous English Poets* (1687), Facsimile Edition with an Introduction by William Riley Parker (Gainesville: Scholars Facsimiles and Reprints, 1963), 101–2.

11. I am citing Crashaw's 1652 version of "The Weeper" here.

12. Compare Caroline Walker Bynum's *Holy Feast and Holy Fast: The Religious Significance of Food to Medieval Women* (Berkeley and Los Angeles: University of California Press, 1987). Discussing the remarkable physical explicitness that characterizes the writings of medieval female saints and mystics, Bynum remarks: "Scholars have, of course, suggested that such reactions were sublimated sexual desire, but it seems inappropriate to speak of 'sublimation.' In the eucharist and in ecstasy, a male Christ was handled and loved; sexual feelings were, as certain contemporary commentators (for example, David of Augsburg) realized, not so much translated into medium as simply set free" (p. 248). I have learned much from Bynum's rich and revisionary treatment of the place of the body and the range of metaphorical significances assigned to it in Christian devotional experience. I do, however, have a number of differences with her interpretive practices and agendas, which will be made clear in the third section of this essay.

13. Michael C. Schoenfeldt, *Prayer and Power: George Herbert and Renaissance Courtship* (Chicago: University of Chicago Press, 1991), 249–50. Schoenfeldt cites the English translations of these Latin poems offered in Mark McCloskey and Paul R. Murphy, *The Latin Poetry of George Herbert: A Bilingual Edition* (Athens, Ohio: Ohio University Press, 1965).

14.   Schoenfeldt, *Prayer and Power*, 249. Schoenfeldt does not completely ignore the homoerotic in his important and otherwise powerfully illuminating treatment of sexuality and spirituality in *The Temple*. See p. 269: "In its eroticized love for a God addressed both as 'Lord' and 'my dear,' Herbert's 'Love (III)' . . . allows the culturally suppressed homoeroticism of the male love for a traditionally masculine deity to surface." Regrettably, however, Schoenfeldt introduces this notion of Herbert's devotional homoerotics by seeming first to pathologize homosexuality: "In a patriarchal and misogynist culture such as the Renaissance, where women are valued primarily as agents of reproduction or as units of exchange, male homosexuality is the inevitable if brutally repressed outlet of the highest social bonds" (ibid.).

15.   Schoenfeldt, *Prayer and Power*, 249. Janet Mueller similarly reads "The Bag" as "constitut[ing] the high point of this feminization of Christ" in her "Women among the Metaphysicals: A Case, Mostly, of Being Donne For," *Modern Philology* 87 (1989): 153.

16.   *The Works of George Herbert*, ed. F. E. Hutchinson (Oxford: Clarendon Press, 1941). All citations of Herbert's English poetry are taken from this edition.

17.   Schoenfeldt, *Prayer and Power*, 249.

18.   Compare Jonathan Goldberg's reading of "Artillerie" and other of Herbert's "Sacred Poems and Private Ejaculations" (as they are termed on the title page of *The Temple*) in *Voice Terminal Echo: Postmodernism and Renaissance Texts* (New York and London: Methuen, 1986), 110–11: "A scene of scattered seed, shooting stars, and the ejaculative traces of a forestalled and productive path: how to enter the poem, how to be on the page, where the words stay, yet nonetheless come."

19.   Despite the fact that "The Bag" depicts an all-male world, Schoenfeldt discerns the feminine surfacing in the poem in terms of an allegorized female figure of Despair, remarking that "Robert Graves perhaps overstates the case, but he is close to the truth when he suggests that 'the Divine Figure in the "The Bag" is fused with the figure of the temptress and at the end of the poem subordinate to her, when it has distinct feminine characteristics'" (p. 249). (The reference here is to Graves's *Poetic Reason and Other Studies* [London: Cecil Palmer, 1925], 62.) But it is far from indisputable, however, that "The Bag" is indeed offering a personification of the emotional state of despair. Moreover, even if we are dealing with a personification here, it is quite a further stretch for Schoenfeldt and Graves to gender Despair as female, as "the temptress." For why should Despair have to be female? In *The Faerie Queene*, for instance, Spenser imagines his personification of Despair as male.

20.   On the sexual meaning of "come" in the Renaissance, see Eric Partridge, *Shakespeare's Bawdy* (London: Routledge, Kegan and Paul, 1955), 376.

21.   Schoenfeldt, *Prayer and Power*, 250.

22.   William Empson places Crashaw's epigram under the heading of his seventh and final type of ambiguity: "This is to show the unearthly relation to earth of the Christ, and with a sort of horror to excite adoration. . . . The second couplet is 'primitive' enough; a wide variety of sexual perversions can be included in the notion of sucking a long bloody teat which is also a deep wound. The sacrificial idea is aligned with incest, the infantile pleasures, and cannibalism; we contemplate

the god with a sort of savage chuckle; he is made to flower, a monstrous hermaphrodite deity, in the glare of a short-circuiting of the human order." See *Seven Types of Ambiguity* (New York: New Directions, 1947), 221. Though his views continue to be much resisted by most Crashavians, Empson remains one of Crashaw's best readers, matching in his criticism the poet's extravagances with his own.

23. See Judith Butler, *Gender Trouble: Feminism and the Subversion of Identity* (New York: Routledge, 1990), especially section 4 of chapter 3, "Bodily Inscriptions, Performative Subversions": "The construction of coherence conceals the gender discontinuities that run rampant within heterosexual, bisexual, and gay and lesbian contexts in which gender does not necessarily follow from sex, and desire, or sexuality generally, does not seem to follow from gender—indeed, where none of these dimensions of significant corporeality express or reflect one another" (pp. 135–36). I have also found Butler's discussion in this section of bodily boundaries and permeabilities useful in my thinking about the depiction of wounds and bodily orifices in Crashaw's poetry.

24. These formulations are cited from (in order): Mueller, "Women among the Metaphysicals," 153; E. Pearlman, "George Herbert's God," *English Literary Renaissance* 13 (1983):107; Schoenfeldt, *Prayer and Power*, 250; Marcus, *Childhood and Cultural Despair*, 148.

25. I say I am speaking anachronistically here because, as Michel Foucault and other historians of sexuality have shown, it is a relatively recent invention to conceive of individuals as subject to—and subjects of—particularized "sexualities" that are polarized around the binary models of heterosexuality and homosexuality. See Foucault's *The History of Sexuality*, vol. 1, *An Introduction*, trans. Robert Hurley (New York: Vintage Books, 1978), as well as Alan Bray, *Homosexuality in Renaissance England* (London: Gay Men's Press, 1982). See also David M. Halperin's powerfully and relentlessly argued essay "One Hundred Years of Homosexuality," in the book of the same title (New York: Routledge, 1990): "Where there is no such conception of sexuality, there can be no conception of either homo- or heterosexuality—no notion that human beings are individuated at the level of their sexuality, that they differ from one another in their sexuality or belong to different types of being by virtue of their sexuality" (p. 26).

In calling for readings that can shift across what we now call sexuality as well as across gender, I am not so much invested in imposing later analytical categories on early modern experience, though I also wouldn't be too hasty in declaring such gestures wholly untenable either. That is to say, I do not think in our investigation of early modern notions of gender and the erotic we can rely wholly and "purely" on how these notions would have been conceptualized in the Renaissance itself. (On the need to see early texts in ways that sometimes vary from the ways in which those texts seem to understand themselves, see Louise O. Fradenburg, "Criticism, Anti-semitism, and the *Prioress's Tale*," *Exemplaria* 1 (1989):69–115, especially pp. 69 and 75.) In calling for readings of Crashaw, Herbert, and Donne that shift across sexualities, I am instead criticizing the unwarranted imposition of normativizing scenarios of heterosexuality—which, as we conceive of it now, of course no more exists in the Renaissance than does homosexuality—on the devotional couplings imagined by these poets. Despite the insistence of certain critics that someone— whether Christ or the male poet—be "female" in these insistently erotic sacred poems, Crashaw, Herbert, Donne, as well as a number of other seventeenth-century religious writers, compose poems which envision erotic unions with Jesus in which both the deity and the poet are indicatively male.

26. Bynum, *Holy Feast and Holy Fast*, 294.

27. Among the critics who have been applying Bynum's work on medieval female piety to Renaissance lyric poetry are: Schoenfeldt, *Prayer and Power*; Thomas F. Healy, "Crashaw and the Sense of History," in *New Perspectives on the Life and Art of Richard Crashaw*, ed. John R. Roberts (Columbia: University of Missouri Press, 1990), 49–65; and Eugene R. Cunnar, "Crashaw's Sancta Maria Dolorum," also in *New Perspectives*, pp. 99–126.

28. Caroline Walker Bynum, "The Body of Christ in the Later Middle Ages: A Reply to Leo Steinberg," in *Renaissance Quarterly* 39 (1986):399–407. This essay has now been reprinted in Bynum's *Fragmentation and Redemption: Essays on Gender and the Human Body in Medieval Religion* (New York: Zone Books, MIT Press, 1991).

29. Bynum, "The Female Body and Religious Practice," in *Fragmentation and Redemption*, 182.

30. Leo Steinberg, *The Sexuality of Christ in Renaissance Art and Modern Oblivion* (New York: Pantheon, 1983).

31. Bynum, "The Body of Christ," 406.

32. See Bynum, "The Body of Christ," 405. See also Arnold I. Davidson, "Sex and the Emergence of Sexuality," *Critical Inquiry* 14 (1987):16–48, especially p. 26.

33. Steinberg, *The Sexuality of Christ*, 47–48.

34. Bynum, "The Body of Christ," 407.

35. Bynum, *Holy Feast and Holy Fast*, 178.

36. Ibid.

37. Bynum, "The Body of Christ," 438.

38. Ibid., 439.

39. Bynum, *Holy Feast and Holy Fast*, 302.

40. Little Gidding was so termed in Puritan attacks on its popish doctrines and "super-stitious practices," such as devotion to the Blessed Virgin. See Paul A. Parrish, "The Feminizing of Power: Crashaw's Life and Art," in *"The Muses Common-Weale": Poetry and Politics in the Seventeenth Century*, ed. Claude J. Summers and Ted-Larry Pebworth (Columbia: University of Missouri Press, 1988), 151.

41. Here is T. S. Eliot: "Crashaw's images, even when entirely preposterous . . . give a kind of intellectual pleasure—it is a deliberate perversity of language. . . . Crashaw is quite alone in his peculiar kind of greatness." *For Lancelot Andrewes* (Garden City, N.Y.: Doubleday, 1929), 134–35, 137. Likewise, Empson finds "Something weird and lurid" in Crashaw's poetry. See *Seven Types of Ambiguity*, 222. Adams, discussing "The Weeper" remarks: "The transformation of salt tears to milk is queer; raising the butterfat content to make cream is odder yet" ("Taste and Bad Taste in Metaphysical Poetry," 66).

42. William Kerrigan, "The Fearful Accommodations of John Donne," *English Literary Renaissance* 4 (1974):340.

43. Ibid., 351–52.

44. Ibid., 335.

45. Stanley Fish, "Masculine Force: Donne and Verbal Power," in *Soliciting Interpretation: Literary Theory and Seventeenth-Century English Poetry*, ed. Elizabeth D. Harvey and Katharine Eisaman Maus (Chicago: University of Chicago Press), 242. A notable exception to the tendency to heterosexualize Donne's "Batter my heart" is Arthur F. Marotti's treatment of it: "The sexualization of the speaker's relationship to God at the end of the sonnet is shocking partly because it has the shape of a passive homosexual fantasy." See *John Donne, Coterie Poet* (Madison: University of Wisconsin Press, 1986), 259–60. However, the implications of this insight for a consideration of gender and desire in Donne's poetics are left unexplored by Marotti in the elaboration of his larger "Love is not Love" argument that what appears to be amorous courtship in Renaissance poetry is actually an encoded solicitation of aristocratic patronage in a homosocial order: "Being loved in the spiritual homoerotic context of 'Batter my heart' corresponded to being favored in the political order" (ibid.).

46. *Thomas Traherne: Selected Poems and Prose*, ed. Alan Bradford (London: Penguin Books, 1991).

47. See Leonard Barkan, *Transuming Passion: Ganymede and the Erotics of Humanism* (Stanford: Stanford University Press, 1991), 26. Mignault, Barkan remarks, "may be operating out of such a peaceful orthodoxy that none of the (somewhat risible) implications that occur to us would occur to him. That we cannot know, nor does any amount of History of Ideas qualify us to limit what a person in a certain age is capable of thinking. But we do not have the warrant to assume that only we are clever enough—or sufficiently unblinded by belief—to be aware of the difficulties in the equation between pederasty and sacred rapture" (ibid.).

48. See *Thomas Traherne: Selected Poems and Prose*, ed. Thomas Bradford, p. 338.

My Two Dads: Collaboration and the Reproduction of Beaumont and Fletcher

JEFF MASTEN

What strange Production is at last displaid,
(Got by Two Fathers, without Female aide)
Behold, two *Masculines* espous'd each other,
   Wit and the World were born without a *Mother.*
—*"On the happy Collection of Master* FLETCHER'S
Works, never before PRINTED"[1]

THIS essay takes as its point of reference the erotics of male relations inscribed by Renaissance conduct-book writers and theorists of friendship—writers who were also, in large part, concerned with the practice and conduct of writing. In the larger project from which this essay derives, I demonstrate the conjunction of friendship, eroticism, and collaboration in, for example, Montaigne's essay "Of Friendship," as influentially translated into English by John Florio. "Of Friendship" centers on a relationship that is demonstrably homoerotic[2] and that overflows the bounds of what we now think of as "the individual."[3] What has *not* often been recognized is the essay's simultaneous emphasis on a collaborative textuality. "In the amitie I speake of," Florio translates, male friends "entermixe and confound themselves one in the other, with so universall a commixture, that they weare out, and can no more finde the seame that hath conjoyned them together."[4] These words also apply to the textual relationship Montaigne describes with his friend—a relationship Montaigne figures as "bound" up in the friend's writing, in an essay that proposes to introduce, reproduce, and incorporate the friend's texts.[5] This sort of collaborative textuality finds an apt emblem in the figure of "Acquaintance" prefacing Richard Brathwait's conduct book, *The English Gentleman* (fig. 1); in that engraving, the identical gentlemen-friends are also collaborators, voicing simultaneously a motto they select by "consenting consort" and "mutuall interchoice."[6]

Francis Beaumont and John Fletcher's living/writing arrangements in the early decades of the seventeenth century may have resembled this configuration; this essay focuses, however, on the historical aftermath of their relationship and textual production—the attempt, thirty years later, to understand their writing practice within a discursive universe where dramatic writing was increasingly imagined more as singular fatherhood than as collaborative, "consenting consort," and where the male homo-erotic friendship I have briefly described was increasingly coincident with an idea of companionate marriage that had begun to be articulated in remarkably similar terms.[7] As I hope to show, these shifts are related in

FIGURE 1.
"Acquaintance"
emblem from
Richard Brathwait,
The Englsih
Gentleman
(1633).

complicated ways; we will have the opportunity to see the inseparability, in this century, of what we now think of as the distinct discourses of textual production and property, and discourses of sexuality and gender. Put simply, I argue that, in the course of the seventeenth century, there is a shift in the printed and performative apparatus of drama away from homoerotic collaboration and toward singular authorship on a patriarchal-absolutist model.[8]

The site of this investigation is the first folio collection of Beaumont and Fletcher's plays (1647), a volume that registers a retrospective view of same-sexual collaboration within this newly emergent discourse of patriarchal-absolutist authorship. In this sense, as we will see, Beaumont and Fletcher's collaboration registers as early as 1647 as a "strange Production" within a tradition of dramatic folio collections increasingly organized around singular, fathering authors (most importantly the Shakespeare folios of 1623 and 1632, and the Jonson folios of 1616 and 1640).[9] Though Beaumont and Fletcher were participants in the theater's earlier standard collaborative mode of production,[10] by midcentury they have become a distinctively odd couple. This is not to say that the construction of singular authorship in drama was a fait accompli with the publication of the Shakespeare and Jonson folios; as we will see, the terms of patrilineal organization continue to be contested well into the seventeenth century. This essay begins with a general discussion of the problematics of textual property and authorship in the Beaumont and Fletcher folio, then proceeds to analyze in more detail the volume's implication in, and reproduction of, the sexual rhetorics of Renaissance authorship.

Double-take

Immediately upon opening the 1647 first folio collection of Beaumont and Fletcher plays, one is struck by the coexisting figurations of authorship and collaboration as modes of textual production. Entitled *Comedies and Tragedies Written by Francis Beavmont and Iohn Fletcher Gentlemen*, the volume juxtaposes this dual attribution with a portrait of Fletcher alone on the facing page (fig. 2). Rising as a classically sculpted bust out of a natural scene, Fletcher is both accoutred in and surrounded by the conventions of authorship in the recognizably classical mode utilized by Jonson's 1616 volume; he wears a toga and crown of laurels, the figures of Tragoedia and Comoedia recline above him on the margins of the engraving, and his

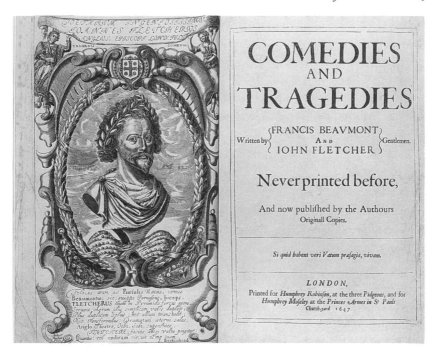

FIGURE 2. *Title page and facing page from* Comedies and Tragedies Written by Francis Beavmont and Iohn Fletcher Gentlemen *(1647)*.

portrait is both under- and over-written with Latin inscriptions denoting his position as poet.[11] The volume both stresses the plurality of its attribution by bracketing its writers as "Gentlemen" in a fashion familiar from earlier title pages of collaborative plays published in quarto form[12] and at the same time visualizes its attribution as a singular author in classical garb. Though the title page would suggest that its term "Authours" is dual in this context ("now published by the Authours Originall Copies"), the juxtaposition of frontispiece and title page opens the possibility that "Authours" may function here as either singular or plural possessive.[13] The volume's seeming vacillation between singular authorship and dual collaboration is by no means stabilized by the extensive preliminary materials that lie between the title page and the plays themselves. Of the folio's thirty-seven commendatory poems, only seven are addressed to Beaumont and Fletcher together; twenty-three are addressed to Fletcher alone, without (or with merely momentary) reference to Beaumont. Beaumont is the subject of three poems. And (as we will see) a number of the commendatory poems are addressed to one man but speak at length of the writers' collaboration.

Traditional bibliography has sought traditional bibliographical explanations for this ambiguity;[14] on the basis of some statements in the volume, one might propose a narrative explaining the conflicting claims of the title page and engraving. In his preface "The Stationer to the Reader," Humphrey Moseley (one of the volume's two publishers) writes, "It was once in my thoughts to have Printed Mr. *Fletcher's* workes by themselves, because single & alone he would make a *Just Volume*: But since never parted while they lived, I conceived it not equitable to seperate their ashes" (A4v). One might argue that Moseley had intended to print the Fletcher-only volume and indeed had solicited commendatory poems for that purpose, but for some reason unknown to us decided instead to print the plays of both men together. But, in such a case, one would also have to posit a Moseley so oblivious in his function as collector and collator that he did not notice the apparent contradiction between engraved portrait and title page, or the fact that the majority of the commendatory poems in the volume are addressed to Fletcher alone.

In his prefatory discussion of the frontispiece, Moseley devotes some attention to the apparent conflict: "I was very ambitious to have got Mr. *Beaumonts* picture; but could not possibly, though I spared no enquire in those *Noble Families* whence he was descended, as also among those Gentlemen that were his acquaintance when he was of the *Inner Temple*: the best Pictures and those most like him you'l finde in this *Volume*" (A4v). Like Moseley's aborted attempt to separate Fletcher's plays into a "Just Volume," "single & alone," his effort here to differentiate the two writers (the attempt to supply two portraits, to provide separate genealogies of family and "acquaintance") eventuates not in distinction but in inseparability: Beaumont's "best Pictures and those most like him" are to be found in this volume of (undifferentiated) Beaumont and Fletcher plays. The impetus of this statement toward differentiation (i.e., read Beaumont's texts as his best likeness) is itself a convention, as readers of the Shakespeare first folio preliminaries will immediately recognize; the lack of Beaumont's portrait in Moseley's collection resonates with the concluding lines of the poem accompanying the engraved portrait in the Shakespeare volume: "Reader, looke / Not on his Picture, but his Booke."[15] Literally unable to look on Beaumont's picture, the reader of Moseley's volume is sent in a direction that both fails to differentiate Beaumont from Fletcher and alludes to the conventionality of such attempts. Apparently compensating further for this lack, Moseley attests that Fletcher's portrait accurately depicts him (it was "cut by severall Originall Pieces"), or at least "As much as could be, you have here, and the *Graver* hath done his part" (A4v). In what is only apparently a non sequitur, Moseley then proceeds without interruption to retrace the trajectory he had mapped for desirers of Beaumont's image; where earlier he had sent readers from the (lacking) portrait to the book, here he sends readers in the direction of Fletcher's manuscript practice: "What ever I have seene of Mr. *Fletchers* owne hand, is free from interlining; and his friends affirme he never writ any one thing twice: it seemes he had that rare felicity to prepare and perfect all first in his owne braine; to shape and attire his *Notions*, to adde or loppe off, before he committed one word to writing, and never touched pen till all was to stand as firme and immutable as if ingraven in Brasse or Marble." The thrust of the passage is against duality and iterability ("free from interlining . . . never writ any one thing twice"). Yet, as Margreta de Grazia has noted, this too is a conventionally iterated statement, drawing on "a long history extending back to the pre-print era of classical rhetoric"[16] and alluding to its more recent inscription in the Shakespeare folio where, in a familiar claim, Heminge and Condell attest that Shakespeare's "mind and hand went together: And what he thought, he vttered with that easinesse, that we haue scarse receiued from him a blot in his papers" (A3). Fletcher's portrait cannot fully secure "his unimitable Soule" (the "Painters confessed it, was not easie to expresse him"), and the evidence produced to supply that lack ("Mr. *Fletchers* owne hand") itself alludes heavily to a prominent precursor volume—other hands describing another hand. The very demonstration of Fletcher's "rare felicity" is its conventionality.

Both narratives—the narrative of the oblivious publisher and the story of the careful stationer who attempts but is unable to secure the individuality of his two writers—seem untenable. There is, instead, another possibility beyond the confines of a binary opposition that depends upon the publisher's reliability or unreliability as a witness.[17] Moseley's preface isolates for us a moment in which the attempt to differentiate writers of collaborative texts written earlier in the century, to identify singular authors and organize volumes accordingly, is nascent in English culture, but that urge is neither universally prescriptive (it does not exclude other claims) nor internally consistent. Moseley's preface begins by discussing Beaumont and Fletcher as a corporate entity, attests that it is "not equitable to seperate their ashes," and proceeds to attempt precisely that. Abruptly ending his ruminations on Fletcher's manuscript practice and introducing the commendatory verse-writers who will further introduce the collaborative volume, he concludes his preface in the singular: "But I keepe you too long from those friends *of his* whom 'tis fitter for you to read" (my emphasis).

We can read the excesses and contradictions of Moseley's claims (and those of the larger volume) as inscriptions of a particularly pivotal moment in English cultural history—a moment when collaboration (and the attendant lack of concern, in certain discourses, over authorial attribution) has not yet been fully supplanted by the regime of the singular, proprietary author within which we now write. The liminality of this moment is illustrated by the articulation of what now appear to us as conflicting positions, and the Beaumont and Fletcher first folio is particularly interesting in the way that it attempts to work out conflictual discourses of writing.

Like Moseley's preface, many of the commendatory poems addressed to Fletcher or Beaumont (singly) attempt to emphasize their singularity and the self-sufficiency of their creations. Joh. Earle, for example, argues that Beaumont's writing is "all so borne within thy selfe, thine owne, / So new, so fresh, so nothing trod upon" (c3v), and Jos. Howe writes that "Fletcher now presents to fame / His alone selfe and unpropt name" (f2)—a dubious proposition, following as it does the volume's title page and several poems that discuss in detail the pair's collaborative practice. Other commendatory verses display more locally this larger tension of the volume. Listing the ways in which one can praise and distinguish Fletcher, T. Palmer concludes: "What shall I doe? all Commendations end, / In saying thou wert BEAUMONTS Friend?" (f2v). The discourse of male friendship enters the poem at this climactic point, and the highest proof or compliment of Fletcher's singularity comes in saying that he is Beaumont's friend. Fletcher's singularity is thus paradoxically anchored in the doubleness and constitutive reflexivity evident in other period formulations of friendship discourse.

At the same time, however, we can see in a statement like Earle's ("all so borne within thy selfe, thine owne, / So new, so fresh, so nothing trod upon" [c3v]) the emergent discourse of patriarchal authorship recently identified in the Shakespeare first folio. De Grazia's rereading of the preliminary materials in that earlier volume has detailed its tropes of affiliation, filiation, and consanguinity; "the 1623 preliminaries," she writes, "work to assign the plays a common lineage: a common origin in a single parent and a shared history of production."[18] Though new to the production of printed drama, this model would have been familiar to Renaissance readers of other folio volumes—including, for example, the 1598 edition of Chaucer's *Workes*, the title page of which advertised not only "Arguments to euery Booke gathered," but also "His Portraiture and Progenie shewed"; or the insistent patriarchality of King James's 1616 *Workes*, dedicated to "Prince CHARLES, *THE ONELY SONNE OF* OVR SOVERAIGNE LORD The King," and elaborately deriving James's authorship from that of his God/father/maker.[19]

A moment like the end of Palmer's poem ("all Commendations end, / In saying thou wert BEAUMONTS Friend") thus illustrates the anomalousness of the Beaumont and Fletcher collection—how quickly its claims within an emerging patriarchal-absolutist paradigm of singular authorship break down, how close those formulations remain to the discourses of collaboration and male friendship, how collaboration is nevertheless increasingly inexplicable (here "all Commendations end"). While several of this volume's preliminaries attempt to proceed with the patriarchal tradition of the Shakespeare folios—we have already witnessed both Fletcher and Beaumont giving birth within their (singular) brains—a significant number of the commendatory verses wrestle suggestively with the problem we might describe as follows: how to explain collaborative textual production within the emerging consensus of patriarchal-absolutist authorship? The contested discourses of seventeenth-century sexuality figure centrally in this question.

Strange unimitable Intercourse

We can begin with a poem falling early in the preliminaries, Jo. Pettus's "Upon the Works of Beaumont, and Fletcher" (a4v). Pettus speaks of an entity "Beaumount-Fletcher," "whose strange unimitable Intercourse / Transcends all Rules." He argues that Beaumount-Fletcher alone have reached the "*Mysteries* of Wit," that they speak "The *Intellectuall Language*" unknown in his troubled era, and that "from *Wit, Sweetnesse, Mirth*, and *Sence*, / This Volume springs a new true *Quintessence.*" Pettus's vocabulary of transcendence is one way of marking collaboration's perceived exceptionality—it is mysterious (in a quasi-religious sense), speaks a higher language, and gives birth to elevated substance that is both "new" and "true." Pettus's figuring of this collaboration's textual offspring as "new" is striking (given its centrality to the theater earlier in the seventeenth century), and his term "strange" emphasizes this. *Strange* of course originally meant "foreign," but it subsequently accrued the meanings "diverse," "different," "unusual," and (relevant here) "unknown, unfamiliar; not known, met with, or experienced before." The word's appearance in this poem, that is, denotes the extent to which collaboration is being marked as a new and different phenomenon within the regime of singular authorship, even though it has historically preceded it. The text thus produced is introduced in the reproductive terms of patriarchal authorship ("This Volume springs . . .") but is new and anomalous. Another period meaning of *strange* is relevant here as well: "Unfamiliar, abnormal, or exceptional to a degree that excites wonder or astonishment; difficult to take in or account for; queer, surprising, unaccountable" (*OED*, 10). "Strange unimitable intercourse" in this sense might be considered a redundancy: exceptional and unimitable.

Pettus's word "intercourse" is central to his description of collaboration, and it is difficult for us as modern readers to separate out the apparently obvious sexual valence. The *OED* does not record the word *intercourse* as referring to sexual activity (at least between differently gendered persons) until late in the eighteenth century. There is the possibility that *intercourse* could refer to same-sex transactions;[20] nevertheless, it may be in the word *strange* that we will, strangely enough, find the stronger suggestion of sexual discourse. Michael Warner has recently explored the geographical particularity of the seventeenth-century term *sodomy*—its reference to an act originating in a specific geographical location that is pointedly elsewhere (Sodom)—and, as Alan Bray's work has suggested, there is ample documentation of the period's tendency to identify sodomitical activity as outside English culture, or imported by alien figures within it.[21] In Warner's investigation, too, the word *strange* has recurred in the sodomitical context of at least one seventeenth-century treatise.[22] I want to suggest here that Pettus's use of *strange*, and the word's recurrence in several verse-writers' discussions of the Beaumont and Fletcher collaboration, signal both the apparent newly "strange" (odd, unusual, queer) status of collaboration within a nascent authorial paradigm and the rumblings of dissonance between a sexually valenced discourse of male friendship and an (again, nascent) articulation of companionate marriage that tended to use friendship's vocabulary.[23] Here Beaumont and Fletcher begin to register as "queer," in the more recent sense of that term.

There are a number of commendatory verses that attempt simply to refigure this strangeness within a patriarchal absolutist model of singular authorship. John Web, for example, applies the familiar discourse of male friendship ("two wits in growth / So just, as had one Soule informed both"), but he also resorts to a modified patriarchal model, imagining the "rich Conceptions of your twin-like Braines." The conveniently early death of Beaumont allows him, furthermore, to consolidate the twins in one: "Thence (Learned *Fletcher*) sung the muse alone, / As both had done before, thy *Beaumont* gone" (c2v). The pronoun ("thy *Beaumont*") may cast a glance in both directions: it signals a sort of monogamous coupling (Fletcher's Beaumont, and no one else's), and a hierarchy of possession, in which Fletcher as surviving author mono / polizes dramatic creation. Jasper Maine emphasizes the indiscernibility of the collaborative texts— "we, / In all things which you did[,] but one thred see; / So evenly drawne out, so gently spunne" (d1)—and yet his statement registers the increasing urgency of authorial identification and his distance from the process of undifferentiated collaboration earlier in the century. Concluding his poem, Maine performs a consolidation similar to Web's in his description of the volume's publication:

> . . . what thus joyned you wrote, might have come forth
> As good from each, and stored with the same worth
>
> · · ·
>
> In you 'twas League, in others impotence;
> And the Presse which both thus amongst us sends,
> Sends us one Poet in a paire of friends.
> (d1v)

Depicting collaboration (from his authorial perspective) as usually "impotent," Maine implicitly figures singular authorship as "potent"—a word that resonates not as sexual discourse (until the late nineteenth century) but as a term of absolute power (cf. *potentate*, or, more resonantly, the phrase from the Latin credo, *patrem omnipotentem*). Maine concludes by making this doubly authored volume the product of a singular poet, in a sense mystifying collaboration into the author-function.[24] He thus at-

tempts to make sense of the volume's opening contradiction; as its frontispiece suggests, this book might be read as "one Poet in a paire of friends."

Roger L'Estrange's poem "On the Edition of Mr *Francis Beaumonts*, and
Mr *John Fletchers* PLAYES never printed before" attempts simply to interpo-
late collaboration into a poem apparently written about Fletcher alone.
The title suggests, with its separately possessive forms of the playwrights'
names, the uneasy conjunction of doubleness and singularity, and in the
poem itself, the name "Beaumont" appears suddenly and extra-lineally,
bracketed with "Fletcher" (cɪ):

> For (in *Me*) nothing *leſſe* then *Fletchers Name*
> Could have *begot*, or *juſtify'd* this *flame*.
> *Beaumont* ⎫
> *Fletcher* ⎬ *Return'd* ? methinks it ſhould not be.
> *No*, not in's *Works : Playes* are as *dead* as *He*.

The poem uses the familiar convention of the collaborative title page, the
bracket, but the interjection of Beaumont's name disrupts the meter, without concern for the ensuing disparity in pronouns, which remain singular:
"his" works, "as dead as He." Furthermore, the poem uses the convention
of a resurrected author ("Fletcher Return'd?"),[25] merely attempting to
interpose collaboration within this newer paradigm, in a way that the text
itself exhibits as afterthought and contradiction.

A more complex version of this interpolation, and one we will now
examine in detail, is suggested by Berkenhead's poem "On the happy
Collection of Master *FLETCHER'S* Works, never before PRINTED" (Eɪv).
The historically early appearance of an apostrophe marking Fletcher's
possession of his works in the title may serve to introduce the poem's
ostensible emphasis; it begins by commanding Fletcher to "arise" and
defend his sovereign textual property against the pilfering of "Usurpers."
Fletcher does not arrive from the afterworld unaccompanied, however
("Nor comes he private, here's great *BEAUMONT* too"), and the poem proceeds to comment at length on the process of their collaboration. In a way
that prefigures the work of twentieth-century critics of Beaumont and
Fletcher, who separate the plays into singly authored acts, scenes, and
lines,[26] Berkenhead writes, "Some thinke Your Witts of two Complexions
fram'd, / That One the Sock, th'Other the Buskin claim'd" (a mode of
criticism that would divide the plays by genre), but he rejects this description of collaboration in the familiarly reflexive discourse of friendship:

> But you were Both for Both; not Semi-witts,
> Each Piece is wholly Two, yet never splits:
> Y'are not Two *Faculties* (and one *Soule* still)
> He th'*Understanding*, Thou the quick free *Will*;

Refusing to divide up plays into scenes and the playwrights into attributes (though at the same time registering the urge to do so), Berkenhead instead identifies them, in a phrase that resonates with the reflexive discourse of other Renaissance theorists of friendship, as "Two, full Congeniall Soules."

The long middle section of the poem takes account of Beaumont's early death in terms familiar from other commendatory poems; Fletcher functions as both men, and the poem invokes absolutist language to describe this process: "Imperiall *FLETCHER!* here begins thy Raigne / Scenes flow like Sun-beams from thy glorious Brain" (E2). The middle section's departure from the earlier description of collaboration is signaled by its insistence on a competition between authorial figures ("Brave *Shakespeare* flow'd, yet had his Ebbings too, / Often above Himselfe, sometimes below; / Thou Always Best"), the policing of plagiarism (other playwrights steal from Fletcher's work), and the author's corresponding originality and self-sufficiency: "When did'st *Thou* borrow? . . . / Thou was't thine *owne* Muse" (E2). Comparing Fletcher on a number of bases with other playwrights, the section concludes with a statement that resolutely differentiates Fletcher: "Thou hadst no Sloath, no Rage, no sullen Fit, / But *Strengh* and *Mirth*, *FLETCHER'S* a *Sanguin* Wit" (E2v).[27]

It is something of a surprise, then, that after this lengthy excursus on Fletcher's distinction and difference, the last section of the poem begins with a moment of unearned logical conjunction: "Thus, two great *Consul*-Poets all things swayd, / Till all was *English* Borne or *English* Made" (E2v). The logically tenuous link between the poem's sections ("Thus") receives emphasis in the construction of Beaumont and Fletcher as "Consul-Poets." The previous section of the poem had elaborated the power of "Imperiall" Fletcher and his singular "Raigne" / "Brain"; here, though the imperial(ist) theme is retained in making all things English, the rhetoric is not that of absolutist monarchy but of Roman republicanism—"Consuls" being "the two annually elected magistrates who exercised conjointly supreme authority."[28] The stanza moves immediately to elaborate further the pair's inseparability, finding in their work "*Miter* and *Coyfe* here into

One Piece spun, / BEAVMONT a *Judge's*, This a *Prelat's* sonne." This rhetoric both introduces and erases the idea of separate patrimonies; Beaumont and Fletcher unite their fathers' occupations, as symbolized by the head-dress of the church and the law. Union (importantly, at the figure of the father) leads immediately into the final lines of a poem that is, it is useful to recall here, ostensibly written about "Master FLETCHER's Works":

> What strange Production is at last displaid,
> (Got by Two Fathers, without Female aide)
> Behold, two *Masculines* espous'd each other,
>   *Wit* and the World were born without a *Mother.*
> (E2v)

In this final burst of overdetermination, the poem exhibits the dialectic that has enabled it thus far, the attempt to explain within an increasingly authorial framework the production of collaborative texts. Enlarging on its tracings of patrimony, the poem clearly employs a patriarchal model of textual reproduction; the text is begotten by, and born of, its fathers. Yet the phrase "Got by Two Fathers"—two patriarchs, dual authorities—is virtually an oxymoron in this period. The *OED* glosses the verb "to get" as "to beget, procreate (said of the male parent)," and the definition's explan-atory parenthesis illustrates the problematic of the doubly fathered text at this cultural moment: of which male parent may we say this? That "got" was often followed by "on"—that is, that the hierarchy of the patriarchal model of reproduction was often (re)produced at the minute level of a preposition signaling the relative position of differently gendered par-ents—only further complicates the use of such rhetoric here; the passage glances at this problem (by exempting "Female aide" from the process) but does not offer further clarification. In sum, the poem attempts to perform here what it has unsuccessfully essayed thus far, an absorption of collaborative textual production within the realm of the author.

The difficulty of this consolidation, its apparent novelty, is signaled (as before) by the resonant term *strange.* The word *masculine* may also register here incipient discomfort with male-directed male sexuality in a new context. This appearance of *masculine* actually precedes by five years the *OED*'s first recorded instance of the word as a full-fledged noun meaning a "person of the male sex," but the *OED*'s 1652 quotation (from a tract condemning magicians and astrologers) may signal the extent to which the word marks the increasing notability of such a sexual relation: "If he had abused himselfe with a masculine . . . he was forced . . . to kill himselfe."[29] As with the word *get*, the difficulty of the phrase "two *Masculines* espous'd" lies in the traditional female-directed action of the verb; as the *OED* makes clear, *espouse* was only occasionally used in a context where the woman was the espouser rather than the espoused, and the first recorded use of the term in a reciprocal sense occurs in 1700. "Two Masculines espous'd each other" thus avoids the question of hierarchy resident in its very language of betrothal and marriage; at the same time, by keeping its fathers on equal, friend-ly terms, it may gesture toward the language of emergent companionate relations between men and women.[30]

As is perhaps obvious by this point, Berkenhead's negotiation of these models of textual production has radically marginalizing effects on representations of women. In its phrase "Got by Two Fathers, without Female aide," the poem appropriates female generative power for male purposes (this process is not restricted to a sexual sense, for "to get" also meant "to acquire wealth or property"). Furthermore, the poem aligns two important categories upon which the construction of the folio heavily depends, both art and nature ("*Wit* and the World"), with male procreation.[31] Stressing the erasure of female generativity ("without Female aide . . . without a *Mother*") in this context implicitly elides the possibility of female authorship; given the earlier notion that Beaumont and Fletcher's fathers' occupations are united in their sons, the poem's last line may suggest that the sons and their texts were "born without a *Mother*." Texts and authors both seem to be patriarchally generated.[32]

This misogynist fantasy is by no means restricted to Berkenhead's poem; at a number of points in the commendatory verses it is accomplished by the silencing of the female muses ("When did'st *Thou* borrow? . . . Thou was't thine *owne* Muse") in contexts that often associate borrowing or textual sharing with effeminacy. George Lisle's poem "To the memory of my most honoured kinsman, Mr. *Francis Beaumont*," for example, works like Berkenhead's, moving from the singular writer of the title to a consideration of collaboration, and it culminates in a similar appropriation of female generativity:

> Behold, here's *FLETCHER* too! the World ne're knew
> Two Potent Witts co-operate till You;
> For still your fancies are so wov'n and knit,
> Twas *FRANCIS-FLETCHER*, or *JOHN BEAUMONT* writ.

> Yet neither borrow'd, nor were so put to't
> To call poore Godds and Goddesses to do't;
> Nor made Nine Girles your *Muses* (you suppose
> Women ne're write, save *Love Letters in prose*)
> But are your owne Inspirers,. and have made
> Such pow'rfull Sceanes, as when they please, invade.
> (b1)

Like Berkenhead's, this poem collates a number of strands we have been analyzing: a masculinity allied with discourses of absolute power ("Two Potent Witts . . . pow'rfull Sceanes . . . invade"), authorial self-sufficiency and autonomy ("neither borrow'd"), and the reflexivity of friendship in the chiastic formulation of the names ("*FRANCIS-FLETCHER,* or *JOHN BEAU-MONT*"). The indeterminacy of the phrase "your owne Inspirers" may again signal the tension between "co-operation" (the two writers inspire each other) and authorial self-sufficiency (each inspires his "owne" work himself). Again: "Thou was't thine *owne* Muse." Yet, despite its slightly different approach to these issues, this poem parallels Berkenhead's in carefully policing the gendering of writing, at least in drama. The "Nine Girles" (this diminution of the usual terminology is itself significant) are held in abeyance; female writing is relegated to the decidedly unelevated domain of prose love-letters, and this alternative is proffered only as a qualification of the generalization that "Women ne're write." The potentiality of female dramatic authorship in the seventeenth century is a subject to which we will turn briefly below, but here it is important to note that the exclusion of such writing in this period occurs not only at the level of material practice (the restriction and manipulation of literacy, the manifold deprivations that Woolf long ago identified) but also in the discursive constitution and negotiation of those material circumstances, the erection and maintenance of generic boundaries.[33]

Self-estranging artifacts

Thus far I have argued that, in describing Beaumont and Fletcher and their plays, the folio's preliminary materials negotiate two modes of textual (re)production. The problematic status of collaboration is also an issue for the larger volume and its own practice; the book is self-evidently a collaborative enterprise, with introductory texts attributed to: the actors from whom Moseley secured the rights to print the plays after they could no longer make performative use of them; fellow-playwright James Shirley in a preface; Moseley in another preface; the thirty-six poets (most living, some dead) who wrote the thirty-seven commendatory verses; the unnamed and unenumerated "others" who (according to Moseley) wrote some of the plays' prologues and epilogues; the "severall Printers" (according to Moseley), as many as eight (according to R. C. Bald). And then there are the Beaumont-Fletcher plays themselves.[34]

Though only one of the preliminary texts is, according to its attribution, collaborative (the multiply signed actors' dedicatory letter), the negotiation of collaboration and authorship is not limited in these preliminary materials to playwrights long dead and only presently resurrected in their texts. The poets of the commendatory verses, inscribing themselves as both readers of and writers about Beaumont and Fletcher's texts, work to figure a relation between themselves and the "*Authours* of this *Volume*," in terms familiar from their construction of those authors themselves. The sexualities of collaboration and authorship are contested not only in descriptions of prior textual productions, but in those of the volume's present moment as well.

Though, in general, the verse writers tend to inscribe their own roles as more authorial (agonistic and competitive, emphasizing a singular poetics over collaborative drama), these inscriptions too are complicated. John Harris writes of the difficulty of commending Fletcher after his death ("Singly we now consult our selves and fame, / Ambitious to twist ours with thy good name" [f3v]), a situation he figures in strikingly gendered terms:

> And but [that] thy Male wit like the youthfull Sun
> Strongly begets upon our passion,
> Making our sorrow teeme with Elegie,
> Thou yet unwep'd, and yet unprais'd might'st be.
> (f4)

Constructing the belated elegists as female matter fertilized by Fletcher's "Male wit" (they are "strongly begot upon"), Harris places current poets in an agonistic relation with Fletcher—desiring but unable to approach his greatness in the very poems that attempt to praise him. Harris furthermore associates the paucity of these poetic inscriptions with female generativity, writing that the poems in Fletcher's praise

> are imperfect births; and such are all
> Produc'd by causes not univocall,
> The scapes of Nature, Passives being unfit,
> And hence our verse speakes only Mother wit.
> (f4)

Univocal could describe terms or signs signifying unambiguously (the author as patriarchally constituted would speak with one voice), but "univocal generation" was also the term used to signify reproduction between male and female members of the same species (*OED*). Harris writes that his textual reproduction with Fletcher is not univocal—that is, that they are not members of the same poetic species, a mixture that results in malformed offspring, "scapes of Nature"; it is relevant too that *scape* could mean an error in speech or print, a breach of chastity, or flatulence. More interesting, perhaps, is Harris's misogynist gendering of his own otherness *in specie* as female, as a way of marking both the superiority and the patriarchality of Fletcher; in the end, Harris and his contemporaries can produce "only Mother wit"—common sense.

Not content to remain in the effeminized category he has established, however, Harris proceeds immediately to expose again the agonism of this model:

> Oh for a fit o'th Father! for a Spirit
> That might but parcell of thy worth inherit;
> For but a sparke of that diviner fire
> Which thy full breast did animate and inspire.

Harris here refers back to the inadequacy of his "Mother wit" and puns on the contemporary term for hysteria, "fit of the Mother," which took its name from the supposed wandering of the womb ("the Mother").[35] Harris desires instead a disease that is not one (this is the only occurrence of the term "fit of the father" that I know of); it is precisely not a disease in a patriarchal culture because it might hypothetically be said to consist of a super-abundance of the phallus. The sexual valence of these lines is only strengthened by evidence that in contemporary discourse "spirit" often signified both penis and semen (the "spirit generative").[36] The poem thus inscribes a fantasy in which ensuing poets "inherit" (again, it would seem, "without Female aide") a "spirit" from the author as patriarchally conceived, and it aligns this suggestion in a parallel construction with what will in subsequent centuries become a dominant authorial model, the internally generating genius (in incipient form): "a sparke of that diviner fire."

A similar configuration appears in T. Palmer's tribute to Fletcher, which culminates, as we saw earlier, in the paradoxical claim that the highest praise of Fletcher lies in labeling him Beaumont's friend. The poem proceeds from there to develop a moment of imagined collaboration with Fletcher:

> What shall I doe? all Commendations end,
> In saying only thou wert *BEAUMONTS* Friend?
> Give me thy spirit quickely, for I swell,
> And like a raveing Prophetesse cannot tell
> How to receive thy *Genius* in my breast.
>
> (f2v)

Like Harris, Palmer asks for Fletcher's "spirit," but again the apparent homoeroticism of this configuration (a resonance strengthened by the reference to male friendship discourse and what may in this context be a suggestion of phallic swelling) is avoided in a shift that genders the speaker of the poem as a female receptacle for the (quickening) authorial spirit of genius. The conclusion of George Buck's poem, "To the desert of the Author in his most Ingenious Pieces," likewise swerves away from a collaborative model of male textual intercourse. Comparing Fletcher to other canonized dramatists of the period, Buck writes:

> Let *Shakespeare*, *Chapman*, and applauded *Ben*,
> Weare the Eternall merit of their Pen,
> Here I am love-sicke: and were I to chuse,
> A Mistris corrivall 'tis *Fletcher's* Muse.
>
> (c3)

Having disposed of Shakespeare, Chapman, and Jonson, the sentence would seem logically to require its "love-sicke" writer to choose Fletcher, a formulation that would place the writer in a situation not unlike the often homoerotic configuration of collaboration earlier in the century. Nevertheless, the poem establishes this possibility only to efface it: the proposed partner is not Fletcher but "Fletcher's Muse," and the relation is rendered (gendered) in what we would now call heterosexual terms. And yet, we can perhaps see the vestigial traces of the collaborative model in the unusual appearance here of the term "Mistris corrivall"; a *corrival* (or co-rival) was a rival suitor, usually male, and Buck's term is in a sense oxymoronic. Though the sentence may thus sketch a configuration in which Shakespeare *et al.* are gendered as female rival mistresses to Fletcher's muse, there is also the implication (not entirely avoided by the word "Muse") of collaborative male intercourse.

In each of these instances, commendatory poets inscribe their relation to the dead Beaumont and Fletcher in the discourses used to figure the relation between the dramatists themselves. But I want also to suggest that these moments in the Beaumont and Fletcher folio make emphatic a notion that has been implicit in this argument from the beginning. I have noted elsewhere the tenuousness in a collaborative paradigm of borders between what we now call "individuals," and we have seen the ways in which collaborative texts and texts figuring collaboration often slip easily between identities, frustrating modern attempts to discern separate authors, divergent persons, or distinct characters. The authorial paradigm with which we are more familiar, of course, depends upon the construction and policing of the borders of personhood, an identification of the textual parent. In the Beaumont and Fletcher volume, however, the apparatus guaranteeing the identification of separable individuals and their discrete textual properties is very much in flux. We have noted in passing the occasional appearance of the apostrophe in its new role delimiting textual property; plays are attributed to one writer, the other, or both; Fletcher is said to become Beaumont-and-Fletcher after Beaumont's death. In other words, just as this volume occupies a liminal status between collaboration and authorship, between collective making imagined homoerotically and patriarchally individuated textual properties, the book is also situated, in a way I can only suggest here, at a crucial moment in the history of the subject. This applies not only to the complicated emulation and agonism inscribed by the book's commendatory verse writers (who are also of course its readers), but also to the larger book-consuming audience for this volume. Addressing this audience in his preface, James Shirley suggests the instability of the categories: "You may here find passions raised to that excellent pitch and by such insinuating degrees that you shall not chuse but consent, & go along with them, finding your self at last grown insensibly the very same person you read, and then stand admiring the subtile Trackes of your engagement" (A3v). We might take as a marker of the sort of estrangement Shirley here de-

scribes the fact that, as in many Renaissance texts, the personal pronoun of possession (in this case, "your") has not yet become inseparably,
typographically fused with the "self," and the passage resonates with the
sort of self-reflecting "consenting consort" and "mutuall interchoice"
inscribed in Richard Brathwait's definition of friendship, or Montaigne's
textual friendship. And yet, there are also in this passage hints of a new
dispensation of self-possession: the self views its own misleading "engagement"; it stands outside the text, warily, if admiringly noting the insensibility and "insinuating degrees" of its (momentary) dispossession. The
thrill of insensibility, the pleasures of self-identification and momentary
self-estrangement, have become a selling point. There is even a hint here
of the language of collaborative intercourse we have read elsewhere in the
volume: "passions," in / sinuation, "engagement."[37]

Mistris corrivall

I know there are many Scholastical and Pedantical persons that will condemn my
writings, because I do not keep strictly to the Masculine and Feminine Genders,
as they call them, as for example a Lock and a Key. . . . but I know no reason but
that I may as well make them Hees for my use, as others did Shees, or Shees as
others did Hees.—Margaret Cavendish, "To the Readers," *Playes*, 1662[38]

Margaret Cavendish's entrance into a genre constructed within an almost
entirely male institution and conceived of either as a conversation between
men and / or as patriarchal generation—her publication of not one but
two elaborate folios in the 1660s—is an important and undernoted development in the publication of English drama, central to an understanding
of the gendering of authorship in the Renaissance and after, and worthy
of more analysis than I can provide in this context. I cite her here, however,
because her negotiations of gendered models of collaboration and authorship (her observations on the gender of lock and key are more than
arbitrary examples in a grammar lesson) illustrate the real queerness, to
our modern eyes, of Renaissance modes of textual reproduction.

In the multiple self-authored preliminary letters in her 1662 volume,
Cavendish largely avoids the sexual discourses of writing we have examined, relying on a model that recalls the patriarchal (in its emphasis on
singularity and self-sufficiency) but that is stripped of its reproductive
language. Her single reference to her writing within sexualized discourse

occurs, importantly, in her description of her husband's participation in a volume she otherwise emphasizes as her own. "My Lord," she writes,

> was pleased to illustrate my Playes with some Scenes of his own Wit, to which I have set his name, that my Readers may know which are his, as not to Cozen them, in thinking they are mine; also Songs to which my Lords name is set, for being no Lyrick Poet, my Lord supplied the defect of my Braine; thus our Wits join as in Matrimony, my Lords the Masculine, mine the Feminine Wit, which is no small glory to me, that we are Married, Souls, Bodies, and Brains, which is a treble marriage, united in one Love. (no sig.)

Read alongside the Beaumont and Fletcher preliminaries, this passage is interesting for a number of reasons. Cavendish uses the sexualized language of male-male collaboration already marked as "strange" in the Beaumont and Fletcher folio, but here reproduces it within the newly emergent discourse of companionate marriage. The passage is startling to the modern reader acquainted with the Beaumont-Fletcher materials, for it demonstrates the emergence of male-female collaboration out of the prior discourse of homoerotic friendship; furthermore, we are witnessing, in this under-read volume, the (re)construction of heterosexual marriage out of a particular vocabulary of Renaissance homoeroticism. The normative mode of textual intercourse in drama in the early decades of the century ("two Masculines espous'd") had become by 1647 "strange Production"; at the same time, what would have signified as radical production in, say, Florio's Montaigne (that is, the presumptive impossibility, even perversity, of men and women writing together) is here written into the discourse of marriage: not "two Masculines," but Masculine and Feminine "espous'd."[39]

As I have already noted, by quoting only Cavendish's brief discussion of collaboration, I am reversing the emphasis of her volume, which concentrates on the construction of an authorial self-sufficiency that works to escape gendered paradigms. But even in the passage cited above, we can see how the regendering of the collaborative partnership functions to separate out authorial shares in the collaboration; where an earlier, homoerotic discourse of collaboration insisted upon the undifferentiation of style and subjectivities, Cavendish's model of collaboration (written within an increasingly patriarchal authorial framework) emphasizes the differentiation of textual material by sex: "being no Lyrick Poet, my Lord supplied the defect of my Braine . . . my Lords the Masculine, mine the Feminine Wit." This insertion of (sexual) difference within a collaboration imagined earlier in the century as "twin-like" is, finally, accompanied in Cavendish by a careful regulation of textual property within the paradigm of singular authorship. Cavendish says she has "set [her husband's] name" to his texts (to do otherwise is to "Cozen" her readers); her identification of her husband's relatively small contributions serves simultaneously to identify and accentuate her own.

Living arrangements

I have outlined in this essay the inseparability of discourses we would now think of as distinct—sexuality and reproduction, on the one hand, and textual production and property on the other—and I have argued that, by the mid-seventeenth century, the emergent discourse of singular authorship only tenuously supplants an earlier model of homoerotic collaboration (simultaneously marking that prior model as "strange" in a sense that resonates as "queer"). While noting these conjunctions and historical shifts, it is important to stress the need not to romanticize the period's conceptions of homoeroticism, collaboration, or their alignment. (This model carries with it other significant political valences I have been unable fully to delineate here, not least of which are its class-specificity and its marginalization and erasure of women). Instead, we can use this material to emphasize the very unnaturalness of (that is, the constructedness of) the patriarchal model of singular authorship in which, largely, we continue to write, conceptualize individuated style, and imagine texts as property and progeny.[40]

The discussion above also illustrates the inappropriateness of using the materials we have read toward an "outing" of Renaissance figures. The modern political utility of demonstrating that Beaumont and Fletcher were "gay" is of course mitigated by their lack of current cultural significance; the more central figure in this regard is Shakespeare, who also participated in the collaborative discourses/practices I have analyzed here, though the intersecting phobias of collaboration and homoeroticism have largely protected him from such a consideration thus far. The larger point is, nevertheless, the impossibility of such an "outing" in this context. We would want to remember first the complexities of using documents deployed to organize a volume to ascertain the sexuality of its dead subjects. At the same time, the language we have been examining suggests the extent to which our own models of sexuality seem inapplicable to the persons here represented (and here I mean Beaumont and Fletcher, the poets who write about them, and the readers they imagine and construct). Not only do these materials significantly complicate the ideas of individuation upon which our notions of essential and identifiable sexuality are based; they also provide a glimpse into an era that includes and encodes a number of intersecting sexual discourses and systems.[41]

In another sense, outing Beaumont and Fletcher is the mildest of possible claims one might make on the basis of the evidence we have read, because it locates gaiety only in specific individuals (again, I would point out the difficulty of the term in this context), working effectively to quarantine other dramatists and writers of the period from the threat of homosexuality. In a largely heterosexist economy of value, Beaumont and Fletcher become sexual suspects, but Shakespeare, Massinger, Middleton, Webster, and Ford profit from their labeling. Instead, by making a discursive argument—by emphasizing that these were the discourses in which collaboration and authorship were understood—I want to claim a much larger effect for the languages we have been reading within Renaissance English culture. By denaturalizing authorship and common-sense notions of writing, we are beginning to recognize the prevalence of collaboration, as a practice, in the Renaissance theater; by training ourselves to read the discourses that both inscribed and re-produced that practice, we will begin to notice their prevalence elsewhere in the culture: in conduct books, essays, letters, commonplace books, plays (written in collaboration or alone). We might take as a metaphor of this disseminative process Fletcher's own wide-ranging textual practice; he wrote alone, with Beaumont, with Shakespeare, with Middleton and others, and was buried with Massinger, in a single grave.[42] "Since never parted while they lived," Moseley wrote of Beaumont and Fletcher, "I conceived it not equitable to seperate their ashes" (A4v). The sifting of these ashes into "straight" and "gay" remains problematic.[43]

The point, then, is not to bring the Renaissance out of the closet, but rather to bring the closet out of the Renaissance. For it is clear from the materials above that certain kinds of male-male sexuality are only beginning to be marked as "strange" by 1647, only beginning to be isolated in the privacy of the closet, the sanctity of the bedroom. It is interesting here to note, finally, one of the few surviving descriptions of Beaumont and Fletcher's relationship outside of the folio, John Aubrey's recollection that

> There was a wonderfull consimility of phansey between [Francis Beaumont] and Mr. John Fletcher, which caused the dearnesse of friendship between them. . . . They lived together on the Banke side, not far from the Play-house, both batchelors; lay together . . . had one wench in the house between them, which they did so admire; the same cloathes and cloake, &c., between them.[44]

Aubrey is often discounted as unreliable, but (as with any reading that attempts to account for the textuality of history) I think it is important to take seriously the terms in which he frames his discussion of dramatic and domestic collaboration in the period. At a lecture I gave recently, a member of the audience insisted on the basis of this description that Beaumont and Fletcher "must be gay"; the woman "between them," this person argued, "must be a cover." Though we have become accustomed, in modernity, to read the apparent lack of sexuality as homosexuality's surest sign,[45] it is important to point out this description's seeming obliviousness to the public/private distinctions we have come to see as central to a modern discourse of sexuality, the way in which there seems to be nothing to cover, no need for closet space in this shared household. What we can see here, instead, is that the terms in which Aubrey describes dramatic collaboration resonate with the others we have seen contested in the highly public venue of the folio: the "dearnesse of friendship," the doubly reflexive "consimility of phansey," the collaborative theatricality and intersubjective indiscernibility of two playwrights who (in a culture where clothes literally and legally made the man) share the "same cloathes and cloake, &c., between them." Aubrey's "&c." may both open further erotic possibilities and gesture toward what he may take as the absolute conventionality of his statement: so obvious as not needing to be named among Christians.[46]

Finally, in a way that may help us distance ourselves from a modern paradigm of artistic creation (in which writing transcends living, in which textual production and the enculturated forms of eroticism are held to be strictly separate), this anecdote does much to obliterate our sense of separate living, working, sleeping, and writing space. Living near the Playhouse; playing house. Writing together; lying together. Only eventually: "strange Production."

Notes

For critique and collaboration, I wish to thank Margreta de Grazia, Jay Grossman, Carol Mason, and Peter Stallybrass.

1. Francis Beaumont and John Fletcher, *Comedies and Tragedies* (London: for Humphrey Robinson and Humphrey Moseley, 1647), sig. E2v. All subsequent references to this volume will appear parenthetically. In transcribing typography, I have often reversed the usual transcription of italic and roman text—especially where the folio's "default" font is italic. It cannot be assumed that the titles of the volume's commendatory verses were, or were not, written by the poets to whom the verses are attributed (in this case, Berkenhead), or by the publisher Moseley, or by someone else.

2. I use *homoerotic* in order to avoid the overtones of modern identity in the term *homosexual.* For critiques of the use of *homosexual* in historical work, see David M. Halperin, "One Hundred Years of Homosexuality," in *One Hundred Years of Homosexuality and Other Essays on Greek Love* (New York: Routledge, 1990), and Jonathan Goldberg, "Colin to Hobbinol: Spenser's Familiar Letters," *South Atlantic Quarterly* 88 (1989):107–26. At the same time, I would point out that Montaigne differentiates friendship from sodomy, excluding from the former what he calls "this other Greeke licence . . . because according to use it had so necessarie a disparitie of ages and differences of offices betweene lovers, [it] did no more sufficiently answer the perfect union and agreement, which we here require"; *The Essays of Montaigne,* trans. John Florio, with an introduction by George Saintsbury, 3 vols. (London: David Nutt, 1892), 1:200. The essay suggests, in other words, that there were multiple homoeroticisms in the Renaissance—some condemned, some privileged.

3. On the problematic history of this term, see Raymond Williams, *Keywords: A Vocabulary of Culture and Society* (New York: Oxford, 1976), 133–36; and Peter Stallybrass, "Shakespeare, the Individual, and the Text," in *Cultural Studies,* ed. Lawrence Grossberg, Cary Nelson, and Paula Treichler, with Linda Baughman, and with assistance from John Macgregor Wise (New York: Routledge, 1992), 593–610.

4. Montaigne/Florio, 1:202.

5. "To . . . his pamphlet I am particularly most bounden, forsomuch as it was the instrumentall meane of our first acquaintance" (Montaigne/Florio, 1:197).

6. In a larger project I read both the Montaigne/Florio and the Brathwait texts in detail; *Textual Intercourse: Collaboration, Authorship, and Sexualities in Renaissance Drama* (forthcoming). Richard Brathwait, *The English Gentleman,* 2nd ed. (London: Felix Kyngston for Robert Bostocke, 1633); the engraving in figure 1 illustrated the initial printing of Alan Bray's "Homosexuality and the Signs of Male Friendship in Elizabethan England." My understanding of male friendship in the period is greatly indebted to Bray's essay.

7. On companionate marriage, see Lawrence Stone, *The Family, Sex and Marriage in England, 1500–1800*, abridged edition (New York: Harper, 1977), 100–101, 217–18. Though the first and third editions of Brathwait's *The English Gentleman* (cited above) are separated by only eleven years, it is possible to read in the details of its publication history this shift in the sex-gender system in microcosm. Where the engravings to the first two editions depicted "acquaintance" as two men hugging, the 1641 engraving substitutes two disembodied hands shaking. The 1641 edition furthermore brings together two conduct books, *The English Gentleman* and *The English Gentlewoman*, in one volume; it seems to be a textual marriage of male and female companion volumes, the word made one flesh—or in the words of the title: *The English Gentleman and English Gentlewoman, Both in one Volume couched* (London: John Dawson, 1641). That Brathwait speaks even in the early editions of a wife as a variety of "acquaintance," however, also suggests the simultaneous circulation and overlapping of sex-gender discourses in this culture (within a single text)—a situation that a word like "shift" too easily simplifies. This is not to say that homoeroticism disappears with the emergence of companionate marriage but rather that its form(s) and articulation(s) change.

8. This formulation departs from and attempts to specify two important arguments of Michel Foucault; see "What Is an Author?" trans. Josué V. Harari, *The Foucault Reader*, ed. Paul Rabinow (New York: Pantheon, 1984), 101–20, and *The History of Sexuality: Volume I: An Introduction*, trans. Robert Hurley (New York: Vintage, 1980). *Patriarchal* has often been used in contemporary feminist discourse to signify any gender-stratified social system that is male-dominated. I follow Gayle Rubin in restricting its use here to a specific sex/gender system, one headed by a patriarch; see Rubin, "The Traffic in Women: Notes on the 'Political Economy' of Sex," *Toward an Anthropology of Women*, ed. Rayna Reiter (New York: Monthly Review Press, 1975), 166–68. I rely here on more specific analyses of patriarchal systems in Renaissance England: Susan Dwyer Amussen, *An Ordered Society: Gender and Class in Early Modern England* (Oxford: Basil Blackwell, 1988); Gordon J. Schochet, *Patriarchalism in Political Thought: The Authoritarian Family and Political Speculation and Attitudes Especially in Seventeenth-Century England* (Oxford: Basil Blackwell, 1975); and Jonathan Goldberg, "Fatherly Authority: The Politics of Stuart Family Images," in *Rewriting the Renaissance: The Discourses of Sexual Difference in Early Modern Europe*, ed. Margaret W. Ferguson, Maureen Quilligan, and Nancy J. Vickers (Chicago: University of Chicago Press, 1986), 3–32. Importantly, patriarchal absolutism continues to circulate as a discourse of textual property and writing long after its currency as a discourse of familial and national government.

9. See Margreta de Grazia's discussion of patrilineage as an organizing principle in the Shakespeare folio in *Shakespeare Verbatim: The Reproduction of Authenticity and the 1790 Apparatus* (Oxford: Clarendon, 1991), 37–42. See also Timothy Murray, *Theatrical Legitimation: Allegories of Genius in Seventeenth-Century England and France* (New York: Oxford University Press, 1987).

10. On the prevalence of collaboration, see G. E. Bentley, *The Profession of Dramatist in Shakespeare's Time, 1590–1642* (Princeton: Princeton University Press, 1971); Stephen

Orgel, "What Is a Text?" in *Staging the Renaissance: Reinterpretations of Elizabethan and Jacobean Drama*, ed. David Scott Kastan and Peter Stallybrass (New York: Routledge, 1991), 83–87; Jeff Masten, "Beaumont and/or Fletcher: Collaboration and the Interpretation of Renaissance Drama," *ELH* 59 (1992):337–56.

11.   On the portrait as a collation of art and nature—organizing tropes in the folio's two important predecessors, the Jonson and Shakespeare folios (respectively)—see de Grazia, *Shakespeare Verbatim*, 46–47. On the classicism of the Jonson folio, see Peter Stallybrass and Allon White, "The Fair, the Pig, Authorship," in *The Politics and Poetics of Transgression* (Ithaca: Cornell University Press, 1986), 27–79; Joseph Loewenstein, "The Script in the Marketplace" *Representations* 12 (1985):101–14; and Murray, *Theatrical Legitimation*.

12.   For example, see the title pages to: John Fletcher and William Shakespeare, *The Two Noble Kinsmen* (London: Tho. Cotes for Iohn Waterson, 1634) and Francis Beaumont and John Fletcher, *A King, and No King* (London: A.M. for Richard Hawkins, 1631).

13.   On this ambiguity in other collaborative texts, see Masten, "Beaumont and/or Fletcher."

14.   In large part, discussion of this volume, and the canon of Beaumont and Fletcher plays it establishes (with its 1679 successor), has centered on the question of why the publishers did not more carefully separate and identify plays of differing authorship. See, for example, R. C. Bald, *Bibliographical Studies in the Beaumont and Fletcher Folio of 1647*, Supplement to the Bibliographical Society's Transactions, no. 13 (Oxford: Oxford University Press for the Bibliographical Society, 1938 [for 1937]). The plays' standard edition, *The Dramatic Works in the Beaumont and Fletcher Canon*, general editor Fredson Bowers, 7 vols. (Cambridge: Cambridge University Press, 1966–), rearranges the plays "chiefly by authors" (1:vii).

15.   *Mr. William Shakespeares Comedies, Histories, & Tragedies* (London: by Isaac Iaggard and Ed. Blount, 1623). Subsequent citations will appear parenthetically.

16.   De Grazia, *Shakespeare Verbatim*, 44.

17.   For a vindication of Moseley (an effort to correlate his statements with the bibliographical evidence that is clearly in the familiar New Bibliographic genre of defenses of Shakespeare's collectors Heminge and Condell), see Bald, *Bibliographical Studies*, 114 and passim.

18.   De Grazia, *Shakespeare Verbatim*, 39.

19.   *The Workes of our Antient and Learned English Poet, GEFFREY CHAVCER, newly Printed* (London: by Adam Islip at the charges of Bonham Norton, 1598); *The Workes of the Most High and Mightie Prince, Iames . . .* (London: Robert Barker and Iohn Bill [for] Iames, Bishop of Winton, 1616), sig. a3.

20.   The *OED* cites 1798 as the first usage of *intercourse* in a sexual sense, but also restricts that usage to intercourse between differently sexed persons. The first recorded use of *sexual intercourse* dates from 1799, and it is useful to recall here that *sexual* first meant what we now call "gender" or "sexual difference." That is, when the term *sexual intercourse* was first used, it apparently applied only to heterosexual activity. As is well known, sexual activity between men was no new thing in the Renaissance; it

only came to be labeled as new and different, as many following Foucault have argued, later, around the time this terminology emerged. (See, for example, Alan Bray's chapter, "Molly," in *Homosexuality in Renaissance England* [London: Gay Men's Press, 1982].) Therefore, it is possible that *intercourse* has a same-sexual valence in 1647, though I know of no examples.

21. See Bray's suggestive remarks on travel narratives (p. 75), and the imprisonment of a black man, Domingo Cassedon Drago, for "a buggery" in 1647 (pp. 72–73), in *Homosexuality in Renaissance England.*

22. Michael Warner, "New English Sodom," in this volume.

23. Lawrence Stone provides evidence for the terminological intersection I am describing (*Family, Sex and Marriage in England*, 218–19). Foucault makes a related suggestion when he argues that sex between men only comes to be viewed as problematic with the demise of a certain type of "intense" male friendship: "As long as friendship was something important, was socially accepted, nobody realized men had sex together. You couldn't say that men *didn't have* sex together—it just didn't matter . . . The disappearance of friendship as a social relation, and the declaration of homosexuality as a social / political / medical problem, are the same process" ("An Interview: Sex, Power and the Politics of Identity," *The Advocate*, Aug. 7, 1984, 30).

24. On the author-function, see Foucault, "What Is an Author?"

25. Incipient forms of this resurrection are staged, for example, by Gower in *Pericles*, and Homer in Heywood's *Ages* plays.

26. For a critique of traditional attribution study in collaborative plays, see Masten, "Beaumont and / or Fletcher."

27. Here the apostrophe may function either as contraction or possessive.

28. On absolutism and its contestation in the folio, see note 37 below.

29. See *OED masculine* (sb.2). The quotation is from John Gaule's *The Mag-astro-mancer, or The Magical-Astrologicall-Diviner Posed, and Puzzled* (London: for Joshua Kirton, 1652), 265. A discussion of diverse sexual practices in different cultures (examples that disprove the astrologer's contention that stars govern all human behavior), the passage also cites the ancient Greeks, who "were not ashamed to pursue specious boyes."

30. I am suggesting, in other words, the coexistence and contestation of discourses of hierarchical (patriarchal) marriage, male friendship, and companionate marriage.

31. See de Grazia, *Shakespeare Verbatim*, 46–47.

32. A significant amount of the literature of reproduction in this period assumes male fertilization of inert female matter; see Thomas Laqueur, *Making Sex: Body and Gender from the Greeks to Freud* (Cambridge: Harvard University Press, 1990); Angus McLaren, *Reproductive Rituals: The Perception of Fertility in England from the Sixteenth Century to the Nineteenth Century* (London: Methuen, 1984).

33. Virginia Woolf, *A Room of One's Own* (San Diego: Harcourt Brace Jovanovich, 1929). On the relation of the material practices of handwriting in this period and their discursive constitution, see Jonathan Goldberg's important study, *Writing Matter: From the Hands of the English Renaissance* (Stanford: Stanford University Press, 1990).

34. On the actors' relation to the publication of the play-texts and the collaborative printing of the volume, see Bald, *Bibliographic Studies.*

35. *OED* and Laqueur, *Making Sex,* 108–10.

36. See Stephen Booth, *Shakespeare's Sonnets* (New Haven: Yale University Press, 1977), 441–43.

37. Although one would want to be careful not to situate too precisely the emergence of a proto-bourgeois individualism in the civil wars of this period, resultant changes in modes of government, and adjustments in the definition of political "subjects," the shift I am describing can usefully be seen in the context of the tumultuous political events of the 1640s through the 1660s. A fuller account of the Beaumont and Fletcher folio in this context would consider the politics of the volume—its insistent royalism and alignment of singular, fatherly authorship with the political authority of Stuart absolutism and, at the same time, the tenuousness of such claims in the context of a collaboratively produced volume. On shifts in the notion of individual, see Peter Stallybrass, "Shakespeare, the Individual, and the Text"; on the ineffectuality of traditional attribution studies based on individual style in the literature and propaganda of the civil wars, see Lois Potter, *Secret Rites and Secret Writing: Royalist Literature, 1641–1660* (Cambridge: Cambridge University Press, 1989), 14, 122.

38. *PLAYES Written by the Thrice NOBLE, ILLUSTRIOUS AND Excellent Princess, THE LADY MARCHIONESS OF NEWCASTLE* (London: by A. Warren for John Martyn, James Allestry, and Tho. Dicas, 1662), no sig.

39. This is not to say that companionate marriage has fully displaced more hierarchical notions of marriage in Cavendish's discourse (as her repetition of the term "My Lord" suggests) or that, more generally, companionate marriage was equitable in seventeenth-century practice.

40. Although the notion of patriarchal authorship has clearly become less gender-specific, Western culture in general still relies in certain discourses on the notion of texts as the progeny of a singular parent (whatever his/her gender). For the central feminist demystification of patriarchal authorship, see Sandra Gilbert and Susan Gubar, *The Madwoman in the Attic: The Woman Writer and the Nineteenth-Century Literary Imagination* (New Haven: Yale University Press, 1984). For discussion and critique of singular authorship from a number of legal, literary, historical, and theoretical perspectives, see *Cardozo Arts & Entertainment Law Journal* 10, no. 2 (1992), an issue devoted to "Intellectual Property and the Construction of Authorship."

41. Eve Kosofsky Sedgwick's *Epistemology of the Closet* (Berkeley: University of California Press, 1990) brilliantly argues this point for the nineteenth and twentieth centuries.

42. See T. W. Baldwin, *The Organization and Personnel of the Shakespearean Company* (Princeton: Princeton University Press, 1927), 51.

43. The preceding paragraphs may suggest the extent of my disagreement with Wayne Koestenbaum's recent *Double Talk: The Erotics of Male Literary Collaboration* (New York: Routledge, 1989). As Koestenbaum makes clear in his introduction, he is uninterested in the historicity and materiality of authorship, collaboration, the individual, and sexuality (8–10). A number of the categories central to his analysis—the psy-

choanalyzable subject, the "integrity of the author"—are largely inappropriate to the Renaissance, though he argues for the extension of his method transhistorically (p. 12). This is not to deny the importance of a book that has usefully opened up the possibility of discussing the erotics of collaboration.

44. *'Brief Lives,' Chiefly of Contemporaries, set down by John Aubrey, between the years 1669 and 1696,* ed. Andrew Clark, 2 vols. (Oxford: Clarendon Press, 1898), 1:95–96. My ellipsis between "lay together" and "had one wench" elides only Aubrey's attribution of his source.

45. On the importance of the secret and privacy for modern conceptions of homosexuality, see Sedgwick, *Epistemology.*

46. See Foucault, note 23 above.

Fighting Women and Loving Men: Dryden's Representation of Shakespeare in ALL FOR LOVE

MARCIE FRANK

ALL for Love (1678), John Dryden's version of William Shakespeare's *Antony and Cleopatra*, is the only play by Dryden that critics like without qualifications.[1] Nevertheless, much contemporary critical discussion evaluates *All for Love* in comparison to *Antony and Cleopatra*.[2] If these discussions have been invited by Dryden himself, who remarks in the preface, "In my Stile I have profess'd to imitate the Divine Shakespeare" (13:18), elsewhere, both in the preface and in the play, Dryden also presents his relation to Shakespeare differently. My aim in the pages that follow is not so much to advance (or call into question) estimations of Dryden's worth, as to raise a corollary concern, not how Shakespeare enabled Dryden's dramatic practice, but how Dryden's relation to Shakespeare shaped his criticism. Although the topic is not unfamiliar—from Samuel Johnson to Gary Taylor, critics find in Dryden's appreciation of Shakespeare grounds for recognizing Dryden as an important predecessor critic—the relationship between Dryden as a critic and as a dramatist, and how one practice relates to the other, is new territory. Moreover, by reading these practices together, I will be suggesting that the prevailing models of Dryden's relation to Shakespeare need to be called into question.

In his *Life of Dryden*, Johnson says, "Nothing can be added" to Dryden's account of Shakespeare in the "Essay of Dramatick Poesy" by the subsequent critics whose practice he inaugurates.[3] If Johnson can be said to ignore the ambivalences and contradictions in Dryden's treatment of Shakespeare, Gary Taylor proposes that Dryden's relation to Shakespeare is filial, as a way to explain and therefore resolve any problems raised by Dryden's ambivalence.

> Some readers have concluded that Dryden's criticisms were conventional but his praise sincere; others decide that his praise was hypocritical and his contempt genuine. I suspect instead that a real admiration cohabited with a real contempt, and that the two attitudes tortured each other for the length of Dryden's life. In 1668 [in "Essay of Dramatick Poesy"] Dryden could say "I love Shakespeare" and mean it—in the same way that an adolescent can honestly abstractly say, "I love my parents" while in practice hating them much of the time. It was Davenant who liked to believe and let others believe that he was Shakespeare's bastard, but it was Dryden who acted like a son—or, rather, an orphan—a posthumous child of uncertain paternity constantly measuring himself against the image of his dead father, testing his legitimacy by his success, finding himself wanting, professing "respect" while chafing for some form of independence, hating what he loved, and hating himself for hating it.[4]

Neither Johnson nor Taylor is interested in analyzing the uses to which Dryden puts Shakespeare in his establishment of a critical practice. In this essay, I ask after these uses in order to show both the inadequacies of Taylor and Johnson's accounts—they are inappropriately and exclusively oedipalized—and the ways in which Dryden invites this response. I take my cues from Dryden's critical remarks in the preface to *All for Love*.

The preface ends: "But since I may not be over-confident of my performance after him [Shakespeare], it will be prudence in me to be silent. Yet I hope I may affirm, and without vanity, that by imitating him I have excell'd myself throughout the Play and particularly, that I prefer the Scene betwixt *Antony* and *Ventidius* in the first Act, to any I have written in this kind" (19). Imprudently, perhaps, Dryden does not remain silent; remarkably, he praises a scene of his own invention. In this addition to Shakespeare's play, the characters alternate between long set speeches and short, rapid interchanges in which each metrically finishes the other's lines. The scene begins when Ventidius announces his previously unnoticed presence to Antony.

> *Ant.*   [starting up] Art thou Ventidius?
> *Ven.*   Are you Antony?

I'm liker what I was, than you to him
I left you last.

Ant.   I'm angry.
Ven.   So am I.
Ant.   I would be private: leave me.
Ven.   Sir, I love you,
And therefore will not leave you.
Ant.   Will not leave me?
Where have you learnt that Answer? who am I?
Ven.   My Emperor; the Man I love next Heav'n:
If I said more, I think 'twere scarce a Sin.

(1.1.248–54)

Their emotions soon escalate to include tears and blushes.

Ant.   Now thou hast seen me, art thou satisfy'd?
For if a Friend, thou hast beheld enough;
And if a Foe, too much.
Ven.   [weeping] Look, Emperor, this is no common Deaw,
I have not wept this Forty year; but now
My Mother comes afresh into my eyes;
I cannot help her softness.
Ant.   By Heav'n he weeps, poor good old Man, he weeps!
The big round drops course one another down
The furrows of his cheeks. Stop 'em, Ventidius,
Or I shall blush to death: they set my shame,
That caus'd 'em, full before me.

(1.1.259–70)

The scene climaxes when Ventidius, having declared his love, persuades Antony to rally his forces. Their mutual interruptive style measures their merger and the scene ends with their embrace.

Although this scene is dramatically impressive, Dryden singles it out on the basis of the critical expertise he has claimed for himself in the rest of the preface, primarily through his negative assessment of another scene of his own creation, one in which Octavia and Cleopatra confront each other, each vying for the title of Antony's legitimate "wife." Both of Dryden's innovative scenes dramatize unconventional interactions between members of the same sex: in the scene Dryden criticizes as the major flaw in his play, two women fight, and in the scene Dryden selects as his favorite, two men declare their love for each other. The critical compensation that exists between the two same-sex scenes suggests that matters of gender inform Dryden's representation of Shakespeare; as I will show, these, in turn, shape his critical practice.

Indeed, from his earliest rewriting of Shakespeare, the collaboration with Sir William Davenant on *The Tempest: or the Enchanted Island* (performed 1667, published 1669), Dryden represents his relation to Shakespeare through a set of connections between theatricality and gender. A well-known feature of Shakespeare's stage is that boy actors took women's parts; perhaps less well known is that actresses, new to the English stage after the Restoration, often took male parts.[5] In their *Tempest*, Dryden and Davenant employ this casting practice for a character of their invention, Prospero's adopted son, Hippolito. The male counterpart to Miranda, Hippolito has never seen a woman (because Prospero has raised him in a cave). Hippolito provides the opportunity for Dryden and Davenant to multiply the number of potential couples in the play; accordingly, they give Miranda a sister, Dorinda, who becomes "his" mate. The preoccupation in Restoration drama with the regulation of gender roles is epitomized in Hippolito: although the play teases a number of possible combinations out of the naive characters' sexual expectations, their assumption of heterosexual gender roles at the play's conclusion relies on the staged illusion that the actress is a man. In the prologue to the play, Dryden contrasts the theatrical impenetrability of the breeches part with the actress's sexual penetrability. The combination is emblematic of the changes wrought on Shakespeare's play; as such, it initially prompts him to ask for the audience's pity.

> But if for Shakespeare we your grace implore,
> We for our theatre shall want it more:
> Who by our dearth of youths are forced t'employ
> One of our women to present a boy.
> That's a transformation, you will say,
> Exceeding all the magic in the play.
> Let none expect in the last act to find
> Her sex transformed from man to womankind.
> Whate'er she was before the play began,
> All you shall see of her is perfect man.
> (27–36)[6]

Although Dryden proposes that opposite casting practices epitomize his relationship to Shakespeare, the different relations between theatrical representation and gender in Dryden's and Shakespeare's theaters problematize the opposition. In Dryden's play, theatrical illusion will not be broken by the kind of self-referential gestures performed in some of Shakespeare's plays. (Not only does Shakespeare's Cleopatra have a speech about her greatness being "boyed" in Rome, but women such as Portia and Viola disguise themselves as men, thereby reminding the audience that they are male actors disguised as women.) Whereas the texture of representation in Shakespeare's theater is discontinuous and self-referential, in Dryden's it is seamless and illusionistic.

The prologue promises that in the course of Dryden and Davenant's play, "Her sex [will not be] transformed from man to womankind," that is to say, "her" "true" gender will neither be revealed nor indicated. But at the same time, this line states both that such a transformation across gender lines won't occur because it is theatrically undesirable and that the transformation necessitated by the "dearth of youths" has already occurred; the sex that won't be revealed is "her[s]." In other words, the difference between Shakespeare and Dryden's casting practices reflects a difference in their understandings of gender identity. Thomas Laqueur describes this difference as the shift from a hierarchical understanding of gender differences (in which women are lower on the scale than men), to an oppositional understanding of gender differences (in which men and women are incommensurable, that is, weighed on different scales).[7]

Notwithstanding Dryden's dismissal of the "real"—what he calls, "Whate'er she was before the play began"—he challenges his spectators to see if they can detect the "real" woman under the male disguise. The spectators' visual perceptions mark the limits of representation in Dryden's theater, and a new understanding of gender identity is proposed that conforms to these perceptual limits: "All you shall see of her is perfect man." Theatrically, she is male, but epistemologically, linguistically (i.e., pronominally), she is female. Thus Dryden's announcement that this transformation will not take place is paradoxically consistent with his commitment to the representability of a "true" identity. The contradiction between what is presented and what is known is resolved in the appeal to physical contact where carnal "knowledge" provides the ultimate proof. The "real" is recuperated at the prologue's end in the bawdy invitation to Charles II: "Or if your fancy will be farther led / To find her woman, it must be abed" (37–38). Whatever may have been lost in the "dearth" is thereby transformed into a gain, or more precisely, into a sexual conquest, where there can be no uncertainty as to "her true sex." Dryden proposes that his literary achievement supersedes Shakespeare's because he substitutes heterosexual opportunity in place of a "dearth of youths."

But the seamless "real" of Dryden's theater also displays its "seam" in this prologue: in exchange for the king's "grace" (1.27), Dryden offers the sexual gift of the actress, but she also stands for another gift, that of his text to the king. In this way, much as Dryden figures his text as "perfect man," and himself as Shakespeare's improver, text and author accomplish these feats insofar as they are best represented by a woman. Moreover, text and author are further conflated: the "perfect man" is Dryden's extension of his self-presentation as Neander, the new man of "Essay of Dramatick Poesy" who admires Jonson but "loves" Shakespeare.[8]

The substitutions of heterosexual opportunity for "dearth of youths," of Dryden for Shakespeare, are complex and multivalent because they are asymmetrical even though both occur in the same gestures. The confluence of substitutions permits Dryden to depict his relationship to Shakespeare as an instance of cultural transmission in which Dryden both receives and improves Shakespeare. The substitutions inform his critical stance in relation to Shakespeare; to the extent that we accept Samuel Johnson's identification of Dryden as "the father of criticism in English," these substitutions also shape our own practices.[9] But the asymmetry between substitutions, best registered, perhaps, in Dryden's ambiguous "love" of Shakespeare, suggests that under the smooth surface of a patrilineal bequest lie complicated gender representations that potentially disrupt the filial relation. In what follows, I emphasize the disruptive moments in *All for Love* and its preface in order to make visible that underwriting Dryden's representation of Shakespeare as a cultural inheritance is the suppression of any relations between poets except an oedipal one and to note the strategies by which they are suppressed.

Dryden's preface begins:

The death of *Antony* and *Cleopatra*, is a Subject which has been treated by the greatest Wits of our Nation, after *Shakespeare*; and by all so variously, that their example has given me the confidence to try my self in this Bowe of *Ulysses* amongst the Crowd of Sutors; and, withal, to take my own measures, in aiming at the Mark. I doubt not but the same motive has prevailed with all of us in this attempt; I mean the excellency of the Moral: for the chief persons represented, were the famous pattern of unlawful love; and their end was unfortunate. (10)

We should not let Dryden's displacement of the motive for rewriting the Antony and Cleopatra story from literary competition to "the excellency of the Moral" distract us from the curious gendering of an otherwise oedipal conception of literary relations. When Dryden discusses the motive for the "greatest Wits of our Nation, after Shakespeare" to treat the subject of Antony and Cleopatra's death, he proposes an analogy that captures the decidedly non-neutral nature of literary competition.

At first glance, Dryden's proposal to take up the bow of Ulysses describes literary competition in terms of sexual competition and seems quite unexceptionable. However, a second look brings to light a peculiar failure that the classical analogy builds in: as we know from Homer, no one but Ulysses can wield his bow. Moreover, another question needs to be asked about this scene of literary competition: if Shakespeare is Ulysses, who is the Penelope to whom the best writer will have literary or sexual access?

According to the analogy, none of the succeeding wits can successfully vie with Shakespeare for the body of his unnamed "wife." Although the analogy seems to portray Dryden's self-insertion into the classical scene of rivalry with Shakespeare as Ulysses in the paterfamilias position and Dryden in the role of Telemachus, literary failure must result.[10] When we turn to the scene in *All for Love* that Dryden characterizes as his literary failure, we can see, however, that it resituates the patrilineal contest in other terms. Indeed, I would argue that the scene Dryden calls attention to as a failure is the true scene of literary competition. The emotional and dramatic center of his play, the scene depicts the competition between Octavia and Cleopatra over the title of "wife." Dryden thereby manipulates the positions made available by the classical analogy to arrive at an alternate scene: he replaces the rivalry between men by a rivalry between women, and he depicts Cleopatra as a paradigm of wifeliness, the virtue most closely associated with Penelope.

Dryden's Cleopatra offers a famous contrast to Shakespeare's "riggish" queen. She says of herself, "Nature meant me / A Wife, a silly harmless household Dove" (4.1.91–92).[11] Over the course of *All for Love*, by virtue of winning her struggle with Octavia for the title of Antony's wife, Cleopatra comes to embody domestic literary success of the sort that Dryden achieves for himself when he joins the ranks of "the greatest Wits of our Nation."

I propose that Dryden identifies his literary success with the domestic success of Cleopatra as a result of having displaced the competition between himself and Shakespeare from the generational model presented in the preface onto the scene of competition that occurs in his play between Cleopatra and Octavia. The scene of rivalry is not only the sentimental centerpiece of the play, it is also the prime object of Dryden's critical attention in the preface. This coincidence suggests, moreover, that there are connections to be drawn between the development of the sentimental drama and the beginnings of a professional practice of criticism in late seventeenth-century English culture.[12] Identifying the scene between women as his flaw, Dryden has it both ways: he criticizes the scene of women fighting in which he has dramatized his competition with Shakespeare, and thereby both figures and denies the competition. He both identifies himself as "wife" and castigates the scene of female rivalry, preferring instead the scene between Antony and Ventidius, the scene of loving men.

I earlier suggested that Dryden puts himself into a female position both to make himself subservient to the king and to "exceed" Shakespeare. The battle between women in *All for Love* displaces Dryden's competition with Shakespeare, and, as a result, Dryden doesn't put himself in a female position in the preface to the play; as we have seen, he presents himself as Telemachus. The battle between women also encodes matters of class in matters of gender and this aspect of the scene also relates— again in a displaced fashion—to the question addressed in the preface; it affects the way Dryden describes the position of the critic.

In the preface to *All for Love*, Dryden engages in a bitter battle with Rochester over the status of poetry as the privilege of the aristocracy. Rochester, famed libertine poet and arbiter of the wits, had put in question Dryden's self-inclusion among "the greatest Wits of our Nation."[13] In "The Allusion to Horace" (which circulated in manuscript in 1676), Rochester equates Dryden's criticism of Shakespeare and Jonson with the presumptions of a social climber.

> But does not Dryden find ev'n Jonson dull;
> Fletcher and Beaumont uncorrect, and full
> Of lewd Lines, as he calls 'em; Shakespeare's style
> Stiff and affected; to his own the while
> Allowing all the justness that his pride
> So arrogantly has to those denied?[14]

In response, Dryden calls into question the access those men of "wretched affectation," drunken debauchery, and privilege have to wit. Over and against wealth and libertinage, he presents poverty and modesty as his poetic and critical qualifications.

> And is this not a wretched affectation, not to be contented with what Fortune has done for them, and sit down quietly with their estate, but they must call their Wits in question and needlessly expose their nakedness to public view? If a little glittering in discourse has pass'd them on us for witty men, where was the necessity of undeceiving the World? . . . We who would write, if we want the Talent, yet have the excuse that we do it for a poor subsistence; but what can be urg'd in their defence, who not having the Vocation of Poverty to scribble, out of mere wantoness take pains to make themselves ridiculous? (14)

The nakedness to which Dryden refers has a notorious historical referent: it is that of Sir Charles Sedley, one of Rochester's circle. The reference is particularly significant in this context, since Sedley was a "Wit" who wrote an *Antony and Cleopatra* that was performed the same year as Dryden's *All for Love* to greater popular acclaim.[15] Sedley had been arrested in 1663 for appearing nude on the balcony of a tavern to give a mock-sermon.[16] In Dryden's attack, public nakedness is a crime, but baring the absence of wit is an even greater one. He invokes poverty, and with it, modesty, as corollary virtues that paradoxically permit the poor writer to dress better than the naked aristocrat.

The topic of modest dress comes up earlier in the preface, when, defending the propriety of representing women fighting, Dryden claims to have kept himself within the bounds of modesty.

> 'Tis true, some actions, though natural, are not fit to be represented; and broad obscenities in words, ought in good manners to be avoided: expressions therefore are the modest cloathing of our

thoughts, as Breeches and Petticoats are of our bodies. If I have kept myself within the bounds of modesty, all beyond is but nicety and affectation; which is no more than modesty deprav'd into a vice: they betray themselves who are too quick of apprehension in such cases and leave all reasonable men to imagine worse of them, than of the Poet. (11)

Expressions are the modest clothes available to the poor writer, preventing him from appearing naked either out of destitution or aristocratic vice. But nakedness is not the only vice; so is the overinvestment in modesty which depraves it: curiously, both fashion and puritanism present such dangers. Despite the precariousness of the situation, Dryden keeps himself within the bounds of modesty by registering, apparently effortlessly, the difference of the body beneath the "modest cloathing" as the gender difference between breeches and petticoats. Counterpointing Dryden's ease is the figure of Sedley, who appears in another anecdote that reveals how his class position and appearance make his gender identity sufficiently "problematic" to require his violent self-defence.

Edward Kynaston, one of the last male actors to take women's roles, was cast in a play that included a satirical portrait of Sedley. However, Kynaston did not only appear on stage in the elaborate lace collars that were Sedley's sartorial signature, he also promenaded in St. James Park so attired. In what very well may have been an instance of "gay-bashing" and was certainly an exercise in threatened class prerogative, Sedley had Kynaston beaten up by hired hands.[17] This anecdote tells as much about changing theatrical casting practices as it does about changing class and gender boundaries in the Restoration.[18] If Sedley provides an example of aristocratic anxieties about matters of both class and gender, Dryden exemplifies what we might call bourgeois attitudes. The smooth facade of facile gender distinctions prefaces the dramatized scenes of male-male and female-female dynamics; Dryden appears to propose that in place of class anxieties, the bourgeois prerogative is a critical mastery of heterosexual codes.

Unlike Sedley, who is either naked or richly appointed in elaborate clothes, Dryden locates himself within the bounds of modest dress in an attempt to nullify class hierarchies and naturalize gender distinctions and decorum. The "bounds of modesty" rule out affectation and depravity as well as "broad obscenities," which, however natural, are "not fit to be represented." Dryden proposes to render void the qualitative distinctions supposedly provided by birth; proper gender distinctions will thus be drawn only in the well-mannered critical discourse of those positioned securely within modesty's bounds.

Dryden routinely substitutes gender for class terms in order to facilitate his claims to critical expertise. Moreover, these claims have specific reference to his literary antecedents. With this in mind, we can, perhaps, arrive at a better understanding of the scene he singles out for critical attention in the preface. For the scene of female rivalry that he added to Shakespeare's play is of such importance to Dryden that he founds his claims as a critic, including those of "modesty" and "poverty," on his understanding of it.

Dryden knows that the French poets would have criticized his literary choice. They "would not, for example, have suffer'd Cleopatra and Octavia to have met; or if they had met, there must have only pass'd betwixt them some cold civilities, but no eagerness of repartée, for fear of offending against the greatness of their Characters and the modesty of their Sex" (11). Drawing our attention to his awareness as the grounds for self-praise rather than self-condemnation, Dryden redirects the critique of his work against those who would object.

> This objection I foresaw, and at the same time contemn'd: for I judg'd it both *natural* and *probable*, that Octavia, proud of her new-gain'd Conquest, would search out Cleopatra to triumph over her; and that Cleopatra, thus attacqu'd, was not of a spirit to shun the encounter: and 'tis not unlikely, that two exasperated Rivals should use such Satyre as I have put into their mouths; for after all, though one were a Roman, and the other a Queen, they were both Women. (11)

Dryden's paradoxical reasoning is more remarkable than his self-promoting rhetoric. Part of the reason to condemn the spectacle is the whole reason that Dryden defends it: it is not suitable for *great women* to fight because they are great, that is, highly placed, but nevertheless, "after all, though one were a Roman, and the other a Queen, they were both Women." Dryden replaces the social categories, queen and Roman, by the gender category "women," and by subsuming matters of class and nation under matters of gender, he is able to maintain his status both as an imitator of "nature," and as a critic.

Although Dryden observes that what offends in the representation of

Octavia and Cleopatra fighting is precisely that one is a queen and the other a Roman, none of his contemporaries seems to have complained. Nevertheless, Dryden himself feels the need to comment: "But this is an objection which none of my Critiques have urg'd against me; and therefore I might have let it pass, if I could have resolv'd to have been partial to myself" (11). Significantly, Dryden presents his critical qualification as his ability to remain impartial; he can observe what has escaped other people's attention. His ostensible indifference to his own flaws informs his claim to critical, indeed, moral superiority. The high cost of this claim, criticizing his own play, can be attributed in part to the ongoing class battle over who has access to literary judgment and, in part, to his understanding of the threat of competing with Shakespeare.

Dryden's criticism of the scene between Cleopatra and Octavia underwrites his preference for the scene between Antony and Ventidius. From this point of view, it is significant that the friendship between Antony and Ventidius registers homoerotically. Both Antony's interactions with Ventidius and his more pronounced homoerotically charged relationship to Dollabella exemplify a hyper-desirability: both men and women compete over him.[19] Indeed, Dryden's noncritical representations of male-male eroticism may be facilitated by the scenes of fighting women.

Dryden's women are domesticated heroines whose combat may be shrill but is also nonphysical. In the following exchange, Cleopatra and Octavia compete for the title of "wife":

> *Cleo.*   Yet she who loves him best is Cleopatra.
> If you have suffered, I have suffered more.
> You bear the specious title of a wife
> To gild your cause, and draw the pitying world
> To favor it; the world contemns poor me,
> For I have lost my honor, lost my fame,
> And stained the glory of my royal house,
> And all to bear the branded name of mistress.
> There wants but life, and that too I would lose
> For him I love.
>
> (3.1.458–67)

Octavia concedes: "Be't so, then; take thy wish" (3.1.468). But the closest Octavia comes to Cleopatra is to look in her face, to "view nearer / That face which has so long usurped my right, / To find th'inevitable charms that catch / Mankind so sure, that ruined my dear lord" (3.1.435–38). The fight between Dryden's women has a more violent counterpart in *The Rival Queens*, a contemporary play by Dryden's sometime collaborator Nathaniel Lee.[20] Because it stages direct and physical conflict between the titular rivals and more explicit scenes of homoeroticism between Alexander and Hephestion, *The Rival Queens* clarifies the relation between representations of female rivalry and male homoeroticism.

In it, Roxana actually stabs Statira to death. Where Octavia registers Cleopatra's "inevitable charms," Roxana is more willful: she "like[s]" Statira's appearance, but the erotic overtones of the physical clash between the women in Lee's play can hardly be understood as "lesbian," or offered for the consumption of the female viewer. On the contrary, when Roxana brandishes her dagger, the spectator is threatened by the possibility of the horrid spectacle—the sight of Statira's breasts transformed from containers of milk to containers of blood:

> *Rox.* I like the port imperial beauty bears;
> It shows thou hast a spirit fit to fall
> A Sacrifice to fierce Roxana's wrongs.
> Be sudden then, put forth these royal breasts,
> Where our false master has so often languished,
> That I may change their milky innocence
> To blood, and dye me in a deep revenge.
>
> (5.1.53–59)

Their lurid battle serves to bolster the authority of the monarch over whom they fight. But meanwhile, Alexander the Great, the man in question, is too preoccupied with his favorite and lover, Hephestion, to notice either the disruption caused by the women, or the revolutionary coup that is being plotted against him.

If fighting women facilitate the representation of loving men, they are also displaced representations of male-male aggression. In both *All for Love* and *The Rival Queens*, the fighting women register in order to deflect male anxieties about loss of power and the threat of loss entailed by power. The anxieties raised by the specter of seeing a breast cut off are more easily allayed than castration anxiety, especially for the men in the audience. Scenes of fighting women can be said to perform a cultural function: they are a symptom of the "degeneration" from a past heroic moment of hand-to-hand combat. It is important to realize that this past moment is only ever ostensibly "heroic"; "though Nobility makes a difference of persons, yet injury acknowledgeth none."[21] According to Lawrence Stone, "Duelling, which spread to England in the late sixteenth century, was kept in check by the joint pressure of the Puritans and the King before 1640, but became a serious social menace after the Restoration."[22] If the advent of duelling before the Civil War was an attempt to resolve the "crisis of an aristocracy" whose ability to muster personal armies was reduced and redefined, after the Restoration, its resurgence must have been an even more belated attempt to fix aristocratic codes to those of honor. The arena of fighting women, in which castration is not possible, is even more highly charged when, in addition to those of gender, it is marked by such issues of class.

At this point, the connections between Dryden's depictions of male anxieties about both political and sexual power and the professional critical discourse that he inaugurates can be made clear. *All for Love* focuses on the contest between *women* as the determination of male political power and value, thereby displacing male rivalry onto a "safe" sphere. As we have seen, in the preface to *All for Love*, Dryden bases his critical claims on his own partiality. Castigating and defending his sentimental scene of female rivalry, Dryden stakes his claim to critical expertise by stating that he might have let his fault pass, "if I could have resolv'd to have been partial to myself" (11). The condition is strange: if he could have resolved to be partial, he would have allowed his play to be uncriticized, that is to say, his play would have remained "whole" (i.e., uncriticized) if he had remained partial; but if he had remained partial, he would have lacked the reconstitution that criticism supplies. Criticism reconstitutes the fragmented play, with the added advantage of constituting Dryden as *im*partial, i.e., "whole." His lack of resolve is dissolved in the reconstituted wholeness of authority that critical judgment expresses.

Dryden thus redeems his integrity as a playwright even as he poses his critical judgment against his own play. He stakes out two roles which correspond to that of playwright and critic, one inside and one outside the play: on the inside, he is the wifely Cleopatra, a dramatist who can compete with a Shakespeare who is regendered as Penelope or Octavia; on the outside, he is Telemachus, an impartial critic and judge of Shakespeare/Ulysses. Threatened by competition with Shakespeare, he criticizes one of his innovative scenes, the scene of fighting women, and his negative criticism validates his critical expertise. It supplies the position out of which he can prefer his other innovative scene, the scene between men. Staging a scene of literary competition as rivalry between women, he creates an object of criticism, a fetish, which is significantly a fight in which there is no threat of castration.[23] He can be critical of his own play because his self-criticism "remasculinizes" him.

Reading Dryden's dramatic and critical practices together shows the ways in which Dryden's criticism is structurally oedipal, which explains but does not justify later critics' depiction of his relation to Shakespeare in straight genealogical terms. Whether he is portrayed as a loving son by critics like Johnson, or as a son in the midst of oedipal crisis by critics like Taylor, these accounts simplify the underlying complexities still visible in Dryden's relation to Shakespeare in the service of establishing and maintaining the literary tradition as a patrimony. But my reading also highlights the ways Dryden's evaluative energies are drawn from and directed toward same-sex scenes. How are we to understand this? Lee Edelman describes Lyndon Johnson's reaction to the news that his chief of staff, Walter Jenkins, had been arrested for "indecent gestures" with another man in a Y.M.C.A. bathroom, and it exhibits striking similarities to Dryden's treatment of homoeroticism; the three centuries that separate Johnson from Dryden also offer helpful contrasts. In 1964, Johnson claimed, "I was as shocked as if someone had told me my wife had murdered her daughter."[24] As Edelman points out, Johnson's figuration of his shock puts into play notions of marital intimacy and domestic crime—these are absent from *All for Love* and its preface. But Johnson's translation of the scene of homosexuality into familial terms has enough in common with Dryden's achievement of a critical filial relation to Shakespeare by means of his representations of same-sex scenes to invite further investigation. Although it would be ahistorical to find the "uncontrollable figuralizing effects" (277) of homosexuality in which Edelman is interested in the late seventeenth century, when "homosexuality" cannot properly be said to exist, his observation that "the unspeakable scene of desire between two men must be represented through a scenario of violence between two women" seems as true of Dryden as it is of Johnson (275).

However, Edelman's "must" applies differently to Johnson and Dryden for historical as well as textual reasons. Edelman accounts for Johnson's substitutive representation of homosexual eros in terms of violence in the context of McCarthyism, momism, and cold war demonology. For Edelman, Johnson's evocation of violence between his wife and daughter participates in the abjection of homosexuality, since there is a "slippage from 'wife,' a position of subordination within the dynamics of heterosexual marriage, to mother, a position of power within the mother-child dyad" (276). In Johnson's substitution, homosexuality is understood as analogous to domestic murder, which, according to Edelman, expresses its paradoxical status: it is something that at once cannot be seen and something that is desired to be seen (in the form of state surveillance) (278).

Dryden's violent women are not mother and daughter; they are rivals for Antony's love. They cannot properly be said to displace the scene of loving men, although, as I have argued, they figure Dryden's literary competition with Shakespeare in displaced fashion and thus enable him to present himself as Shakespeare's loving critic. Furthermore, the competing women do not render invisible the homoerotic scenes in the play, possibly because in Dryden's substitution we do not have the transumption of erotic energy into murderous impulses; instead, erotic desire is maintained, though it is directed at Antony more emphatically by competing women than it is by men. Finally, the field of the visible in Dryden's writing is not put in crisis by the disruptive spectacle of homosexuality, as Edelman describes, although the ease with which the homoerotic scenes get taken as homosocial marks the accuracy of his analysis for twentieth-century critics.[25]

If Dryden's substitutive representation is a disavowal that permits a filial (or oedipal) relation to Shakespeare to become the critical norm, the disavowal also enables him to express his evaluative preference for the homoerotic scene between Antony and Ventidius. In Dryden's substitution, the scene of homoeroticism between men occupies preferred status under the conditions that I have outlined, conditions which become more stringent, exclusionary, and exacting over the course of the eighteenth century.[26] From this perspective, Dryden's substitution can be said to mark an early and transitional moment on the way to Edelman's paradigm.

What, then, is to be made of the oedipal critic who prefers homoerotic scenes? Answering this question would involve historicizing together the discourses of aesthetics and sexuality. The vocabulary of preference, central in both the aesthetic and the sexual domains, presupposes a Lockean subject whose will is freely directed toward the object of choice. However, the freely directed will can be shown to be exercised within confines loosely described as available options, and more rigorously understood as social and psychic conventions, the organizing structures of class and gender. The tension in my question between the psychoanalytic adjective "oedipal" and the verb "prefers" is telling, but as Foucault has shown, the psychoanalytic discourse on sexuality is more of an outgrowth than an overthrowing of the autonomous subject who seeks the freedom to discuss sex.[27] Putting equal historical pressure on notions of aesthetic evaluation and sexuality as forms of voluntarism would be a way to begin this enterprise. Critics and theorists like Eve Kosofsky Sedgwick, Judith Butler, and others have interrogated the applicability of categories such as will, choice, or preference to matters of sexuality and gender.[28] Applying their insights to historical questions about aesthetic evaluation remains to be done.

Notes

I want to acknowledge John Guillory's patience, care, and tact, and Jill Frank's sense of timing, which helped shape this essay.

1. Moody E. Prior claims that "Dryden's *All for Love: or the World Well Lost* is generally acknowledged as his best play, and without much question it is the best tragedy of its age." "Tragedy and the Heroic Play," in *Dryden: A Collection of Critical Essays*, ed. Bernard Schelling (New Jersey: Prentice-Hall, 1963), 93. N. J. Andrew, an editor of the play, says, "Recognition of the theatrical purity and structural beauty of *All for Love* accounts for some of its appeal, but not for its power to arouse strong emotional responses even on a casual reading" (London: A. and C. Black Ltd., 1986), xxviii. Maximillian E. Novak, another editor, comments, "*All for Love* was an artistic triumph." Novak also notes that Samuel Johnson "called upon 'universal consent' in praising *All for Love*." *The Works of John Dryden* (Berkeley: University of California Press, 1984), 13:363–64. I cite the play from this edition; page numbers and act, scene, and line references are given in the text.

2. All but a few essays in *Twentieth Century Interpretations of "All for Love": A Collection of Critical Essays*, ed. Bruce King (New Jersey: Prentice-Hall, 1968), set out to evaluate Dryden's achievement in terms of Shakespeare's. Indeed, the comparison seems impossible to avoid, even in those critics who claim that Dryden's play should be evaluated on its own terms. For example, Norman Suckling writes, "I wish to suggest that the quality of *All for Love*, as representing a different but equally interesting dramatic *genre* from that of *Antony and Cleopatra*, is of greater importance than the fact that it was written by a lesser poet" (46).

3. Johnson continues, "Nor can the editors and admirers of Shakespeare, in all their emulation of reverence, boast of much more than of having diffused and paraphrased this epitome of excellence, of having changed Dryden's gold for baser metal, of lower value, though of greater bulk." *Lives of the Most Eminent English Poets: with Critical Observations on their Works* (Edinburgh: Peter Hill, Printer to the Church of Scotland, 1815), 2:62.

4.   Gary Taylor, *Reinventing Shakespeare: A Cultural History from the Restoration to the Present* (New York: Weidenfeld and Nicolson, 1989), 44–45.

5.   Scholars who discuss the gender dynamics of this Renaissance stage practice include Stephen Orgel, " 'Nobody's Perfect': Or Why Did the English Stage Take Boys for Women?" *South Atlantic Quarterly* 88, no. 1 (1989):7–30, and Katharine Eisaman Maus, "Playhouse Flesh and Blood: Sexual Ideology and the Restoration Actress," *ELH* 46 (1979):595–617.

6.   John Dryden, *Of Dramatic Poesy and Other Critical Essays*, ed. George Watson (New York: Dutton, 1962), 1:133.

7.   Thomas Laqueur describes the "biology of incommensurability" in *Making Sex: Body and Gender from the Greeks to Freud* (Cambridge: Harvard University Press, 1990). See also Maus, "Playhouse Flesh and Blood," 614.

8.   "Essay of Dramatick Poesy," Watson, 1:70.

9.   Samuel Johnson, *Lives*, 2:60. I argue more fully in "Staging Milton, Staging Criticism: John Dryden's *The State of Innocence*," *The Eighteenth Century: Theory and Interpretation* 34 (Spring 1993):45–64, that Dryden's rewriting of Milton is key to the development of a critical vocabulary that ensures the transmission of the literary inheritance which he describes as a patrimony. Dryden's anxieties about inheriting from the previous generation are best seen in "Astrea Redux" (1660), Dryden's poem celebrating the return of Charles II:

>   Youth that with Joys had unacquainted been
>   Envy'd gray hairs that once good days had seen:
>   We thought our Sires, not with their own content,
>   Had ere we came to age our Portion spent.

The Poems and Fables of John Dryden, ed. James Kinsley (New York: Oxford University Press, 1970), 16. In the epilogue to *The Conquest of Granada, Part Two*, Dryden explicitly links the privilege that writers of the previous age had to his own critical imperative:

>   Fame then was cheap, and the first comer sped;
>   And they have kept it since by being dead.
>   But were they now to write when Critiques weigh
>   Each Line, and ev'ry word, throughout a Play,
>   None of 'em, no not Jonson, in his height
>   Could pass, without allowing grains for weight.
>   Think it not envy that these truths are told,
>   Our Poet's not malicious, though he's bold.
>   'Tis not to brand 'em that their faults are shown,
>   But by their errours, to excuse his own.
>   (Kinsley, 134)

10.   In *John Dryden and His World* (New Haven: Yale University Press, 1987), 331, James Winn, Dryden's biographer, reads the Ulysses analogy "straight": he sees Dryden casting himself as Telemachus, playing son to a literary father. This observation makes the classical analogy into another example of Dryden's self-presentation as weaker than his literary forefathers. Like Gary Taylor, Winn oedipalizes Dryden's

relation to Shakespeare. Neither Taylor's nor Winn's account gives a sense of how Dryden manipulates being a weak son to his own, i.e., critical, advantage.

11. Eugene Waith observes this contrast in his discussion of *All for Love* in *Ideas of Greatness: Heroic Drama in England* (New York: Barnes and Noble, 1971), 231–35. Although in Shakespeare's play Cleopatra claims her wifely title in death, saying "Husband I come," in Dryden's play she aspires to wifehood throughout.

12. As Laura Brown points out, Restoration rewritings of Shakespeare occupy a privileged place in the evolution of what she calls "affective tragedy," that is, the sentimental. *English Dramatic Form, 1660–1760: An Essay in Generic History* (New Haven: Yale University Press, 1981), 99–100.

13. James Winn also describes the conflict in class terms. *Dryden and His World*, 248–55, 302–11.

14. *The Complete Poems of John Wilmot, Earl of Rochester*, ed. David M. Vieth (New Haven: Yale University Press, 1968), 120–26.

15. Sedley's *Antony and Cleopatra* was licensed and performed in 1677. *The Poetical and Dramatic Works of Sir Charles Sedley*, ed. V. de Sola Pinto (London: Constable and Co., 1928).

16. V. de Sola Pinto, *Sir Charles Sedley, 1639–1701: A Study in the Life and Literature of the Restoration* (London: Constable and Company, 1927), 61–63.

17. V. de Sola Pinto, *Sir Charles Sedley*, 111–12.

18. In *Homosexuality in Renaissance England* (London: Gay Men's Press, 1982), Alan Bray claims that homosexual culture per se only comes into visibility at the end of the seventeenth century. Homosexuals are only then subject to systematic attack of the sort enacted in the raids on the Molly Houses beginning in 1699. In *Sexual Suspects: Eighteenth-Century Players and Sexual Ideology* (Princeton: Princeton University Press, 1992), Kristina Straub demonstrates that the actor is a crucial figure in the emergence of regulatory definitions of gender, sexuality, nationality, and class. Sedley and Kynaston's interaction can be seen as an early example of the transition to visibility and the definitional struggles that Bray and Straub describe.

19. David Vieth characterizes the relationship between Antony and Dollabella as explicitly homosexual in the introduction to his edition of *All for Love* (Lincoln: University of Nebraska Press, 1973), xxiv–xxv. Initially Ventidius welcomes the return of Dollabella since it increases the pressure on Antony to break with Cleopatra, but in act 4, scene 1, he eavesdrops on Dollabella, who has been sent by Antony to say goodbye to Cleopatra for him, and recognizes a better opportunity to kill two birds with one stone. He falls into Alexas's plot to inflame Antony's jealousy, but by representing Dollabella as usurping Cleopatra's affections Ventidius also attempts to eliminate two of his rivals for Antony's affections.

20. Nathaniel Lee, *The Rival Queens*, ed. P. F. Vernon, *The Regents Restoration Drama Series* (Lincoln: University of Nebraska Press, 1970). Dryden collaborated with Lee on *Oedipus* (1679) and *The Duke of Guise* (1683). Vernon discusses the fact that, to a large extent, *The Rival Queens* and *All for Love* shared a cast: Charles Hart played both Alexander and Antony, Elizabeth Boutell played Statira and Cleopatra, and Mohun played both Clytus and Ventidius (pp. xiv–xvi).

21. Lawrence Stone quotes Patrick Ruthven's comment to Algernon, Earl of Northumberland in *The Crisis of the Aristocracy* (Oxford: Clarendon Press, 1965), 245.

22. Lawrence Stone, *The Family, Sex and Marriage in England, 1500–1800*, abridged ed. (New York: Harper and Row, 1979), 77. In *The Duel: A History of Duelling* (London: Chapman and Hall, 1965), 68–70, Robert Baldick points out that Cromwell passed an ordinance against duelling in 1654. He corroborates Stone's perception that after the Restoration duelling regained its prestige.

23. Jay Caplan argues that a link between castration and tears underwrites the sentimental. The sentimental tableau "depends upon the power of fragments to invest the imagination, the ability of the part (which psychoanalysis calls the fetish) to make an ideal whole (the phallus)." Moreover, "All of the actors in the dialogic relationship that defines the [sentimental] tableau share a certain partiality or partialness: the author or maker, the represented characters, and the beholder or remaker all take sides, and all are parts of the incomplete whole." *Framed Narratives: Diderot's Genealogy of the Beholder* (Minneapolis: University of Minnesota Press, 1985), 19.

24. Lee Edelman, "Tearooms and Sympathy, or The Epistemology of the Water Closet," *Nationalisms and Sexualities*, ed. Andrew Parker, Mary Russo, Doris Summer, and Patricia Yaeger (New York: Routledge, 1992), 266.

25. To most critics, the homoeroticism between Antony and Ventidius is understood as a platonic bond between soldiers. As I noted earlier, David Vieth characterizes the homoeroticism between Antony and Dollabella as homosexual, but Maximillian Novak responds to this suggestion with an invitation to critical silence that is more representative: "Such an interpretation is less important for throwing light on Dryden's tragedy than for pointing to certain historical problems about Dryden's milieu, about which we know very little" (13:386).

26. Kristina Straub describes various understandings of masculinity in the contests over literary authority that occur forty years later in "Men from Boys: Cibber, Pope and the Schoolboy," ch. 4 of *Sexual Suspects*. She analyzes the kinds of sexual and economic power associated with patriarchal, homosexual, and homosocial positions and makes clear the next stages in the process that defines male homoeroticism as disempowering.

27. Michel Foucault, *The History of Sexuality. Volume I: An Introduction*, trans. Robert Hurley (New York: Pantheon, 1978).

28. Eve Kosofsky Sedgwick, *Epistemology of the Closet* (Berkeley: University of California Press, 1990); Judith Butler, *Gender Trouble: Feminism and the Subversion of Identity* (New York: Routledge, 1990).

New English Sodom

MICHAEL WARNER

W HEN John Winthrop was considering emigration to America, one of his first arguments was that divine judgment on England was imminent.[1] He had already written to his wife that a "heavye Squorge and Judgment" could be expected. Like so many others around him, he drew the obvious parallel, arguing that those who were considering emigration should take care not to "imytayte Sodom."[2] In response to Winthrop's arguments, his neighbor Robert Ryece used the same analogy: "[In England] where every place mourneth for wante of Justice, where the cryenge synnes goe unponished, or unreproved . . . and what so ever is evyll is cowntenanced, even the leaste of these, is enowghe, and enowghe to make haste owte of Babylon, and to seeke to dye rather in the wyldernes then styll to dwelle in Sodome."[3] Thomas Hooker wrote that England had become "literally *Babel, and so consequently Ægypt and Sodome,*" ready to be "abased and brought down to hell."[4] Talking about Sodom in this way became one of the telltale signs that a Puritan was on the verge of migration. Puritans referred to Sodom as an example of judgment and a warning for England; they referred to themselves as a possible "saving remnant" of the kind that Abraham bargained for with God; and they referred to the American migration as the journey of Lot into Zoar ("If the Lord seeth it wilbe good for us," Winthrop wrote in 1629, "he will provide a shelter and a hidinge place for us and ours as Zoar for Lott").[5] The language was familiar even to the unsympathetic but shrewd Thomas Morton, who has a jab at it in *New English Canaan*: "In gods name," he writes, "let the people have their desire, who write to their friends to come out of Sodome to the land of Canaan, a land that flowes with Milke and Hony."[6]

The Puritans of the Great Migration relied on the myth of Sodom in their self-understanding to a degree that is probably without parallel in history. The fable of Sodom had, however, a familiar element that is not clearly integrated in this rhetoric. In the standard exegesis of the time, Sodom had been destroyed primarily because its male citizens were disposed to have sex with each other, a taste they showed when they demanded to "know" the undercover angels who were Lot's guests. The Anglo-American rhetoric of Sodom clearly derived its force from the scandal attached to this shared anecdote about anathematized sexuality— "the filthy lustes of the Sodomites," as the Geneva Bible has it.[7] Yet no matter how much this common lore was drawn upon in Puritan rhetoric, sexual proscription was not the overt content of the language about Sodom. Although many Puritans remained visibly if inadmissibly interested in sodomy, as we shall see, and although they could also be lethally explicit about the connection between their idea of Sodom and their idea of sodomy, the main—or at least most explicit—source of their interest lay in a different line.

The Puritan rhetoric of Sodom had begun as a language about polity and discipline. As early as 1583, a petition from Northampton had called for new church discipline and had cautioned the queen about divine retribution: "We can not see how the Lord should holde his revenging hand from punishing this slackenes in the rulers and most horrible and grievous sinne in the subjects, which aboundeth infinite waies more then it should doe, if we had this discipline."[8] Because Sodom was the most prominent example of judgment passed upon a polis in all the lore of Christendom, this call for discipline soon made Sodom a commonplace. In 1609, for example, one English preacher declared, "If God once visit this land and citie, for the sinnes of the inhabitants thereof, . . . neither the largeness of their territories, nor their beauty, excellence, riches, or multitude of people shall excuse them, but he will make them as Sodom, and like unto Gomorrha."[9] Presumably "as Sodom, and like unto Gomorrha" means destroyed, not sodomitical. It is an argument not for what we would call heterosexuality but for public regulation. The fable of Sodom represented, in a way that no other image could, an entire society open to discipline and in need of saving.[10]

In modern culture the fable of Sodom and the term *sodomy* have come to be directly linked in the public imagination with the topic of sexuality per se; sodomy is understood as a quasi-technical term with no necessary relation to the eponymous city.[11] In seventeenth-century New England, by contrast, the topic of sodomy was linked primarily to the topic of national judgment. Sodomy could not be securely distinguished from its notorious precedent—especially in the discourse culture of Puritanism, which tended anyway to collapse the collective and the individual, the literal and the metaphoric. The anathematized sexuality of Sodom was therefore never quite irrelevant, only held in reserve as an ambiguous referent.

It is of course impossible to know how much sexual activity was going on among New England males—one scholar claims that the court records are "statistically insignificant"[12]—but where records do exist they show that Puritan officialdom took a keener interest than usual.[13] Sexual bodies had been redefined by Puritan thought as social bodies in a way that required public collective management, and many of the earliest complaints about the English church becoming a Sodom were backed up with complaints about unmanaged and unofficial sex—not because of a theory about sex per se but because the management of the body had been made publicly indicative in a spiritual order.[14] As the Geneva Bible put it, in a significant marginal note to the Sodom episode, endlessly elaborated in Puritan sermons, "Nothing is more dangerous, then to dwel where sinne reigneth: for it corrupteth all."

It must be added, however, that it would be easy to overdraw the contrast between Puritan and modern usages. Like the much later coinage *lesbianism*, *sodomy* still implies, at however fantasmatic a level, a map of sexual knowledges and exotic origins. No other terms in the language of sexuality have a comparable etymology, as though unlike all other sexual acts—if they even *are* acts—these two were practiced not by individuals but by cities, islands, or nations.[15] This hidden fantasy about the geography of sex continues to exert some influence, primarily in the assumption that sodomitical and lesbian sex are more germane to public politics than other kinds of sex. The prominence of the term *sodomy* in the discussions around *Bowers v. Hardwick* (1986), for example, helped to legitimate the state's regulation of sex between consenting same-sex adults. The Supreme Court was able to point to a long tradition of defining sodomy as a uniquely public concern, a tradition in which fantasy geographies have often been invested with apocalyptic vehemence.[16] The public imagination of sex brought about in Puritanism continues to mark national discourse.

The Sodom on the Hill

Collective destiny and discipline seemed throughout the seventeenth century to be the most relevant aspects of Sodom. "When I read the story of *Sodom's overthrow*," wrote Samuel Willard in 1673, "me thinks I see the Son rising in glorious brightness, the *Sodomites* sporting and pleasing themselves in their *opulence and security*; when on a sudden, me thinks I see the heavens covered with those sable clouds, and hear the great Cannon of heaven thundring down tempests upon them, and the streams of fire with horror and dread, till I behold a proud City, on a sudden become a *desolate heap*." [17] Willard uses "Sodomite" to mean both "resident of Sodom" and "performer of sodomy," and the difference hardly seems relevant to him. When the Sodomites are said to be "sporting" about, they may or may not be having sex. The connection between private act and public judgment is so close that the gap need not be mentioned.

By the time of Willard's writing, it had become clear that such language could refer to sex—even in New England. But unlike the emigrants of the 1620s and 1630s, Willard does not simply oppose Sodom to New England. His point is to stir New England into a renewed sense of mission. He writes in the high style of the late-seventeenth-century jeremiad, as his title suggests: *Useful Instructions for a professing People in Times of great Security and Degeneracy.* Willard's pamphlet does not ostensibly describe sexual practice and makes no reference to any instance of what we would call sodomy. It relies on the commonplace claim that New England was a site of "degeneracy," a claim that, regardless of how undegenerate people might in fact have been, gave the rhetoric of Sodom a somewhat different emphasis after the beginning of the English civil wars. It presented Sodom as a shadow-image within New England rather than as a point of contrast between old England and New.

One consequence of this imagery of place, however, is to give the sexual content of the Sodom story a relevance uncannily close to home. Willard's imaginary vision of Sodom is given in present tense, with no Atlantic distance of recollection: "Sion affords no more security to sinners then Sodom, Shiloh is as dangerous a place to sin in, as any in the world; if a people in covenant with God, be found rebellious, he will spare them no more then any other people, nay he will begin with them" (16). Sodom, in other words, is we.[18]

In 1674 Samuel Danforth, who a few years earlier had preached his famous jeremiad on the "errand into the wilderness," took up the same theme in a sermon published as *The Cry of Sodom*. Where Willard's sermon had taken up questions of national judgment in theory, Danforth's responded to a case of sexuality in practice. The occasion for *The Cry of Sodom* was the execution of one Benjamin Goad, not for sodomy per se but for bestiality. Even bestiality, however, does not seem to worry Danforth as much as masturbation. After commenting at length on the vileness of Goad's habits, he turns aggressively toward the audience, announcing that onanism was widespread among them: "What, art thou a compleat Sensualist? Thou withholdest thy heart from no carnal joy, or fleshly delight. Thou hast two eyes, and two hands, and two feet; thou canst not endure to maim and mangle the body of sin, and render thy self absurd and ridiculous to the world: Verily, thou hadst better go a Creeple to Heaven, then being a perfect Epicure to be cast into Hell."[19] Rather brilliantly, Danforth seems to recognize the crippling effects of what we would call heterosexuality, achieved only by those willing to "maim and mangle" the body. The proliferating pleasure he worries about here finds its simplest version in onanism, but Danforth claims that onanism leads to all the other forms of "sodomitical uncleanness," among which he lists "self-pollution," "nocturnal Pollutions," "impure thoughts and fancies in the day-time," "whoredome," adultery, incest, sodomy, and "Bestiality, or Buggery."

Sodomy is nevertheless singled out as a representative term for all such sins, both in Danforth's title and in phrases such as "sodomitical uncleanness." One reason for this, I would suggest, is that the geographical reference embedded in the term *sodomy* lends itself to Danforth's communalist rhetoric, authorizing the publicity of sexual practice. He defines sodomy, in a quasi-technical gesture, as "filthiness committed between parties of the same sex: when Males with Males, and Females with Females work wickedness"; and in the next sentence he says, "This sin raged amongst the Sodomites, and to their perpetual Infamy, it is called Sodomy." The civic significance of sodomy, he goes on to say, is more than etymological: "Repentance it self cannot so throughly heal this Wound, but some Scar will remain in this world . . . Yea, it pollutes and defiles the

Land where it is committed, and causeth it to spue out its Inhabitants" (7). Only after making this point does Danforth address the secret uncleanness that he supposes to be general among the audience, revealing that he is, in fact, rather uninterested in the hapless individual standing on the scaffold. As in his jeremiad four years earlier, he wants to purify the collectivity. "Do not linger nor defer thy Repentance," Danforth tells his hearers, "but hasten out of Sodom" (20).

Hasten where? Surely the analogy with Sodom must have been partly uncomfortable at this point. For if his audience dwells in a degenerate and onanistic New English Sodom, how shall they hasten out of it but by leaving New England itself? They had come there because old England, as they called it, was becoming Sodom. The figurative spatialization of sodomy and its knowledge only protects the local community if Sodom is somewhere else. To speak of sodomy in New England is to create a confusion of inside and outside. Thus, according to the preface of *The Cry of Sodom*—which is subscribed by John Sherman, Urian Oakes, and Thomas Shepard—"Amongst many other [things], this might have been looked at as astonishingly strange, that the worst of sins should be perpetrated, in some, the best of Places and Societies; that Enormities not so much as named amongst Gentiles, should be found among Christians." If the character of a society is indicated in large part by the presence or absence of such enormities, then the best and worst of societies interpenetrate.

The boundary between them can only be marked by a marveling rhetoric. Astonishingly strange, as the ministers say. Or just strange, as Samuel Whiting puts it over and over in *Abraham's Humble Intercession for Sodom*, a treatise on prayer in which the rhetoric of Sodom is all the more remarkable in that it does not seem to have been occasioned by any specific case of sodomy or bestiality:

> *Unnatural Uncleanness: Strange flesh*, as it is called, *Jude* ver. 7. when *men with men commit filthiness, and women with women*, as the Apostle expresseth it, *Rom.* 1.26, 27. and this makes men ripe for ruine. *Strange lusts* bring *strange punishment*; *strange fire* kindled upon earth, brings *strange fire* from heaven. Fire naturally *ascends*, but the fire that destroyed the Sodomites *descended*, Gen. 19.24. the *sin* was strange, and the *destruction* strange: God proportions the *punishment* to the *sin*, payes men in their own *coin*; they have *fire* for *fire*, and not onely so, but *strange fire*, for *strange fiery lusts*.[20]

Like Danforth and Willard, Whiting uses "sodomite" to mean resident of Sodom as well as a man of strange flesh, and *strange* partly means foreign. Like Danforth and Willard, he also believes that sex and urban geography are connected in this case: God only punishes an entire community, he tells us, "When their sins are universal: so were the sins of Sodom . . . General sins bring general destruction with them" (44). Whiting's conclusion from this lesson is that old England, which had recently restored monarchy and the episcopate, is ripe for destruction and in need of intercession (66–67). But he also suggests that New England, which he like Danforth believed was in declension, stood at risk of becoming Sodom itself. Hence Whiting recognizes the same hazard of interpenetration with Sodom that his fellow ministers worried about. "The most excellent of Saints have been found amongst the most wicked sinners: their black makes the godlies white more conspicuous. How eminent was Lot in Sodom" (34).

Late in *Of Plymouth Plantation*, William Bradford's account of some trials and executions for sodomy and bestiality in Plymouth begins on the same note of an interpenetration between Sodom and Canaan. The only protection is shock: "Marvelous it may be to see and consider how some kind of wickedness did grow and break forth here, in a land where the same was so much witnessed against and so narrowly looked unto, and severely punished when it was known, as in no place more, or so much, that I have known or heard of." Puritan society, defined so fundamentally by its comparison with other "Places and Societies," loses its own rationale more completely than any other society if it turns out to be like them. And sodomy, of all practices, most conjures the image of the other societies that this one has willed itself not to be. Confronted with a bugger and a sodomite, the Plymouth authorities worry about the inside/outside boundary of their colony. Their first response is to demand of the men "how they came first to the knowledge and practice of such wickedness." Luckily, "one confessed he had long used it in old England"; the other claimed to have heard through the grapevine "of such things from some in England." "By which it appears," Bradford remarks, "how one wicked person may infect many."[21] In his version of the scapegoating hunt for Patient Zero—mastered in our own day by Randy Shilts—Bradford rests content not with an original sinner but with old England as a site of knowledge.[22] Yet he still thinks it "may be marvelled at" that wicked persons should come to New England from old, and another five paragraphs are devoted to explaining how this penetration could have come about.

Bradford has difficulty explaining the presence of wickedness in general in New England, but no other kind of wickedness had posed this problem in his text until this chapter, which he begins by marveling: "Even sodomy and buggery (things fearful to name) have broke forth in this land oftener than once" (316). In this relatively brief paragraph at the opening of the chapter, Bradford uses the same verb three times, changing only the tense: wickedness is said to "break forth," to be "breaking out," and to have "broke forth." If this hammering repetition suggests a too-penetrable boundary, made even more spatially troublesome by its confusing temporality, it also echoes the breaking forth of the separatist church itself, in the opening sentence of the first chapter, where Satan is said to have attacked the church since its "first breaking out." Indeed, the chapter on sodomy and bestiality contains the book's most sustained reflection, at least in part two, on New England's world-historical position. Aside from an afterthought about the final bargain with Plymouth's English shareholders, the breaking forth of sodomy and bestiality is the only event that Bradford records for the entire year of 1642—a year in which civil war broke out in England, in which New England consequently ceased to be the vanguard of Puritan reform, and in which immigration dwindled to a trickle, making the entire colonial venture of doubtful purpose and success.

Bradford's anxieties about these developments are not exactly absent from the chapter. But they are expressed only in his discussion of sodomy. "The Devil may carry a greater spite against the churches of Christ and the gospel here," he speculates, again echoing his opening chapter, "by how much the more they endeavour to preserve holiness and purity amongst them and strictly punisheth the contrary when it ariseth either in church or commonwealth; that he might cast a blemish and stain upon them in the eyes of [the] world, who use to be rash in judgment" (316). Besides, he adds, in New England "the churches look narrowly to their members" (317).[23]

New England's nervousness about the eyes of the world on its stained members can be read either as an anxiety about becoming a Sodom or as an echo of Winthrop's famous image of the city on the hill. For Winthrop's city-on-the-hill paragraph is dominated by the same creepy erotics of visibility. He tells the other men on his ship to go about "allwayes haveing before our eyes . . . our Community as members of the same body," and to consider themselves as a city upon a hill *because* "the eies of all people are uppon us." Under so global an inspection, any blemish or stain almost gives off a sulphuric odor: "Wee shall be made a story and a by-word through the world, wee shall open the mouthes of enemies to speake evill of the wayes of god and all professours for Gods sake; wee shall shame the faces of many of gods worthy servants, and cause theire prayers to be turned into Cursses upon us till wee be consumed out of the good land whether wee are goeing."[24]

Sodom is a ghostly anxiety here in Winthrop's 1630 text; it would only gain pertinence for Bradford in 1642. In fact, it seems to make regular appearances in texts that deploy the city-on-a-hill theme. Peter Bulkeley makes the connection almost explicit when he tells New England, "Take heed . . . lest being now as *a Citie upon an hill*, which many seek unto, thou be left like *a Beacon upon the top of a mountaine*, desolate and forsaken"; only a few paragraphs earlier, he had reminded New Englanders of those other ex-emplary cities: "The filthinesse of *Sodome and Gomorrah* is known, they were *exceeding* sinners against the Lord, *Gen.* 13.13. their sins were not of the common sort, but exceeded; and therefore they perished not by the com-mon visitation of all men, but their judgement was exemplary, to stand as a warning to all ages; *a fire not blowne by man* (as it is in *Job* 20.26.) consumed them, the fire of God fell upon them from heaven."[25] Likewise, in 1673 Urian Oakes would repeat the "City upon an Hill" theme in a pamphlet that also cautions against becoming like Sodom.[26]

In a recent essay on the homopanic of Puritan poets whose medita-tions bring them, desirably and undesirably, into too great a proximity to God's Rod (as Wigglesworth always says), Walter Hughes makes a joke about the uncanny resemblance between the New England mission and Sodom. "The city on the hill," Hughes writes, "had become the city on the plain."[27] Hughes actually does not seem to have in mind the sodomitic overtones in Winthrop's sermon or its successors, so the joke may be more telling even than he intended. But even more telling, the connection is made (or nearly made) in Bradford's account itself. Having just remarked his stain in the eyes of the world, Bradford continues: "Besides, here the people are but few in comparison of other places which are full and populous and lie hid, as it were, in a wood or thicket and many horrible evils by that means are never seen nor known; whereas here they are, as it were, brought into the light and set in the plain field, or rather on a hill, made conspicuous to the view of all" (317). Bradford's notion of being set conspicuously on a hill probably echoes Winthrop's sermon, which had long circulated in manuscript. But he does not arrive at that image without first going through a rhetorical stammer, imagining that the colonial city is set not on a hill but, conspicuously, "in the plain field." The image stands out all the more since Bradford has passed over the obvious analogy between the New World wilderness and the "wood or thicket" in which something may be hid. In the context of (a) sodomy in its "literal" sense; and (b) the making of a people into a byword, can the reference to the cities on the plain not be audible here? Only maybe. Bradford's mid-sentence indecision makes the city on the hill only more notorious than the city on the plain.

A Modell of Christian Sodomy

In Winthrop's "Modell of Christian Charity," the reference to Sodom seems to be relevant in another way as well. The new colony threatens to resemble Sodom not only because of its global notoriety but also because of the intensity of its affective bonds among males. When Winthrop speaks of "allwayes haveing before our eyes . . . our Community as members of the same body," he is not primarily speaking of or to women. The burden of his argument is that society has been so constituted "that every man might have need of other, and from hence they might be all knitt more nearly together in the Bond of brotherly affeccion" (283). By "brotherly" he means male; the women aboard the *Arbella* are not specifically addressed by this social vision, and in fact Winthrop's language here derives almost unchanged from an earlier text in which he addressed an expressly all-male audience. On that occasion, in his first address to the Massachusetts corporation as its governor, he laid the same emphasis on male affection: "my speeche leads cheifly to this end, that being assured of eache others sincerity in our intentions in this worke, and duely considering in what new relations we stand, we might be knit togither in a most firm bond of love and frindshippe."[28] Both in that speech and in the more famous sermon aboard the *Arbella*, the theme of "love and frindshippe" among men is linked to the need for a visible solidarity under the inspection of the world: "Consider your reputation, the eyes of all the godly are upon you, what can you doe more honorable for this Cytye" (176). The community defined in both texts is a male one—despite the presence of women on the *Arbella*—formed in affection and in a hazardous specularity.

Of course brotherly affection is not always the same as sex, especially given the complex ways in which, as Alan Bray has shown so well, such language did not in this period conform to modern patterns of sexualization.[29] The Sodomites were notorious for something much more particular than mere "love and frindshippe," which can be thought of in relatively general, nonaffective, and nonerotic ways. Winthrop in fact contrasts Christian charity with the desires of the Sodomites by saying it "was practised by Abraham and Lott in entertaineing the Angells" (284). And critics have certainly never seen anything remarkable about Winthrop's affective community. Yet if Winthrop seems unquestionably to have in mind only such sanitized and nonerotic bonds, his text also tends to invoke bonds and attractions between men on a much more literal level than he would seem prepared to avow.

It is certainly very peculiar that he goes on, in "Modell of Christian Charity," to explain his "Bond of brotherly affection" by means of a theory of erotic attraction. In a passage that has received almost no commentary by critics—especially when compared to the ubiquitously cited "city on the hill" paragraph—Winthrop derives the social impulse from attraction.[30] And the attraction at the heart of the social is based on likeness:

> Simile simili gaudet or like will to like; for as it is things which are carved with disafeccion to eache other, the ground of it is from a dissimilitude or [blank] ariseing from the contrary or different nature of the things themselves, soe the ground of love is an apprehension of some resemblance in the things loved to that which affectes it, this is the cause why the Lord loves the Creature, soe farre as it hath any of his Image in it, he loves his electe because they are like himselfe, he beholds them in his beloved sonne: soe a mother loves her childe, because shee throughly conceives a resemblance of herselfe in it. Thus it is betweene the members of Christ, each discernes by the worke of the spirit his owne Image and resemblance in another, and therefore cannot but love him as he loves himselfe. (290)

Here Winthrop goes farther than his Latin proverb, farther than medieval notions of analogy, asserting that the similitude of things not only underlies social order but also creates the very bonds of the social by acting as a force of desire.[31] He even implies that Christian charity, like social attraction in general, will typically be a same-sex bond. Each member of Christ will be drawn to another and will "love him as he loves himselfe."

Of course one might still object that this theory of social attraction is not necessarily erotic. Winthrop's examples, after all, come from (same-sex) parent-child relations. But again the way he continues is surprising:

> Now when the soule which is of a sociable nature findes any thing like to it selfe, it is like Adam when Eve was brought to him, shee must have it one with herselfe this is fleshe of my fleshe (saith shee) and bone of my bone shee conceives a greate delighte in it, therefore shee desires nearenes and familiarity with it: shee hath a greate propensity to doe it good and receives such content in it, as feareing the miscarriage of her beloved shee bestowes it in the inmost closett of her heart, . . . shee setts noe boundes of her affeccions, nor hath any thought of reward, shee findes recompence enoughe in the exercise of her love towardes it. (290–91)

By this point, the boundless affection Winthrop describes as the fundamental social passion has an unmistakably erotic cast. That much would be clear from the choice of Adam and Eve as examples; only more striking is the consistent reference to the desirable body as "it," the desiring soul as "shee," especially since the latter pronoun is introduced immediately after the introduction of Eve. Though Winthrop ostensibly describes Adam's desire when Eve was brought to him, his language seems to concretize Adam's body, through Eve's point of view, as an object of desire.

In any case, how does this example illustrate the origins of love in resemblance? It would seem to suggest that Winthrop finds the attraction of likes best exemplified in male / female marriage. This expectation would fit with the idea, tirelessly repeated in the historical scholarship at least since Morgan's *The Puritan Family*, that Puritan ideas of society are based in the model of the family.[32] It would further seem likely, given the premise at the beginning of Winthrop's sermon, that God has ordained hierarchical relations among humankind, "some highe and eminent in power and dignitie; others meane and in subjeccion" (282). The erotic relations of the sexes could have been interpreted as such a natural relation of attraction in subjection. That at least would be Milton's strategy, almost forty years later; he deliberately and sharply *contrasts* Eve's desire for Adam with her desire for her own image. Adam's entrance disturbs her narcissistic reflection in what Milton understands as a progress toward divine intention.[33]

But that is not the argument in Winthrop's text. Far from it. Not only is Eve's attraction to her own image in Adam's body unpathologized by Winthrop; he also continues the same sentence that concludes the account of Eve by showing that the purest example of attraction would in fact not be Adam and Eve at all, but rather a same-sex bond: "wee may see this Acted to life in Jonathan and David." Again, we might be tempted to think that a sanitized, nonphysical, and nonerotic understanding of Jonathan's love for David is what allows him to use this example. But Winthrop does not hesitate to offer enthusiastic detail, considerably elaborating his scriptural sources in a passage that all but the most complete modern editions omit:

> Jonathan a valiant man endued with the spirit of Christ, soe soone as hee Discovers the same spirit in David had presently his hearte knitt to him by this linement of love, soe that it is said he loved him as his owne soule, he takes soe great pleasure in him that hee stripps himselfe to adorne his beloved, his fathers kingdome was not soe precious to him as his beloved David, David shall have it with all his hearte, himselfe desires noe more but that hee may be neare to him to reioyce in his good hee chooseth to converse with him in the wildernesse even to the hazzard of his owne life, rather then with the greate Courtiers in his fathers Pallace; when hee sees danger towards him, hee spares neither care paines, nor perill to divert it, when Injury was offered his beloved David, hee could not beare it, though from his owne father, and when they must parte for a Season onely, they thought theire heartes would have broake for sorrowe, had not their affeccions found vent by aboundance of Teares: other instances might be brought to shewe the nature of this affeccion as of Ruthe and Naomi [!] and many others, but this truthe is cleared enough.

The verb that Winthrop uses here for Jonathan's love of David, "knitt," is always his favorite verb for the operation of Christian charity, endlessly repeated in the *Arbella* sermon as well as in the earlier address to the corporation. The source of the phrase is in fact the account of David and Jonathan in I Samuel 18.[34] And in the biblical assertion that Jonathan loved David "as his owne soule," Winthrop might have found confirmation that love is based in reference to the self-image.

But Winthrop's interest in I Samuel is more than theoretical. As he later says, "This love among Christians is a reall thing not Imaginarie" (292). And indeed we might surmise that while describing David and Jonathan aboard the *Arbella* Winthrop was thinking back to a letter that he had written to his friend Sir William Springe before departing from England:

> I loved you truely before I could think that you took any notice of me: but now I embrace you and rest in your love: and delight to solace my first thoughts in these sweet affections of so deare a friend. The apprehension of your love and worth togither hath overcome my heart, and removed the veil of modestye, that I must needes tell you, my soule is knitt to you, as the soule of Jonathan to David: were I now with you, I should bedewe that sweet bosome with the tears of affection: O what a pinche will it be to me, to parte with such a freinde! if any Embleme may expresse our Condition in heaven, it is this Communion in love: I could, (nay I shall) envye the happinesse of your deare brother B[arnardiston] that he shall enjoye what I desire. nay (I will once let love drive me into an extacye) I must repine at the felicyty of that good Lady (to whom in all love and due respecte I desire to be remembered) as one that should have more parte then my selfe in that honest heart of my deare freinde.[35]

There is, as far as I can discern, not a single remark in the Winthrop criticism about this letter or its relation to the *Arbella* sermon.[36] Many writers have commented on the affectionate letters between Winthrop and his wife, but Winthrop seldom if ever lets love drive him "into an extacye" in those letters as he does here, going so far as to express envy toward Springe's wife in her proximity to the "sweet bosome" that Winthrop wants to bedew.

The letter to Springe is the source not only for the Jonathan and David passage of the *Arbella* sermon but also for the bond of brotherly affection in general. The letter concludes with an ecstatic appeal to Christ, in which Winthrop uses the language of seduction, possession, and marriage to describe once again how he wants to be "knitt," perhaps even bodily, to Springe:

It is tyme to conclude, but I knowe not how to leave you, yet since I must, I will putt my beloved into his arms, who loves him best, and is a faithfull keeper of all that is Committed to him. Now thou the hope of Israell, and the sure helpe of all that come to thee, knitt the heartes of thy servantes to thy selfe, in faith and puritye: Drawe us with the sweetnesse of thine odours, that we may runne after thee, allure us, and speak kindly to thy servantes, that thou maist possesse us as thine owne, in the kindnesse of youthe and the love of mariage: sealle us up by that holy spirit of promise, that we may not feare to trust in thee: Carrye us into thy Garden, that we may eate and be filled with those pleasures, which the world knows not: let us heare that sweet voyce of thine, my love my dove, my undefiled: spread thy skirt over us and cover our deformitye, make us sicke with thy love: let us sleep in thine armes, and awake in thy kingdome: the soules of thy servantes, thus united to thee, make as one in the bonde of brotherly Affection. (206)

My love, my dove, my undefiled—only by an elaborate displacement of rhetorical address does this text manage to avoid being in explicitness the love letter that it continually implies, diverting its erotic language (here derived from Song of Solomon) from the addressee of the letter, to whom it nevertheless addresses itself. Christ's arms become prostheses for Winthrop's caresses. Christ's skirts become a cover for the physical union of the two men, knit together in that nether space, rapt and allured by the odors there, "possessed" and "filled" in nothing less than "the love of mariage."

Despite the intensity of this language I do not mean to speculate on Winthrop's physical relations to Springe, much less to suggest that he would have understood the letter as advocating sodomy. The point is rather that Winthrop's bond with Springe, the "bonde of brotherly Affection" upon which he would later base the social vision of "Modell of Christian Charity," involves broadly erotic possibilities that he violently repudiates in any other context. When William Plaine was executed for sodomy in 1646, for example, Winthrop could not voice his approval too strongly, calling Plaine "a monster in human shape."[37] Perhaps Plaine had not enough skirts to cover his deformity. At any rate Christian charity, with its affective/erotic knitting of males, can be voiced by Winthrop only on the condition that he repudiate or displace its resemblance to

Sodom and sodomy. This is pathetic enough on its own, but it should also be remembered that the violence of the contradiction was unleashed on the bodies of William Plaine and others like him.

Some of those others may have been closer to hand as a context for "Modell of Christian Charity": at the moment of delivering the *Arbella* sermon, Winthrop might have been thinking not only of the sweet bosom of William Springe but also of the "5 beastly Sodomiticall boyes" detected aboard the *Talbot* in the previous June.[38] The *Talbot*, like the *Arbella*, had been carrying emigrants in service of the Massachusetts Bay corporation. Five "boys" of unknown age were detected in acts of "charity" and were remanded "to the company to bee punished in ould England, as the crime deserved." When the boys returned to England in September, the company was evidently uncertain what the crime deserved, for they voted twice—on 19 September and again on 29 September—to seek legal advice on "what punishm^t may bee inflicted upon them, and how the Comp$^~$ may bee legally discharged of them."[39] Winthrop was present at both of these meetings. Three weeks later, with the matter still evidently unresolved, Winthrop was himself elected governor and so became responsible for the administration of their punishment. Thereafter the boys disappear from the official record, perhaps because their fate was still in doubt when Winthrop took the records with him to Massachusetts in the following spring.

The *Arbella* sermon was thus delivered in the very space of the repudiation of sodomy, en route to the New Canaan. When Winthrop worries aloud to his shipmates that the world's prayers will "be turned into Cursses upon us till wee be consumed out of the good land whether wee are goeing," shall we not hear his own curses on those who were consumed out of this good land—or, in the case of those five boys, never made it to the good land whither they were going? And shall we not also hear those curses at the very moment when, in the conclusion of the letter to Springe, they become prayers?

The Covenant of Sodom

It may seem that we have moved, in these considerations of Winthrop's sermon and the letter to Springe, into a private realm fundamentally different from the rhetoric of Sodom. For the latter is, after all, essentially a function of official discourse and public consumption, while Winthrop's texts suggest a more personal arena of meaning for the erotic. These two levels are brought together in the *Arbella* sermon, joined in the theoretical claim that affectionate male-male bonds can sustain a disciplined public body. In Winthrop, in Bradford, and in Puritan culture more generally, discipline and attraction—the national judgment of Sodom and the private bonds of fraternal men—were two sides of the same coin, twin aspects of the formation of the church. Winthrop's rhetoric about the English Sodom is meant to develop an ideal of a true church as a disciplined church, keeping its covenant with God; his rhetoric about brotherly affection is meant to develop an ideal of a true church as a quasi-voluntary association, its members keeping covenant with each other. "A Modell of Christian Charity" is above all else a Congregationalist performance, describing and enacting the formation of a contractual society; and its contradictory investments on the topic of male-male desire have much to do with that context.

From its beginnings in the Elizabethan period, English Puritanism had been centrally a struggle over patterns of association: conventicling, the classis, the congregation. This is especially true of the branch of Puritanism that came to be dominant in New England, with the fundamental role that the doctrine of the covenant played there. The American Puritans believed that God had entered into a quasi-contractual agreement, not just with individuals but with a people, and that a church was formed by a similar quasi-contractual convenant among its members. This latter strand came to be institutionalized in the federative practices of Congregationalism, especially in the years following the *Arbella* sermon.

The Puritans were anything but voluntarists at the level of the individual. At the level of the social, however, covenant theory pioneered the legitimacy of elective ties modeled in contract relations and merging to form a society of affinity and common purpose, subject to collective self-reflection and self-direction under divine judgment. From the perspective of modernity, this "inadvertent" liberalism is the most significant and compelling feature of American Puritanism, as Perry Miller and Edmund Morgan long ago argued.[40] In the words of a more recent historian, "Gradually, a discovery was being made: quite apart from polity, the culture of the age offered a multitude of means to draw people voluntarily into a disciplined life and a purposive society."[41]

This discovery occasioned deep ambivalence. In Winthrop's sermon, the male erotics of Christian charity produces a model of the social based on affection, likeness, and affinity; the erotics of that model was therefore in tension with another model of the social equally important in the Puritan imagination—one based on natural order, hierarchy, the family, and reproduction. The two models tended to be interwoven in practice, but their tendencies conflicted: the one toward voluntarism in the formation of social groups, the other toward the rightness of the given, humanly unwilled order as the expression of divine will.

Alan Bray has recently argued that sodomy became the subject of tension in English culture during Winthrop's day precisely because the Elizabethan conventions of intense affection between male bedfellows were less and less stabilized by class and rank hierarchies; male-male affective relations were stigmatized as sodomitical, as in the case of Francis Bacon, not when they seemed too intimate but when they seemed to take precedence over status relations.[42] Bray's evidence suggests that Winthrop's relation to Springe, with all its apparent erotic intensity, may nevertheless have been acceptably conventional in this Elizabethan context of male friendship and unthreatening within the status hierarchy that the *Arbella* sermon nominally justifies. In that context it would have found a protected place within the economy of favor and allegiance among gentlemen.

But the associative practices of Puritanism, as elaborated in Winthrop's theory of charity and attraction, could be seen as placing society on a footing other than given status. Winthrop is able to single out attraction and similitude as a basis for social life in large part because the social relation of covenanting parties has been made the basis of the church and of God's relation to a people. Jonathan, after all, is said in I Samuel to "covenant" with David. Implicitly male contract relations—for that is what covenant theology was modeled on—were becoming paradigmatic of God's own behavior.[43] At least in part, mutuality and interest were becoming the principles of the social bond, not hierarchy and divine command. The conventions of male friendship took on different meanings in this changing context, as a system of status-based personal service gave way to systems of voluntary and contractual association.[44]

Puritan public rhetoric about Sodom also derived from covenant theology and its contractarian premises. In the words of Sacvan Bercovitch, "God's national judgments, bringing temporal, material blessings or disasters, followed from certain contractual agreements."[45] The social group defined in that contract is available to reflection as an object, amenable to theory, corrigible in practice. It is in this sense that Sodom serves as the great object lesson for the constitution of a society. In Peter Bulkeley's *The Gospel-Covenant*, for example, Sodom is the example of a society offered a covenant and destroyed for refusing it. Abraham's intercession for Sodom, in Whiting's sermon, is presented as an example of the contractual negotiation involved in the convenant, as Abraham bargains with God for the conditions of Sodom's redemption. In these readings of Genesis, Sodom primarily represented a people held responsible for its disposition as a people, a disposition of which sexual behavior was indicative. What stands out in Puritan exegesis is the fateful voluntarism implied at the social level by God's covenant. It could hardly have seemed accidental that the story of Sodom embeds, in the text of Genesis 13 through 19, the story of the covenant with Abraham and his seed in chapters 17 and 18.

That so much of Puritan theology and social theory boiled down to exegesis of Genesis 17 and 18 no doubt helps to explain further why the Puritans were so well versed in the story of Sodom. Like many others, Thomas Shepard first began to hear the call of Puritan preaching when, as a student at Cambridge, he says, "I heard Mr. Dickinson commonplace in the chapel upon those words—I will not destroy it for ten's sake (Genesis 19)." Shepard, however, here makes a not insignificant slip. The passage he has in mind is Genesis 18:32. Genesis 19 describes the Sodomites' demand for the angels and consequent destruction.[46] I say the slip may not be insignificant because two paragraphs earlier he has remarked "what a woeful estate I had been left in if the Lord had left me in that profane, ignorant town of Towcester where I was born, that the Lord should pluck me out of that sink and Sodom." And in the same paragraph that mistakenly cites Genesis 19, he goes on to describe the crisis in his own degeneracy, the turning point in his life:

> I drank so much one day that I was dead drunk, and that upon a Saturday night, and so was carried from the place I had drink at and did feast at unto a scholar's chamber, one Basset of Christ's College, and knew not where I was until I awakened late on that Sabbath and sick with my beastly carriage. And when I awakened I went from him in shame and confusion, and went out into the fields and there spent that Sabbath lying hid in the cornfields where the Lord, who might justly have cut me off in the midst of my sin, did meet me with much sadness of heart and troubled my soul for this and other my sins which then I had cause and leisure to think of.

Of course there is little ground for speculation about this evening in Basset's room, since Shepard covers it so thoroughly with conspicuous oblivion and satisfying shame, though the phrase "I went from him in shame" seems to suggest that Shepard had more than drunkenness to think about in his "beastly carriage." He later adds an interesting gloss to his own manuscript; referring to the same period at Cambridge, he says, "I was once or twice dead drunk and lived in unnatural uncleanesses not to be named and in speculative wantonness and filthiness with all sorts of persons which pleased my eye" (72). Though he does not say just how "unnatural" those "uncleanesses not to be named" were, nor which "sorts of persons" pleased his eye, his language has an unmistakable tendency to frame his conversion against the background of Sodom and sodomy. At any rate, he does tell us that it was the proximity of these pleasures to Genesis 18—or was it 19?—that induced him to leave that sink and Sodom where he was born and migrate westward, to that city on a hill in New England, never looking back. In *The Sincere Convert* of 1641, moreover, Shepard tells the reader that sodomy is latent in every sinner: "thy heart is a foul sink of all atheism, sodomy, blasphemy, murder, whoredom, adultery, witchcraft, buggery; so that, if thou hast any good thing in thee, it is but as a drop of rosewater in a bowl of poison; where fallen it is all corrupted. It is true thou feelest not all these things stirring in thee at one time . . . but they are in thee like a nest of snakes in an old hedge. Although they break not out into thy life, they lie lurking in thy heart."[47]

The temptation to read Shepard's autobiography, like Winthrop's sermon, as indicating in its gaps something like a repressed desire raises once more the question of the personal and subjective dimension to the Puritan imagination of sodomy. Yet even here the corporate context of covenant theology must have helped in more ways than one to give Sodom and sodomy such a powerful charge. Private anxieties about affinitive male relations could only have been intensified within this strand of Puritanism, as the personal relations of the covenant and of Winthrop's charity were generalized to a theory of social bonds. What Shepard calls the pleasures of the eye, after all, Winthrop calls the elemental form of Christian charity: *simile simili gaudet*. The same theology, however, allowed any private anxieties about the affinitive character of male relations to be played out in public anxieties about the world-historical standing of the community, directly indexed in Puritan culture by the bearing of the body.

Winthrop's "Modell of Christian Charity" also shows how the federal strand in Puritan theology could throw into relief, as a paradigm for social bonds in general, nonreproductive erotics unmoored from natural hierarchy—even in a sermon ostensibly dedicated to justifying natural hierarchy and patriarchal familialism. Covenant theology doubtless did not bring about for anybody a conscious legitimation of alternative sexualities. But it did move into a central ideological role elements of social life that could not fully be squared with the ideology of patriarchal-familial sexuality—so much so that one of the deepest tensions in colonial New England was that between the covenant and the traditional rhetoric of generational transmission, or what Philip Gura has called "the intricate genetics of salvation."[48]

Thomas Lechford noted this potential as early as 1642. In a pamphlet critical of the New Englanders, he argues that given congregational practice—which he beautifully describes—the Puritans "in short time shall have their children for the most part remain unbaptized: and so have little more priviledge then Heathens, unlesse the discipline be amended and moderated."[49] The problem was that if church membership were contractual in nature it could not be passed along within a family. Thus the contractual side of covenant theology conflicted with its national promise, rooted in Genesis 17 and 18 where God covenants with Abraham and his "seed." Lechford cites a controversy surrounding a parishioner named Doughty, who claimed that the covenant being with Abraham and his seed, children of church members should be baptized. But such a reading of the language in Genesis seemed to do away with the covenant itself, than which few things could have been more important to American Puritans. Doughty was physically dragged out of the church and was then "forced to goe away from thence, with his wife and children" (41).

Puritan theologians differed on what to make of Abraham's seed. Peter Bulkeley argues that just as the old covenant "did include the seed," so also the new covenant "belongs to the seed." He distinguishes between the literal and figurative seed of Abraham: "not onely that many Nations should spring from his loyns by naturall generation, but that the Nations of the world (though not springing from him by naturall meanes,) should be counted to him as his children, and that he should be called *their Father*."[50] In short, children of church members were covered in their parents' covenant. But John Cotton, and many with him, took the other emphasis in the covenant to be supreme, arguing that it applies only to those who are "confederate," who bring themselves in agreement with its terms.[51] Eventually, of course, this tension within the concept of the covenant would result in the compromise of the "Half-Way Covenant."

In its radical implications contractarian theology provoked deep anxieties. Cotton himself had warned the first emigrants to "have a tender care that you looke well to the plants that spring from you, that is, to your children, that they doe not degenerate as the Israelites did; after which they were vexed with afflictions on every hand. . . . Your Ancestours were of a noble divine spirit, but if they suffer their children to degenerate, to take loose courses, then God will surely plucke you up."[52] It was the very importance of the covenant, requiring new acceptance and compliance, that brought the specter of Sodom and its judgment between any two generations.

The tension in covenant theology was never resolved, and was at any rate no mere dispute over church doctrine. There was a contradiction between the two models of society implicit in these two aspects of covenant theory, a contradiction that continues to be a fundamental site of conflict to the present day. In *Bowers v. Hardwick*, for example, Justice White's majority opinion dismisses the relevance of precedents that prevent the state from interfering in decisions about whether or not to reproduce. With truly ghoulish disingenuousness the court declares, "No connection between family, marriage, or procreation on the one hand and homosexual activity on the other has been demonstrated, either by the Court of Appeals or by respondent." In our time such claims become more and more fraudulent and vindictive because people have fought so long for the ability *not* to make such a connection; the institutions of generational transmission are no longer everywhere necessary in order to legitimate either sexual pleasure or social affinity. In seventeenth-century New England the possibility of this separation could only be uncertainly glimpsed—in Winthrop's erotics of affinitive society or in the vexed destiny of Abraham's seed.

The possibility of a society no longer imagining itself through familial and reproductive institutions has been lost from view not only in law but in much American literary criticism. Critics have instead been content to produce untiring enthusiasm for the rhetoric of the city on the hill—an enthusiasm obligingly taken up in speeches over the past four decades by the same president, appropriately enough, under whose administration *Bowers v. Hardwick* was prosecuted. Although the deployment of New England's legendary history in support of a homophobic and heterosexist agenda has been powerful in recent years—even overwhelmingly so—it nevertheless scarcely remains the only possible use of Puritan history, as I have tried to show. Could we make more familiar a history of American Puritanism that clarified rather than obscured the critical possibilities glimpsed in the social erotics that the Puritans, despite their best intentions, began to imagine?

Notes

This essay first appeared in *American Literature* 64, no. 1 (March 1992): 19–47. Copyright © 1992 by Duke University Press.

1. "All other Churches of Europe are brought to desolation, and it cannot be, but the like Judgment is comminge upon us." From the texts known variously as "Arguments," "General Observations," and "Considerations" "for the Plantation of New England," in the variant called version "B" by the editors of the Winthrop papers. Stewart Mitchell, ed., *The Winthrop Papers*, 5 vols. (Boston: Massachusetts Historical Society, 1929–47), 2:106–27, 114.

2. 1629 fragment in John Winthrop's hand, evidently from a letter, arguing in favor of emigration, *Winthrop Papers*, 2:121–24, 122.

3. Robert Ryece to John Winthrop, *Winthrop Papers*, 2:127–32; 129–30.

4. Quoted in Sacvan Bercovitch, *The Puritan Origins of the American Self* (New Haven: Yale University Press, 1975), 102.

5. *Winthrop Papers*, 2:91–92. Compare this to Thomas Hooker's remark in March 1631: "God makes account that New England shall be a refuge for his Noahs and his Lots." Quoted in Stephen Foster, *The Long Argument: English Puritanism and the Shaping of New England Culture, 1570–1700* (Chapel Hill: University of North Carolina Press, 1991), 110.

6. Thomas Morton, *New English Canaan*, ed. Charles Francis Adams (1637; rpt., New York: Burt Franklin, 1967), 230.

7. Contrary to this gloss, John Boswell has argued that the text of Genesis 18 and 19 should not be read as attributing any sexual practice at all to the Sodomites. In his view, this is a much later misreading, institutionalized since the Romans coined the term *sodomia*. Where the citizens of Sodom demand to "know" the angels, Boswell argues, the verb does not necessarily imply sex and demonstrates instead an unpardonable breach in the etiquette of hospitality. See *Christianity, Social Tolerance, and Homosexuality* (Chicago: University of Chicago Press, 1980), 92–98.

8. Quoted in Foster, *The Long Argument*, 50.

9. Robert Gray, *An Alarum to England* (London, 1609), quoted in Edmund Morgan, *The Puritan Dilemma* (Boston: Little, Brown, 1958), 20.

10. To this day the popular imagination associates Puritanism with the phrase "fire and brimstone," commonly thought to refer to hell but actually deriving from the destruction of Sodom in Genesis 19:24. "*Sodom*," as one writer needlessly reminded his readers, "was destroy'd with *fire & brimstone* from Heaven." Benjamin Wadsworth,

    Unchast Practices Procure Divine Judgments (Boston, 1716), 16. Puritans often made the connection between the destruction of Sodom and metaphysical hell, as did Samuel Mather in citing Sodom and hell as type and antitype. Mather points out in support of this typology that the phrase "fire and brimstone" is repeated in Revelation to describe hell. Samuel Mather, *Figures and Types of the Old Testament*, 2nd ed. (London, 1705), 57, 83, 163.

11.   The definition of sodomy has been notoriously problematic, leading Foucault once to call it "that utterly confused category" (Michel Foucault, *History of Sexuality*, vol. 1, trans. Robert Hurley [New York: Vintage, 1980], 101). On the meaning of "sodomy" in colonial usage, see Robert Oaks, " 'Things Fearful to Name': Sodomy and Buggery in Seventeenth-Century New England," in *The American Man*, ed. Elizabeth Pleck and Joseph Pleck (Englewood Cliffs, N.J.: Prentice-Hall, 1980), 53–76. More generally on the political history of "sodomy" and the law, see Ed Cohen, "Legislating the Norm: From Sodomy to Gross Indecency," *South Atlantic Quarterly* 88 (Winter 1989): 181–217.

12.   Roger Thompson, *Sex in Middlesex: Popular Mores in a Massachusetts County, 1649–1699* (Amherst: University of Massachusetts Press, 1986). Thompson goes on to interpret this nonevidence as follows: "Men and women of the middle and lower orders took their pleasures straight . . . sexual experimentation and libertinism were the outcome of sophisticated, leisured, privileged, and urbanized groups, such as court or literary coteries; these prerequisites would effectively exclude the population of Middlesex County, Massachusetts" (74–75). It does not seem to occur to Thompson that the scarcity of court evidence might indicate nonreporting from any of a number of causes. Nothing would be less surprising than that sex among men or among women would be less visible than other kinds, given (a) the different and less public contexts in which it might come about, and (b) the capital punishments provided by law and the extreme, even terroristic rhetoric of the culture. But from anyone who is capable of using the word *straight* without irony in this context, we should hardly be surprised to see such stale and ideological images of urban decadence and rural simplicity, of natural sex and deviant "complications" (his term). Farm boys know better. I might note, moreover, that Thompson's association of "deviant" sex with urban geography gives yet another instance of the rhetorical tradition I am tracing in this essay.

13.   The results of that interest were sometimes lethal and always oppressive, as we know from recent work such as the following: Jonathan Ned Katz, *Gay American History* (New York: Harper and Row, 1976); Robert Oaks, " 'Things Fearful to Name' "; Kathleen Verduin, "Our Cursed Natures," *New England Quarterly* 56 (1983): 220–37; Walter Williams, *The Spirit and the Flesh: Sexual Diversity in American Indian Cultures* (Boston: Beacon Press, 1986); Walter Hughes, " 'Meat Out of the Eater': Panic and Desire in American Puritan Poetry," in *Engendering Men*, ed. Joseph A. Boone and Michael Cadden (New York: Routledge, 1990), 102–21. I am particularly indebted to Jonathan Goldberg, "Bradford's 'Ancient Members' and 'A Case of Buggery . . . Amongst Them,' " in *Nationalisms and Sexualities*, ed. Andrew Parker, Mary Russo, Doris Sommer, and Patricia Yaeger (New York: Routledge, 1991); and

his "Sodomy in the New World," *Social Text* 29 (Fall 1991): 46–57. Goldberg is astute on the mystification involved by celebrations of the Puritan legacy—such as Wayne Franklin's—that diminish the importance of violence, whether homophobic or racist or misogynist, in the nation's founding texts.

Unfortunately these scholars' work has as yet scarcely made a dent in narratives and origin myths offered by cultural historians, as Michael Moon observed in remarks to a panel at the Modern Language Association, 30 December 1990. Perhaps one reason is that we have not grasped the connections—condensed into the very term "sodomy"—between unofficial sexualities and the more prestigious themes of Puritan history: the city on the hill, the errand into the wilderness, the social covenant, declension and redemption, the jeremiad.

14.   For some examples of these complaints, see Edmund Morgan, *Visible Saints: The History of a Puritan Idea* (1963; rpt., Ithaca, N.Y.: Cornell University Press, 1987). More generally on discipline and the body in Puritan New England, see Kai Erikson, *Wayward Puritans: A Study in the Sociology of Deviance* (New York: Macmillan, 1966). For an especially strong statement of the relationship between sexual behavior and national judgment, see John Cotton's 1636 sermon at Salem, in *John Cotton on the Churches of New England*, ed. Larzer Ziff (Cambridge: Harvard University Press, 1968), 67.

15.   The exception might seem to be French kissing. But Frenching doesn't make you French, as sodomizing makes you a sodomite. (Interestingly, but not surprisingly, there is no corresponding verb for being a lesbian.)

16.   The Supreme Court's majority decision in that case, by Justice Byron White, continually refers to "homosexual sodomy." It argues that there can be no "fundamental right" for "homosexuals to engage in acts of consensual sodomy. Proscriptions against that conduct have ancient roots. Sodomy was a criminal offense at common law and was forbidden by the laws of the original 13 states when they ratified the Bill of Rights." Chief Justice Burger wrote a concurring opinion in the case expressly in order to endorse the premodern associations of the term *sodomy*: "As the Court notes, the proscriptions against sodomy have very 'ancient roots.' Decisions of individuals relating to homosexual conduct have been subject to state intervention throughout the history of Western civilization. Condemnation of those practices is firmly rooted in Judeo-Christian moral and ethical standards. Homosexual sodomy was a capital crime under Roman law. . . . During the English Reformation when powers of the ecclesiastical courts were transferred to the King's Courts, the first English statute criminalizing sodomy was passed. Blackstone described 'the infamous crime against nature' as an offense of 'deeper malignity' than rape, an heinous act 'the very mention of which is a disgrace to human nature,' and 'a crime not fit to be named' " (*Bowers v. Hardwick*, from *New York Times*, 1 July 1986). Both in choice of nomenclature and in anathematization the Supreme Court chooses not to deviate from the early Christian exegesis of the Sodom episode in Genesis.

17.   Samuel Willard, *Useful Instructions for a professing People in Times of great Security and Degeneracy* (Cambridge, 1673), 12.

18. David Cressy argues that, given the social conditions of migration, the congregationalist venture was from the outset coupled with colonial requirements that could only be registered by Puritans as corruption. The company wrote to Endecott in 1629, for example, saying that it was sending him mostly godly persons, but that " 'notwithstanding our care to purge them, there may still remain some libertines.' " "Newcomers to Massachusetts," Cressy continues, "complained of 'the prophane and dissolute living of divers of our nation.' " As Cressy points out, this effect of degeneracy was unavoidable given the importance of kinship and patronage networks for emigration. David Cressy, *Coming Over: Migration and Communication between England and New England in the Seventeenth Century* (Cambridge: Cambridge University Press, 1987), 40–48.

19. Samuel Danforth, *The Cry of Sodom Enquired into: Upon Occasion of the Arraignment and Condemnation of Benjamin Goad, for his Prodigious Villany* (Cambridge, 1674), 22. There is an important discussion of this text in John Canup, *Out of the Wilderness: The Emergence of an American Identity in Colonial New England* (Middletown, Conn.: Wesleyan University Press, 1990).

20. Samuel Whiting, *Abraham's Humble Intercession for Sodom* (Cambridge, 1666), 46.

21. William Bradford, *Of Plymouth Plantation*, ed. Samuel Morison (New York: Knopf, 1952), 321.

22. The reference is to Randy Shilts, *And the Band Played On: Politics, People, and the AIDS Epidemic* (New York: St. Martin's Press, 1987). For a good critique of this book's scapegoating rhetoric (and homophobia) in its construction of Gaetan Dugas, see Douglas Crimp, "How to Have Promiscuity in an Epidemic," *October* 43 (Winter 1987): 237–71, esp. 238–46.

23. For an excellent discussion of the themes of specularity and male bonds in Bradford, see Jonathan Goldberg, "Bradford's 'Ancient Members.' "

24. "A Modell of Christian Charity," *Winthrop Papers*, 2:282–95, at 294–95. In these texts by Winthrop and Bradford the link between homoerotics and panicky visibility may call to mind the classic instance of that link in Freud's analysis of the Schreber case. I owe to Eve Sedgwick, however, the observation that Schreber's fantasies of visibility can be read as struggles to articulate desires and possibilities otherwise inexpressible; for this reason, Freud's pathologizing account of paranoia as a symptomatic displacement of homoerotics must be seen as inadequate at best.

25. Peter Bulkeley, *The Gospel-Covenant*, 2nd ed. (London, 1651), 11, 16.

26. Urian Oakes, *New-England Pleaded With* (Cambridge, 1673). Oakes makes several references to Sodom (e.g., 15) in order to make the point that it is a people's duty to "understand and consider their latter end" (7), especially when that people has become "degenerous" (24), and guilty of "monstrous deportment of a Covenant people" (33).

27. Walter Hughes, " 'Meat Out of the Eater,' " 113. For a related but somewhat different reading of Puritan male sexual panic, see Eva Cherniavsky, "Night Pollution and the Floods of Confession in Michael Wigglesworth's Diary," *Arizona Quarterly* 45 (Summer 1989): 15–33.

28. Address of John Winthrop to the Company of the Massachusetts Bay, *Winthrop Papers*, 2:174–77, at 176.

29. Alan Bray, *Homosexuality in Renaissance England* (London: Gay Men's Press, 1982), esp. 58–80.

30. One significant exception is Andrew Delbanco, who briefly discusses the passage in *The Puritan Ordeal* (Cambridge: Harvard University Press, 1989), 74.

31. The sources of Winthrop's thinking here have not yet been identified, though he clearly draws on a broad tradition that includes such un-Puritan thinkers as Bonaventure and Aquinas. "Up to the end of the sixteenth century, resemblance played a constructive role in the knowledge of Western culture. It was resemblance that largely guided exegesis and the interpretation of texts; it was resemblance that organized the play of symbols, made possible knowledge of things visible and invisible, and controlled the art of representing them" (Michel Foucault, *The Order of Things* [New York: Vintage, 1973], 17).

32. Edmund Morgan, *The Puritan Family: Religion and Domestic Relations in Seventeenth-Century New England* (New York: Harper and Row, 1966).

33. For a good if not very critical account of this logic in Milton, see Jean Hagstrum, *Sex and Sensibility: Ideal and Erotic Love from Milton to Mozart* (Chicago: University of Chicago Press, 1980), 24–49.

34. The language of this account, as Winthrop takes it up, remains consistent in the Geneva and King James Bibles. In the Geneva version it runs: "And when he had made an end of speaking unto Saul, the soule of Jonathan was knit with the soule of David, and Jonathan loved him, as his owne soule. And Saul toke him that day, and wolde not let him returne to his fathers house. Then Jonathan and David made a covenant: for he loved him as his owne soule. And Jonathan put of the robe that was upon him, and gave it David, and his garments, even to his sworde, & to his bowe, and to his girdle" (I Samuel 18:1–4).

35. Winthrop to Sir William Springe, 8 Feb. 1629/30, *Winthrop Papers*, 2:203–6, 205.

36. The historian Stephen Foster is a near exception. He writes that "To [Winthrop] and his generation love to God and man was not just the English translation of some New Testament Greek, but a real, vivid passion in which *agape*, *philos*, and *eros* were all combined." Winthrop's letter to Springe is cited as an example of this. Stephen Foster, *Their Solitary Way: The Puritan Social Ethic in the First Century of Settlement in New England* (New Haven: Yale University Press, 1971), 48–49.

37. Winthrop, *Journal*, quoted in Jonathan Katz, *Gay American History*, 22.

38. Francis Higginson's *True Relacion*, in *The Founding of Massachusetts*, ed. Stewart Mitchell (Boston: Massachusetts Historical Society, 1930), 71. Historians, when they have noted this incident at all, have shown an alarming tendency to identify with Higginson's horrified reaction. See, for example, David Cressy, *Coming Over*, 101. Interestingly, Cressy later observes, apropos of Winthrop's interest in charity's bonds: "Confined for eight to twelve weeks or more to a tiny wooden world, the travellers were thrust into intimacies that might never have developed on land" (151).

39. Nathaniel Shurtleff, ed., *Records of the Governor and Company of the Massachusetts Bay*, 6 vols. (Boston: 1853–55), 1:54.

40. Perry Miller, *Orthodoxy in Massachusetts, 1630–1650* (Cambridge: Harvard University Press, 1933); Perry Miller, *The New England Mind*, vol. 1 (1939; rpt., Cambridge: Harvard University Press, 1982), esp. 398–431; Edmund Morgan, *Visible Saints: The History of a Puritan Idea*. The notion of inadvertent liberalism is in Miller, *New England Mind*, 1:418. On the social character of the covenant, see also Foster, *Their Solitary Way*; and Larzer Ziff, "The Social Bond of the Church Covenant," *American Quarterly* 10 (1958): 454–62.

    Miller's version of this history has of course been much contested, partly because it has defined the field so fundamentally. For some examples of the revisions of Miller's theses that are relevant to the point made here, see David D. Hall's introduction to the 1970 Harper Torchbooks edition of *Orthodoxy in Massachusetts*; also Philip Gura, *A Glimpse of Sion's Glory: Puritan Radicalism in New England, 1620–1660* (Middletown, Conn.: Wesleyan University Press, 1984); and Darrett Rutman, *Winthrop's Boston: A Portrait of a Puritan Town, 1630–1649* (1965; rpt., New York: Norton, 1972).

41. Foster, *The Long Argument*, 64.

42. Alan Bray, "Homosexuality and the Signs of Male Friendship in Elizabethan England," an essay reprinted in this volume. "As a social form," writes Bray, "the personal service of early Tudor England was in decay by the end of the sixteenth century but as a cultural form it was not; here the language of 'friendship,' as a set of assumptions and expectations, was still very much alive. There was though now a disparity between the two in precisely those elements that protected the intimacy it involved from a charge of sodomy" (53). A further connection here is the denunciation of Bacon's sodomy, cited by Bray, in the autobiography of Sir Simonds D'Ewes, whose affiliations with the early New England Puritans were many.

43. On this point see Miller, *New England Mind*, esp. 1:413.

44. In saying this I am trying to suggest one historical framework for modern homosociality and its proscription of the homoerotic, as classically analyzed in Eve Kosofsky Sedgwick, *Between Men: English Literature and Male Homosocial Desire* (New York: Columbia University Press, 1985). For a more theoretical statement of the issues raised by such a historical claim, focused especially on the liberal ego, see my "Homo-Narcissism; Or, Heterosexuality," in *Engendering Men*, ed. Boone and Cadden, 190–206.

45. Bercovitch, *Puritan Origins*, 81.

46. Thomas Shepard, autobiography and journal, ed. by Michael McGiffert as *God's Plot: The Paradoxes of Puritan Piety* (Amherst: University of Massachusetts Press, 1972), 40.

47. *The Works of Thomas Shepard*, vol. 1 (Boston, 1853), 28.

48. Gura points out that Puritanism could not eliminate a tendency to radicalize itself in a way that undermined generational logic. "If the baptists had their way," he writes, "the intricate genetics of salvation on which the New England Puritans believed the continuity of their churches depended, with the children of church members guaranteed the right to baptism by their virtue as the 'seed' of believers

and so placed under the spiritual watch and care of the church, would simply crumble. . . . [The baptists'] implicit premise was that no one could inherit membership in the Church" (*A Glimpse of Sion's Glory*, 95, 217).

49.   Thomas Lechford, *Plain-Dealing: Or, Newes from New-England* (London, 1642), 39–40.

50.   Bulkeley, *The Gospel-Covenant*, 151, 154–55.

51.   See especially the 1636 Salem sermon, in *John Cotton on the Churches of New England*, ed. Larzer Ziff (Cambridge: Harvard University Press, 1968).

52.   *God's Promise to His Plantation* (London, 1630), 19. Compare this with *The Covenant of Gods Free Grace* (London, 1645), in which Cotton lays much emphasis throughout on family duties and relations, especially those of parent and child, as the arena of grace and the covenant. Cotton's text, 2 Samuel 23:5, leads him to cite especially David's children, and the recurrent theme is that of the generational transmission of the covenant: e.g., "it may teach every righteous Housholder and Parent, to take more care to leave a good covenant to their children and servants than any thing else" (26). Cotton's language consistently tries to ambiguate the relative weight of chosen and unchosen relations, covenants made and covenants left behind. "If you be not in the Covenant, but your whole desire is, that you may, you must labour to bring your selves into a good family, and that you may be fitted for any service, you must deny your selves, and give up your mindes, wills and affections unto God" (20).

Afterword

MARGARET HUNT

THIS volume has sought to chart a new course for the study of sexuality in the Renaissance and early modern period,[1] and implicitly for a larger enterprise that includes lesbian/gay studies, but whose ambitions are more expansive still. Yet the point of embarkation is a quite particular one, the recent demonstration, in *Bowers v. Hardwick*, of how ready conservatives are to invent their own version of history to use against us. What we have here, then, is an attempt to claim a usable history in the face of an all too easily abusable past.

It should come as no surprise that this present move has come out of Renaissance studies. The European Renaissance presents us with a series of societies sufficiently different from our own as to destabilize a number of received assumptions about, among other things, gender, sexuality, politics, religion, language, and identity. Yet it is also a period to which twentieth-century people almost reflexively appeal when they wish to validate whatever passes at any given time for "mainstream values." The Supreme Court's discovery, or rather invention, in *Bowers v. Hardwick*, of full-fledged modern-style "homosexuals" already drawing universal obloquy and moral retribution onto themselves as far back as Henry VIII's sodomy statute of 1533 is an example of the latter move. In the face of these sorts of attacks the reconsideration represented by this volume is more than timely; it is essential.

The contributors to this volume show brilliantly how very different the cultural terrain of the Renaissance was from the historical fantasy which conservatives on and off the Supreme Court are using to justify repressive measures in the present. Acceptable desire had a markedly different social location in the Renaissance than it does today, in Valerie Traub's words, "flow[ing] rather freely between homoerotic and heterosexual modes." It was a setting in which it was taken for granted that religious devotion had a strongly erotic component,[2] and where deep emotional bonds between men (at least the right sorts of men), including physical displays of affection, sleeping in the same bed, etc., were esteemed rather than disparaged. And it was one in which "sodomy" itself was less an "utterly confused category" (to use Michel Foucault's famous phrase) than one whose unstable meanings mirrored the shifting preoccupations of groups in power, or, at times, those ambitious to replace them. Certainly the fact that the word *sodomy* was used to refer to such disparate activities as bestiality, heterosexual anal intercourse, *both* priestly celibacy and clerical concubine-keeping, an adult man's sexual abuse of a young girl, sexual intercourse between Christians and Jews,[3] masturbation, coitus interruptus, birth control, pederasty, and luxurious consumption belies the assertion that the presence of laws forbidding "it" signaled the existence of a unified "homosexual" identity or subjectivity in the Renaissance. (Ironically, one thing the category of sodomy almost certainly did *not* include in the Renaissance was fellatio, the act that brought Michael Hardwick to the attention of the Georgia judiciary in the first place.)[4]

Yet if this volume exposes the historical fallacies and perhaps deceits of the *Hardwick* court, some of its contributors also go further, to make a critique of a certain strand of gay historiography. The argument, in effect, is that by focusing too exclusively on the rise of homosexual identities and subcultures,[5] and by constructing an overarching narrative that focuses on the progressive attainment of a unitary homosexual identity, historians have inadvertently contributed to the unhealthy climate in which decisions like *Bowers v. Hardwick* could thrive. Even more unfortunate, or so this critique goes, scholars have failed to examine the ways that the permissions and prohibitions that surround sexuality and gender, indeed the shifting boundaries of what constitutes the erotic, are implicated in what used to be called "larger" systems, including various heterosexual family forms, male supremacy(ies), modern (and past) class divisions, and the like.

It is debatable how much the problem (which I am convinced is a real one) inheres in specific pieces of writing by gay scholars and how much it is a product of the way the gay studies has come to be taught. It is true that an older historiography did search obsessively for famous people to "out" in the past. It is also the case that the standard narrative of the history of homosexuality in the West (perhaps most visible in "history of homosexuality" or "introduction to lesbian/gay studies" courses) still sees the Greeks as confusing teases, treats everything up through the early modern period as foreplay, finally gets down to it with Whitman and Havelock Ellis, and climaxes with the Mattachine Society and the Stonewall riots.

The clear complicity of some, if by no means all, of those who pioneered sexual "categories" in the nineteenth and early twentieth centuries with repressive regimes and campaigns has made it difficult to view the rise of the category of "homosexual" as an unproblematic development, even for those quite heavily invested in the narrative of progress I just outlined. But the resulting tactical (and especially pedagogical) confusion has rather often simply transformed itself into interminable debates about whether the rise of a homosexual identity is more good than bad rather than into attempts to examine larger sexual/social systems.

Finally, in privileging historical figures who appear most closely to approximate "the" idealized modern self-identified gay person (a project in which, in my experience, students enthusiastically join), historians can easily embrace an unwarrantably narrow and compartmentalized view of "homosexuals" and "homosexuality" in the present, at the same time setting themselves up to overlook the very different, often more fluid and at least comparably diverse ways that desire is organized in societies and time-periods other than our own. But whether it comes in the first instance out of the scholarship or out of gay/lesbian pedagogy, or, as is more likely, a combination of the two, there is a definite strain within gay and lesbian history that is narrow, presentist, and (using Eve Kosofsky Sedgwick's useful terminology) minoritizing, rather than broad, culturally sensitive, and universalizing, whether in its overarching chronologies, its preferred objects of study, or its methodological preoccupations.[6]

Historians of the Renaissance and early modern period may have fallen into some of the same traps. There has been considerable interest of late in the rise of "the molly," typically seen as a kind of forerunner of the modern homosexual man, and in the growth of identifiable sexual subcultures in cities like Amsterdam and London at the end of the seventeenth and beginning of the eighteenth century. It is possible that this focus has elbowed out some broader approaches to the history of sexuality in the period. On the other hand, no historian of the period thinks molly houses, or the public toilets of Amsterdam and the Hague, apparently hotbeds of homosexual activity in the early eighteenth century, exhaust the sites for homoerotic activity in these societies, and several articles explicitly seek to contrast coexisting erotic regimes (here I think particularly of L. J. Boon's exemplary, and alas posthumously published, essay "Those Damned Sodomites: Public Images of Sodomy in the Eighteenth Century Netherlands").[7] The very fact that "subcultures" (if that is what they were) emerged in a period of rapid political, economic, and demographic change has encouraged some historians to seek linkages between changing understanding of the heterosexual family and new kinds of homosexual panic—and between more "modern" conceptions of gender and new linkages between sexuality and identity.[8] Still, in the face of the considerable uncertainty that currently reigns as to "what really happened" to women, the heterosexual family, the economy, and "the individual" in the early modern period, there is a real temptation to retreat to a simple model of "find the homosexuals, in or out of their subcultures, and see how badly society treats them."

A compelling rejoinder to the charge that historians are engaged in an ultimately damaging, or at best short-sighted form of identity-inflected history can be mounted from the rather different vantage point of lesbian history. The search for subcultures or for a "lesbian" identity (or indeed any kind of female identity) is a significantly more challenging enterprise among lesbian historians, or women's studies scholars in general, than it is for those who study the history of male homosexuality. At the same time the search for the linkages between regimes of sexual control and male supremacy (and more lately, their linkages with race and class oppression and imperial domination) is and has been absolutely central to the enterprise of feminist studies. This can be seen in any number of historical and theoretical works, from Adrienne Rich's suggestively titled 1978 article "Compulsory Heterosexuality and Lesbian Existence" to one of the most influential pieces of "lesbian" history ever done, Carroll Smith-Rosenberg's "Female World of Love and Ritual: Relations between Women in Nineteenth-Century America" (1975). Smith-Rosenberg focuses precisely upon what she argues is the normative and functional role of feminine homoerotics within white middle-class American families in the late eighteenth through the second half of the nineteenth century. A "lesbian identity" or an identifiable subculture is conspicuously absent from, indeed largely precluded by, this approach, and in the almost two decades that have elapsed since the first appearance of this essay numerous other studies have followed this lead, though, and here the critique may hold, without always placing it within a larger critical framework, or restoring the race- and class-interested erasures present in the original paradigm.[9]

In fact, subcultures have only very recently made an appearance in lesbian historiography: literally their "coming of age" might be said to be Madeline Davis and Elizabeth Lapovsky Kennedy's long-awaited book on the Buffalo lesbian community in the 1940s, 50s, and 60s.[10] The turn to "subculture" history in lesbian studies is part of a conscious effort to reclaim a racially diverse, working-class lesbian history in which explicit eroticism is valued, and in which women resist efforts to embed them within kin networks, or at least seek to define such connections on their own terms. In historical terms this project conceives itself as being in re-action to a middle-class, largely white, and usually sexually reticent model of "romantic friendship" that derives from the work of Smith-Rosenberg, Lillian Faderman, and others.[11] In political terms it definitively rejects the naive calls for "universal sisterhood" made by (mostly) white feminists—straight and lesbian alike—in the 1970s (of which works like Adrienne Rich's *Compulsory Heterosexuality*, formative as it was, is quite representative) in favor of more skeptical and more eclectic political visions like those of the African-American, Latina, Asian-American, and Native-American contributors to *This Bridge Called My Back* or of white working-class writers like Joan Nestle.[12]

These are visions which, to the extent that one can find common ground between them, do appear to view a self-conscious sexuality as an important constituent of identity, though not necessarily the sole or even main component. But what is more significant about them is that they see "identity" as being of recent origin, the fruit of hard struggle, and under continuing assault. The subject that emerges from all this cannot be said to be "stable"; in fact it is very much a collective construction, one in which each joist and each beam bears the marks of a diachronic free-for-all between the repressive, the liberatory, and everything in between. There is considerable potential here for simply reproducing Enlightenment concepts of identity, to which, however, the counterargument would be that such concepts were never originally intended for "us" anyway, and that to insist on expanding them to cover people of color, or women, or colonial subjects, or queers, or the poor so explodes their content, indeed their very reason for being, as to render them unrecognizable.

These more lesbian-modulated concerns also have their place in Renaissance and early modern European studies, despite the fact that it is virtually impossible to find distinct lesbian or, at least in Protestant countries, even women's collectivities, much less subcultures, in this period. One fact that is well established is that the rise of concepts of identity was so irrevocably tied to being male, above the servant class, and, in practice, of European stock, that pairing the concept to anyone else would have been an oxymoron. The classical, Renaissance, and early modern antecedents of what came to constitute a modern "identity" included a self-affirming public voice (often called "citizenship"),[13] an identification with a vocation (e.g., he is a carpenter),[14] personal autonomy, standardly defined in the Renaissance and early modern period as the ability to deploy the labor, reproductive and otherwise, of inferior family members (who, in the more expansive definition of "family" that then prevailed, included women, children, and, at least rhetorically, servants, slaves, and workers)[15] and some measure of bodily self-control, a central attribute of which was the ability to initiate and to definitively refuse sexual intercourse. All these were difficult or impossible to attain for married women, slaves, or servants (and these categories cover the overwhelming majority of all women), and most were ontologically incompatible with what a married woman, a slave, or a servant "was." Slaves did not deploy others, they were themselves deployed. Women did all kinds of jobs, but were not, except in the case of the most lowly or undesirable jobs, permitted to train for or identify themselves with an occupation, and this was also true historically for most men of color, slave or free. A wife did not have the legal right to refuse to have sexual intercourse with her husband, nor, in most cases, could a slave or servant refuse to sexually service her master. None of these people had a legitimate "public" voice. None of them were full persons in the eyes of the law. Their hold on anything resembling an identity was tenuous at best.

Similarly, the dispersion of women, slaves, and servants across patriarchally organized households, the sustained efforts by their social superiors to control the movements of social inferiors outside those households, and the strong legal and cultural injunctions against their organizing into trans-familial collectivities made it difficult, well into the nineteenth century, for most non-elite groups to construct anything resembling a "subculture." These various strictures did not, of course, always have their desired result. But their very ubiquity suggests some of the reasons why subcultures and other collectivities, as well as the elusive notion of identity, still have such resonance today in the historiography of communities of color and women.

Queer historians have a double mandate. Clearly they have a responsibility to examine "minority" experiences, to trace the ways new "minorities" emerge out of the definitional sludge, to celebrate the artful methods that the stigmatized use to transform and improve their threadbare estate, and to engage the theoretical and tactical perplexities that accompany inescapably the experience of living in two (or more) cultures. But they also have to adopt a more universalizing standpoint, one that goes beyond what can be a rather insular tendency within gay and lesbian history. The present volume has especially sought to explore the latter, hoping to suggest ways of studying Western history that, while destabilizing our notions of what sexuality is or has been, place the rise of specific sexualities squarely at the center of larger historical narratives. I will devote the remainder of this essay to exploring the new historical landscape that this approach opens up for us.

For Renaissance and early modern scholars the enterprise might be summarized as follows: to chart the emergence of modern Western social/political systems in a way that acknowledges the intermingling of normative notions of gender and sexuality with the preoccupations of power at every step along the way. If we adopt the view which is implied in the above formulation, that authority itself is in a constant state of flux, we will want to know how societies sustain themselves at all. How do concerns about the stability of particular social and political arrangements get articulated culturally, judicially, and sexually? Sodomy fears (and also fears about women seizing power from men) have for some time had a prominent place in the anxious communications that surround times of social and political flux. This was true during the period of the Glorious Revolution of 1688–89 in England and during the political and economic crises of the 1720s in the Netherlands. (The latter crisis coincided with the largest homosexual pogrom of the early modern period, in which hundreds of men were tortured or executed or sought self-exile.)[16] And we are depressingly familiar with such formations in our own day. We need more work for the Renaissance and early modern period that focuses on the language of sexuality and gender in political and religious rhetoric as well as on the rhetoric and visual display of governance and religion.

One of the things this volume does magnificently is to establish how very different same-sex relationships were in the Renaissance from what they are today, at least in Britain and the United States. The specificity of these contributors' findings casts into stark relief the huge number of constraints upon physical and emotional displays of affection between men that help make up modern regimes of social control. I hope that future work will take up more directly the problem of why Renaissance culture was so permissive on this issue. Was it simply a matter of a society that couldn't be bothered to oversee relationships that hurt no one, as a rather naive, modern civil libertarian might have it, or, more plausibly (and this, I think, is what most of the contributors are driving at, some more explicitly than others), were passionate male friendships, at least among elites, one of the linchpins of the complicated system of patronage, faction, protection, and jockeying for status and preferment that largely constituted the "governance" of the Renaissance? I hope that queer scholars, building on the current volume, will redouble their efforts toward discovering the very different ways that power and passion intersected in the Renaissance. But I also hope that they will work toward giving us a clearer sense of how passionate male friendship worked among non-elites (were they celebrated in similar ways, or seen as problematic?) as well as of the ways that real-life friendships between women, even elite women, did and did not fit the patterns for men. For instance, one would like to know a great deal more about the passionate attachments between the English Queen Anne, last of the Stuart monarchs, and, successively, Sarah, Duchess of Marlborough, and Abigail Masham in the early 1700s, connections that had everything to do with the distribution of power and status during Anne's reign.

We also want to know, and here Alan Bray, with his usual perspicacity, is already showing the way, what happened to the ideal and practice of male friendship over the long run. Bray traces a slippage, beginning in the late sixteenth century, between the convention of male friendship and an increasingly complex and heterogeneous society. More recently he has been searching for some of the ways the "consumption revolution" in eighteenth-century England may have blurred the boundaries between socially respectable forms of male friendship and forbidden sodomy.[17] Future scholarship will, perhaps, look into the ways changing notions of personal privacy and hygiene, often heavily marked by class, altered what kinds of human connections were considered appropriate,[18] and some of

us are already examining the rise of new kinds of "rational" male sociabil-
ity in the late seventeenth and early eighteenth centuries in the form of all-
male voluntary associations and clubs. These most "enlightened" of institutions apparently extended the distribution of political and economic
influence to a somewhat wider circle of men, at the same time reconfigur-
ing the exclusion of women and people of the laboring class from social
and economic power, and providing a locus for distinctively new, differently ritualized, and, probably, more physically distant relations among
middle and upper-class men.[19]

Male friendship has not died out, but it clearly has changed its style
and social location in the modern era. There are still settings where passionate same-sex friendships (or cultural depictions of them) are, to a
degree, permissible, though always hedged about with phobic prohibitions; these include, or have in the recent past included, both boys' and
girls' schools, same-sex colleges, many of the evangelical churches,[20] male
sports teams, American westerns, and, not least, the armed forces. Conversely, openly celebrated same-sex passion is far less acceptable today
than it was during the Renaissance in the realm of business and civilian
work generally, in government, in most of the main-stream religious de-
nominations, in high culture productions, and when the principals are
above the age of about twenty-five. How has this exiling of the overtly
homoerotic from the power center of society out to more liminal zones
taken place, and what does it signify in the larger scheme of things? Some
work has been done on these topics for the twentieth century, and it is to
be hoped that queer historians of earlier periods will soon begin to address these issues more directly than they have tended to so far.

Thanks in large part to the work of Lawrence Stone and Randolph
Trumbach, the Western heterosexual family has a historicity it did not
have before.[21] There have, it is true, been compelling criticisms raised
against both scholars' work. Women's historians have argued persuasively
that, whether or not the "rise of companionate marriage" ever actually
took place, or took place when Stone says it did, it certainly did *not* go
along, as both Stone and Trumbach claim it did, with sexual egalitarianism. Historians of the family also point, with some justice, to the reduc-
tionist character of Stone's schema, to the dearth of evidence in both
books about any except elite families (Trumbach's book focuses exclusively on the English peerage), and to the pitfalls of the kind of "trickle
down" sociology that informs both works. But that having been said,

these books make it very much more difficult than it was to make facile claims about the universality of the modern "family" and they also mark the Renaissance and early modern period as key sites for the scholarly study of the construction of heterosexuality.

This challenge has been taken up with brio by queer scholars in recent years,[22] and several contributions in the current collection add to that growing body of work. One of the more interesting of these, in my view, is Valerie Traub's "The (In)significance of 'Lesbian' Desire in Early Modern England." It is, I believe, exemplary of a type of scholarship that underscores the losses incurred by women as a result of compulsory heterosexuality, as well as painstakingly uncovering traces of the sparse but poignant connections they may occasionally have managed to establish. As Traub and several of the authors in this collection show, passionate friendships (or indeed any friendships) between women, unlike, for the most part, those between elite men, were viewed with considerable official and popular disfavor in the Renaissance. What Traub may underestimate is the degree to which these feminine dyads, even in the mythic and elegiac forms in which they turn up in male-authored texts, represented a form of resistance to dominant mores. The sense of numbing physical and emotional loss that infuses many of the homoerotic texts Traub is studying has numerous echoes in women's novels, feminist writings, and real women's lives in succeeding centuries, and has some claim to being among the earliest indications we have of, if not a "lesbian" consciousness, at least a series of statements by women that link a specifically female experience of erotic and emotional deprivation to the institution of heterosexual marriage.

A really thorough critique of compulsory heterosexuality today or in its rather different Renaissance forms demands that we establish its essential instability along such axes as who is thought to make up a "family"; where and between whom in a given society the most powerful emotional and erotic ties are thought to subsist; the centrality (or not) within "families" of reproductive concerns; the range of variation within which it is still possible to be considered "a family"; and the responsibilities and entitlements accruing to different types of "families." But it also demands that we look closely at the differential distribution of benefits within families, at the reciprocal complicities of particular types of families and systems of political and cultural control, at sites of resistance both within and deliberately distinct from whatever definition of "family" is in the ascendancy at any given historical moment, and at the ways the category itself shifts and changes in the heat of political controversy. A queer history of the Renaissance and early modern period must deal with these kinds of questions, but it must do so under unusually challenging circumstances. Particularly before 1700 the sources are largely (though never entirely) silent about huge sections of the population. Moreover there is an extremely high level of disagreement among social historians about chronologies of change in relation to gender, class, marriage, sexuality, and the economy. It is also a time period in which, as Jonathan Goldberg shows especially well in his piece on *Romeo and Juliet,* areas of unclarity are especially likely to be filled in with facile fantasies designed to support reactionary political agendas. Queer scholars have a special responsibility to address these issues in the sort of nonparochial way that characterizes this present volume, and it is to be hoped that even more expansive efforts will be forthcoming.

The intersection of fears about homosexuality with colonial expansion and European racism has only recently begun to receive sustained attention from scholars of the Renaissance and early modern period.[23] Though several contributors in the present volume note the already commonplace tendency (by the sixteenth century, at least) to project unusual sexual practices onto foreigners, there is much more to be said about the ways forbidden eroticisms came, in this first great age of European imperialism, to *define* peoples that Europeans were bent upon conquering or controlling. For instance, Valerie Traub's throwaway note about the imputation of tribadism to women in "the Indies" and Egypt fits into a developing orientalist discourse that dwells obsessively upon comparisons between the allegedly low status and low sexuality of foreign, especially Middle Eastern, women and the allegedly high status and sexual respectability of Western European women. In time this came to be used both to discredit Western feminists' political demands *and* to enlist European women's support for a wide range of coercive colonial projects allegedly aimed at "protecting" non-Western women from the savage sexual practices of their countrymen—and from themselves.[24] It is notable, too, that here lesbianism is assumed to derive from frustrated heterosexual desire as well as from decadence, an important series of linkages that can still be found in mainstream views of female homosexuality to this day.

Much more work is needed on these sorts of topics if we are to begin to understand the connection between sexual discourses and European expansionism as well as European racism.

As I suggested earlier, the thrust of the present volume is away from the study of early subcultures toward a more "universalizing" approach to issues of sexuality in society. It is not, in my view, very likely that urban homosexual subcultures are going to lose their appeal for historians, both because they have left a relatively large number of traces in the records, and because they speak to a sense of fractured identity and enforced confinement within at best uncongenial and at worst profoundly oppressive heterosexual systems that is still a feature of gay and lesbian experience today. But it *may* be possible to examine "minority" history in a more universalizing way than we have done so far.

I myself am not at all sure that the so-called "homosexual subcultures" that have been discovered in late seventeenth- and early eighteenth-century Amsterdam and London—at the very end of the period being discussed in this volume—are best characterized as "homosexual" or even as "subcultures." Arguably they might be better represented as communities that were relatively tolerant of sex outside the patriarchal nuclear family, and which organized the exchanges of money, resources, and mutual support that accompany sexual relations in many societies in ways that differed from the norm. (The exchange of sex for money was not, in itself, the sticking point, since this was a society in which both licit and illicit sexual activities were associated with overt monetary exchanges.)

This community was made up of a quite heterogeneous collection of people, from men who engaged in transvestism and various kinds of homosexual sex, and female prostitutes who catered to heterosexual men, to sexually nonconformist groups with strong traditions of mutual support, such as actors and actresses or soldiers and sailors. It drew substantially from the ranks of the unrespectable poor, and also contained lodging housekeepers, dressmakers, and coffeehouse, tavern, and brothel owners who serviced all these peoples' diverse social and sexual needs while benefiting from their fairly high level of access, in a cash-poor society, to ready money. Finally it included significant numbers of spouses, parents and grandparents, sons and daughters, and sisters and brothers. If this was a subculture, it bore little resemblance to urban gay subcultures today (or at least to the image of them purveyed by the gay press) with their emotionally and geographically distant relations with blood kin, their gay-owned services, their elaborate stratification by class and race, and their rhetorical separation, at least at the "respectable" end, from other sexually "deviant" groups, such as female prostitutes.[25]

While these communities differed in many respects from today's "gay communities," there were, nevertheless, some affinities that may permit (and there is nothing intrinsically wrong with this) a degree of identification with these urban forms of a past time. Early modern cities certainly drew sexual and other "refugees" from abusive or disapproving families and villages, and people then, as now, gravitated toward particular communities and/or neighborhoods in order to protect themselves against the abuse that often accompanied unconventionality, to find a supportive circle of people, or to facilitate social, sexual, and economic contacts. There were, moreover, distinctly "countercultural" and subversive elements within these ragtag collectivities that could respond violently to external challenges.

In London one of these challenges came in the form of a novel sort of men's organization, the Societies for Reformation of Manners, which, in the late seventeenth and early eighteenth centuries, launched a series of moral crusades against, among other things, prostitutes and "molly-houses" (houses of assignation favored by homosexuals and transvestites). In the face of these attacks it seems to have been relatively common for family members and neighborhood mobs to attack Society for Reformation of Manners agents as they sought to arrest prostitutes (at least two agents were actually killed in the course of such disturbances) and on at least one occasion in 1725 the customers of a Covent Garden molly house, some of them in drag, fought violently with a group of agents who came to close the house down.[26]

One may read such episodes as being about local communities trying to protect their own or as evidence of early homosexual subcultures defending a way of life—and both positions have merit. But a more universalizing approach would encourage us to look carefully at the question of why such sexually unrespectable communities, or more often subsets of them, came under repressive scrutiny at just this time. Both prostitutes and sodomites had long inspired fears of "national judgments": Sodom and Gomorrah symbolized not just the detestable character of homosexual sex, but God's penchant for visiting large-scale calamities on nations that tolerated unregulated sex in any form. But in the post-1689 era older concerns about these two groups took on a new salience. To a politically, economically, and militarily insecure nation, newly obsessed with "family values," both groups became powerful symbols of the obverse of a new vision of sexual, familial, and gender "respectability" even then being clarified in discernibly modern terms.

Early modern reformers created new forms of cultural alterity for *some*, but not all of the people who inhabited this more generally sexually nonconformist milieu. And over the long run it may well have been the fissures that selective stigmatization and repression created within larger, more heterogeneous communities that led to the defensive rise of a homosexual identity "on the ground," as well as to homosexual subcultures in the modern sense.[27] But in the short run we may well ask what role the idea of sexual "minorities," just then in the process of being invented, played in deflecting attention from other sorts of homoerotic relations thriving at the very heart of a patriarchal, heterosexist society. The lived experience behind these alleged sodomite subcultures may have been deeply and complexly embedded in mainstream culture, but the propaganda and enforcement activities of groups like the Societies for Reformation of Manners were already setting in motion that conceptual splitting off of social and sexual "deviance" from "respectable" society that is so prominent a feature of modern Western societies. We also need to know a great deal more than we do about how ideas about immoral subcultures (such as, for instance, the apparently fanciful thieves' subculture said by contemporaries to thrive in sixteenth-century London) fit into developing notions of the city. It strains credulity to think that they played no role in the complex programs of containment and control of the unrespectable poor and of various ethnic and racial groups that have so occupied Europeans and Euroamericans ever since.

The study of subcultures supplies opportunities to address "minoritizing" concerns in the best sense, but it also provides the chance to pursue truly universalizing historical and theoretical questions. Most of us will continue to feel some cautious kinship with mollies, transvestites, sodomites, "female husbands,"[28] and other sexual seekers, especially when they come down on the wrong side of the law. Yet, as this collection shows so well, particularly in its examination of passionate same-sex friendship, we should also be seeking to scramble the definitions and blur the boundaries of the erotic, both so as to forestall the repressive uses to which rigid understandings of it almost inevitably lend themselves, and to gain access to a much larger analytical arena. This is the usefully paradoxical approach that *Queering the Renaissance* adopts, and it is one from which all of us, whatever our disciplinary perspective, can learn.

I have been outlining some of the parameters of an emerging "queer history," with special reference to the Renaissance and early modern period. Before I conclude, there are a few dangers of which I think we need to be aware. There is a strong tendency in Western culture to idealize the Renaissance, and those of us who are deeply critical of the ways "the Renaissance" has been understood are hardly immune to this disease. It would not be hard for a "queer history" to reinstate the Renaissance as an ideal site of, this time, polymorphous eroticisms and loosely constructed gender boundaries, and to construct new theories of decline that advance this view. It is essential that we resist this tendency. The era of the Renaissance also saw the first flush of modern European imperialism, the birth of the slave trade, and some of the earliest discernible "capitalist" institutions. Its palette of acceptable eroticized activities included numerous rituals of humiliation, especially of women and the poor, the public torture of people and animals, and public executions. Queer histories need to cast their nets widely if they hope to decipher the connections between sexuality and power, and they cannot shrink from some of its less palatable manifestations, whatever society they are studying.

We must also take care not to concentrate our energies too narrowly. Take for example the expansive term *sodomy*, which has grown still broader thanks to this collection. Ample as the category of sodomy is, it is very rarely applied to forbidden or "antisocial" acts perpetrated by women. Why is this? Plainly it is because there is an already well-established set of precepts, practices, and discursive conventions at both the elite and popular levels devoted to the supervision and confinement of women, and particularly to controlling their sexual and reproductive lives. If we really wish to understand sexuality and power in the Renaissance, it would be unwise either to proceed as if "sodomy" were a more gender-inclusive category than it actually is (or was),[29] or to fall into the trap of idealizing a phenomenon like passionate male friendship, divorced from its gendered social context. Instead we should focus our attention precisely on the intersections between sodomy fears, the discourse of male friendship, and the domination of women, a more challenging and more deeply subversive course, but one for which this collection has already pointed the way.

"Queer history" combines "gay and lesbian" history, social history, intellectual history, the study of the rise of modern literary genres, and a host of other subdisciplines, into something that is far more than the sum of its parts. This volume represents an exhilarating example of this kind of cooperation, drawing in specialists in Renaissance literature, legal and social history, women's studies, sexuality, and religion, and dealing with topics as different one from the other as pedagogical misreadings of *Romeo and Juliet*, the birth of modern science, the marginalizing of Renaissance women poets, Erasmus's letter-writing technique, Spenser's views of female friendship, and one influential historian's heterosexist readings of ecstatic religious language. What a long way we have come, and what exciting possibilities still await us.

Notes

My thanks to Michèle Barale for her comments and her friendship.

1. In deference to the literary bent of the present collection, I use "early modern" to mean the period approximately 1660 to 1800. Historians generally use the term to refer to a longer expanse of time that includes the Renaissance.

2. It is conceivable that a writer like Crashaw and/or his readers were unconscious of the "sexual" suggestions in his poetry. But I think it unlikely. Sixteenth- and seventeenth-century people were far more attuned to sexual double-entendre and to erotic metaphor than modern people (even post-Freudians) tend to be. They were hardly innocent about these matters; rather they found it reasonable and, most of the time, appropriate that transcendent religious experiences be expressed in terms evocative of more earthly raptures.

3. Theo van der Meer, "The Persecutions of Sodomites in Eighteenth-Century Amsterdam: Changing Perceptions of Sodomy," in Kent Gerard and Gert Hekma, eds., *The Pursuit of Sodomy: Male Homosexuality in Renaissance and Enlightenment Europe* (New York: Harrington Park Press, 1989), 265.

4. The relative absence of fellatio as a sexual practice or sexual category in the premodern period has been noted by Theo van der Meer, ibid., 290–91. Randolph Trumbach, in "Sodomitical Assaults, Gender Role, and Sexual Development in Eighteenth-Century London," in Gerard and Hekma's *Pursuit of Sodomy*, finds some instances of it, however (pp. 416–17).

5. I use the terms *identities* and *subcultures* advisedly; they are clearly not the same thing, though they are generally thought to be closely linked. In fact, gay historiography has tended to locate the former in the mid to late nineteenth century, especially with the rise of sexology and the invention of categories such as "homosexual." On the other hand, subcultures (in the specific sense of *urban* subcultures) have been moving back in time, but seem to have stabilized in the very late seventeenth and early eighteenth century, at least for England and Holland, the two countries that have spawned the largest body of scholarship on the subject. For useful discussions of the historiography see Alan Bray, *Homosexuality in Renaissance England* (London:

Gay Men's Press, 1982), 134–37, and Randolph Trumbach, "Sodomitical Subcultures, Sodomitical Roles, and the Gender Revolution of the Eighteenth Century: The Recent Historiography," *Eighteenth-Century Life* 9 (1985):109–21.

6. Eve Kosofsky Sedgwick, *The Epistemology of the Closet* (Berkeley: University of California Press, 1990), 1, 9, 26–27, 40–44. Sedgwick defines a minoritizing view as "seeing homo/heterosexual definition . . . as an issue of active importance primarily for a small, distinct, relatively fixed homosexual minority" and a universalizing view as "seeing [homo/heterosexual definition] . . . as an issue of continuing, determinative importance in the lives of people across the spectrum of sexualities" (p. 1).

7. L. J. Boon, "Those Damned Sodomites: Public Images of Sodomy in the Eighteenth Century Netherlands," in Gerard and Hekma, eds., *Pursuit of Sodomy*, 237–48. Boon usefully compares the remote village of Faan in Groningen, where homoerotic and homosexual acts were apparently seamlessly integrated into the fabric of mainstream life, and the large towns and cities of Holland (Amsterdam, the Hague, Delft, etc.) where a discourse that was both minoritizing and persecutory had already transformed the meaning of the same sorts of acts.

8. See for example Randolph Trumbach, "The Birth of the Queen: Sodomy and the Emergence of Gender Equality in Modern Culture, 1660–1750," in Martin B. Duberman, Martha Vicinus, and George Chauncey, Jr., eds., *Hidden from History: Reclaiming the Gay and Lesbian Past* (New York: NAL Books, 1989), 129–40.

9. Carroll Smith-Rosenberg, "Female World of Love and Ritual: Relations between Women in Nineteenth-Century America," *Signs: Journal of Women in Culture and Society* 1, no. 1 (1975): 1–29. Smith-Rosenberg could be faulted for overstressing the degree of complicity of these women, as well as for making male supremacy within and without the family essentially disappear in the face of loving bonds between women. Moreover, the narrow race and class provenance of this study and some of its successors is very palpable. Smith-Rosenberg herself works to resist the application of the category "lesbian" to these women in much the same way that the contributors to the current volume do, and for much the same reason: she is trying to stress their embeddedness in their society.

10. Elizabeth Kennedy and Madeline Davis, *Boots of Leather, Slippers of Gold: The History of a Lesbian Community* (New York: Routledge, 1993). See also Joan Nestle, *A Restricted Country* (Ithaca, N.Y.: Firebrand Books, 1987).

11. Lillian Faderman, *Surpassing the Love of Men: Romantic Friendship and Love between Women from the Renaissance to the Present* (London: Junction Books, 1982). Faderman's most recent book, *Odd Girls and Twilight Lovers: A History of Lesbian Life in Twentieth-Century America* (New York: Columbia University Press, 1990), is much more comprehensive. See especially pp. 67–81 and 159–87 on black and white working-class lesbian communities from the 1930s to the 1960s.

12. Cherríe Moraga and Gloria Anzaldúa, eds., *This Bridge Called My Back: Writings by Radical Women of Color* (New York: Kitchen Table: Women of Color Press, 1983). *This Bridge Called My Back* wants to speak to all women of color, not just lesbians. However lesbian contributors speak powerfully within it, and there is a concerted effort

to link issues of homophobia to racism, imperialism, gender discrimination, and issues of class.

13.   The literature on women's lack of access to citizenship is vast. See especially Joan Landes, *Women and the Public Sphere in the Age of the French Revolution* (Ithaca, N.Y.: Cornell University Press, 1988).

14.   See Michael Roberts, " 'Words They Are Women, and Deeds They Are Men': Images of Work and Gender in Early Modern England," in Lindsey Charles and Lorna Duffin, eds., *Women and Work in Preindustrial England* (London: Croom Helm, 1985), 122–80.

15.   Margaret Hunt, "Women and Trade," in *Middling Culture in Eighteenth-Century England* (Berkeley and Los Angeles: University of California Press, 1993).

16.   Theo van der Meer, "The Persecutions of Sodomites in Eighteenth-Century Amsterdam," 263–65, 271–74, et passim.

17.   Alan Bray, "Why Was the Sodomite Effeminate?" Delivered at the Fifth Annual Lesbian and Gay Studies Conference, Rutgers University, November 1–3, 1991. Laura Brown has been doing important work on the connections between consumption, colonialism, and femininity in the early eighteenth century. See especially her *Alexander Pope* (Oxford: Basil Blackwell, 1985).

18.   Norbert Elias, *The Civilizing Process*, vol. 1, *The History of Manners*, trans. Edmund Jephcott (Oxford: Basil Blackwell, 1978).

19.   Margaret C. Jacob, *The Radical Enlightenment: Pantheists, Freemasons and Republicans* (London: Allen and Unwin, 1981), 182–214.

20.   The world of evangelism is ripe for examination from the perspective of the history of homoeroticism and homosexuality. For some preliminary forays see Randolph Trumbach, "Sodomitical Assaults, Gender Role, and Sexual Development in Eighteenth-Century London," in Gerard and Hekma, eds., *Pursuit of Sodomy*, 419–21, and Henry Abelove, *The Evangelist of Desire: John Wesley and the Methodists* (Stanford: Stanford University Press, 1985). A most thought-provoking autobiographical account from a later period is Claude Hartland, *The Story of a Life: For the Consideration of the Medical Fraternity* (San Francisco: Grey Fox Press, 1985; originally published 1901).

21.   Lawrence Stone, *The Family, Sex, and Marriage in England, 1500–1800* (New York: Harper and Row, 1977); Randolph Trumbach, *The Rise of the Egalitarian Family: Aristocratic Kinship and Domestic Relations in Eighteenth-Century England* (New York: Academic Press, 1978).

22.   Important contributions include Eve Kosofsky Sedgwick, *Between Men: English Literature and Male Homosocial Desire* (New York: Columbia University Press, 1985), and her *Epistemology of the Closet*. A recently historical intervention is Henry Abelove, "Some Speculations on the History of Sexual Intercourse during the Long Eighteenth Century in England," in Andrew Parker, et al., *Nationalisms and Sexualities* (New York: Routledge, 1992).

23.   Literary critics have been quicker to engage this topic than historians. See especially Jonathan Goldberg, *Sodometries: Renaissance Texts, Modern Sexualities* (Stanford: Stanford University Press, 1992). On the topic of sexuality more generally and imperial / colonial ideology, see Karen Newman, *Fashioning Femininity and English Renaissance*

Drama (Chicago: University of Chicago Press, 1991); Laura Brown, "The Romance of Empire: *Oroonoko* and the Trade in Slaves," in Felicity Nussbaum and Laura Brown, *The New Eighteenth Century: Theory, Politics, English Literature* (New York: Methuen, 1987), 41–61; and Laura Brown, *Alexander Pope.*

24. On the centrality of issues of gender within Victorian racist and colonialist discourse, as well as efforts to attract European feminists to the imperial cause by focusing on the allegedly degraded position of Muslim women, see Leila Ahmed, *Women and Gender in Islam: Historical Roots of a Modern Debate* (New Haven: Yale University Press, 1992), 151–55.

25. This picture of urban gay communities (much less other gay communities) is, of course, an idealized one. Subculture publications, such as, say, the *Advocate*, exaggerate gays' and lesbians' lack of connectedness to kin and separation from other "deviant" groups. This section has benefited from Eve Kosofsky Sedgwick's discussion of "what [we think] we know today" in *Epistemology of the Closet*, 44–48.

26. Randolph Trumbach, "London's Sodomites: Homosexual Behavior and Western Culture in the Eighteenth Century," *Journal of Social History* 11, no. 1 (Fall 1977–78): 22.

27. Here I wish to acknowledge my indebtedness to Judith Walkowitz's *Prostitution in Victorian Society: Women, Class and the State* (Cambridge: Cambridge University Press, 1980), which traces an analogous series of developments as a result of the increased surveillance of working-class communities that accompanied the Contagious Diseases Acts.

28. See Rudolph M. Dekker and Lotte C. van de Pol, *The Tradition of Female Transvestism in Early Modern Europe* (New York: St. Martin's Press, 1989).

29. It is, however, important to recall that, while sodomy was generally understood to be a crime perpetrated by men, it could be either homosexual or heterosexual (or bestial).

Notes on Contributors

Alan Bray is a British civil servant and the author of *Homosexuality in Renaissance England.*

Marcie Frank is Assistant Professor of English at Concordia University in Montreal, Canada. She has published essays on John Dryden, David Cronenberg, Susan Sontag, and Valerie Solanas, and is currently working on a book about the relations between aesthetic evaluation and sexuality in late seventeenth- and early eighteenth-century literary criticism by men and women.

Carla Freccero is Associate Professor of Literature and Women's Studies at the University of California, Santa Cruz. She is the author of *Father Figures: Genealogy and Narrative Structure in Rabelais* (1991), and numerous articles on early modern culture. She has also written on contemporary popular icons such as Madonna and Two Live Crew. She is currently working on a book entitled *Marguerite de Navarre and the Politics of Maternal Sovereignty.* Her forthcoming "Cannibalism, Homophobia, Women," in Margo Hendricks and Patricia Parker, eds., *Women, Race, and Writing in the Early Modern Period,* forms the basis for a future project on early modern masculinities.

Jonathan Goldberg is Sir William Osler Professor of English Literature at The Johns Hopkins University. He is the author of *Sodometries: Renaissance Texts, Modern Sexualities; Writing Matter: From the Hands of the English Renaissance; Voice Terminal Echo: Postmodernism and English Renaissance Texts; James I and the Politics of Literature: Jonson, Shakespeare, Donne, and Their Contemporaries;* and *Endlesse Worke: Spenser and the Structures of Discourse.* He is the editor of *The Sodomy Reader* and an editor of Series Q.

Janet E. Halley is Associate Professor of Law at Stanford Law School. Among her publications on the early modern period are "Equivocation and the Legal Conflict over Religious Identity in Early Modern England," *Yale Journal of Law and the Humanities* 3 (1991), and "Heresy, Orthodoxy, and the Politics of Religious Discourse: The Case of the Family of Love," *Representations* 15 (Summer 1986). She has also published several articles on sexual orientation in the law, including "Misreading Sodomy: A Critique of the Classification of 'Homosexuals' in Federal Equal Protection Law," in *Bodyguards: The*

Cultural Politics of Gender Ambiguity, ed. Julia Epstein and Kristina Straub (1991), and "The Politics of the Closet: Towards Equal Protection for Gay, Lesbian, and Bisexual Identity," *UCLA Law Review* 36 (1989). She is on the Editorial Advisory Board of *GLQ: A Quarterly of Gay and Lesbian Studies.*

Graham Hammill is Assistant Professor of English at North Carolina State University. He is currently completing a book entitled *Consum'd To Nought: Subjectivity in "The Faerie Queene."*

Margaret Hunt is Associate Professor of History and Women's and Gender Studies at Amherst College. She is the author of a number of articles and short pieces on early modern European history, women's history, feminist theory, and lesbian and gay studies. Her book *Middling Culture in Eighteenth-Century England* is forthcoming.

Donald N. Mager is Assistant Professor of English at Johnson C. Smith University, former Co-Chair of the Gay/Lesbian Caucus of the Modern Language Association, and former Executive Director of the Michigan Organization for Human Rights. He is also a poet, with two books: *To Track The Wounded One* and *Glosses.*

Jeff Masten teaches English at Harvard University. He has published essays on manuscript circulation, gender, and subjectivity in Wroth's sonnets (in *Reading Mary Wroth*), and on collaborative drama and traditional attribution studies (in *ELH*); an essay on the editorial erasure of the 1603 *Hamlet* ("Rossencraft and Gilderstone are dead") is forthcoming; and he is editing *The Old Law*, a collaborative play, for Oxford's *Collected Works of Thomas Middleton.*

Elizabeth Pittenger is a graduate student in the Humanities Center at The Johns Hopkins University and works on the technologies of representation and gender in late medieval and early modern cultures; her "Dispatch Quickly: The Mechanical Reproduction of Pages" recently appeared in *Shakespeare Quarterly.*

Richard Rambuss is Assistant Professor at Tulane University, where he teaches Renaissance literature and cultural studies in the English department. He is the author of *Spenser's Secret Career* and is currently writing a book on performances of embodiment, gender, and sexuality in the early modern prayer closet of Christian devotion.

Alan K. Smith, a graduate student in the Department of Comparative Literature at Cornell University, is writing a dissertation on political and gender signification in the French Petrarchan lyric. He is also coediting an anthology of essays on psychoanalysis and early modern culture.

Dorothy Stephens is Assistant Professor of English at the University of Arkansas. She received the Spenser Society's 1992 Isabel MacCaffrey Award for an earlier version of the article that appears in this volume. She is currently working on a book, *"But if ye saw that which no eyes can see": Conditional Erotics in the English Renaissance*, which will address female poets' responses to male poets' complicity with the feminine imagination.

Forrest Tyler Stevens, an English graduate student at The Johns Hopkins University, is completing a dissertation entitled "Body Seizures: Sexuality and Moral Philosophy in Nineteenth-Century English Literature."

Valerie Traub is Assistant Professor of Renaissance Drama and Gender Studies in the English department at Vanderbilt University. She is the author of *Desire & Anxiety: Circulations of Sexuality in Shakespearean Drama* (1992), and is at work on *Staging Desire: Discourses of Female Erotic Pleasure in Early Modern England*.

Michael Warner teaches English at Rutgers University. He is the author of *The Letters of the Republic: Publication and the Public Sphere in Eighteenth-Century America* (1990). He has edited *Fear of a Queer Planet: Queer Politics and Social Theory* (1993), and, with Gerald Graff, *The Origins of Literary Studies in America* (1988). He is currently editing, with Myra Jehlen, a collection of colonial writing entitled *The English Literatures of America*.

Index

Library of Congress Cataloging-in-Publication Data
Queering the Renaissance / edited by Jonathan Goldberg.
p.   cm. — (Series Q)
Includes index.
ISBN 0-8223-1381-2 (cloth). — ISBN 0-8223-1385-5 (paper)
1. Homosexuality—Europe—History.   2. Homosexuality in
literature—Europe.   3. Renaissance.   I. Goldberg, Jonathan.
II. Series.
HQ76.3.E8Q44   1994
306.76'6'094—dc20   93-28955 CIP